DWIGHT D. EISENHOWER

DWIGHT D. EISENHOWER

Soldier, President, Statesman

Edited by Joann P. Krieg

Prepared under the auspices of Hofstra University

Contributions in Political Science, Number 183

Greenwood Press
New York • Westport, Connecticut • London

The publication of the Dwight D. Eisenhower Conference Proceedings
has been made possible by a generous grant from the
Eisenhower World Affairs Institute, Washington, D.C.

Library of Congress Cataloging-in-Publication Data

Dwight D. Eisenhower, soldier, president, statesman.

(Contributions in political science, ISSN 0147–1066 ;
no. 183)
Bibliography: p.
Includes index.
1. Eisenhower, Dwight D. (Dwight David), 1890–1969—
Congresses.   2. Presidents—United States—Biography—
Congresses.   3. Generals—United States—Biography—
Congresses.   4. United States. Army—Biography—
Congresses.   5. United States—Politics and government
—1953–1961—Congresses.   I. Krieg, Joann P.   II. Hofstra
University.   III. Series.
E836.D84   1987   973.921'092'4   87–7511
ISBN 0–313–25955–0 (lib. bdg. : alk. paper)

British Library Cataloguing in Publication Data is available.

Library of Congress Catalog Card Number: 87–7511
ISBN: 0–313–25955–0
ISSN: 0147–1066

First published in 1987

Greenwood Press, Inc.
88 Post Road West, Westport, Connecticut 06881

Printed in the United States of America

The paper used in this book complies with the
Permanent Paper Standard issued by the National
Information Standards Organization (Z39.48–1984).

10   9   8   7   6   5   4   3   2   1

Contents

THE PRESIDENT: FOREIGN POLICY

REVIEWING THE EISENHOWER YEARS

Preface

The Dwight D. Eisenhower Conference held at Hofstra University in March 1984 was the third in a series of Presidential Conferences marking a five-year celebration of Hofstra's fiftieth anniversary. The aim of the series was to offer a centralized effort to study the lives, careers, and administrations of the Presidents of the United States who held office during the years of our University's life.

The preceding conferences, on Presidents Franklin D. Roosevelt and Harry S. Truman, established a high standard of scholarly excellence which was continued in the third of these events. In addition to the formal presentations, our knowledge of Dwight David Eisenhower was enhanced by the presence and participation, in forums and roundtable discussions, of Eisenhower biographers, military colleagues, former officials of the Eisenhower administration, leaders of other governments, and, of course, the Eisenhower family. We are enormously grateful to all of them for their invaluable and good-spirited assistance.

Eric J. Schmertz
Dean, Hofstra University School of Law
Director, Dwight D. Eisenhower Conference

Acknowledgments

It is with considerable gratitude that I acknowledge the assistance of the Dwight David Eisenhower Library, Abilene, Kansas, in the preparation of this book, and the encouragement of the Honorable John Eisenhower.

The order in which the papers appear in this volume is the result of an editorial decision. Regrettably, roundtable discussions and forum materials have had to be eliminated, and some of the papers have appeared in print elsewhere. The conference program, reprinted in full at the end of the book, is both an acknowledgment of all who participated and an expression of appreciation for their contributions.

Joann P. Krieg

THE CANDIDATE

1

The Reluctant Candidate: Dwight Eisenhower in 1951

Joseph M. Dailey

In 1951, Dwight Eisenhower, then military commander of the North Atlantic Treaty Organization (NATO), was convinced that NATO's success was doubtful without wholehearted support from all quarters of the American government. By that time, Eisenhower's name had been heard repeatedly in connection with the 1952 presidential campaign. Years before, President Truman had offered his support if Eisenhower would run for the presidency in 1948 as a Democrat. After that, the requests, the pleadings, even the enticements to get the General to run in 1952, were continual. Eisenhower occupied his time at his NATO headquarters near Paris with defense plans, training, field exercises, and polite visits with a stream of at least seventy-eight politicians and friends, most of whom urged him to seek the Republican nomination. To all of them Eisenhower replied that he was not interested in politics, and he complained that sometimes he could not do his work because of all the visitors who came to talk politics.

Much has been made of Eisenhower's having claimed that he did not want to run for the presidency, without ever having stated categorically that he would not run under any circumstances. Eisenhower later explained that his refusal to say in public what he had been saying in private—that he would never run for the presidency—was a bit of impression management. Eisenhower wrote in *Mandate for Change* that he hoped an aura of mystery about his plans would help achieve congressional support for the collective defense of Europe.[1]

Before, during, and after his first presidential campaign, it was widely believed that throughout 1951 (and perhaps earlier) Eisenhower desired the presidency. He was sometimes seen as being coy. His rejections of a candidacy in 1952 were regarded as strategic. Were those ideas correct? Or was Eisenhower sincerely reluctant to run?

This chapter investigates (1) precisely how reluctant Eisenhower was before and during 1951; (2) whether his stay in Europe before the 1952 Republican National Convention was strategic; and (3) the effect of Eisenhower's reluctance to declare himself a candidate on his eventual candidacy.

While General Dwight David Eisenhower was avoiding politics at NATO, an influential group in New York, a spinoff of the Dewey organization, was discussing the possibility of making him the GOP candidate in 1952. The group was composed of Thomas E. Dewey, General Lucius Clay, Herb Brownell, Barak Mattingly, and Tom Stephens. Eventually, though they had no commitment from Eisenhower, the group called in Senator Henry Cabot Lodge to ask him to be Eisenhower's campaign manager.[2]

The very fact that Eisenhower had to be drawn into making a commitment made the group feel that Lodge would be the ideal manager. Because of enormous antagonism toward Dewey from the Republican right wing, it would have been poor strategy to suggest a potentially important role for Dewey in the Eisenhower candidacy. Neither Dewey nor Brownell knew Eisenhower as did Lodge, who had resigned from the Senate to serve in the military during World War II. It was Lodge then, who was in the best position to persuade Eisenhower to run, and so he took on the job as manager at the risk of losing his Senate seat to John F. Kennedy.

At subsequent meetings, the group discussed the main problems of recruiting Eisenhower as a candidate: Eisenhower did not conceive of himself as a politician, and he was also less than keen about being President. It seemed likely that Eisenhower's recruitment to candidacy could easily fail, and the slightest misstep could reinforce his desire to stay out of politics. Eventually, the group decided to stress the notion that it was Eisenhower's duty to run. Max Rabb, who worked closely with Lodge during this period, later explained that the group honestly felt that Eisenhower had a duty to run and that it did not intend to use Lodge as "a confidence man" who would set out to get Eisenhower with talk of duty.[3]

Lodge was dispatched to Europe to visit Eisenhower on September 4, 1951. There he told Eisenhower of the group's desire to organize a nationwide nomination movement, arguing that the victory of a divided minority party was possible only if its standard-bearer was a unifier who could attract large numbers of Americans who had customarily voted Democratic. Lodge claimed that Eisenhower was the only Republican who could win, and he asked the General to permit the use of his name in the primaries. Eisenhower agreed only to think it over, but it was the first time he had not given a flat refusal to seek the presidency. This marked the beginning of the process that would draw the reluctant Eisenhower into the campaign.[4]

It has been alleged that Eisenhower remained in Europe on the advice of his managers; there, shielded by his uniform and his reticence, it has been said, he could be safe from partisan attack.[5] Actually, his managers thought it was imperative that he come home. Assuming incorrectly that Eisenhower was willing to leave NATO and that seeking the "higher duty" of the presidency was first on his list of priorities, Lodge advised the General in a letter of December 3, 1951, that the time had come for him to return home. One reason was clear: GOP National Chairman Guy Gabrielson had invited Eisenhower to attend an important meeting of Republican big-wigs from eleven Western states.[6] For the candidates, this was the greatest single opportunity before the convention to meet with members of the Republican National Committee, state chairmen and vice-chairmen, and leaders of the Young Republicans—that is, with the people who would control the delegates. With Robert Taft the odds-on favorite, Eisenhower's appearance at this meeting could have marked the turning point. The party leaders at this meeting were the cornerstone of Taft's strength. Under the weight of Eisenhower's charm and obvious ability to work at the highest levels of government, combined with Lodge's arguments that only Eisenhower could guarantee a Republican victory in November, the cornerstone might have crumbled. In the hope that this might happen, Lodge wrote to Eisenhower:

I can't emphasize too strongly my hope that you will be able to attend this meeting. . . .

From a political standpoint you have everything to gain and nothing to lose by getting into it early. You'll be better off politically being back in this country in civilian clothes, free to discuss even the most difficult issues, than you would remaining much longer in your present status where you are a helpless target for all whispering attacks which the supporters of Senator Taft are making upon you.[7]

Eisenhower's reply must have come as a jolt to Lodge. The General countered that if the effort to win the nomination was doomed to failure by his absence, then so be it. In a letter to Lodge dated December 12, Eisenhower said that he was convinced that it was impractical to try to nominate someone who would remain politically inactive before the convention. Hence, Lodge and his associates should abandon their efforts to win an Eisenhower nomination.

The recruiting process had gone sour; the candidate-to-be wanted out before he had gotten in. Lodge, Dewey, and the others could continue without Eisenhower or they could hand Taft the nomination. They chose to continue.[8] Eisenhower had asked those most loyal to his candidacy to drop the idea, but instead of becoming a former possible candidate as he wished, he became the beneficiary of a large, complex, and well-thought-out public relations operation.

The events of early January showed how genuinely reluctant Eisenhower was. On January 1, 1952, he wrote to President Truman, who had asked for a statement of Eisenhower's political intentions. This was his reply:

I do not feel that I have any duty to seek a political nomination, in spite of the fact that many have urged me to the contrary. Because of this belief I shall not do so . . . (and) because particularly of my determination to remain silent you know, far better than I, that the possibility that I would ever be drawn into political activity is so remote as to be negligible.[9]

On Sunday, January 6, Lodge met the press at the Eisenhower-for-President headquarters at the Shoreham Hotel in Washington. With about fifty of the one hundred reporters present squeezed into the main room of the suite, Lodge made his announcement: Eisenhower had authorized him to enter the General's name in the New Hampshire primary. "I am speaking for the General and I will not be repudiated," Lodge concluded, though he offered no hope that Eisenhower would actively campaign.[10]

Being drawn into politics was frustrating and burdensome to Eisenhower who was so involved in the work of NATO that he was sometimes unable to think of other matters.[11] If it was essential for the future security of Europe that he stay in NATO headquarters, there could be no doubt that he had to remain aloof from partisan politics. To become a candidate would create an obvious alliance with the party that opposed the party of his Commander in Chief. It mattered little that Eisenhower endorsed Truman's policy toward Europe and its collective defense. In politics it is the purpose of the opposition to oppose, and this famous General could not very well stand before the world in the uniform of his country and appear to oppose his President.

Eisenhower was very unhappy about Lodge's press conference and sent General Clay a "fiery telegram" (Clay's words) saying so. Lodge's speech had involved him in a way he had not wanted. He had hoped that the absence of repudiation would be the only effort that would be required of him.[12]

On the day after Lodge's press conference, Eisenhower addressed the situation for the record by claiming that Lodge's announcement had reflected his convictions and Republican voting record. But he also said that Lodge was correct in stating that he would not seek nomination to political office. Eisenhower said: "Under no circumstances will I ask for relief from this assignment in order to seek nomination to political office and I shall not participate in the pre-convention activities of others who may have such an intention with respect to me."[13]

In the face of continued pressure to become an active candidate, Eisenhower sought and found his solution easily. It grew from his genuine conviction that Europe was fragile, that it could crumble in the face of communist aggression, and that as the leader of the free world he could prevent such a disaster.

It is impossible to document what Eisenhower guessed would happen if he did not run in 1952, but several facts are clear. He had good reason to believe that the race would be between Truman and Taft. This was the assessment of many well-informed advisers and the most logical conclusion to reach at the time. Furthermore, there was good reason to believe that Truman would beat Taft and continue his resistance to isolationism from the White House. Under those circumstances, Eisenhower could expect to continue as military commander of NATO and thereby help the collective security of Western Europe. Undoubtedly, a Truman presidency was not ideal for Eisenhower, but in his judgment it was better than the abandonment of NATO.[14]

Two alternatives faced Eisenhower: he could resign from NATO to seek the nomination, or he could risk the chance that his silence would ultimately guarantee Taft's nomination. He vastly preferred silence. To Eisenhower, partisan politics was at best distasteful. When Lodge had first broached the possibility of his being President, Eisenhower had replied, "It would be the bitterest day of my life if I ever had to become involved in party politics, and it would be a complete departure from everything I had ever said. It would be like a man who has been a Catholic up until the age of fifty suddenly becoming a Protestant."[15] The priority which Eisenhower placed on NATO left his more nervous political supporters with little cause for joy.

One such supporter was *New York Times* publisher Arthur Hays Sulzberger, who wanted to pressure Eisenhower into a greater awareness of his potential opponent, Senator Robert Taft. Sulzberger, fearing that the voter would have to choose between Taft and Truman, took it upon himself, singlehandedly if necessary, to persuade Eisenhower to leave NATO. In a series of six letters, he tried relentlessly to change Eisenhower's mind.

The arguments coming from Times Square were logical, and a congenial rapport existed between the two men, but when Eisenhower replied to Sulzberger, he was unmoved and unmoving. Convinced that politicking at home could be done without him, he replied to the pleadings from the *Times* offices with calm. He saw no crisis. He would continue to attend to his current responsibilities and leave the business of politics to others.[16]

Like a bulldog in the pit, Sulzberger held on, repeated his position, and stated:

If you agree with me that it's likely to be Taft if it isn't Eisenhower, then it would seem to me that you have to go along with my statement that the crisis is now and not in June, for those of us who feel that we cannot afford to wait.[17]

There was really no precedent for the Eisenhower forces to follow; they had a candidate but were denied his voice and his presence on American soil. Eisenhower's prestige was measurable in the public mind, though not in the secret heart of the county chairman. The public does not nominate; delegates do. Dewey had won his nominations in 1944 and 1948 by wooing professional politicians. How was Eisenhower to translate public popularity into delegate votes? This was the central problem at Eisenhower-for-President headquarters in Washington.

Some leaders were understandably upset with Eisenhower's absence and unconvinced that he could win the nomination. Polls showed that two-thirds of the professional politicians who would control delegates wanted Taft. Day by day the professionals were being convinced that Taft could win not only the nomination but also the election. Previously, the most persuasive argument working for Lodge was that Eisenhower was the only Republican who could win the election. If that argument were ever lost, the nomination might well be lost with it.[18]

The Eisenhower headquarters in Washington concluded that the only thing to do was to build an organized public opinion that could be dramatized. This was to be done by building Eisenhower clubs across the country and by creating a "promotion organization." A media strategy on behalf of the General would be constructed and executed whether or not Eisenhower wanted it. Eisenhower clubs were to be the heart of a volunteer effort that would be engineered by politicians and paid media professionals. The Eisenhower clubs were to build local pro-Ike sentiment to a dramatic climax just before delegates departed for the convention. The promotion organization was to send highly organized propaganda drives into strategic states like Michigan, Pennsylvania, and Texas.[19]

At Eisenhower headquarters at the Shoreham, former members of the Dewey organization met with Lodge, Max Rabb, Mason Sears, and Senator James H. Duff, who became the nucleus of a group that would construct preconvention campaign strategy for Eisenhower.[20] They constructed a public relations effort that was partly voluntary and partly run by paid professionals. On the volunteer side was an organization called the "TV Plans Board" composed of media professionals who set out to enlist members of the television industry in the Eisenhower movement, to "create *en masse* pro Eisenhower TV impressions," to elicit mail replies from the public in order to gain names of potential petition canvassers, and to provide TV evaluation. The paid professionals, headed by Sig Larmon and some of his staff at the Young and Rubicam advertising agency, intended to create a pro-Eisenhower sentiment so great that a "true draft movement" would exist until Eisenhower declared his candidacy.[21]

Presidential candidates usually generate news by speaking on the issues, but this was not the usual campaign, and so the public relations planners were to assemble a picture of Eisenhower from old speeches and personal letters.[22] Eventually a public relations master stroke allowed Eisenhower to speak for himself while not speaking out of turn. The opportunity came in a series of articles by Kevin McCann in the *New York Herald Tribune* entitled "Eisenhower's Creed." The twelve-part series revealed Eisenhower's views by making his personal letters public. Eventually, the McCann series was published as a thirty-one-page booklet and made available from the *New York Herald Tribune* for a dime.

Creating news about the absent General was for the most part limited to speaking engagements and press conferences by Lodge and Duff and to distribution of booklets explaining where the General stood on the issues. Eventually, the Eisenhower people, with the help of their ad agency, developed a bold plan for a spectacular public relations push.[23] By early January 1952, Young and Rubicam had outlined a media program to create a "true draft movement" until Eisenhower declared his candidacy. It would hammer away at the theme that only Eisenhower could save the nation. The raw stuff of the campaign was to come from a biography to be prepared under the direction of Young and Rubicam which would serve as a campaign bible and speaker's handbook. It was hoped that this book, distributed to newspaper editors across the country, would stimulate favorable, or at least factual, commentary.[24]

In January the strategy group planned the public drama that was to unfold. Across the country, Ike fans were to demonstrate their support at locally designed whoop-and-shout rallies which were to be promoted by Young and Rubicam-designed ads placed in the newspapers of each rally city as well as by radio and television spots. The main kickoff event was to be in New York City. To get maximum mileage out of the spectacle, Madison Square Garden was chosen, so that the crowd would come in on the heels of a prize fight. To hold them in place, prominent fight personalities such as Gene Tunney, Jack Dempsey, and Joe Wolcott would be special guests. Television coverage of the rally would be especially easy at the Garden since cameras would already be in place to cover the fight, and contributions were to be solicited to pay for local station time to join the Madison Square Garden television hookup.[25]

To pump energy into the grass roots, Republican leaders and party workers were to be invited to New York and then encouraged to sell the Ike story back home. Entertainers would serve as bait for them. It was important to woo these party workers because, although the Gallup Poll for 1951 had shown Eisenhower to be far ahead of all other candidates, the January 2, 1952, poll of GOP county chairmen, many of whom would be delegates or would control delegates, showed Taft ahead by a margin of three to one. As a result, Republican leaders and key work horses from around the country were to be specially invited to the rally. Carloads, trainloads, and planeloads of rally-bound Republicans, placards waving, were to embark from their hometowns and converge on New York in a wild spontaneous demonstration of support for Ike.

The whole dramatic plan eventually became reality, and by the time it was all over the Eisenhower-for-President organization had spent more than $55,000 for newspaper ads, rent, and other expenses. What was produced at Madison Square Garden was the second paid-for political TV program and the first of the big political money to be spent on television.[26] The Garden was jammed to capacity with Eisenhower supporters from around the country who were entertained by beauty queens and Philadelphia mummers, by singers and celebrities. The entertainment was not the best, but the crowds loved it and it was often enough to spark a raucous demonstration that would fill the ring with waving, screaming spectators.[27]

The rally's organizers had delighted in the fact that the Republicans could virtually trap the fight crowd inside the arena to give the illusion of a larger political crowd. With 15,000 packed into the Garden, there were thousands left on the street in the 30-degree cold of the night. One master of ceremonies asked if those who had not been invited would please leave. They would not leave. It was chaos. Mrs. James Doolittle had to be rescued from a policeman, and the city had to call out the fire department to help handle the crowd.

A few days after the Madison Square Garden event, Jacqueline Cochran, a tireless Eisenhower worker, showed a movie of the rally to Eisenhower in his livingroom at Villa St. Pierre, near Paris.[28] Later, Eisenhower described what it was like watching the film, "I think for the first time, there came home to me something of what it means to be the object of interest to a great section of packed humanity."[29] He said he was "profoundly affected" by the film, which impressed him more than all of the arguments he had been hearing for months.[30] To Cochran's arguments that if he did not send some public statement home he would frustrate the work of all the people he had seen on the film, Eisenhower explained that he would make no public statement, but she was to carry a message to Jock

Whitney, to Lucius Clay, and to William Robinson. She was to tell them that he would return to run before the convention.[31]

The reluctant Eisenhower had been recruited. What he had earlier described as the bitterest day of his life, the day in which he would become involved in party politics, had arrived.

Just how reluctant was Eisenhower during 1951? Is there a chance that Eisenhower's statements about not wanting to be involved in politics were less than sincere?

One could argue that by 1951 Eisenhower had a long-standing intention to run. Clear evidence, one could say, can be found in Eisenhower's refusal to publicly and categorically close the door on a presidential candidacy. In a 1948 letter to Leonard Finder, the publisher of the *New Hampshire Evening Leader* who had tried to draw Eisenhower into a race, Eisenhower argued that lifelong professional soldiers should avoid seeking high public office. Even in that letter he qualified his objections, saying professional soldiers should stay out of campaigns "in the absence of some obvious and overriding reason."[32]

It is true that he never closed the door on a candidacy, but the evidence seems overwhelming that Eisenhower was for a long time genuinely opposed to his own candidacy. Conservatively, one might say that throughout 1951 Eisenhower was extremely reluctant to be a candidate, since it was in December of that year that he urged Lodge and his other close supporters to abandon their efforts to win an Eisenhower nomination. In other words, at that point Eisenhower took action to oppose his own nomination. It was not until February of 1952 that he decided to come home to campaign.

But what can we make of Eisenhower's refusal to shut the door on a candidacy?

In *Mandate for Change*, Eisenhower writes about a meeting between himself and Senator Taft. Eisenhower asked Taft about his views on strengthening Europe; Taft seemed to avoid the question. Years later, when recalling the meeting with Taft, Eisenhower told his Press Secretary James Hagerty that he would have made a public statement taking himself irrevocably out of any political race in 1952, but, because he could get no commitment to NATO from Taft, he settled on an "aura of mystery" tactic. We have no reason not to accept Eisenhower's own explanation on this matter.

Was Eisenhower's stay in Europe before the 1952 Republican National Convention a strategic move? Was he in fact using his uniform to hide behind because public exposure in the political arena would harm his campaign?

The answer is obviously *no*. Eisenhower's political managers were begging him to return home.

What effect did Eisenhower's reluctance have on his candidacy?

The chief effect of Eisenhower's reluctance was his own unpreparedness for campaigning. In his first campaign experience, a well-publicized speech in Abilene, Eisenhower fumbled with ideas and with language. He showed that he could look strangely undignified out of uniform. But those early campaign flaws cost him little. Eisenhower was dedicated to living with a minimum of campaign image-building. His intuition told him that the public would see him as a decent man sincerely concerned about the nation and its people. Time proved that intuition to be correct. Since he had the support of a top-notch campaign organization, Eisenhower could afford the few rough edges that were the price of his reluctance.

But before the convention Eisenhower had benefited from a dramatic public campaign that had been designed and executed mostly by people he did not know. His own role in the construction of the drama had been minimal. As his party's nominee he would have to work directly with the drama makers, with surrogates who would help his performance; and he would have to play the lead role in a complex drama, a role he was still reluctant to play even in the ensuing campaign.

NOTES

1. Dwight David Eisenhower, *The White House Years: Mandate for Change, 1953–1956* (Garden City, N.Y.: Doubleday and Co., 1963), p. 12.

2. Sherman Adams, transcript of a tape-recorded interview, Dwight D. Eisenhower Library. Lucius Clay, transcript of a tape-recorded interview, Dwight D. Eisenhower Library.

3. July 16, 1975. Max Rabb interview.

4. Eisenhower, *Mandate for Change*, pp. 17–18.

5. Leonard Lurie, *The King Makers* (New York: Coward, McCann and Geoghegan, 1971).

6. Letter, Henry Cabot Lodge to Dwight D. Eisenhower, December 3, 1951, Dwight D. Eisenhower Library, Lodge microfilm.

7. Ibid.

8. Letter, Dwight D. Eisenhower Library, Lodge microfilm.

9. Eisenhower, *Mandate for Change*, pp. 17–18.

10. *New York Times*, January 7, 1952, pp. 1, 9.

11. Letter, Dwight D. Eisenhower to Arthur Hays Sulzberger, January 14, 1952, Dwight D. Eisenhower Library, Eisenhower Correspondence, 1916–1952, Box 104, Sulzberger #1.

12. Lucius Clay, transcript of a tape-recorded interview, Dwight D. Eisenhower Library.

13. *New York Times*, January 8, 1952, p. 15.

14. Henry Cabot Lodge, memo for record dated November 30, 1950, Dwight D. Eisenhower Library, Henry Cabot Lodge Microfilm.

15. Henry Cabot Lodge, *The Storm Has Many Eyes* (New York: W. W. Norton, 1973), p. 77.

16. Letter, Arthur Krock to Arthur Hays Sulzberger, December 5, 1951; Memorandum, Turner Catledge to Arthur Hays Sulzberger, December 11, 1951; Letter, James B. Reston to Arthur Hays Sulzberger, December 12, 1951; Letter, Arthur Hays Sulzberger to Dwight D. Eisenhower, January 7, 1952; Letter, Arthur Hays Sulzberger to Dwight D. Eisenhower, January 13, 1951; Letter, Arthur Hays Sulzberger to Dwight D. Eisenhower, January 23, 1952; Letter, Arthur Hays Sulzberger to Dwight D. Eisenhower, January 28,

1952; Letter, Arthur Hays Sulzberger to Dwight D. Eisenhower, January 29, 1952; Dwight D. Eisenhower Library, Eisenhower Correspondence, 1916–1952, Box 104, Sulzberger #1. Editorial, *New York Times*, January 7, 1952, p. 8.

17. Letter, Arthur Hays Sulzberger to Dwight D. Eisenhower, January 31, 1952, Dwight D. Eisenhower Library, Eisenhower Correspondence, 1916–1952, Box 104, Sulzberger #1.

18. "Memorandum following discussion with Lodge, Vanderberg, Larman and Brownell . . . ," unsigned, January 28, 1952, Dwight D. Eisenhower Library, Documents RE 52 Campaign, Box 1, 52 Election Spring and Summer.

19. Ibid.

20. Undated memorandum, Dwight D. Eisenhower Library, Lodge microfilm. Max Rabb interview.

21. Memorandum, TV Plans Board to Henry Cabot Lodge and Associates, December 17, 1951, Dwight D. Eisenhower Library, folder marked "RNC 1952 (Speakers . . . TV, etc.)" Tom Stephens Collection, Box 6. Letter, Howard Chase to Sig Larmon, May 2, 1950, Dwight D. Eisenhower Library, folder marked "Correspondence of Sig Larmon," Young and Rubicam, Box 1. Item, January 8, 1952, p. 1, Dwight D. Eisenhower Library, folder marked "Correspondence of Sig Larmon and others pertaining to the nomination of General Eisenhower in 1952 . . . ," Young and Rubicam, Box 1.

22. Memorandum, Tony Zaghi to Sig Larmon, February 8, 1952, Dwight D. Eisenhower Library, folder marked "Correspondence of Sig Larmon," Young and Rubicam, Box 1.

23. Kevin McCann, *Eisenhower's Creed* (*New York Herald Tribune*), pp. 5–6.

24. Item, January 8, 1952, pp. 1–5, Dwight D. Eisenhower Library, folder marked "Correspondence of Sig Larmon and others pertaining to the nomination of General Eisenhower in 1952 . . . ," Young and Rubicam, Box 1.

25. Ibid.

26. U.S. Congress, House of Representatives, *Campaign Expenditures*, p. 33. "Video Election," *Newsweek*, February 18, 1952, p. 68.

27. "Midnight Serenade for Ike," *New York Times*, February 9, 1952, pp. 1 and 8. Hugh A. Bone "Campaign Methods of Today," *Annals of the American Academy of Political and Social Science* 283 (September 1952): 132. Department of Marketing, Miami University, Oxford, Ohio, *The Influence of Television on the Elections of 1952* (Oxford, Ohio: Oxford Research Associates, 1954), p. 5.

28. Jacqueline Cochran, transcript of a tape-recorded interview, Dwight D. Eisenhower Library.

29. Letter, Dwight D. Eisenhower to Lucius Clay, February 12, 1952, Dwight D. Eisenhower Library, folder marked "Clay #3," 1916–1952, Box 1.

30. Eisenhower, *Mandate for Change*, p. 20. Transcript, Cochran interview.

31. Letter, Eisenhower to Clay, February 12, 1952.

32. Lurie, *The King Makers*, p. 5.

2

Eisenhower and Robinson: The Candidate and the Publisher in the 1952 Campaign

Steve M. Barkin

The 1952 presidential campaign transformed the process of running for national office in America. It was the first national campaign in which the airplane, television, and professional public relations were significant factors.[1] The Republican campaign of Dwight D. Eisenhower was particularly sensitive to these innovations, especially to the role television might play. Still, the cultivation of newspaper support was an important part of the Eisenhower strategy, initially to gain the nomination and later to defeat the Democratic nominee, Adlai E. Stevenson.

Much of the nomination campaign was waged in Eisenhower's absence. Saying that he had no intention of initiating a run for the presidency, Eisenhower chose to remain in Paris as Supreme Commander of NATO until June of 1952. As a consequence, public opinion was crucial in building momentum for an Eisenhower candidacy. Newspapers, magazines, radio, and television were all utilized to persuade the General to run (or at least give the appearance of a national mandate) and enable him to wrest the nomination from Ohio Senator Robert A. Taft.

The pillar of the newspaper strategy was the *New York Herald Tribune*. The *Herald Tribune*'s editorial policy represented the moderate wing of the Republican party, more specifically the views of Thomas E. Dewey, former Governor of New York, and the leadership of the New York State Republican Committee.[2] The president of the *Herald Tribune*, Helen Rogers Reid, was an influential behind-the-scenes figure in Republican politics in the East.[3] The Reids, along with other moderates in the party, were interested in finding an alternative to the conservative Taft in 1952. Personally, Dwight Eisenhower had an even stronger

This research was supported by a grant from the University of Maryland's General Research Board.

connection to the paper. One of his closest personal friends was William E. Robinson, the newspaper's executive vice-president and general manager. Documents at the Dwight D. Eisenhower Library reveal that William Robinson and his newspaper played a key role in the development of Eisenhower's campaign strategy and his relationship with the press, especially in the critical period between September 1951 and October 1952.[4]

Robinson's newspaper career began in 1931 on the *New York World Telegram*. He was later advertising director for the *New York Evening Journal* and, in 1936, joined the *Herald Tribune*, where he remained for eighteen years. His friendship with Eisenhower was based on golf and bridge, as well as politics. Robinson first invited Eisenhower to play golf at the Augusta National course, and through Robinson, he met men who were to become his closest personal advisers, among them the investment banker Clifford Roberts.[5]

Acting as an advocate of Eisenhower became a familiar role for Robinson. Peter Lyon notes that Robinson was

on terms of easy familiarity with newspaper publishers and editors; since 1948 he had been diligently promoting the Eisenhower cause with the Scripps-Howard, Hearst, Knight, and other newspaper chains and with publishers of the more widely circulated magazines as well.[6]

Robinson was also busy building bridges to Walter Lippmann, Joseph Alsop, David Lawrence, Roscoe Drummond, Arthur Krock, and other political writers of syndicated columns.[7]

The two men first met in 1944. A day or two before the Battle of the Bulge, Robinson found the General "the only unworried, unharassed man I had met in four days."[8] The relationship resumed after the war, when Eisenhower was serving as Army Chief of Staff. With Douglas M. Black, the president of Doubleday, Robinson persuaded Eisenhower to write his memoirs of the war years; *Crusade in Europe* was published in 1948. Eisenhower reflected later that although the offers to do a book were "annoying," Black and Robinson presented a convincing argument.

They showed me, or reminded me of, a number of books which had been written hurriedly, so as not to "miss the market." . . . Mr. Black and Mr. Robinson, who were functioning as partners for the proposal, pointed out errors in these publications and said that since these were written in my lifetime and were not denied or corrected by me, the historians of the future might give them a high degree of credibility. "You owe it to yourself, to the country, and to history, to tell the personal story of your European campaigns." . . . This reasoning impressed me.[9]

The meeting at the Pentagon on October 17, 1947, to discuss the publication of Eisenhower's memoirs had a strong effect on Robinson as well. He wrote to Helen Reid: "[Eisenhower] was natural, alive, alert, spirited, and gave the impression of having an intense amount of unloosened energy, both intellectual and physical.'' Moreover, Robinson observed that ''if one of the major political parties could demonstrate a clear preponderance of opinion in his favor, he would accept the nomination.''[10]

Over a period of almost three years, Robinson continued to sound out Eisenhower on his political convictions and personal philosophy, and reported his impressions to Helen Reid—that Ike's political philosophy was essentially Republican, that he could be persuaded to run, and that he would win.[11] William Ewald, Jr., who served in the Eisenhower White House, writes that the dialogues with Robinson were pivotal in the General's own decision-making:

[Robinson] was indispensable to Eisenhower, who, like all normal men, required friendship. Robinson gave it in abundance. And through the early post-war years, Dwight Eisenhower had confided to him his innermost political secrets, confided them in conversations of frequently volcanic candor.[12]

Robinson was reassured to learn that Eisenhower was opposed to the New Deal and the Fair Deal, and that the General shared his belief that the Truman administration was ''committed to Socialist doctrines.''[13] Nonetheless, he argued against a 1948 campaign as a Republican, especially after Eisenhower became president of Columbia University. Robinson wrote to Clifford Roberts that ''strong leftish elements'' in the Columbia student body and faculty would ''harass and badger'' Eisenhower if he declared his candidacy as a Republican.[14]

In 1951, there were no such misgivings. Robinson and Roberts visited Eisenhower in Paris and urged him to publicly declare he was a Republican. The *Herald Tribune*'s chief Washington correspondent, Bert Andrews, also urged Eisenhower to declare his party affiliation. Andrews sent a cable to Paris when Oregon Democrats *and* Republicans filed petitions to place him on the primary ballot. Eisenhower responded that, while the cable ''was inspired by the friendliest of motives,'' a statement of his political beliefs would damage his ability to serve ''objectively and earnestly'' in a nonpartisan capacity.[15] Before Eisenhower announced that he was a Republican, however, the *Herald Tribune* publicly declared its support in a front-page editorial. In a letter to Boston businessman Maxwell Bessell, Robinson outlined the reasons for the endorsement:

1. Through personal and unrestricted conversations over a period of several years, we were completely convinced of the General's basic republican philosophy.

2. We were confident that he could win the election by a majority that would transcend anything in Republican Party history—and that he would help elect to office Republican candidates for Congress. . . .

3. We were impressed by his primary devotion to America's economic and military security and his concept of a foreign policy that would insure this.

4. [He understands] clearly that the cost of government and especially the cost of defense must be drastically reduced as a primary measure against an accelerated inflation.

5. General Eisenhower's miraculous gift for reconciling the most contradictory and conflicting points of view would develop a spirit of unity within the party and the country which is desperately needed.

And finally, his great integrity and high sense of moral and spiritual values would bring a regeneration to government at all levels.[16]

Eisenhower was, of course, a national hero and, according to opinion polls, was the most widely admired American then living.[17] He had been seriously regarded as a possible presidential candidate since 1948, when Harry Truman reportedly offered to run as his vice-president on a Democratic ticket. (Truman denied that he had made such an offer.)[18] As late as 1951, however, Eisenhower had disdained politics as a pretty "sordid" business.[19]

His public position on seeking the presidency was that he would respond to a "call of duty" only if it were demonstrated by the country, in effect forcing a convention to nominate him. The movement to draft Eisenhower was led by Massachusetts Senator Henry Cabot Lodge (who at one time had been a reporter for the *Herald Tribune*), together with Senators James H. Duff of Pennsylvania, Frank Carlson of Kansas, and Governor Dewey. Actually, the effort was not a genuine draft, for Eisenhower had to come home from Europe in June to strengthen his cause by direct appeal.[20]

On January 7, 1952, Senator Lodge announced that Eisenhower had given his permission to have his name entered in the New Hampshire primary as a member of the Republican party. The next day, Eisenhower issued a statement that he would not campaign, but confirming that he was a Republican and would accept the nomination if chosen by the convention. Robinson congratulated Eisenhower on his decision, and expressed his delight "with this sincere and honest clarification of your position." Robinson offered his assistance in press relations and in creating the campaign organization, despite the fact that Eisenhower had expressly dismissed any personal involvement in the campaign efforts of Lodge and others. Drawing a very fine distinction between keeping the candidate informed and encouraging his active participation, Robinson reminded the General:

Needless to say, this letter requires no answer—in line with our plan to keep you free of political discussion or correspondence. I'm assuming you will have no objection to some one-way correspondence whenever I think I have something to say that might not be in your routine information.[21]

Without the overt cooperation of the candidate, Robinson enlisted the services of his newspaper. On February 28, the *Herald Tribune* began a twelve-part serialization of excerpts from *The Man from Abilene*, an unabashedly supportive biography written by Kevin McCann, Eisenhower's chief civilian assistant from 1946 to 1951, and afterward president of Defiance College.[22] Robinson made it his job to personally arrange for the syndication of the series, obtaining the rights from Douglas Black, who was McCann's publisher as well as Eisenhower's. Robinson eventually placed the series in sixty-four newspapers in the United States, six in South America, and two in Europe.[23] The *Herald Tribune* published a booklet of the twelve articles titled ''Eisenhower's Creed.''

While placing the McCann series, Robinson took time to survey the political landscape. On one of several trips to New Hampshire, where the first primary would be held on March 11, Robinson wrote to Eisenhower in Paris:

I succeeded in placing the McCann series with four of the seven regional daily papers. Of the weeklies, 50% of them are definitely for you and came out accordingly in last week's issue, or will in this week's edition. I would say 25% of them lean in your direction but will not take any position. I could find only two out of the sixteen weeklies I contacted that have or will come out for Taft.[24]

Success in the New Hampshire primary was vital for Eisenhower. Taft had established a substantial lead in delegate strength, perhaps as many as 400 votes. (There were 1,205 convention delegates, with 603 votes needed for the nomination.) In his correspondence with Eisenhower, Robinson noted the perception of voters in New Hampshire that Taft's campaign organization was a ''well-oiled, well-heeled machine'' compared to the disorganized appearance of his opposition. That, he told the General, could be ''more of an asset than a liability'' in appealing to the ''fair-minded average voter.''[25] Indeed, Robinson reported that a close Eisenhower victory was likely, although there were problems in the state. William Loeb, the arch-conservative publisher of the *Manchester Union*, the only morning daily in New Hampshire, had long before endorsed Taft. Robinson wrote to Eisenhower on March 3 that Taft had ''made some real gains in the state. . . . He is especially strong in the reactionary, dyed-in-the-wood Republican areas.''[26] Eisenhower's strength was ''predominant'' among Independents, but Robinson pointed out that the Independents would have to register as Republicans to make their preferences count in the primary, and would thereby lose their independent status.[27]

Taft had one other advantage in New Hampshire; he was in a position to actively campaign in the state while Eisenhower was committed to remain in Paris, striking an above-the-battle pose. Reflecting on that problem, Robinson shared the *Herald Tribune*'s editorial intentions with Eisenhower:

We are planning to do a prominent editorial here, once more setting forth the reasons why you cannot come home to engage in this campaign, and why you should not. If for no other reason, it's about time we told the Eisenhower forces that they ought to take pride in the fact that their candidate is devoting his whole time and effort (at great personal sacrifice) to develop a defense for the free world and to prevent another war.[28]

Robinson gave Eisenhower his prediction of the outcome in New Hampshire: ''My crystal ball tells me that the preferential primary would show you leading

Taft in the ratio of 5–to–4.''[29] It was an uncannily accurate forecast; on March 11, Eisenhower received 46,661 votes to Taft's 35,838. A week later, in Minnesota, more than 100,000 write-in votes were cast for Eisenhower, whose name had not been entered on the ballot. The campaign was underway.

Robinson was among the most influential of all Eisenhower's advisers in planning his return from Europe. After Eisenhower announced that he would leave his European post in June, Robinson confessed to Milton Eisenhower, the General's youngest brother and the president of Pennsylvania State College: ''I don't suppose there's a free moment in the day or night—and I could include some unfree ones—when I'm not thinking about Ike's problems between June 1 and the convention.''[30]

The keynote of the entire campaign, Robinson believed, would be sounded in Eisenhower's formal announcement of candidacy in his boyhood home of Abilene, Kansas, on June 4. Elaborate materials were prepared for reporters covering the events over two days in Abilene, a town with a population of approximately 7,000. For the major address, which was televised live by CBS and NBC, 2,600 stadium seats were reserved for VIPs.[31] The theme of Eisenhower's remarks was the relationship between citizenship and world peace. Robinson had suggested in February that Eisenhower should discuss peace at Abilene:

I can hear you saying at Abilene that you are dedicating your life to the proposition that this Abilene memorial [which later became the Eisenhower Library and Museum] will be the last war memorial that anyone will dedicate. You know the strategy and the sinews of peace as well as those of war. You can make it a practical program to implement the great dream of mankind. This needs doing. There can be no more appropriate place than Abilene.[32]

In May, Robinson told Eisenhower that ''no speech made in recent years will have had such public interest as this one.''[33]

Perhaps fortunately for the Eisenhower campaign, the speech received far less attention than Robinson anticipated. The address itself was a notable disappointment, the General had to speak in a driving rain and delivered his announcement in a halting, uninspired manner as rain cascaded off a nearby umbrella onto his glasses. The next day's press conference went almost as poorly. Print journalists tried to bar television cameras from the Abilene movie house where the session was held. Finally, David Schoenbrun of CBS was allowed in as a pool reporter but had to broadcast live with no return circuit from New York. Robinson had tried to prepare the candidate for this first meeting with reporters. He had drawn up a list of likely questions from a number of reporters, including James Reston, Roscoe Drummond, Marquis Childs, and Bert Andrews of the *Herald Tribune*, for Eisenhower to review beforehand.[34]

Robinson had less direct involvement in the campaign after the Abilene homecoming. When Eisenhower won the Republican nomination in July, Robinson offered his assistance and that of his newspaper to Sherman Adams, the campaign chief of staff: ''If, in the tremendously vital work ahead, you think there is anything I or any of us on the Herald Tribune can do to be of the slightest service to you, please do feel free to command us."[35] During the remainder of the campaign, Robinson consulted on personnel matters and provided the Eisenhower staff with the results of public opinion polls and other information.[36]

The relationship between Eisenhower and Robinson during the campaign underwent its most severe test over the vice-presidential candidacy of Richard Nixon. Robinson was reportedly "furious" when it was revealed that the California Senator had been the beneficiary of an $18,235 political expense fund.[37] On September 20, the *Herald Tribune* called upon Nixon to formally withdraw from the campaign. Two days later, Robinson wired the Eisenhower campaign train, then in Owensboro, Kentucky: "My own personal view is that Nixon's continuation on the ticket seriously blunts the sharp edge of corruption issue and burdens you with heavy and unfair handicap. This view shared by Cliff [Roberts]."[38] Robinson and the *Herald Tribune* did not prevail. Instead, according to one account, Robinson "turned . . . 180 degrees" when Nixon defended himself on television in the "Checkers" speech of September 23.[39]

Following Eisenhower's election, Robinson maintained his friendship with the President, joining him frequently for games of golf or bridge. On one occasion, Eisenhower wrote to complain about the press, particularly syndicated columnists (with the exception of David Lawrence, whom Eisenhower described as "sensible and usually very close to fact").[40] Robinson answered not as a political ally, but as a journalist, with a defense of press performance:

You have had and still have the most favorable press of any man in my lifetime. Why? Did you curry favor with them like Baruch? No. Did you flatter them like Roosevelt? No. Did you become pal-ly like Truman? No. You were honest—forthright—faithful—and in a way, admiring. Before 1952 the cynics said, "But wait until he gets into politics." What happened? You still saw the press reported the truth or at least what they knew of it—but now they seem strangely arrogant and demanding beyond their deserts or the call of duty. This is what causes distaste for newspaper people among all political leaders, and I can understand it. As President you have access to information that reporters cannot possibly get. Therefore you very properly have disdain for their deliberations. And it's no comfort when sometimes they reach sound conclusions from a deficiency of fact. . . . The news columns of the press of the country since your election have been objective and eminently fair.[41]

In 1955, Robinson left the *Herald Tribune* to become president of Coca-Cola, Inc. His relationship with Eisenhower remained personally close, but, according to Lyon, "circumspect, in the middle distance."[42] Four years earlier, there had been very little distance between Eisenhower, Robinson, and the *New York Herald Tribune*. The nature of their cooperation was not unprecedented: an alliance of New York bankers, businessmen, and publishers had first promoted the Republican candidacy of Wendell Wilkie, then Thomas Dewey, then Eisenhower.[43] "So influential in the Party, so close were the Reids and William Robinson to Eisenhower," Herbert S. Parmet notes, "the paper was virtually a

Pravda of the Eastern Establishment.''[44] It seems clear that Robinson saw no essential conflict between his advocacy of Eisenhower and the management of the *Herald Tribune*. In 1951, as Eisenhower privately considered his future, and in the early stages of the 1952 campaign, the *Herald Tribune* had become almost naturally the political instrument of Robinson's friendship and high regard.

NOTES

1. See, for example, Charles A.H. Thomson, *Television and Presidential Politics* (Washington, D.C.: Brookings Institution, 1956) and Melvyn H. Bloom, *Public Relations and Presidential Campaigns: A Crisis in Democracy* (New York: Thomas Y. Crowell, 1973).

2. For a discussion of the *Herald Tribune*'s tradition of liberal Republicanism, see Kenneth Stewart and John Tebbel, *Makers of Modern Journalism* (New York: Prentice-Hall, 1952), pp. 253–56. See also Oswald Garrison Villard, *The Disappearing Daily* (New York: Alfred A. Knopf, 1944), pp. 93–102.

3. See Herbert S. Parmet, *Eisenhower and the American Crusades* (New York: Macmillan Co., 1972), p. 135. See also Blanche Wiesen Cook, *The Declassified Eisenhower: A Divided Legacy of Peace and Political Warfare* (New York: Doubleday and Co., 1981), pp. 76–77.

4. A number of documents concerning Eisenhower's political deliberations are found in the William E. Robinson Papers, Box 2. Other materials concerning the election of 1952 are in Boxes 6–9. See also the Personal File of Dwight D. Eisenhower: 1916–1952, Box 91.

5. See Peter Lyon, *Eisenhower: Portrait of the Hero* (Boston: Little Brown, 1974), pp. 383–84.

6. Ibid., p. 427.

7. Ibid.

8. Quoted in William Bragg Ewald, Jr., *Eisenhower the President: Crucial Days, 1951–1960* (Englewood Cliffs, N.J.: Prentice-Hall, 1981), p. 251.

9. Dwight D. Eisenhower, *At Ease: Stories I Tell to Friends* (Garden City, N.Y.: Doubleday and Co., 1967), p. 325.

10. William Robinson to Helen Rogers Reid, October 17, 1947, William E. Robinson Papers, Box 9, Eisenhower Library.

11. See Robinson to Reid, 21 June 1948, William E. Robinson Papers, Box 9.

12. Ewald, *Eisenhower the President*, p. 42.

13. Quoted in Lyon, *Eisenhower*, p. 406.

14. Ibid.

15. Andrews to Eisenhower, August 27, 1951; Eisenhower to Andrews, August 31, 1951, William E. Robinson Papers, Box 8, Folder on Election of 1952 (1951).

16. Robinson to Maxwell E. Bessell, January 31, 1952, William E. Robinson Papers, Box 2, Folder on Eisenhower—Personal, January-March 1952.

17. Louis Harris, *Is There a Republican Majority? Political Trends, 1952–1956* (New York: Harper and Brothers, 1954), p. 56.

18. See Relman Morin, *Dwight D. Eisenhower: A Gauge of Greatness* (New York: Simon and Schuster, 1969), p. 128.

19. Several journalists interviewed Eisenhower during this period, on and off the

record, and his comments to each of them were essentially the same. The statement that politics was a "sordid" affair was made to C. L. Sulzberger and is cited in *A Long Row of Candles: Memoirs and Diaries, 1934–1954* (New York: Macmillan Co., 1969), p. 703. See also Arthur Krock, *Memoirs: Sixty Years on the Firing Line* (New York: Funk and Wagnalls, 1968), p. 284. Eisenhower discusses his reluctance to run in Robert H. Ferrell, ed., *The Eisenhower Diaries* (New York: W. W. Norton, 1981), p. 206.

20. See Eugene H. Roseboom and Alfred E. Eckes, Jr., *A History of Presidential Elections from George Washington to Jimmy Carter*, 4th ed. (New York: Macmillan Co., 1979), pp. 217–29.

21. Robinson to Eisenhower, January 14, 1952, p. 2, Personal File of DDE: 1916–1952, Box 91, Folder 2 on William E. Robinson.

22. See David F. Schoenbrun, "The Ordeal of General Ike," *Harper's* 205, no. 1229 (October 1952):25–34.

23. Robinson to Douglas Black, April 14, 1952, William E. Robinson Papers, Box 2, Folder on Eisenhower—Personal, April-June 1952.

24. Robinson to Eisenhower, March 3, 1952, p. 1, William E. Robinson Papers, Box 2, Folder on Eisenhower—Personal, January-March 1952.

25. Ibid.

26. Ibid.

27. Ibid.

28. Ibid., p. 2.

29. Ibid.

30. Robinson to Milton Eisenhower, April 18, 1952, p. 1, William E. Robinson Papers, Box 2, Folder on Eisenhower—Personal, April-June 1952.

31. "Welcome to Abilene" (Eisenhower Day Press Kit), June 4, 1952, William E. Robinson Papers, Box 8, Folder on Election of 1952—Spring and Summer 1952.

32. Robinson to Eisenhower, February 18, 1952, p. 2, Personal File of DDE: 1916–1952, Box 91, Folder 2 on William E. Robinson.

33. Robinson to Eisenhower, May 15, 1952, William E. Robinson Papers, Box 2, Folder on Eisenhower—Personal, April-June 1952.

34. See Lyon, *Eisenhower*, p. 438.

35. Robinson to Sherman Adams, July 23, 1952, William E. Robinson Papers, Box 9.

36. Robinson suggested, for example, that Eisenhower use the Young and Rubicam advertising agency in the campaign, and recommended its president, Sigurd Larmon, to Eisenhower.

37. See Lyon, *Eisenhower*, pp. 454–55. See also Cook, *Declassified Eisenhower*, p. 142.

38. Robinson to Thomas Stephens, September 22, 1952, p. 2, William E. Robinson Papers, Box 6.

39. See Ewald, *Eisenhower the President*, p. 55.

40. Eisenhower to Robinson, December 20, 1952, William E. Robinson Papers, Box 6.

41. Robinson to Eisenhower, July 22, 1953, p. 2.

42. Lyon, *Eisenhower*, p. 503.

43. See Theodore H. White, *America in Search of Itself: The Making of the President, 1956–1980* (New York: Harper and Row, 1982), p. 55.

44. Parmet, *Eisenhower and the American Crusades*, p. 503.

3

Eisenhower's Two Presidential Campaigns, 1952 and 1956

L. Richard Guylay

In his lifetime, Dwight David Eisenhower undertook two presidential campaigns which were markedly different in form, style, and content. In 1952, he ran as the enormously popular war hero, but it was apparent that at first he was unsure of the issues, and at times uncomfortable with the rambunctious elements that make up a national political organization. Even in 1956, after four years as Chief Executive, he once told National Chairman Len Hall to "order" the state chairmen to do something he wanted. Hall said, "Mr. President, you can't order state chairmen to do anything, I have to ask or suggest."

Politics was a new environment for this lifelong soldier, but he drew great confidence from the plaudits of the crowds and the dedication and skill of the many powerful friends who won for him the nomination for President. Furthermore, he was a quick learner and it didn't take him long to find out what politics was all about, and, having learned that, to take charge.

The learning process began when the 1952 campaign got off to an uncertain start, which alarmed the candidate as well as his supporters. It began on September 2 with a quick trip to Georgia, Florida, and Alabama, and back to New York, where national headquarters had been set up in the Commodore Hotel. The next morning, the entire entourage, including a sizable group of reporters, were off on a seven-day swing to Philadelphia, Chicago, Minneapolis, Cleveland, Indianapolis, Washington, and New York. These trips, perhaps, were too fast and ambitious for a shakedown cruise, and the crowds were disappointing and apathetic. The Scripps-Howard newspaper, which had supported Ike for the nomination, ran a first-page editorial in all editions sharply criticizing the campaign effort, entitled "Running like a Dry Creek."

It was obvious that the party "regulars" who held most of the state and local offices and controlled the party machinery were still licking their wounds. They had worked hard for Senator Taft as their choice for the nomination, and the final Gallup Poll before the convention had given Taft a narrow lead, as did the *Newsweek* panel of fifty leading newspaper correspondents.

Senator Taft, the leader of the Senate, was known as "Mr. Republican," and his supporters felt he was fully qualified to follow his father, William Howard Taft, as President. The crucial incident of the convention which ended Taft's chances for the nomination concerned his capturing of the Texas delegation, which the Eisenhower strategies labeled the "Texas Steal." The victory was overturned in an acrimonious battle in the credentials committee. Taft's loss on that key vote turned the tide and ultimately resulted in Eisenhower's nomination.

Taft spent the three months following the convention tidying up the unfinished business of the Senate and taking his customary vacation with his family at Murray Bay, Canada, but staying in touch with his supporters in Congress and throughout the forty-eight states. In the serene weeks at Murray Bay his disappointment slowly subsided. His fears that an Adlai Stevenson-Estes Kefauver administration would be a continuation of the Truman years, which he had opposed with all his power, led him to believe that Eisenhower would be infinitely better for the country.

Taft tried to convey his feelings to his followers, but they were adamant and Taft despaired of ever bringing the two wings of the party together. He felt that Eisenhower might not get the presidency without the enthusiastic support of the powerful regular Republican organizations in most of the key states. Such support was necessary to overturn the unbroken Democratic regimes of Roosevelt and Truman going back to 1932.

If only Taft could persuade Eisenhower to move slightly more to the right in support of conservative fiscal policy, including a balanced budget and economy in government, a strong foreign policy, and support of the Taft-Hartley Law (which Taft had pressed through Congress over the opposition of President Truman and most of organized labor), the rancor that had split the Republicans at their convention could be healed. So Taft reasoned. If Eisenhower would agree to these measures, Taft felt he could swing his following into line. After discussions between Taft and his Senate colleague, Frank Carlson of Kansas, and other moderates of the two camps, Carlson went to Governor Sherman Adams of New Hampshire, who had acted as Eisenhower's manager, and to Senator Henry Cabot Lodge of Massachusetts. All agreed that a meeting between Eisenhower and Taft would be highly desirable, and a date was set for September 12 at Columbia University.

Eisenhower brought Jim Hagerty and one other aide to the meeting, and Taft brought two of his closest colleagues, Jack Martin and me. All of the aides left the room immediately after the General greeted the Senator.

Eisenhower read Taft's document slowly and carefully and, except for a few minor corrections, said that he could accept the document in its entirely. He made no substantive corrections, deletions, or additions. He also agreed not to discriminate against Taft supporters in making appointments in his administration.

After the business end of the meeting was over, the two leaders fell into small talk. Altogether, the meeting lasted only about 30 minutes. The General informed the press that he would leave the announcement of the meeting to the Senator, and a large press conference was held across the street in a hotel ballroom. The press immediately labeled the conference, "The Surrender at Morningside Heights," but the Republican presidential campaign was finally on track.

The change in the mood of the Republican campaign was immediate. The party had lost five successive presidential elections. The Depression and Roosevelt's three-plus administrations had reduced the GOP to minority status. But now the party was finally united, and all hands pitched in with vigor and enthusiasm to get the job done. The GOP campaign themes were "cleaning up the mess in Washington" and "ending the war in Korea." The battle cry was "Win with Ike." To contrast with this belletristic style, the Democrats relied heavily on Stevenson's polished rhetoric and on their slogan, "You Never Had It So Good."

The Republican managers laid out a strenuous campaign for Eisenhower and Nixon, who went in separate directions. Most of the barnstorming was by train, with a large entourage of headquarters officials and workers, and national press people. Local press and party dignitaries would join the train briefly for a ride to the next stop. There were brief rear-platform appearances, but major addresses were generally given "offtrain" at local hotels, city hall steps, or state capitols. Motorcades from the train stations to downtown destinations were a means of getting crowds of citizens to catch a glimpse of the candidates. There were local broadcasts of speeches over radio and television hookups, and regional simulcasts carried some important speeches on radio and television. Network television was in its infancy, however—at least as far as national politics was concerned—and was used infrequently.

Whistlestop campaigning in 1952 was gruelling and not a very efficient way of getting the message to the country's voters. Two key incidents of the Republican campaign, however, drew nationwide attention. These were the Nixon "Checkers" speech and Ike's promise to go to Korea.

The Nixon Fund controversy occurred early in the campaign when a syndicated columnist, Peter Edson, revealed that a group of California businessmen had collected a "secret" fund for Nixon. Indeed, Dan Smith, who had been treasurer of Nixon's 1950 successful campaign for the Senate, came up with the idea of financing Nixon's expenses for off-season politicking, which could not be paid out of his $12,000 salary or from formal campaign treasuries. Smith and the others felt that Nixon had to stay active in California politics even while Congress was in session, and that the fund would permit him to maintain a reasonable level of political activity back home. The budget was $16,000, and contributions were limited to $100 to $500.

The story broke on September 18, 1952, the very day that General Eisenhower, campaigning in Iowa, promised to drive the "crooks and cronies" from power and bring a Republican Honest Deal to Washington to replace the Democratic Fair Deal. "When we are through," he declared, "the experts in shoddy government operations will be on their way back to the shadowy haunts in the subcellars of American politics from which they came."

The Nixon story provoked a raging controversy. Pickets showed up at Nixon's appearances hurling epithets. Eisenhower said that he had "long admired and applauded Senator Nixon's American faith and his determination to drive Communist sympathizers from offices of public trust." Nixon was "an honest man," the General added, "and would prove this by placing 'all the facts' before the people, fairly and squarely." Meanwhile, editorials calling for Nixon's replacement on the ticket began appearing. A hard blow came from the *Herald Tribune* which suggested that Nixon offer to resign, leaving it up to Eisenhower whether or not to accept. At an informal session with some reporters on the President's campaign train, General Eisenhower was asked if "the Nixon thing was a closed incident." Eisenhower frowned and said, "By no means." He said that he had just learned of the controversy and that, although he had not known Nixon very long, the Senator seemed to exemplify the kind of honesty, vigor, and straightforwardness he admired. Furthermore, he couldn't believe that Nixon would do anything crooked or unethical. All the same, he emphasized, Nixon would have to prove it. Then the General added, "Of what avail is it for us to carry on this crusade of what has been going on in Washington if we ourselves aren't as clean as a hound's tooth."

The storm took on renewed fury when Harold Stassen, former Governor of Minnesota, who harbored a long-time ambition to be President, wired Nixon, suggesting that he offer to resign and thus put the decision up to Eisenhower. Then a survey of newspaper editorials showed that they were two to one against Nixon. Finally, Governor Tom Dewey of New York called to say that he had polled the campaign leaders and that most of them felt that Nixon should resign. That call was a blockbuster to Nixon. Meanwhile, Dewey and others agreed that Nixon should go on a national broadcast to tell his side of the story. The Republican National Chairman, Arthur Summerfield, learned that under the rules of the national convention the delegates would have to select a replacement if a vacancy on the ticket occurred. He suggested, therefore, that Nixon ask the listeners to be the judges by wiring the national committee headquarters, yes or no, on his resignation.

Not until three days after the story broke did Eisenhower call Nixon and have their first conversation. Nixon told the General that the important thing was for the Republicans to win. "I want you to know that if you reach a conclusion either now or later, that I should get off the ticket, you can be sure that I will respect your judgment and do so." Eisenhower replied, in effect, that he didn't think he should be the one to make that decision.

Nixon's speech was broadcast on September 23 over a national hookup of 64 NBC television stations, 194 CBS radio stations, and the entire 560 Mutual

Broadcasting radio stations. It was said to be the largest audience for any political figure in history. Nixon had no script, speaking only from notes. He denied that a single cent of the fund went to his personal use. All of it went for campaign expenses, he insisted, and the contributors never received any special consideration. He pointed out that his wife, Pat, didn't own a mink coat but, rather, had a respectable Republican cloth coat. He said that his daughters had received a cocker-spaniel dog, Checkers, as a gift but that he had no intention of returning it. He then asked his listeners to write or wire the Republican National Committee as to whether he should get off the ticket or stay on it. "Whatever your decision, I will abide by it."

General Eisenhower watched the performance and wired Nixon immediately, "Your presentation was magnificent." He added that he wished to see Nixon the following night in Wheeling, West Virginia. Following the broadcast, party headquarters reported the receipt of 300,000 letters, telegrams, and petitions totaling more than a million signatures. The national committee reported that 107 of its 138 members had voted enthusiastically to keep Nixon on the ticket. When Nixon's plane arrived in Wheeling after dusk, Eisenhower was the first to run up the steps and put his arm around Nixon, warmly declaring "Dick, you're my boy."

The campaign now settled down to the nitty-gritty of presidential politics. The Democratic effort was disorganized, with little coordination between state organizations and the national committee. Stevenson stressed civil rights, social welfare, federal-state relationships, political morality, and foreign policy, and used abstract terms and literary quotations. For its part, the Democratic National Committee stuck to its issue, "You Never Had It So Good." In contrast, the Republicans concentrated on the "mess" in Washington and on ending the Korean War. They were successful in turning that conflict into "Truman's War" in the minds of a large part of the American public, and Eisenhower insisted that the tragic blunder could only be remedied by a new administration. "I shall go to Korea," he promised, as millions of Americans thrilled to the drama of his pledge. Soon, huge crowds across the country roared, "We want Ike!" After the election, Truman asked Eisenhower if he "still wanted to go to Korea." This angered Eisenhower who took it as a snide remark. Of course, he wanted to go, he said, and right after the election, he did. The war ended soon thereafter.

The popular vote in 1952 was more than 51 million, the largest in the nation's history. Eisenhower ran far ahead of his party, whereas Stevenson ran far behind the Democratic ticket. Ike won thirty-nine states with forty-two electoral votes; Stevenson had nine states with only eighty-nine votes in the electoral college. Best of all, from the Republican point of view, was the GOP capture of both houses of Congress. On the morning after the election, Democrat Sam Rayburn, Speaker of the House, acknowledged, "We just got the hell beat out of us." Senator Taft was chosen leader of the Senate, and Congressman Joe Martin majority leader of the House. The Republicans looked forward to at least eight years in power.

Eisenhower's popularity during the first two years of his first term remained at a high level. A Gallup Poll found that Ike was the most admired man, worldwide; his rating was higher than the combined total of the next two men, Winston Churchill and Douglas MacArthur. But his coat-tails were not long enough for his party, and in the by-election of 1954 the Republicans lost control of both houses of Congress. This outcome was interpreted as a sign of weakness and promoted the Democrats and the press to attack the President, despite his great prestige and popularity.

It was not Ike's nature to engage publicly in political controversy. Rather, he preferred to emphasize the ties uniting all citizens and to leave the political brawling to others. But the Republican apparatus for this kind of warfare was weak, both in Washington and throughout the country. The problem aggravated the President, and he discussed it at several meetings at the White House and with Leonard Hall, Republican Party Chairman. A committee of some of the President's close friends who had some experience with advertising and public relations was formed to suggest some remedies and to find someone to head the overall promotional effort for the reelection drive. The committee recommended me, and on April 3, 1955, I was appointed director of advertising and public relations for the Republican National Committee, which was to be the vehicle for Eisenhower's second nomination drive. At the same time, John Clifford Folger, a Washington banker, was named chairman of the Finance Committee. Hall, Folger, and I had our first meeting with the President at a White House breakfast on May 5, 1955, to discuss campaign plans.

In broad terms, the campaign of 1956 would not rely on the inefficient, time-consuming whistlestop method. The dramatic gains in radio and television made it possible to reach tens of millions of voters quickly and effectively. It was therefore decided to concentrate on an electronic campaign. One problem arose, however. In the past, campaign speeches on radio and TV had been 30 minutes or more in length and in 1952 had not attracted or held audiences. Furthermore, by 1956 few, if any, half-hour slots were available. The networks did not want to preempt their regular half-hour shows, particularly those in prime time, for fear of losing audiences and revenues. A happy solution was to shorten their regular shows by five minutes and sell those spots to us. Those "piggy-back" spots were very expensive, but with their huge audiences they proved to be a good investment. Since these shows were on film or tape, the scripts had to be redone in the shorter version. Working with its ad agency, BBDO, the national committee tied up the best spots early in the year, leaving the leftovers for the Democrats.

On September 10, 1955, the Republican state chairmen had a meeting at the Brown Palace Hotel in Denver to discuss plans for the coming campaign. The President was on vacation in Denver at the same time, and after the meeting Chairman Hall and I went to his temporary office to give a report. Hall's report was brief, but Ike kept looking at his watch. He was obviously irritated because an Italian diplomat had made an appointment to see him and was already a half hour late. The President had a golf date, and his friends were waiting. Hall and Ike retired to a small anteroom for a private conversation.

As Hall reported after the meeting, the President paced the floor, and his irritation and tenseness grew. The burden of his conversation was: "I've given my whole life up to now to the service of my country—why should I give any more? There are other men just as well qualified to be President of the United States. I should be given a chance to get out and enjoy private life and any of these men will carry on and be just as good as I could be." Among the names he mentioned were Robert Anderson, Richard Nixon, Cabot Lodge, Herbert Brownell, and William Rogers. It was the first time the President had ever indicated such feelings to Hall. How seriously he felt about not running again or whether it was just a fleeting moment of frustration is hard to tell. But the thought was there, and Hall was shaken.

Two weeks later, on September 24, while he was still in Denver, Ike had a heart attack that shook the world. I received the news from Murray Snyder, assistant press secretary, who was in Denver. He had been trying to reach people in Washington including Hall, and it fell to me to relay the news to Hall at his home on Long Island.

A decision was made to avoid the press until the seriousness of the attack became known. As luck would have it, Hall was scheduled to address the Union League Club in New York on Monday. As we entered the club, newspapermen were already gathering on the sidewalk, and TV cameras were being set up. Fortunately, the Club's luncheons are off the record, and the news people were not admitted. Hall struggled through the speech and parried the questions from the club members as best he could, but the press was another matter. There were one hundred or so reporters on the sidewalk, with a dozen TV and still cameras, radio mikes, and tape recorders at the ready.

Over the weekend Hall and I had already discussed the danger of opening up any speculation on who might be likely to announce their candidacy for the nomination. No one had precise information on either the severity of the attack or the prognosis for recovery. More importantly, we felt that if there was any open jockeying for the nomination by the time the President began to rally, he might conclude that the party assumed he would not be a candidate again. The result might then be a bloody free-for-all that would hurt the party's chances to hold the presidency. For these reasons Hall's statement to the press was: "The ticket still will be Eisenhower and Nixon." They snickered, howled, and came at him from every side. But Hall insisted; "As far as I'm concerned, the ticket will be Ike and Dick. And thank you very much."

We flew back to Washington. I was first down the steps, and a group of newsmen pressed forward. Rowland Evans, then the political reporter for the Associated Press, said to me, "The AP has a 'mistake' on its wire from New York. It quotes Len Hall saying that the ticket will be Ike and Dick." I replied "That's no mistake. That's exactly what he said!" Evans looked me in the eye and said, "Hall must be out of his blinking mind."

During the early period of Ike's convalescence, Sherman Adams ran the day-to-day business of the White House. Vice-President Nixon presided over Cabinet meetings and was the chief spokesman for the administration. Meanwhile, Hall kept the lid on the eager aspirants for the top nomination who were popping up all over the country, maneuvering for position in the event Ike would not be a candidate. Hall had deliberately not seen the President during the many weeks following the heart attack, but finally the time seemed to be appropriate after the president was moved from Denver to his home in Gettysburg.

Hall arranged a meeting for November 28, and he and I flew to Gettysburg in a single-engine plane and landed on a small field. Jim Hagerty met us. My first words were, "What does it look like?" Jim said, "No way, the man's not going." We moved on to the President's temporary offices where Sherman Adams was sitting in a small outer room, looking glum and discouraged. The essence of his opinion was that there was no chance that Ike would be a candidate again.

Hall went in alone to see the President and stayed with him some 15 or 20 minutes. He found the President doodling with a pen at his desk. He had never seen the President in lower spirits. "How are you feeling, Chief?"

Ike replied, "Len, you're looking at an old dodo."

Hall told him he knew some friends who had heart attacks, and they all felt low in spirits for a while after, but that it ultimately passed. Ike didn't respond.

Hall spoke a little about politics and then said that every Cabinet officer who had come to see the President in recent days was asked by the press afterwards whether they discussed whether the President would run again. They all said they had not. "As the chairman of the party I can't tell the press I didn't discuss politics with you." The President said, "Len, I'm going to leave that up to you. I don't want to tell you what to say. I don't know what you will say. But go out there and say what you think you should."

Hall came out of the President's office to tell us the President was leaving it up to him. "Now, what do I say?" Adams shrugged his shoulders and turned to his desk. Jim said to me, "It's your baby," and went off to the fieldhouse where several hundred reporters were waiting for Hall's press conference.

I sat down at a table with Len to put some words on paper. I said that the press would be looking for a headline, and we agreed on "*Ike Will Run If He Is Able.*" That was Hall's opinion, and it had the added attraction of implying Ike's satisfactory recovery. The press treated it as a bombshell, and the story was sensationally received across the country. As to how the President received it, we have the word of George Allen, a long-time friend, who came to see the President later that same day. As he went into the office, Hagerty handed him the wire service stories that had just come over the tickers. Allen later told Hall that the President looked at the stories and smiled.

On January 20, 1956, the Republicans staged a series of "Salute to Eisenhower" dinners in fifty-one cities throughout the country, tied together for the first time by closed circuit TV. He was deeply moved by the speakers, especially a lady from Texas who looked into the camera and said, "Mr. President, we need you." On February 29, the President's heart specialist, Dr. Paul Dudley White, said that there was no reason why the President could not carry on his present activity satisfactorily for another five to ten years. On February 29, Ike announced his intention to seek a second term, and on April 26, Nixon, who had been told by the President to "chart his own course," told the President that he wanted to be on the ticket again. Ike was delighted, and it was announced that the Ike and Dick team would seek a second term.

Another setback seemed imminent on June 8, 1956, when the President suffered an attack of ileitis, an inflammation of the smaller intestine, and was operated on that night. The operation was a success, however, and recovery rapid so that campaign plans could move forward.

The Republican National Convention was scheduled for San Francisco beginning August 20, 1956, immediately following the Democratic convention in Chicago. The Republican convention drew a record number of press people, not only from the United States but also from many countries around the world. Six thousand press credentials were issued. The proceedings were televised from "gavel to gavel." The opening statement of the GOP convention, delivered by Chairman Hall, set the theme. He said, "There's one difference between the Democratic convention and ours. Last week in Chicago they nominated a loser. This week in San Francisco we're going to nominate a winner!"

To bring unity to the campaign, Chairman Hall directed that all speeches, literature, press releases, and other activities be cleared by my office. We insisted on a greater reliance on congressional spokespersons, saving the President for major appearances and press conferences. We also organized a highly effective "Murderers Row" on the Hill to answer Democratic speakers as quickly as possible with material we furnished. In the campaign period, we established an Answer Desk headed by Dr. Gabriel Hauge, the President's chief economic adviser, to monitor the Democrats' major speeches and to place answering material in the hands of our spokespersons throughout the country the next morning. We sent out a "Truth Squad" by chartered plane to follow Democratic speakers around the country, answering them on the spot and getting our publicity into the same news cycle. We had an aggressive press relations program and monitored all media, protesting unfair coverage and cheap shots. We had frequent off-the-record background dinners, hosted by the Chairman, to which were invited ten or twelve national correspondents at a time.

Essentially, we structured Eisenhower's campaign around four key elements: (1) prestige, (2) affirmation, (3) repetition, and (4) contagion.

1. *Prestige*: Ike had his great renown as Allied Supreme Commander and fully exploited the accoutrements of the White House. He never did anything to denigrate the mystique of the White House.

2. *Affirmation*: The case for Ike's reelection was concisely stated in the slogan, "Peace and Prosperity." It was effective and expressed what every American understood and appreciated. A variation of the slogan was "Everything's Booming But the Guns."

3. *Repetition*: This phase involved hammering away at the central theme of the campaign, with all possible variations. We played it like an orchestra plays a symphony; the

variations were many, but the theme was always the same: Peace and Prosperity under Ike.

4. *Contagion*: The final phase of the campaign was fed by massive advertising, publicity, endorsement, large crowds, and great excitement. Timing was of the essence as the campaign came to a climax. The result was a tremendous victory for the President, despite the earlier widespread misgivings about his two serious illnesses.

In the landslide of popular votes, Ike carried forty-one of the forty-eight states with 457 electoral votes, leaving Stevenson with only seven states and seventy-four electoral votes. But this time the President's sweep did not carry over into the congressional races, and the Democrats were once again in control of both houses. We had had two campaigns and two victories, and each was marked by its uniqueness.

THE PRESIDENT: DOMESTIC POLICY

4

Regardless of Station, Race, or Calling: Eisenhower and Race

Michael S. Mayer

For many years, historians and the general public alike assumed that Dwight Eisenhower was an ineffective President who had relatively little to do with running the country during the era to which he gave his name. By the late 1960s, in the wake of the tragedy of the American involvement in Indochina, young radical historians grew disillusioned with liberal Democrats and with policies that resulted in the war in Vietnam and riots in America's cities. In their search for alternatives, some discovered Eisenhower, a military man who, as President, ended one war and did not begin another. In the early 1970s, new material in the Eisenhower Library became available to researchers. Renewed interest combined with access to materials, and a new picture of the thirty-fourth President began to emerge. Rather than a doddering caretaker, he appeared to have been a capable, astute politician, but a far more conservative one than most people had imagined. That assessment extended to his record on civil rights and especially to his personal attitudes on racial issues.

In the mid-1970s, however, enormous collections of documents were opened up to researchers. The papers of James Hagerty, Eisenhower's capable Press Secretary, and the so-called Ann Whitman File, which contains Eisenhower's papers as President, were made available for research. From these rich files, yet another picture of Eisenhower emerged. The newly available material reinforced the conception that Eisenhower was a highly capable and articulate man, but forced historians of the period to reevaluate their conclusion that he was a rock-ribbed conservative. This is especially true in the area of civil rights. This chapter evaluates Eisenhower's personal attitudes on the question of race in light of the evidence now available.

In his memoirs, Eisenhower recalled that "since boyhood I had accepted without qualification the right to equality before the law of all citizens of this country, whatever their race or color or creed."[1] One might well question, however, the degree to which he actually confronted the issue of racial discrimination. Few black families lived in Abilene, and there were no blacks at West Point. Eisenhower's early career in the Army provided no more opportunity to establish contacts with black people except those in menial or personal service roles. A number of his early assignments took him to posts in the South, and Southerners dominated the Army's professional officer corps. His tour of duty in the Philippines served only to reinforce stereotypes of racial servility and inferiority.[2]

While Eisenhower seems to have harbored no personal ill-will toward blacks as a group, he was nonetheless a product of his environment. From North Africa, in February 1943, he wrote to his son, "I . . . find myself living in a comfortable house, nicely heated, and staffed by Mickey [Sergeant Michael McKeogh, Eisenhower's orderly] and a group of darkies that take gorgeous care of me."[3] The year before, an official bulletin from the War Department had proscribed the term "darkey."

On the other hand, Eisenhower took pains to insure that black troops received even-handed treatment.[4] In the early days of the war, the Allied High Command was worried that Australia might fall to the Japanese. The island continent needed troops desperately, and Eisenhower assigned several divisions to head down under. Soon after, he received a visit from the Australian ambassador, who explained that his nation had a constitutional stricture prohibiting blacks from entering the country. Eisenhower responded firmly, saying that he would send no troops at all in that case. The next morning, he was inundated with cables from Australia saying that whatever troops he sent would be welcome.[5]

In another instance, the Commander of the United States Service Forces in the European Theatre, Major General John H.C. Lee, countermanded the efforts of white officers to bar black GIs from associating with English civilians by placing towns and pubs off limits to black soldiers. When Lee took the matter to Eisenhower, the Supreme Commander agreed that if blacks could die in the uniform of the United States, they had a right to be entertained in that same uniform. Eisenhower also issued orders desegregating many Red Cross and USO clubs.[6]

During the Battle of the Bulge, spurred by a desperate need for manpower, Eisenhower was willing to offer blacks who volunteered to serve in infantry units assignment "without regard to color or race." However, the War Department and the Chief of Staff, George Catlett Marshall, wanted no part of such an arrangement.[7] Later, near the end of the war, Eisenhower did approve an order sending black replacements into previously all-white units, an action that provoked criticism from his friends and colleagues. As a result of these experiences, Eisenhower concluded that he was a liberal on racial matters.[8]

In April 1948, when he was president of Columbia University and Senior Military Adviser to Secretary of Defense James Forrestal, Eisenhower appeared before the Senate Armed Services Committee's hearings on universal military training. When asked to comment on segregation, Eisenhower responded that the Army, as a mirror of American society, had to face the "incontrovertible fact" of racial prejudice; because of such prejudice, when men of different races "live together under the most intimate circumstances . . . we sometimes have trouble." On the other hand, he observed that segregation prevented the Army from making the best use of its manpower during World War II. Eisenhower proposed organizing blacks into units no larger than platoons. While acknowledging that this might create "certain social problems on a post," he believed that "those things can be handled." He opposed integration beyond that point, however. "In general," he told the senators, "the Negro is less well educated than his brother citizen that is white, and if you make a complete amalgamation, what you are going to have is in every company the Negro is going to be relegated to the minor jobs, and he is never going to get his promotion to such grades as technical sergeant, master sergeant, and so on, because the competition is too tough." Eisenhower made a point of expressing his personal opposition to the "extreme segregation" that existed when he first joined the Army, and he stated his hope that "the human race may finally grow up to the point where it will not be a problem." Segregation, he continued, would disappear "through education, through mutual respect, and so on. But I do believe that if we attempt merely by passing a lot of laws to force someone to like someone else, we are just going to get into trouble."[9]

Today, Eisenhower's position appears paternalistic, perhaps even the mere rationalization of racist attitudes. However, he resisted Senator Richard Russell's attempts to get him to endorse a traditional Southern argument as to why blacks were unfit to be integrated into the armed services. When Russell launched into a discourse on how blacks had higher rates of venereal diseases and criminal offenses than whites, Eisenhower interrupted with an observation of his own. While not challenging Russell's statistics, he attributed them to the lower educational standards of most blacks and said that he found that Russell's figures did not hold true for blacks who had enjoyed greater educational advantages.[10]

During Eisenhower's presidential campaign in 1952, E. Frederic Morrow, a black aide, asked him about his appearance before the Armed Services Committee in 1948. Eisenhower explained that he had called in his field commanders for an opinion and that all had opposed integration. Only later did it dawn on him that practically all of his commanders were from the South. Eisenhower reminded Morrow that Morrow's father had been a preacher and asked if he had ever heard him preach about forgiveness. When Morrow answered yes, Eisenhower asked for his forgiveness. Eisenhower went on to explain that not long after graduating from West Point, he had been assigned as an instructor to a black National Guard unit in Illinois. By his own description a young, spit and polish officer, he was dismayed by the poor performance of his black troops. When his rifle team performed pathetically against white outfits in competition, he was "ashamed and embarrassed." He told Morrow that it had not occurred to him back then that these men had been improperly trained and led by incompetent or indifferent officers, and he admitted that his unfortunate early association with black troops might have affected his thinking on the matter of integration for years.[11]

Eisenhower's tenure at Columbia broadened his experience on the matter of race relations. In 1950, Columbia planned to award an honorary degree to Ralph Bunche. According to custom, the president of the University invited all recipients of honorary degrees to a dinner at his house. Worried that some guests might take offense at Bunche's presence, Eisenhower wondered whether he should follow that custom. He decided to hold the dinner in any case and, much to his gratification, observed that other guests "made a point of seeking out the Bunches."[12]

Later, while Eisenhower was serving as the Supreme Commander of the NATO forces, the eastern, or internationalist, wing of the Republican party began promoting his candidacy for the presidency. Herbert Brownell visited Eisenhower in Paris to attempt to convince the General to seek the nation's highest office. When the issue of civil rights came up, Eisenhower told Brownell that "his record in favor of integration, in any area where the government properly belonged, was clear, that he had been the leader in that, and he felt that the plans for integration in the armed forces had worked out very well." Eisenhower's forceful position took Brownell somewhat by surprise.[13]

When it came time to form a government, Eisenhower included a number of liberals on civil rights issues among his official family. Most important, these men held positions that were most likely to influence the administration's policy on civil rights. Brownell, Morrow, Maxwell Rabb, James Hagerty, Sherman Adams, and Milton Eisenhower stand out as advocates of civil rights within the administration.

If, however, his official family had a liberal tinge, many of the President's personal friends were Southerners, and most of these held racial attitudes that were unenlightened, at best. One of the President's intimates, George Allen, never spoke to Morrow, even though the two men were thrown together in social situations several times.[14] The President also enjoyed spending time with Cliff Roberts. As president of the Augusta National Golf Club, Roberts' views on race became a public issue in the 1960s over the admission of Lee Elder, a black professional golfer, to the U.S. Open. Among his official family, Eisenhower was particularly fond of the company of George Humphrey who probably had the closest personal relationship with the President than anyone in the administration. Eisenhower sometimes vacationed at Humphrey's plantation in Georgia. Both Humphrey and Wilton Persons, another top aide, held conservative views on civil rights.[15]

These friendships exerted a strong influence on Eisenhower. Morrow observed that the President "instinctively did the right thing," and the President's initial response to racial matters often pleased the black aide. If, however, Eisenhower later broached the issue to his personal friends over the intimacy of a bridge game and it offended them, it created a real problem for him.[16] Eisenhower's personal relationships with Southerners caused him much anguish, especially after the Supreme Court's ruling in the school segregation cases. He complained that old friends, like James Byrnes, no longer even spoke to him.[17]

Family as well as friends exposed the President to racial prejudice. He could not help but grow used to criticism from his brother Edgar, a man of profoundly conservative opinions. On civil rights, however, the criticism came not from his brother, but from Edgar's wife, Lucy, whose views reflected not so much her husband's conservatism as her own racism. After the incident at Little Rock's Central High School, she wrote a letter to the President to express her horror. She predicted that if the Supreme Court insisted on enforcing integration, there would be violence. "With the ratio of negroes [*sic*] to whites (in some places as much as 40–60%), if integration is enforced, violence will prevail. We can never upgrade the negro to our level. Consequently, we must drop to his level. And this may be putting it crudely, but I hate to think of the many pretty pink-and-white 'Susan' [Susan Eisenhower, the President's granddaughter] type of girls who will fall victim to the passionate instincts and desires of their coal-black class-mates!!"[18]

Whatever influence his Southern friends and in-laws might have had, unlike several of his predecessors in office, Eisenhower refrained from using racial epithets. Certainly he deserves no award for that modest feat, but Eben Ayers' diary reveals, for example, that Harry Truman regularly used the term "nigger."[19] In addition, Eisenhower tended not to react to situations on the basis of race. For example, Adam Clayton Powell, a black congressman from New York, sent him a public telegram that accused some Veterans Administration hospitals and naval bases in the South of continuing segregation after the President had ordered an end to such practices. The telegram ignited Eisenhower's monumental temper. However, his rage was directed at Powell as a politician; Powell had violated a cardinal rule by taking the matter to the press before bringing the problem to the President's attention, much less giving him a chance to correct it. It is probably worth comparing Eisenhower's response to another, similar, situation in which Powell also figured.

Bess Truman accepted an invitation from the Daughters of the American Revolution (DAR) to a tea in her honor. After she accepted, it was revealed that Hazel Scott, a leading nightclub singer and Powell's wife, had been denied the use of DAR Constitution Hall for a concert because its rules stipulated that the hall could be leased to white artists only. Powell sent a telegram to Truman demanding action. He also sent a letter to the President's wife asking her not to attend the tea and lend the stature of the First Lady to the segregationist policies of the DAR. Bess Truman responded that she was sorry that the conflict had arisen, but she had accepted the hospitality before the situation had come to light and her acceptance was unrelated to the issue. Truman wrote Powell a letter on the day of the tea, condemning racial discrimination, but citing the "impossibility of any interference in the management or policy of a private enterprise such as the one in question."[20] His wife attended the tea. Disappointed and embittered, Powell let slip a reference to the "Last Lady." Upon hearing of it, Truman flew into a rage and unleashed a stream of epithets directed at Powell. He had not cooled off by the following day, when at a staff meeting he railed against "that damn nigger preacher.''[21] Powell never received an invitation to the White House as long as Truman remained President, not even to the annual reception for members of Congress, and Powell had at least given Truman the politician's courtesy of taking the matter up in private first. In contrast, Eisenhower's anger was directed against a politician who had violated the rules of the game as he understood them; it was free from any racial tinge. Indeed, Powell endorsed Eisenhower in the election of 1956.

Throughout his life, Eisenhower demonstrated repulsion at individual acts of bigotry. In high school, a coach harassed a black teammate of Eisenhower's and finally threw the black athlete off the team. Eisenhower, the team captain, threatened to quit and, with support first from his brother Edgar and then from other members of the team, forced the coach to reinstate the black player.[22] Much later in life, the Eisenhowers were vacationing off the coast of Florida with General Lucius Clay and his wife. Clay remembers that they were about to check in when Eisenhower noticed a sign that read "Negroes and Jews not welcome," at which point he told Clay that he would never stay at such a place and the two couples returned to Miami.[23]

This does not mean that Eisenhower was untouched by the racist mores of the time and the environment that produced him. In many ways, he reflected the dominant racism of white society. Morrow cautioned him repeatedly and unsuccessfully not to use the phrase "you people" when speaking to a black audience. In all fairness, however, it should be pointed out that Adlai Stevenson employed the same offensive usage.[24] Arthur Larson's first draft of the speech with which Eisenhower would accept the nomination at the convention of 1956 brought out the more conservative side of the President's personality. The draft referred to "that ugly complex of injustices called discrimination," a phrase that Eisenhower immediately struck from the speech. The President told his writer that he was uncomfortable with the word "discrimination" and was reluctant to use the word "racial." In discussing a later version, Eisenhower said that he wanted to make clear that equality of political and economic opportunity did not require mingling "or that a Negro should court my daughter." Typically, Eisenhower further sought to emphasize the need for extending "good will and understanding" to Southerners as well. After all, they had lived with a ruling of the Supreme Court for two generations and now had to accept a new and contrary ruling that threatened to upset their social order. As the final form of the speech took shape, softer phrases, such as "equal justice," replaced more pointed usages.[25]

Eisenhower's relationship with the black press epitomized in many ways his attitudes toward blacks and racial matters. In mid–1954, he told James Hagerty that he deliberately recognized Ethel Payne, a black reporter, at news conferences because he "did not want to give anybody an excuse to write that he was overlooking the colored press." While he considered many of her questions foolish, he thought it a good thing to give black reporters recognition. "You know, Jim," he said, "I suppose nobody knows how they feel or how many pressures or insults they have to take. I guess the only way you can realize exactly how they feel is to have a black skin for several weeks. I'm going to continue to give them a break at the press conferences despite the questions they ask."[26] That single remark revealed much of the complexity of Eisenhower's feelings and attitudes. Clearly, it expressed a degree of sympathy and even empathy. Indeed, it was almost a cliché of liberal doctrine for the period; after all, this was the era that produced John Howard Griffin's *Black Like Me*. On the other hand, it smacks of paternalism. Moreover, it reflects Eisenhower's dislike for addressing the issue of civil rights in a public forum. Ethel Payne was a particularly aggressive reporter, and her questions often touched on racial discrimination. Eisenhower's response to her may have indicated the extent to which he considered civil rights a peripheral subject, one that detracted from "important" issues such as the economy, national defense, and foreign policy.

After the first presidential news conference recorded by television cameras took place on January 19, 1955, Eisenhower told Hagerty that he had deliberately called on Alice Dunnigan so that a black reporter would have a chance to ask a question on television.[27] In another episode, only incidentally related to the black press corps, Eisenhower once again revealed himself to Hagerty. Louis Lautier of the *Baltimore Afro-American* applied for membership to the National Press Club. When some members actively opposed his admission, Merriman Smith, a reporter friendly to the administration, advised Hagerty to stay out of the upcoming confrontation because it might prove embarrassing to the administration. Hagerty responded that he was a voting member and that he would vote for Lautier's admission. He explained to the President that as a voting member he did not feel that he could duck the issue, and he believed that he had no moral alternative to voting to admit Lautier. Eisenhower assured Hagerty of his support, saying, "Jim, if I were in your place, I'd do exactly the same thing."[28]

Eisenhower's personal attitudes on race combined elements of sympathy, understanding, and empathy with paternalism and some racist notions. The views of this extremely complex man played a large role in shaping his administration's policies on racial issues. While individual acts of bigotry or discrimination never failed to invoke his horror, he could not translate his reaction to specific instances into outrage at the larger issues of racial injustice in American society. Yet his personal approach to the issue of race was not the only consideration in determining his administration's policy. Eisenhower's perception of the federal government's role in settling such questions was also influenced by his convictions regarding the proper role of the federal government in American life. His concerns over federalism were no mere sophistic justification for his reluctance to act forcefully on civil rights. He had no qualms about justifying his position on the substance of the issue. Nor was he alone in his disquietude over the relationship between federal and state governments. Even an activist such as Brownell had his doubts about federal authority to act in certain instances. Such considerations seem strangely archaic today. The 1960s settled the issue on the side of federal action, but in the preceding decade the issue remained very much up in the air.

Eisenhower's personal views about blacks and whites were also balanced by his perception of his duty as President of the United States and his conviction that every citizen, regardless of race, deserved equal treatment at the hands of his government. Whatever his own prejudices, he believed that legally mandated segregation was wrong, and he considered it his duty to make sure that the government practiced equal treatment of all its citizens.

Before his first inauguration, Eisenhower came up with the idea of offering a prayer before beginning his address. He wrote out a brief invocation on a yellow scratch pad. In it, he revealed an acute consciousness of his duty to represent all Americans: "Give us, we pray, the power to discern clearly right from wrong, and allow all our words and actions to be governed thereby, and by the laws of the land. Especially we pray that our concern shall be for all the people, regardless of station, race or calling."[29]

NOTES

1. Dwight D. Eisenhower, *The White House Years: Waging Peace, 1956–1961* (Garden City, N.Y.: Doubleday, 1965), p. 148.

2. Peter Lyon, *Eisenhower, Portrait of a Hero* (Boston: Little, Brown, 1974), p. 556; Steve Neal, *The Eisenhowers: Reluctant Dynasty* (Garden City, N.Y.: Doubleday, 1978), pp. 196–207; Elmo Richardson, *The Presidency of Dwight D. Eisenhower* (Lawrence: Regents Press of Kansas, 1979), p. 105.

3. Dwight Eisenhower to John S.D. Eisenhower, February 26, 1943, *Papers of Dwight D. Eisenhower, The War Years*, Vol. 2, Alfred D. Chandler, ed. (Baltimore: Johns Hopkins, University Press, 1970), p. 997; Lyon, *Eisenhower*, p. 556.

4. Lyon, *Eisenhower*, p. 556.

5. Diary of Ann Whitman (hereafter Whitman Diary), November 23, 1958, Whitman File, Diary Series, November 1958, Dwight D. Eisenhower Library (DDEL).

6. Lee Nichols, *Breakthrough on the Color Front* (New York: Random House, 1954), pp. 65–67; *Waging Peace*, p. 148.

7. Stephen E. Ambrose, *The Supreme Commander: The War Years of General Dwight D. Eisenhower* (Garden City, N.Y.: Doubleday, 1970), pp. 559–60; Lyon, *Eisenhower*, p. 556; Nichols, *Breakthrough on the Color Front*, pp. 67–69.

8. *Waging Peace*, p. 148; Whitman Diary, March 21, 1956, Whitman File, Diary Series, March 1956 (1), DDEL; Richardson *Presidency of Dwight D. Eisenhower*, p. 106; C. L. Sulzberger, *A Long Row of Candles: Memoirs and Diaries, 1934–1954* (New York: Macmillan Co., 1969), p. 616.

9. U.S. Congress, Senate, Armed Services Committee, *Hearing on Universal Military Training*, March 17-April 3, 1948 (Wasington, D.C.: U.S. Government Printing Office, 1948), pp. 995–96.

10. Ibid., pp. 997–98.

11. E. Frederic Morrow, *Forty Years a Guinea Pig* (New York: Pilgrim Press, 1980), pp. 86–87; Columbia Oral History Project, Interview with E. Frederic Morrow (hereafter Morrow COH), pp. 30–31, 79–80; interview with Morrow by the author.

12. Sulzberger, *Long Row of Candles*, p. 409.

13. Columbia University Oral History Project, Interview with Herbert Brownell (hereafter Brownell COH), p. 33.

14. Morrow, *Forty Years*, p. 212.

15. Interview with Morrow; Morrow, *Forty Years*, p. 212.

16. Morrow COH, pp. 29–30.

17. Neal, *The Eisenhowers*, p. 383; Emmet John Hughes, *The Ordeal of Power: A Political Memoir of the Eisenhower Years* (New York: Atheneum, 1963), p. 201.

18. Lucy Eisenhower to Dwight Eisenhower, August 26, 1958, Whitman File, Name Series, Eisenhower, Edgar (1957–1958), DDEL.

19. Diary of Eben Ayers, October 13, 1945, Papers of Eben Ayers, Harry S Truman Library, Independence, Missouri (hereafter HSTL).

20. *Public Papers of the President, Harry S Truman, 1945* (Washington, D.C.: U.S. Government Printing Office), p. 396; Robert J. Donovan, *Conflict and Crisis: The Presidency of Harry S Truman, 1945–1948* (New York: W. W. Norton, 1977), pp. 147–48.

21. Ayers Diary, October 13, 1945, HSTL; Donovan, *Conflict and Crisis*, p. 148.

22. Virgil Pinkley, *Eisenhower Declassified* (Old Tappan, N.J.: Fleming H. Revell, 1979), pp. 47–48.

23. Ibid., pp. 349–50.

24. Morrow COH, p. 102.

25. Arthur Larson, *Eisenhower: The President Nobody Knew* (New York: Scribner's, 1968), pp. 126–28.

26. Diary of James Hagerty, June 16, 1954, Hagerty Papers, DDEL.

27. Hagerty Diary, January 19, 1955, DDEL.

28. Hagerty Diary, June 17, 18, 1955, DDEL.

29. *Public Papers*, 1953, p. 1; Pinkley, *Eisenhower Declassified*, pp. 270–71.

5

Whose Brief? Dwight D. Eisenhower, His Southern Friends, and the School Segregation Cases

James C. Duram

It is sometimes said that good historians ask the right kinds of questions of their sources. Historians involved in the current reassessment of the Eisenhower presidency have formulated a whole series of questions, some of which it is hoped will prove to be the "right" ones. One of the most critical of these asks whether or not President Eisenhower's moderate approach to the school desegregation crisis was rooted in a more realistic perception of the complex implications of that issue than the hindsight of many of those who have since criticized or condemned his response. In pursuit of an answer to that question, it is necessary to examine some of the critical factors shaping Eisenhower's early response to the most controversial domestic issue of his presidency.

The U.S. Supreme Court's June 8, 1953, invitation to U.S. Attorney General Herbert Brownell to file a brief, and/or submit arguments in the pending school segregation cases, guaranteed that President Dwight D. Eisenhower would continue to devote great amounts of time and attention to the issue of desegregation. Attempts to influence the President's thinking on that topic came from many sources. One of the most persistent was the body of conservative Southern Democratic politicians who had supported him in his 1952 presidential campaign. On July 16, 1953, Texas Governor Allan Shivers wrote to the President regarding the Court's invitation to Brownell and warned: "The United States is not a party to this lawsuit except insofar as Truman and former Attorney General McGranery intervened."[1] Shivers then proceeded to warn the President about the dangers of administration involvement.

I see in this unusual Supreme Court invitation an attempt to embarrass you and your Attorney General.

I assume that the invitation to your Attorney General by the Supreme Court will be accepted. I trust that he will see the implications involved and advise the Court that this local problem should be decided on the local and state level.[2]

Shivers' message and others like it from his political allies in the South became the President's justification for caution and reinforced his desire to use federal power sparingly.

A clear expression of what the President regarded as the proper approach appeared in his July 24, 1953, diary notes on his conversation with Governor James F. Byrnes of South Carolina.[3] Eisenhower wrote that Byrnes was convinced that a Court decision might abolish segregation and that such a decision would cause a number of states to immediately cease support for public schools, a consequence which the President's private statements of a later date indicate he came to fear greatly. Byrnes further warned that if the administration took a strong antisegregation stand in hopes of capturing the black vote, it would defeat forever the possibility of developing a viable Republican party in the South.[4]

Eisenhower's response to Byrnes was revealing. After assuring Byrnes that his response to the school segregation cases would not be formed by political expediency, the President proceeded to state his fundamental beliefs about the desegregation issue. He insisted that the South Carolina Governor was

well aware of my belief that improvement in race relations is one of those things that will be healthy and sound only if it starts locally. I do not believe that prejudice, even palpably unjustified prejudices, will succumb to compulsion. Consequently, I believe that Federal law imposed upon our states in such a way as to bring about a conflict of the police power of the states and of the nation, would set back the cause of progress in race relations for a long, long time.[5]

Thus, very early in his administration, Eisenhower stated the guiding principles behind his moderate approach to the race question. Unfortunately, the difference between what the President and his Southern friends understood as allowing the desegregation question to be settled at the local level did not become obvious to him until much later. That misunderstanding, however, is not sufficient reason to charge the President with outright neglect or cowardice.

Another aspect of President Eisenhower's beliefs that had an important effect on shaping his reaction to the desegregation issue appeared in his discussion of the brief which Attorney General Brownell prepared for the segregation cases. In a "Memorandum for the Record," written on August 19, 1953, Eisenhower drew a sharp distinction between the function of the Court and that of the executive branch, and expressed uneasiness about the Court's behavior in the pending segregation cases.

It seems to me that the rendering of "opinion" by the Attorney General on this kind of question would constitute an invasion of the duties, responsibilities and authority of the Supreme Court. As I understand it, the Courts were established by the Constitution to interpret the laws, the responsibility of the Executive Department is to execute them.[6]

The President was sufficiently moved by his concern that he telephoned Attorney General Brownell about it. He did this, he explained,

because it seems to me that in this instance the Supreme Court has been guided by some motive that is not strictly functional. The Court cannot possibly abdicate; consequently, it cannot delegate its responsibility and it would be futile for the Attorney General to attempt to sit as a Court and read a conclusion as to the true meaning of the Fourteenth Amendment.[7]

The President concluded his memorandum by conceding that, regardless of the questions he had raised, the Attorney General would present a complete ''resume of fact and historical record'' about the Fourteenth Amendment.

Further evidence of Eisenhower's emphasis on the limited scope of federal responsibilities in the desegregation area appeared in his November 5, 1953, telephone call to Attorney General Brownell.[8] During their conversation, the President mentioned that he could see why the Attorney General could not duck involvement in this issue in the District of Columbia, but he questioned how the Attorney General could be expected to speak out on the issue of state-enforced segregation.[9]

The President's knowledge of both constitutional history and legal procedure was, of course, limited, based more on theory than on practical experience. The Justice Department had filed briefs in many cases heard by the Court in the past. The Truman administration had already intervened in the segregation cases with a strong brief arguing against the constitutionality of segregation, and it was not unheard of for the Court in significant and controversial cases to invite or permit *amicus curae* briefs.

It appears that Eisenhower's firm belief in the separation of powers, his limited understanding of the judicial process, the influence of his Southern friends, and his growing awareness of the highly explosive nature of the segregation question, all combined to push him toward a position of executive neutrality, one that separated his administration from accountability for the actions of the Court. His assertion that the Court was governed by a motive that was not strictly judicial (reflecting Governor Shivers' warning) indicates that the President's view of the judicial process was a narrow one that emphasized procedure over substance. He suspected the Justices had violated some canon of neutrality. One thing is certain: the President was never enthusiastic about the Supreme Court's invitation for Attorney General Brownell's involvement in the case.[10]

As stated previously, the President was highly disturbed by Governor Byrnes' prediction that a desegregation decision would lead to the closing of the public schools in several Southern states. In a telephone conversation with Attorney General Brownell on November 16, 1953, the President asked him what would happen if the states abandoned public education.[11] Brownell observed that Byrnes was coming to the White House for dinner the following evening and assured the President that he would try to convince the Governor that ''under our doctrine it would be a period of years [before desegregation] and he wouldn't have to 'declare war' so to speak.''[12] Eisenhower then expressed his fear that such a controversy would make education a function of the federal government. Brownell responded that he felt the states would work out the problem in ten to twelve years and that it might be helpful if Governor Shivers talked with Byrnes, since the Texan felt that things had worked out successfully in his own state.

It is apparent that from the beginning the President was less certain than Attorney General Brownell of the wisdom of the administration's involvement in the desegregation cases and more pessimistic about their outcome. His growing fear that the South might close its schools rather than desegregate them increased, to his mind, the possibility of a federal takeover of public education, something he had long abhorred.[13] His desire to avoid such a consequence pushed him away from willing involvement with the desegregation question.

Yet, ironically, he could not escape it. The Court's invitation to submit a brief in the school segregation cases saw to that. Evidence of how closely his words and actions were being weighed by those involved in the case came in the reactions to his November 18, 1953, press conference. When a reporter asked the President whether he planned to confer with the Attorney General prior to the Justice Department's filing of its brief on the school segregation question, he answered: "Indeed I do. We confer regularly. And this subject comes up along with others, constantly.''[14] Despite the President's previously cited private reservations, many people regarded his offhand public remark as an admission that he was personally involved in the shaping of the details of the Justice Department's brief, that it would represent his personal opinions of the desegregation issue.

As a consequence of this misperception, two Southern governors, James F. Byrnes of South Carolina and Robert F. Kennon of Louisiana, wrote letters to the President seeking to convince him of the wisdom of their position on the pending school segregation cases, thus influencing the substance of the Justice Department's brief. Despite their somewhat differing approaches, both Byrnes and Kennon made the same point: the school segregation question would be best solved at the local and state levels with the preservation of the "separate but equal" doctrine.[15] Their letters presented clear articulations of what proved to be the basis of the Southern states' position during the entire desegregation crisis. This merger of constitutional and practical objections to desegregation would be heard again and again.

The strong assertions of state sovereignty and calls for judicial restraint in the letters from Southern politicians reinforced the President's desire to seek a moderate solution to the desegregation crisis. This was very apparent in the personal letter Eisenhower wrote, with Attorney General Brownell's concurrence, to Governor Byrnes, dated December 1, 1953.[16] It should be kept in mind that the President was aware by this time that the Justice Department's brief took a stand against segregated schools.

The President began his letter by emphasizing that he had put much thought and study into the school segregation cases. He expressed the hope that solutions could be found "which would progressively work toward the goals established by abstract principle, but which would not, at the same time, cause such disruption and mental anguish among great portions of our population that progress would actually be reversed.''[17] No better characterization of the President's approach to the desegregation question can be offered than those which he himself provided in his speeches and writings. His problems would come when he sought the middle ground which he needed to implement such an approach.

Continuing, the President complimented Byrnes for his study and knowledge of the segregation problem and assured the Governor that he was sympathetic to the South's problems. As he put it:

I recognize that there are very serious problems that you have to face—regardless of the exact character of the Court decisions in the pending cases. By this I mean that the task of establishing "equal but separate" facilities will involve, I am told, extraordinary expenditures throughout all the Southern states. Incidentally, I sometimes wonder just what officials of government would be charged with the responsibility for determining when facilities were exactly equal.[18]

The President's remarks reveal that he anticipated serious difficulties in the event of a Court decision requiring the Southern states to adhere to a more rigorous definition of the "separate but equal" doctrine. Moreover, he was already concerned lest the Court present his administration with the unenviable task of enforcing such a decision. He then hastened to add that he was not actually involved in preparing the administration's brief because:

In the study of the case, it became clear to me that the question asked of the Attorney General by the Supreme Court demanded answers that could be determined only by lawyers and historians. Consequently, I have been compelled to turn over to the Attorney General and his associates full responsibility in the matter. He and I agreed that his brief would reflect the conviction of the Department of Justice as to the *legal aspects* of the case, including, of course, the legislative history of the enactment of the 14th Amendment. In rendering an opinion as to this phase of the case, it is clear that the Attorney General has to act according to his own conviction and understanding.[19]

Eisenhower had a valid reason for disassociating himself from the preparation of the brief: he was not a lawyer. At this point, however, he appeared to be acknowledging the existence of differences between his personal views and the conclusions of the Justice Department's brief. The President assured Byrnes that no political considerations of any kind would be given any weight whatsoever in the Justice Department's brief and that "no matter what the *legal* conclusions might be, the principle of local operation and authority would be emphasized to the maximum degree consistent with his legal opinions.''[20] Although it did not prevent his Attorney General from presenting a brief rationalizing judicial activism, it is not surprising that the President's emphasis on local responsibility ultimately became the basis of the administration's 1955 brief on how to implement the desegregation decision.

The President concluded his letter to Byrnes with an attempt to prepare the Governor for the Justice Department's forthcoming brief, which supported desegregation. As he put it:

Two or three Court decisions of recent years have, as you know, tended to becloud the original decision of "equal but separate" facilities. One of these decisions, I am told, even held that a Negro in graduate school attending exactly the same classes as whites, but separated from them by some kind of railing, was held to be the victim of discrimination and could not be so separated from the white students. This and other decisions had all, of course, to be considered by the Attorney General and his staff. But I am sure that you have no doubt as to the complete integrity and broad capacity of the Attorney General—even if in this case I suspect you may question his legal wisdom.[21]

Although this letter was revised prior to being sent by the Department of Justice, the original is valuable for what it reveals about the agonizing position in which the President found himself.

By late 1953, Eisenhower was caught between his desires for a moderate approach built on state and local responsibility and gradualism and his own Justice Department's brief, which supported a judicial attack on discrimination. Though helpless to stop it, the President was convinced that the latter approach would lead to bitterness, confusion, and frustration. The situation by March 1954 was such that he was left with few options beyond the exercise of caution and moderation.

The events that occurred after the initial *Brown* decision in May 1954 only served to reiterate what his philosophy and experience had already combined to tell him: that there were strong reasons to doubt the wisdom of the attempt to resolve the desegregation crisis by rapid actions involving judicial and legislative fiat. This belief proved to be a powerful brake on any temptation the President may have had to take strong action. At the same time, it must be remembered that his critics have charged that his failure to provide strong leadership in that crisis contributed greatly to its complexity and its longevity.[22] Whether or not one accepts that stern judgment, there is little doubt that the attitudes the President developed in the early phase of the desegregation controversy stayed with him throughout, and that they explain much of what he did and did not do.

NOTES

1. Allan Shivers to Eisenhower, July 16, 1953, Official File (hereafter cited as OF), Box 731, Dwight D. Eisenhower Presidential Library, Abilene, Kansas (hereafter cited as EPL).
2. Ibid.
3. Eisenhower Diary, July 24, 1953, Whitman File (Diary Series), Box 2, EPL.
4. Ibid.
5. Ibid.; see also Dwight D. Eisenhower, *The White House Years: Waging Peace,*

1956–1961 (Garden City, N.Y.: Doubleday and Co., 1965), pp. 682–83. for excerpt of letter to Byrnes.

6. "Memorandum for the Record," Eisenhower Diary, August 19, 1953, Whitman File (Diary Series), Box 2, EPL.

7. Ibid.

8. Telephone call, Eisenhower Diary, November 5, 1953, Whitman File (Diary Series), Box 3, EPL.

9. Ibid.

10. Contrary to this view, see Eisenhower's somewhat amorphous handling of this point in Eisenhower, *Waging Peace*, p. 150.

11. Telephone call, Eisenhower Diary, November 16, 1953, Whitman File (Diary Series), Box 3, EPL.

12. Ibid.

13. Ibid.

14. Transcript of presidential press conference, November 18, 1953, Whitman File (Press Conference Series), Box 1, EPL.

15. James F. Byrnes to Eisenhower, November 20, 1953, OF, Box 731, EPL; and Robert F. Kennon to Eisenhower, November 20, 1953, OF, Box 731, EPL.

16. Eisenhower to James F. Byrnes, Eisenhower Diary, December 1, 1953, Whitman File (Diary Series), Box 2, EPL. When the President called Brownell regarding a paragraph in his December 1, 1953, letter to Byrnes, the Attorney General informed him that Chief Justice Earl Warren had stated that the administration's brief in the *Brown* case was excellent. Telephone call, Eisenhower Diary, December 2, 1953, Whitman File (Diary Series), Box 3, EPL.

17. Eisenhower to James F. Byrnes, December 1, 1953, Whitman File (Name Series), Box 3, EPL.

18. Ibid.

19. Ibid.

20. Ibid.

21. Ibid.

22. Emmet John Hughes, *The Ordeal of Power: A Political Memoir of the Eisenhower Years* (New York: Atheneum, 1963), p. 243.

6

Dwight D. Eisenhower and Civil Rights Conservatism

Robert F. Burk

The decades since World War II have witnessed the resurgence of civil rights issues as central concerns on the American political agenda. In recent years, a bipartisan consensus has been reached on the legitimacy of black demands for equal citizenship rights and on the nation's need to project an image of racial democracy. Even in the formerly Jim Crow South, overt expressions of white supremacy have lost their political respectability and legitimacy. Hidden behind this consensus on general principles, however, are sharp ideological differences over the means and the proper pace of minority advance. The modern civil rights debate centers on the appropriate role and powers of the federal government in regulating the racial behavior of private citizens, and in pressing for an integrated society as a necessary condition for genuine racial equality.

In contrast to modern liberals, who have advocated accelerated government action to confront both officially sanctioned and private forms of segregation and discrimination, conservatives have argued that the dangers of federal ''coercion'' and ''statism'' outweigh the benefits of a larger federal role in the racial field. The rise of this postwar conservative approach to racial issues, which has jettisoned Jim Crow and has incorporated a limited advocacy of civil rights within a general philosophy of lifting governmental restraints on private citizens, can be traced to the presidency of Dwight D. Eisenhower. From his central position of national leadership, Eisenhower offered an approach to racial issues which criticizes both the traditional official racism of the South and the newer tradition of government intervention in the private sector symbolized by the New Deal. Eisenhower's civil rights philosophy stemmed from a combination of his pre-presidential racial experiences, his evolving views on the role of the federal government, and the partisan needs of his adopted Republican party. His approach to racial issues sought the removal of official sanctions mandating discrimination, but left additional progress to the states and the private sector. The policy product was a civil rights program long on symbolic gestures for racial equality, but intentionally short on effective government enforcement mechanisms.

Dwight D. Eisenhower's background was not marked by many demonstrations of overt bigotry, but neither was it distinguished by sensitivity to black stereotypes and hardships. Although his boyhood experiences rarely put him in contact with black Americans, as a boy Eisenhower did play the game of "black man," or "crack the whip." His education at West Point added few other racial insights, and, although his early tours of duty in Southern camps exposed him to racial segregation, the young officer evidently was not troubled by what he saw. A brief encounter with black Illinois National Guardsmen only fueled his skepticism toward blacks' abilities, and he would later lament, "They just couldn't do anything." Eisenhower's early acceptance of discrimination was made easier by the fact that most of his colleagues had either grown up or had been trained in the South. In addition, Eisenhower's lifelong love of history and military tales had included a deep sympathy for the region and its heroes.[1]

During the period of his greatest military triumphs, the General showed no greater concern for blacks, though on occasion he bent racial rules for the sake of larger objectives. As before, Eisenhower saw blacks most often as servants. In North Africa, he wrote that he was served "by a group of darkies that take gorgeous care of me." At the Battle of the Bulge, Eisenhower did temporarily order the replacement of depleted rifleman units with blacks from the supply services. But at the request of General Walter Bedell Smith he revoked the order because it contradicted Army segregation requirements. Even after the war, Eisenhower refused to take the lead before congressional committees in advocating the integration of military units.[2]

When persuaded to seek the presidency in 1952, Eisenhower found his reluctance to advocate bold measures in the racial field reinforced by his developing views on the limits of federal power. Backed by supporters who feared "unbridled statism," Eisenhower sought to express a political philosophy that would allow both individual freedom and maximum voluntary cooperation for social ends. He stressed the value of private initiative, cautioned against government "paternalism," and sought solutions to national problems, including civil rights, through voluntary cooperation. The art of government was to encourage private groups and individuals to "do the right thing" by themselves. This philosophy reflected the views of former President Herbert Hoover, which was no accident, since Hoover was among those offering counsel to the General. In a message that predicted the course of the Eisenhower presidency, Hoover advised,

Some people will want you to lead them back at full speed to the "good old days." At the other extreme, some will want you to initiate welfare programs regardless of their effect on federal fiscal affairs and on the nation's economy. To go back is impossible, but many will not believe this, and will demand miracles of you. To allow present trends to go on is unwise; they will lead to disaster. All you can do is try to turn away gradually from the path leading to paternalism, until it takes a central course, and then stick with it.[3]

The advice of Hoover and others did not suggest that Eisenhower as President would seek enhanced federal powers in the civil rights field or elsewhere. Reinforcing this reluctance was Eisenhower's own political objective of building a Republican base in the South and in the border states. While listening to the speech of a black supporter in Detroit, the candidate was moved to remark to an aide, "That will sure win us a lot of votes in Houston." Eisenhower built a series of political alliances with leading Southern politicians, including Governors James Byrnes of South Carolina, Robert Kennon of Louisiana, and Allan Shivers of Texas. Among his pledges to the South were support for state tideland oil claims and opposition to a federal fair employment practices commission.[4]

What Eisenhower was willing to do in civil rights was to occasionally assert the principles of equal opportunity, while focusing limited actions exclusively in areas of undisputed federal jurisdiction, the greatest international symbolic value, and the minimum risk of political cost. He was content to carry through the Truman administration's military desegregation program, remove discriminatory sanctions from the nation's capital, and appoint blacks to visible but insignificant executive positions. However, events would not permit Eisenhower to avoid involvement in civil rights controversies indefinitely. Because the Truman administration had committed the Justice Department to "friend-of-the-court" participation in the *Brown* school segregation cases, Eisenhower was to be drawn into the growing controversy over racial integration in the South. He tried to maintain his distance, instructing the Justice Department to file a brief giving the Supreme Court leeway to rule on the constitutionality of segregation without the administration itself taking a public stand. However, the subsequent rulings of 1954 and 1955 put him in the awkward position of having to uphold federal court desegregation orders, even by the use of force if necessary.[5]

Ultimately, Eisenhower's unwilling entanglement in the South's desegregation agonies would lead to the confrontation with Arkansas authorities at Little Rock Central High School. No other civil rights action of the Eisenhower presidency has received as much attention, and yet none was less characteristic of Eisenhower's own civil rights philosophy. Among many ironies of the Little Rock incident, perhaps the most striking is Eisenhower's distaste for intervention which helped set the stage for the final, massive intervention that did occur. Having refused to make contingency plans for a more limited intervention with federal marshals at earlier stages, by September 20, 1957, the administration found itself in the position of either having to use federal troops or of backing down publicly from enforcing the federal court order. Eisenhower's decision to use force at Little Rock was also encouraged by the President's sense of betrayal at the hands of Arkansas Governor Orval Faubus and by the fact that 1957 was not a presidential election year. State officials in Tennessee and Texas had defied federal court authority the previous year, but interventions in those states in 1956 would have carried far greater political risks for the President and his party than a showdown in Arkansas did a year later.[6]

Nevertheless, Eisenhower acted in the Little Rock crisis without enthusiasm. He sought to pull the federal troops out almost immediately, and he refused subsequently even to make any general statements in support of school desegregation. Privately, he predicted that reaching an ideal level of desegregation even in a border state such as Tennessee would take thirty or forty years. After Little Rock, his administration shied away from intervention in the Southern integration struggle until the lame-duck days of late 1960, when the Justice Department did take belated legal action against authorities in New Orleans. Rather than advocate a court of intervention, Eisenhower preferred to encourage voluntary, local solutions to desegregation issues. Privately, he urged Southerners to support token desegregation steps in order to convince the courts of the region's goodwill and thereby encourage more moderate federal court orders.[7]

Even before the Little Rock crisis, the problem of Southern racial violence following the *Brown* implementation decision had led the President and his subordinates to seek a graceful means of federal disengagement while offering blacks a tool for self-protection in the absence of federal force. The answer eventually proposed by Attorney General Herbert Brownell was the enhancement of black voting rights, and the policy results of this "search for a shield" were the Civil Rights Acts of 1957 and 1960. With the power of the vote, Eisenhower reasoned, Southern blacks would have new leverage with which to protect themselves and their rights from violent segregationist resistance. At the same time, the administration could quietly withdraw from the desegregation battle, avoid the political fallout from a Reconstruction-style perpetuation of federal intervention, and still claim to have advanced the cause of black citizenship rights. But even the "two-sided" shield of voting rights law did not succeed in permitting federal disengagement from the South. Instead, it only added new justification for a greater federal presence, since Southern governments and private citizens were as willing to defy federal voting rights law as they were to resist court-ordered racial desegregation.[8]

The Eisenhower tenure in civil rights policy had produced an important, if mixed, legacy. On the one hand, in spite of the administration's uneasiness with the exercise of federal power, the heightened focus on black constitutional rights produced in the 1950s had given Americans a rudimentary "progress chart" of legal equality for minorities. By the time of the Kennedy inauguration, executive orders and regulatory judgments prohibited discrimination in the armed services and in federal hiring. Other rulings prohibited segregation in interstate transportation and in public services in the District of Columbia. National legislation promised equal access to the voting booth and set forth criminal and civil sanctions for the protection of other citizenship rights. The federal courts, with or without the administration's encouragement, had banned enforced public school segregation, restrictive covenant enforcement, discriminatory zoning laws, and racial exclusion from jury service. Because of Eisenhower's decision to employ federal troops at Little Rock, precedent even existed for the military enforcement of federal court desegregation orders.

The Eisenhower approach in civil rights also led to the promotion and institutional expression of a sharply limited form of civil rights advocacy, one that sought to rule out both the vigorous use of federal power to compel integration and the launching of a federally sponsored economic offensive against minority poverty and inequality of opportunity. Eisenhower's civil rights philosophy had jettisoned Jim Crow, only to allow voluntary forms of segregation and discrimination to continue by denying federal responsibility in those areas. By the 1970s, the Eisenhower antistatist doctrine, with its general professions of support for equal rights for minorities, had become so popular among conservative politicians of differing backgrounds on racial issues that even some of Jim Crow's earlier defenders had adopted it. When asked by reporters in the late 1970s why he had "stood in the schoolhouse door," George Wallace of Alabama could argue that he had done so not to oppose integration, but rather to block the excesses of "big government." Dwight D. Eisenhower had not condoned Wallace's open defiance, but he could not have summarized his own civil rights philosophy any more succinctly.

NOTES

1. Peter Lyon, *Eisenhower: Portrait of the Hero* (Boston: Little, Brown, 1974), p. 556; E. Frederic Morrow Oral History, 1977, Dwight D. Eisenhower Library (DDEL), 20.

2. Lyon, *Eisenhower*, p. 556; Elmo Richardson, *The Presidency of Dwight D. Eisenhower* (Lawrence: Regents Press of Kansas, 1979), p. 105; Herbert S. Parmet, *Eisenhower and the American Crusades* (New York: Macmillan Co., 1972), p. 438.

3. Dwight D. Eisenhower, *The White House Years: Mandate for Change, 1953–1956* (Garden City, N.Y.: Doubleday and Co., 1963), p. 441.

4. Lyon, *Eisenhower*, pp. 411–12; Emmet John Hughes, *The Order of Power: A Political Memoir of the Eisenhower Years* (New York: Atheneum, 1963), p. 201.

5. For overviews of Eisenhower's role in the Justice Department *Brown* brief, see James C. Duram, *A Moderate Among Extremists: Dwight D. Eisenhower and the School Desegregation Issue* (Chicago: Nelson-Hall Publishing, 1981), ch. 3; and Richard Kluger, *Simple Justice* (New York: Random House, 1975), chs. 11–12. For important primary source materials, see the Ann Whitman File, Eisenhower Diary Series, Boxes 2–3, DDEL.

6. The Little Rock crisis is recounted in a variety of sources. For Eisenhower's personal role, see the Whitman File, Diary Series, Boxes 9, 16. Among personal accounts, the most useful include Dwight D. Eisenhower, *The White House Years: Waging Peace, 1956–1961* (Garden City, N.Y.: Doubleday and Co., 1963), pp. 166–75; Orval Faubus, *Down from the Hills* (Little Rock, Ark.: Democrat Printing and Lithographing Co., 1980); and Brooks Hays, *A Southern Moderate Speaks* (Chapel Hill: University of North Carolina Press, 1959).

7. Hughes, *Ordeal of Power*, 261; "Memorandum for the Record," August 22, 1958, Whitman File, Administrative Series, Box 35, DDEL: J. W. Peltason, *Fifty-Eight Lonely Men* (New York: Harcourt, Brace and World, 1961), pp. 222–33.

8. Various materials relating to the administration's civil rights proposals of 1956–1957 and 1959–1960 can be found in the Legislative Meetings Series and Cabinet Series of the Whitman Files, and the records of Bryce Harlow, Gerald Morgan, E. Frederic Morrow, and Wilton B. Persons, all at the Eisenhower Library. Important secondary sources include J. W. Anderson, *Eisenhower, Brownell, and the Congress* (Birmingham, Ala.: University of Alabama Press, 1964); Daniel M. Berman, *A Bill Becomes a Law: The Civil Rights Act of 1960* (New York: Macmillan Co., 1962); and Stephen F. Lawson, *Black Ballots* (New York: Columbia University Press, 1976).

7

Eisenhower and the American Medical Association: A Coalition Against the Elderly

Sheri I. David

During the eight years that Dwight David Eisenhower was President, his administration witnessed a domestic crisis over the ability of the elderly to acquire and pay for adequate medical care. In response, a coalition of congressional leaders, with labor and former Social Security Administration officials, organized a legislative effort to provide a national health insurance program for those over sixty-five years of age. Eisenhower's response to this effort was determined in part by his personal attitudes toward welfare and security as well as his trust in private, voluntary organizations to find effective solutions to a crisis. Eisenhower's response was also shaped by his commitment to the American Medical Association (AMA) to which he looked for leadership and ideas. When the AMA failed to rally to the President's aid, Eisenhower failed to look elsewhere for a better approach.[1]

There were several reasons why a focus on the health care problems of the elderly was appropriate during Eisenhower's administration. First, the numbers alone were impressive. As against 3 million American citizens over sixty-five in 1900, there were 14 million by 1957, a growth rate of approximately three times that of the rest of the population. Moreover, the trend of the 1950s was toward a lowering of the retirement age and toward formalizing it at sixty-five.[2] Furthermore, older people were visibly left out of advances made for the rest of the population. During the 1950s, labor unions made significant gains at the collective bargaining table in obtaining health insurance for their workers. Retired employees, however, were not usually included in the new contracts. Employees found that on retirement their policies were automatically canceled, or canceled at their first illness. If by some chance they could keep their insurance, they found their premiums unaffordable. Given their age, they could not qualify for a new policy. The problems of those retiring on a pension were more apparent in the light of the new benefits won by younger workers.[3]

Nor did the elderly benefit very much from the tremendous growth in the 1950s in Blue Cross and Blue Shield coverage. At first, Blue Cross allowed its holders to keep their policies after retirement at the same premium but for greatly reduced coverage. This allowance was made only for those workers who made such a choice early in their careers and who never missed a premium payment.[4] By 1957, with corporations purchasing about one-half of all health insurance from commercial carriers, the nonprofit Blue Cross was left with a larger share of high-risk elderly clients.[5] Blue Cross was eventually forced to raise its premiums for retirees, and by 1958, it too was far out of the price range of those living on a pension or Social Security check.[6]

Because of the expense, employers were loath to include retired workers in union health programs. Nor were private insurance carriers eager to get into the field. Hence, there was a growing gap in this new field of health insurance as only 22 percent of all labor contracts in 1954 provided medical benefits for retired workers, a figure that translated into only 1.8 million persons over age sixty-five. In such contracts, only the retired worker and not his or her spouse was covered.[7]

Another factor contributed to the recognition of the high cost of health care for the elderly. In the field of education, a cultural revolution was underway that affected the plight of the elderly. As more young people went to college, their parents were hard-pressed to purchase their childrens' education and at the same time meet the bills for aging parents' health care.[8] The government was asked to save its citizens from having to choose between their children's education and their parents' health.[9]

In a study made by the Bureau of Old-Age and Survivors Insurance, it was found that only 430 out of every 1,000 senior citizens had any hospital or health policy. Of these 430, 285 had hospital benefits with some surgical reimbursement and 145 persons had hospital coverage only. The study found that very few persons over seventy-three had any coverage. Of those who could afford coverage, it was estimated that the average elderly couple had to spend more than 15 percent of their income for a policy that covered little.[10]

Because Eisenhower was the first Republican President after two decades of Democratic administration, the new President evoked considerable speculation from the press about his plans concerning the elderly.[11] Unfortunately, the press had few guidelines from Eisenhower's 1953 campaign speeches or from his early days in office. While asserting that the ''Republican Party yields to no one its concern for the human needs of human beings,'' Eisenhower insisted that if there were unmet needs they could be best fulfilled by the private sector.[12]

The President, like many Democrats and most Republicans in the 1950s, viewed the problems of poverty and unaffordable medical care as the responsibility of charity, the private sector, or local government. In June 1958, the President told the House Ways and Means Committee, ''If all that Americans want is security, they can go to prison. They'll have enough to eat, a bed, and a roof over their heads.''[13] Eisenhower insisted that any government-sponsored health insurance coverage for the elderly ''would become frozen in a vast and unfair government system, foreclosing future opportunity for private groups, non-profit and commercial, to demonstrate their capacity to deal with the problem.''[14] A year later, in his 1959 State of the Union message, Eisenhower, disturbed by the increasing controversy of Medicare, sent Congress a warning: ''The Social Security system is not intended as a substitute for private savings, pension plans, and insurance protection. It is rather intended as a foundation upon which other forms of protection can be built.''[15]

Eisenhower and most of his staff tended to equate Medicare with socialized medicine. The AMA was so sure of the President's philosophy that it cut its political ''war chest'' from $2.5 million in 1950 to $255,000 in 1952.[16] In his campaign of 1952, Eisenhower spoke vehemently against Truman's proposal for a national health insurance program. The Republican candidate even borrowed the term ''socialized medicine'' to describe any extension of the Social Security system for medical purposes.

As part of his 1954 State of the Union message, the President told the nation: ''It is unfortunately a fact that medical costs are rising and already impose severe hardships on many families. The Federal Government can do many helpful things—and still carefully avoid the specialization of medicine.''[17] The White House seemed to underestimate the severity of the hardships. While Democratic congressmen were presenting evidence in special hearings on the loss of lives because of unaffordable health care, Republican Minority Leader ''Charlie'' Halleck gave his assessment, ''If people were dying right and left for lack of medical care you'd read about it in the papers.''[18] No one from the White House publicly disagreed.

Cooperating with the AMA on health insurance led Eisenhower to one achievement that had eluded Truman: the creation of a new Department of Health, Education and Welfare (HEW).[19] To head the new department, a position that carried Cabinet-level status, Eisenhower chose Olveta Culp Hobby. Hobby immediately reassured the AMA by telling the doctors that she would ''look to the physicians of the country for leadership.''[20] To provide a permanent place for physician leadership, Hobby created a new position of special assistant to health and medical affairs and appointed Dr. Chester Scott Kiersten, chief physician at Massachusetts Memorial Hospital and Professor of Medicine at Boston University, to fill the post. Hobby had every intention of fulfilling the President's promise to the AMA of no government interference and no health insurance for the elderly.[21]

Olveta Culp Hobby, formerly editor and publisher of the *Houston Post*, had gained Republican attention when she led a Texas bolt of Democrats for Eisenhower. She had the additional qualification of heading the Women's Army Corps during World War II. *Business Week* featured Mrs. Hobby on the cover of its May 16, 1953, edition, with what was said to be her credo, ''Welfare, but no welfare state.''[22]

A crisis did exist, however. The elderly could not afford their medical costs. Both Hobby and Eisenhower knew that if they could not find an acceptable solution more drastic programs would be presented. In a 1954 Los Angeles speech, the President suggested guidelines for a program to help the elderly: "Federal compulsion with our health supervised under a Washington stethoscope is not American and is not the answer. The answer is to build on the system of voluntary, non-profit insurance plans, which other people have already developed at an amazing rate."[23] After Eisenhower's statement, Blue Cross, Blue Shield, and other private insurance companies flooded the press with promises and statistics. They claimed that, given time, they had the ability to handle the problem. The White House, assured by the AMA that it was on the right track, waited for the insurance industry to meet the challenge.

Unfortunately, the industry indulged in empty advertising. Only *two* companies developed an actual plan to meet the needs of low-income elderly customers. The Continental Casualty Company of Chicago and the Mutual of Omaha Company ran a limited-time statewide drive to enlist those over sixty-five for a policy that covered thirty-one days in the hospital. The benefits ranged from $5 to $20 per day, and the monthly premium was $6.50.[24]

Despite the poor showing from the insurance industry, Eisenhower and Hobby were determined to have a privately based program. Hobby hired eight insurance executives to serve as consultants to help her work out a Republican alternative to government national health insurance. The result was a piece of legislation that only Hobby, Eisenhower, and the AMA liked. The legislation called for the federal government to subsidize private insurance companies by a system of "reinsurance" for policies that provided health care to the elderly. Not even the insurance industry supported Hobby's plan, and when it rejected Hobby's legislation before a House Ways and Means Committee Hearing, it took the President's persuasion to bring the industry to retract. In the end, Hobby's legislation was rejected anyway by Congress.[25]

Marion Folsom, Eisenhower's second appointee as Secretary of HEW (1955), searched for alternative ways to remain within the White House guidelines and at the same time propose positive legislation. Folsom's idea was to relax the antitrust laws so that insurance companies could pool their resources. This would enable the carriers to better absorb their high-risk customers. As in the case of the Hobby bill, Congress wasn't impressed, and neither was the insurance industry. Only Eisenhower and the AMA favored the proposal.[26]

By the time Arthur Flemming took over responsibility as Eisenhower's third Secretary of HEW in 1958, several liberal Democrats were launching a major legislative offensive, known as the Forand bill after its sponsor, Aime Forand (D-R.I.). The Forand bill used the Social Security method of financing and provided sixty days of hospital care and sixty days of nursing home care to those receiving Social Security benefits.

The AMA responded to this new threat by putting its members on "legislative alert," a warning to doctors of the dangers of the Forand bill. The Association emphasized that doctors never turned down charity cases (a disputed issue) and that there was no need for such extensive legislation.[27] Instead, the AMA began a campaign to correct difficulties in state and local assistance programs for the needy. Their priorities were remarkably similar to the recommendations given by the Surgeon-General, Dr. John Porterfield: more training programs for community health workers, and more research into health programs and services that emphasized preventative techniques. In other words, the AMA's goal was to expand voluntary welfare services and charity-oriented programs.[28]

On August 15, 1960, AMA President-elect Dr. Leonard Larson of Bismarck, North Dakota, announced the results of a survey that found, contrary to popular opinion, that most persons over sixty-five did *not* want a government program of health care. Only 10 percent of those polled favored a compulsory plan. The survey was conducted by Emory University sociologists, James W. Wiggins and Helmut Schoek, and funded by the William Volker Fund. The two professors interviewed 1,500 "representative persons" selected by scientific survey techniques. The survey reported that there was little reason to believe that the elderly were suffering from medical hardship. Of those polled, 60 percent said that, if they sold all they owed and paid all their bills, they would still have more than $7,500 in the bank.[29]

With the upcoming 1960 election and with Medicare the "Number One domestic issue," the Republicans felt public pressure to offer a positive program to go against the Democratic bills. Vice-President Richard Nixon was reportedly eager for the President to support a plan, but did not want to take the initiative to endorse something without Eisenhower's approval. Eisenhower, however, refused to endorse any plan. Secretary of HEW Flemming worked out a list of five possibilities from which the administration could choose, but still the President remained silent.

Nixon stuck by his favorite comment that the President was "searching for an acceptable solution."[30] A letter, drafted April 5 by Nixon's administrative assistant Robert Fitch and mailed to doctors around the country by the AMA, said that the Vice-President favored a program whereby those who desired to do so would be able to purchase health insurance from private companies on a voluntary basis. That meant that the federal and state governments would subsidize the purchase of such policies—one of the five plans suggested by Flemming.[31]

Throughout April and May, Flemming tried to persuade the President to choose a plan. Finally, at the end of June, on the second day of Finance Committee hearings, Eisenhower allowed Flemming to endorse a program. On June 29, Flemming appeared before the finance Committee to explain the new Eisenhower program introduced on June 30 as S3784 by Senator Leverett Saltonstall (R-Mass.). The bill proposed federal and state partnership on a program offering protection against long-term (catastrophic) illness for low-income senior citizens. An income test would determine eligibility; $2,500 yearly income for a couple was the maximum earnings for eligibility. There was also a $24 a year enrollment; a deductible of the first $250 of expenses; and the bill covered only 80 percent of costs after the deductible.

This program would be financed by the federal government out of general tax revenues and by state revenues on a special matching basis. Eisenhower, who equated Social Security taxed plans with socialized medicine, preferred using general taxes to finance any health insurance endeavor. If passed, the administration's plan would do nothing more than expand the public assistance programs. Medical writer Edward Chase wrote, "It is hard to escape the conclusion that the plan is strictly a political gesture, reluctantly taken to ease the politically untenable situation into which sheer negativism had placed the Party."[32]

Eisenhower's eleventh-hour legislation was reflective of the middle of the road course to which he adhered. To the left of the President and within the Republican party, a group of liberal Republicans including Jacob Javits (New York), Clifford Case (New Jersey), George Aiken (Vermont), John Sherman Cooper (Kentucky), Hiram Fong (Hawaii), Kenneth Keating (New York), Hugh Scott, Jr. (Pennsylvania), and Winston Prouty (Vermont) sponsored their own bill in the Senate, S3350. This Javits bill, as it was known, was closer to what the AMA had described as Nixon's favored approach. It called for federal and state subsidies to help low-income elderly purchase private health insurance policies.

Within Eisenhower's administration, Flemming and his Assistant Secretary Elliot Richardson were alone in wanting a more comprehensive health care program. Most of the President's staff, particularly his Budget Director, called for as little as possible in the way of a government program.

There were far more Republicans to the right of the President. To this group *any* government-sponsored health plan would have been objectionable. According to Everett Dirksen (Illinois), even Eisenhower's very limited plan to extend public assistance was "a small hole through which we will be driven, and the government will eventually do it all."[33] By "all" Dirksen presumably meant socialism. For his part, Eisenhower was pleased by the criticism. "I feel pretty good when I'm attacked from both sides," he told reporters. "It makes me feel certain that I'm on the right track."[34]

Both the House and the Senate rejected the Javits bill and the administration's bill. After a long and bitter debate, the Democratic Medicare program, sponsored by Senator Clinton Anderson (New Mexico) and Representative Cecil King (California), was also rejected. The only bill that passed the Senate (74–11) and the House (360–17) and was signed into law by President Eisenhower on September 13, 1960, was a compromise measure known as the Kerr-Mills bill. This particular bill, sponsored by Robert Kerr (D-Okla.) and Wilbur Mills (D-Ark.) provided federal grants to the states to help defray the costs of medical services for those elderly who were not already on public assistance but who were unable to meet their medical expenses. This created a whole new category of welfare recipients known as "medical indigents".

While the circumstances leading up the Kerr-Mills bill are beyond the scope of this chapter, it is important to note that the bill was partially designed to meet Eisenhower's objections and was worded so that the President would have no problem signing it into law. Kerr-Mills eventually became the basis for the 1965 Medicaid program.

The bill that "could do no harm" and "rocked no boats" had difficulty proving that it could do any good. The states, particularly those in the South, which stood to be reimbursed for over 70 percent of their dollars spent, could not or would not budget funds for the remainder.[35] By the time Eisenhower left office, only five states had passed legislation providing for at least some of the benefits under Kerr-Mills: Michigan, Oklahoma, Massachusetts, West Virginia, and Kentucky. Even these five provided benefits that were more apparent than real. Massachusetts, for example, transferred 14,000 persons over sixty-five from other public assistance programs to the new Massachusetts Assistance to the Aged (MAA, Kerr-Mills) program because the federal dollar share was higher. Other states enacted various impediments to Kerr-Mills. New Mexico, Tennessee, and Oregon required a deductible that was out of reach for the poor. Nine states allowed the state to take a lien after death on the property of the MAA recipient.[36]

One of the last major events in Eisenhower's administration was the White House Conference on Aging. In many ways the conference was a summary of Eisenhower's attitudes toward health care for the elderly. Twenty-seven thousand delegates attended about twenty paneled sessions. Discussions were scheduled to cover all issues affecting the elderly, including income, housing, employment, leisure, religion, and health. The subject that received the most publicity was financing health care.[37]

Liberals and labor leaders charged that the conference was "rigged" by the AMA.[38] Labor complained that Eisenhower had stacked the conference with wealthy doctors. George Meany told the press that the AMA "was conducting a reckless campaign of rule or ruin and the public be damned."[39] But Eisenhower staunchly defended the conference. He told reporters "I thought the purpose of a conference . . . was to get opposing sides, to see whether there is a platform that can satisfy the sound . . . logic of people of good will."[40] In fact, the doctors had planned to dominate the discussion of medical care financing. Much to their annoyance, however, they were outmaneuvered by the combined efforts of Arthur Flemming and labor leaders George Meany and Nelson Cruikshank when the three arranged for the agenda to be changed and health care financing was rescheduled to another panel. The AMA tried to have the topic changed again but was ruled out of order by the chairman of the conference, former Republican representative from New Jersey, R. W. Kean.[41] The AMA then charged Soviet dictation by "inner circles" during the planning for the conference.[42]

Although both sides charged that the other had more influence within the conference, two speeches delivered by former Eisenhower staff members had more to do with the outcome on medical care financing than the panel-stacking or agenda manipulations. The two speeches were made by Marion Folsom, former Secretary of HEW and now a director of Eastman-Kodak Company, and Arthur Larson, former Assistant Secretary of Labor and currently director of World Rule of Law Center at Duke University. Both men announced their support of the Democratic Medicare Plan. Folsom gave a "formidable factual analysis establishing the superiority of the Social Security mechanism over public assistance or charity for elderly citizens in need of health care."[43]

After eight years, the Republican administration had made some progress on its record of health care for the elderly. While Eisenhower was adamantly opposed to any program that did not require state cooperation, involve the private sector, or claim voluntary participation, he had signed the Kerr-Mills bill which, at the very least, recognized that the elderly could not pay their medical expenses. More than that, Kerr-Mills set a precedent for government involvement on the federal level for payments involving medical services. Kerr-Mills recognized that the over sixty-five population had special problems. Finally, because Kerr-Mills was acceptable to Eisenhower, it came to be acceptable to the AMA.

On the positive side, too, was Eisenhower's ability to elevate the Social Security Administration to Cabinet-level HEW. During the eight years of Eisenhower's office, HEW steadily increased the dollars spent to help the elderly. Two of the three Eisenhower appointments as Secretary to HEW, Arthur Flemming and Marion Folsom, contributed to the future Medicare program passed in 1965, and Eisenhower himself lent support to the White House Conference on Aging.

On the negative side, the elderly had to wait until 1965 to receive substantial help with their medical bills. Eisenhower remained tied to his own moral stand against social insurance, while looking to the American Medical Association for leadership and ideas. When it failed to provide any solution to the problem of health care for the elderly, Kerr-Mills became inevitable.

NOTES

1. Monte M. Poen, *Harry S Truman Versus the Medical Lobby* (Columbia, Mo.: University of Missouri Press, 1979), p. 211.

2. Richard Harris, *A Sacred Trust* (New York: New American Library, 1966), p. 73.

3. "Paying Health Costs of the Aged," *Business Week* (January 31, 1959), p. 33.

4. "Medical Care for Retired Workers?," *Fortune* 62 (July 1960), p. 211.

5. Raymond Munts, *Bargaining for Health Care: Labor Unions, Health Insurance and Medical Care* (Madison, Wis.: Univ. of Wisconsin Press, 1967), pp. 90–91.

6. Jerome Pollack, "A Labor View of Health Insurance," *Monthly Labor Review* 81 (February 1958):145.

7. "Medical Care for Retired Workers?," p. 211.

8. Aime Forand in a recorded interview with Peter Corning, 1966, in the Columbia University Oral History Program, 11. Hereafter identified as COH.

9. Eugene Feingold, *The Politics of Medicare* (San Francisco: Chandler Publishing Co., 1966), p. 24.

10. "Resources and Health Status of OASI Beneficiaries," *Monthly Labor Review* 82 (August 1959):882.

11. "Finding a GOP Welfare Plan," *Business Week* (May 16, 1953):116.

12. Dwight D. Eisenhower, *The White House Years: Mandate for Change, 1953–1956*, (Garden City, N.Y.: Doubleday, 1963), p. 134.

13. House Ways and Means Committee, *Hearings on Unemployment-Insurance Amendments*, 85th Cong., 2d Sess., June 22, 1958.

14. "Paying Health Costs," p. 33.

15. President Eisenhower message to Congress, *Congressional Quarterly Almanac* 16 (January 1959):618.

16. James G. Burrow, AMA, *Voice of American Medicine* (Baltimore: Johns Hopkins Press, 1963), p. 374.

17. Dwight D. Eisenhower, "State of the Union Message," *New York Times*, January 7, 1954.

18. James L. Sundquist, *Politics and Policy, The Eisenhower, Kennedy, and Johnson Years* (Washington, D.C.: Brookings Institution, 1968), p. 303.

19. Harris, *A Sacred Trust*, p. 65.

20. "Finding a GOP Welfare Plan," p. 118.

21. "The Doctors Arrive," *Newsweek* 42 (August 17, 1953):58.

22. *Business Week*, cover (May 16, 1953).

23. "The Doctors Arrive," p. 58.

24. "Paying Health Costs," p. 33.

25. "The Doctors Arrive," p. 58.

26. Robert J. Donovan, *Eisenhower: The Inside Story* (New York: Harper and Row, 1956), p. 229.

27. Harris, *A Sacred Trust*, p. 57.

28. Senate Subcommittee on Aged and Aging, *Hearings*, 86th Cong., 2d Sess. (April 4, 1960), p. 15.

29. House Ways and Means Committee *Hearings*, 86th Cong., 1st Sess., p. 270.

30. Gilbert Harrison, "Those Old Folks Back Home," *New Republic* 142 (April 18, 1960):9.

31. Ibid., p. 9.

32. Edward T. Chase, "Medical Aid for the Aged," *Commonweal* 72 (May 20, 1960):199.

33. Sundquist, *Politics and Policy*, p. 303.

34. Donovan, *Eisenhower*, p. 229.

35. "Politics of Medicine," *Harper's* 221 (October 1960):124.

36. *Congressional Record* 106 (1960):16425.

37. "Health Care for the Aged: An Unexpected Victory," *Reporter* 24 (February 2, 1961):24.

38. *Wall Street Journal*, December 18, 1960.

39. "Medicare for the Aged: The Logical Solution," *Newsweek* 57 (January 23, 1961):51.

40. "Aging with a Future," *America* 104 (January 28, 1961):558.

41. Harris, *A Sacred Trust*, p. 121.

42. "Aging with a Future," p. 559.

43. "Medicare for the Aged," p. 52.

8

The Eisenhower Administration and Intergovernmental Relations

Carl Lieberman

The policies of the Eisenhower administration regarding intergovernmental relations have generally been characterized as state-oriented, relatively unconcerned about the problems of cities, and inclined toward inaction as compared to those of the Democratic administrations that preceded and followed it. Indeed, it has been suggested that these policies were the result of the President's personal preferences. Thus, William E. Nelson writes:

The election of Dwight D. Eisenhower to the presidency for two terms resulted in a curtailment in the growth of federal-city relations exhibited over the previous two decades. Describing himself as a "dynamic conservative," Eisenhower believed strongly that the states and the cities had the responsibility of solving their own problems without involvement or interference by the federal government.[1]

In a similar vein, Roscoe Martin has stated:

. . . a strong chief executive almost uniformly brings on increased national activity, a weak or complacent one renewed emphasis on the states. Thus a Roosevelt was followed by a Taft, a Wilson by a Harding-Coolidge, a Roosevelt-Truman by an Eisenhower, and Eisenhower by a Kennedy-Johnson. The swing from centralization to decentralization and back is by no means constant, but the over-all trend is clearly discernible.[2]

For the most part, scholars have failed to describe at length the policies of the Eisenhower administration regarding intergovernmental relations or to consider

The author wishes to thank Elaine Barnett, Melanie Blumberg, and Anne Schwarz for their assistance in gathering bibliographical materials and statistical data.

the actual practices of the federal authorities in providing aid to state and local government.[3] An examination of federal aid during the Eisenhower years will show that there was a significant growth in the total amount of monies provided to state and local governments, that aid to local governments increased substantially, and that the national government undertook some important initiatives in the nature and administration of grant-in-aid programs. Although there was not the rapid increase in the number of categorical grants that one saw during the Johnson administration, neither was this merely a period of draft and complacency in intergovernmental fiscal relations.

EISENHOWER'S VIEWS ON INTERGOVERNMENTAL RELATIONS

One reason why Eisenhower has been perceived as a conservative, state-oriented President is that his public positions on intergovernmental relations reflected a desire to reduce the role of the national government in intergovernmental relations. When Eisenhower appointed the Commission on Intergovernmental Relations (the Kestnbaum Commission) during his first year in office, he remarked that it would begin "the elimination of frictions, duplications, and waste from Federal-State relations; the clear definition of lines of governmental authority in our nation."[4] The Commission on Intergovernmental Relations did not prescribe clear distinctions between the wide array of functions to be performed by state and local governments on the one hand and by the national government on the other. It generally supported the existing grant-in-aid system, but it urged some changes in a few specific programs. It suggested that the primary responsibility for civil defense should be reallocated to the national level. A further recommendation was made that the national government pay money in lieu of taxes on properties which it owned in order to assist local communities. Some reduction of federal aid in such areas as vocational education and old age assistance was urged, while the Commission suggested increased national aid for highways of special importance to interstate commerce and national security.[5]

The President created the Joint Federal-State Action Committee in 1957 in cooperation with the Governors' Conference in order to recommend functions that the states could assume, as well as changes in the fiscal system to enable the states to accept these responsibilities. The Committee recommended that the national government transfer support for vocational education and the construction of waste-treatment facilities entirely to the states, while it simultaneously relinquished 40 percent of the local telephone service tax to provide them with an opportunity to secure additional revenue. The Committee suggested an increased state role in urban renewal planning, national disaster relief, and the regulation and promotion of peaceful uses of atomic energy. Eisenhower endorsed these proposals and urged legislation to put them into effect.[6]

The President's proposals concerning national assistance appear to have been governed by four interrelated principles: (1) Aid could be provided in new areas when "State inaction, or inadequate action, coupled with undeniable national need, has forced emergency Federal intervention''; [7] (2) in those areas where aid could be reduced or gradually eliminated, steps should be taken to do so; (3) the states should be prepared to share an increasing part of the burden for domestic activities in order to encourage their continued existence as important components of the federal system and to discourage wasteful spending; and (4) the states should play an important role in aiding local governments.

Eisenhower's reluctance to expand the national share of funding specific programs was justified in part by arguments that increased federal assistance would make the states and localities too dependent on funding from the central government and thus weaken their influence. [8] However, exclusive federal financing was also criticized because it could produce waste:

I believe there should be a partnership between the local government and the Federal, if the Federal must participate. If there is not, then what influence, what incentive, is there for the local government to be economical and efficient in the running of this affair? On the contrary, their incentive is to be extravagant because that brings in more money from the general purse to spend there [9]

Even when Eisenhower proposed additional federal aid, his recommendations were generally not as far-reaching as those of such nationally oriented Presidents as Truman, Kennedy, and Johnson. Thus, his message on health care called for additional funding for research to combat various diseases, but did not urge the creation of a national health insurance system. Instead, he supported a program of federal reinsurance to permit private companies to expand coverage among those parts of the population who were potentially high-risk clients. [10]

With regard to federal aid to education, it was not until 1958, in the wake of the furor over the launching of Sputnik and alleged Russian leadership in science, that Eisenhower called for spending large sums of money in matching grants to improve instruction in science and mathematics. [11] Until that time, his recommendations for general aid to public education were mostly limited to assistance for school construction, much of which would be in the form of federal purchases of school bonds when school districts were unable to sell them on the open market at reasonable rates of interest. [12]

One area in which Eisenhower encouraged a substantial expansion of national assistance to the states was in the construction of highways. Aid was justified on the grounds that national highways would reduce accidents, promote commerce, and assist national defense. There were, of course, precedents for such national intervention, and his program of highway construction was proposed only after consultation with state officials. [13]

PATTERNS OF FEDERAL AID

During the period in which the Eisenhower administration was in power (fiscal years 1954–1961), federal aid grew from 3.7 to about 7.3 percent of federal budgetary outlays. Federal aid increased from 7.6 to 11 percent of total state-local revenues. (See Table 8.1.) Only in fiscal 1954, when the administration sought to reduce nonmilitary expenditures in its first budget, was there a reduction in federal aid from the previous year.[14]

Total federal payments to state and local governments grew at an annual rate of 12 percent. When an adjustment is made for inflation, the growth in federal aid is found to be smaller than in the Truman, Kennedy, Johnson and Ford administrations, as large as in the Nixon administration, and larger than in the Carter years. (See Table 8.2.) Of course, the rate of growth in federal aid was not constant, and it fell during the last two fiscal years, when Eisenhower tried to cut expenditures for such programs as public housing and urban renewal and to return responsibility for their funding to the states.[15]

Federal aid to local governments grew substantially. Precise figures for the amount of federal aid given to cities are not available for all the years of the Truman and Eisenhower administrations. However, direct federal payments to local governments more than doubled from the end of the Truman administration until 1961. Despite the growth of federal grants to local governments, approximately ten out of every eleven dollars of aid went to the states by the end of the Eisenhower administration.[16]

Direct aid to local government grew more rapidly during the Truman administration, increasing almost sixfold from 1946 to 1953. However, federal aid to local government in the Eisenhower years, though sometimes erratic in its growth, increased at a faster rate than state assistance. (See Table 8.3.)

There was a change in emphasis in the programs favored by the Eisenhower administration for urban America. Instead of concentrating on public housing,[17] the federal government introduced an urban renewal program to revitalize cities.[18] Urban renewal stressed rehabilitation and not merely slum clearance. It was designed to consider the needs of the city as a whole, particularly those of an economic nature. As the Advisory Committee on Housing noted, "cleared land [should] be put to its best industrial, commercial, institutional, public, and residential use."[19]

Perhaps as important as direct federal aid to cities is the amount of federal funds that were actually allocated to urban areas. By the end of the Eisenhower administration in fiscal year 1961, $3,893,000,000 of federal aid outlays was being distributed to standard metropolitan statistical areas. This figure represents 54.7 percent of all monies given to state and local governments.

If one compares federal expenditures in metropolitan areas in 1961 with those in fiscal 1964, the last year of the Kennedy administration, one finds that more money was spent in the former year for water pollution control ($24 million as opposed to $8 million). Moreover, a higher proportion of the federal aid outlays to urban areas in 1961 was provided for airports, elementary and secondary education, employment security administration, public assistance, and child nutrition programs. (See Table 8.4.)

By 1964, the Kennedy administration was spending $5,588,000,000 in stan-

Table 8.1 Federal Aid to State and Local Government, 1946–1982

Fiscal Year	(1) Federal Aid in Millions of Dollars	(2) Federal Aid as Percent of Federal Budgetary Outlays	(3) Federal Aid as Percent of State and Local Expenditures (Selected Years 1950–82)	(4) Federal Aid as Percent of Total State – Local Revenues
1946	775	1.3		5.9
1947	1,163	3.1		7.6
1948	1,492	4.1		8.4
1949	1,800	4.4		9.1
1950	2,253	5.3	10.4	10.6
1951	2,434	5.3		10.7
1952	2,604	3.8		9.2
1953	2,857	3.7		8.6
1954	2,657	3.7		7.6
1955	3,207	4.7	10.1	8.3
1956	3,724	5.3		8.9
1957	4,039	5.3		8.8
1958	4,935	6.0		10.0
1959	6,669	7.2		12.4
1960	7,020	7.6	14.7	11.7
1961	7,112	7.3		11.0
1962	7,893	7.4		11.3
1963	8,634	7.8		11.6
1964	10,141	8.6		12.3
1965	10,904	9.2	15.3	12.6
1966	12,960	9.6		13.5
1967	15,240	9.6		14.4
1968	18,599	10.4		14.6
1969	20,255	11.0		14.5
1970	24,014	12.3	19.2	14.6
1971	28,109	13.3	19.9	15.7
1972	34,372	14.8	22.0	16.5
1973	41,832	16.9	24.3	18.0

Table 8.1 continued

Fiscal Year	(1) Federal Aid in Millions of Dollars	(2) Federal Aid as Percent of Federal Budgetary Outlays	(3) Federal Aid as Percent of State and Local Expenditures (Selected Years 1950–82)	(4) Federal Aid as Percent of Total State – Local Revenues
1974	43,354	16.1	22.8	17.6
1975	49,834	15.4	23.0	17.8
1976	59,093	16.2	24.2	18.3
1977	68,414	17.1	25.9	18.5
1978	77,889	17.4	26.8	18.7
1979	82,858	16.9	26.3	18.6
1980	91,472	15.9	26.2	18.4
1981	94,762	14.4	25.0	17.8
1982	88,194	12.1	22.1	N.A.*

*Data Not Yet Available

Sources

Column 1: U.S. Bureau of the Census, Statistical Abstract of the United States, 1948–1960; U.S. Bureau of the Budget, Special Analyses: Budget of the United States, Fiscal Year 1968, p. 148; Executive Office of the President, Office of Management and Budget, Special Analyses: Budget of the United States Government, Fiscal Year 1980, p. 225; and Special Analyses: Budget of the United States Government, Fiscal Year 1984, p. H–16.

Column 2: Statistics based on information provided in Executive Office of the President, Office of Management and Budget, The United States Budget in Brief, Fiscal Year 1975, p. 58; Special Analyses: Budget of the United States Government Fiscal Year 1980, p. 225; and Special Analyses: Budget of the United States Government, Fiscal Year 1984, p. H–16.

Column 3: Executive Office of the President, Office of Management and Budget, Special Analyses: Budget of the United State Government, Fiscal Year 1980, p. 225; and Special Analyses: Budget of the United States Government, Fiscal Year, 1984, p. H–16.

Column 4: 1946–1962, Data computed from statistics in U.S. Bureau of the Census, Statistical Abstract of the United States, 1948–1964.

1963–1981, Data computed from statistics in U.S. Bureau of the Census, Governmental Finances, 1965–66 – 1980–81.

dard metropolitan statistical areas. This was an increase of approximately 43.5 percent over the amount spent in 1961, and represented 55.1 percent of total federal aid to state and local governments. Thus, there was a slight increase in the proportion of federal aid outlays going to urban areas. New programs were instituted for economic development, water and sewer facilities, personnel training, and medical assistance.

The most dramatic increases in the total amount of money going to metropolitan areas occurred during the Johnson administration. Between 1964 and 1969,

Table 8.2 Average Annual Growth Rate in Federal Aid, 1946–1981

Administration	Fiscal Years	Average Yearly Growth Rate in Federal Aid (In Current Dollars)	Average Yearly Growth Rate in Federal Aid (In Constant Dollars)*
Truman	1946-1953	20%	14
Eisenhower	1954-1961	12	8
Kennedy	1962-1964	13	10
Johnson	1965-1969	15	9
Nixon	1970-1975	16	8
Ford	1976-1977	17	9
Carter	1978-1981	8	0

*Average yearly growth rate in constant dollars has been determined by using an implicit price deflator for state and local government purchases of goods and services.

Table 8.3 Federal and State Aid to Local Government, 1946–1961 (in millions of dollars)

Year	Federal Aid	State Aid
1946	53	2092
1948	218	3283
1950	211	4217
1952	237	5044
1953	300	5384
1954	298	5635
1955	368	5987
1956	309	6590
1957	343	7321
1958	404	7974
1959	489	8399
1960	592	9522
1961	719	10185

Source: U.S. Bureau of the Census, Census of Governments: 1962, Vol. VI, No. 4, "Historical Statistics in Governmental Finances and Employment," pp. 44–45.

Table 8.4 Federal Aid Outlays in Standard Metropolitan Statistical Areas, 1961, 1964, and 1969 (in millions of dollars)

Function and Program	1961 $	1961 %	1964 $	1964 %	1969 $	1969 %
National Defense	10	0.3	28	0.5	30	0.2
Agriculture & Rural Development:	155	4.0	271	4.8	417	3.0
Donation of Surplus Commodities	128	3.3	231	4.1	313	2.2
Other	27	0.7	40	0.7	104	0.7
Natural Resources	54	1.4	18	0.3	180	1.3
Water Pollution Control	24	0.6	8	0.1	79	0.6
Other	30	0.8	10	0.2	101	0.7
Commerce and Transportation	1435	36.9	2147	38.4	2539	18.1
Economic Development	----		158	2.8	104	0.7
Highways	1398	35.9	1948	34.9	2225	15.8
Airports	36	0.9	36	0.6	83	0.6
Urban Mass Transportation	----		----		122	0.9
Other	1	*	5	0.1	5	*
Community Development & Housing	213	5.5	348	6.2	1610	11.5
Community Action Program	----		----		432	3.1
Urban renewal	106	2.7	159	2.8	786	5.6
Public Housing	105	2.7	136	2.4	257	1.8
Water and Sewer Facilities	----		36	0.6	52	0.4
Model Cities	----		----		8	0.1
Other	2	0.1	17	0.3	75	0.5
Education and Manpower	561	14.4	732	13.1	2963	21.1
Head Start and Follow Through	----		----		256	1.8
Elementary and Secondary	222	5.7	274	4.9	1262	9.0
Higher Education	5	0.1	14	0.3	210	1.5
Vocational Education	28	0.7	29	0.5	179	1.3
Employment Security Administration	303	7.8	344	6.2	449	3.2
Manpower Activities	----		64	1.1	530	3.8
Other	3	0.1	7	0.1	77	0.5
Health	99	2.5	300	5.4	2278	16.2
Hospital Construction	48	1.2	66	1.2	89	0.6
Regional Medical Program	----		----		19	0.1
Mental Health	4	0.1	8	0.1	150	0.4
Maternal and Child Health	18	0.5	34	0.6	139	1.0
Comprehensive Health Planning and Services	29	0.7	48	0.9	80	0.6
Health Educational Facilities	----		----		106	0.8
Medical Assistance	----		140	2.5	1713	12.2
Health Manpower	----		----		28	0.2
Other	----		4	0.1	54	0.4
Income Security	1341	34.4	1695	30.3	3899	27.8
Vocational Rehabilitation	37	1.0	61	1.1	247	1.8
Public Assistance	1170	30.1	1450	25.9	3022	21.5
Child Nutrition, Special Milk and Food Stamps	131	3.4	168	3.0	482	3.4
Other	3	0.1	16	0.3	148	1.1
General Government	25	0.6	47	0.8	129	0.9
Law Enforcement	----		----		17	0.1
National Capital Region	25	0.6	38	0.6	85	0.6
Other	----		9	0.2	27	0.2
Other Functions	----		2	*	----	
Total, Aids to Metropolitan Areas	3893		5588		14045	

*Less than 0.1% of federal aid outlays

Source: Executive Office of the President, Office of Management and Budget, The Budget for Fiscal Year 1971: Special Analyses, p. 229.

federal outlays increased by 151.3 percent, and funds became available for urban mass transit, the community action program, Model Cities, Head Start, and Follow Through. In general, there were major increases in expenditures for community development, education and manpower, and health.

As noted previously, the Eisenhower administration introduced programs for highway construction and education, both of which went into operation during the President's second term. Although these programs were not as well funded as some of the grants-in-aid established in the 1960s and 1970s, their impact was nevertheless substantial at the time of enactment.

The highway program, as Eisenhower stated, "was the biggest peacetime construction project of any description ever undertaken by the United States or any other country." The more than $30 billion which the administration proposed to give to the states in the form of matching grants over a ten-year period would provide for the construction and widening of a 41,000-mile network of interstate and defense highways linking virtually all cities with a population of 50,000 or more.[20] Between 1955 and 1960, the share of state and local capital expenditures financed by federal grants increased from 8.3 to 23.9 percent largely as a result of the funding of the interstate highway system. During the same period, the proportion of federal aid allocated to commerce and transportation grew from approximately 19 to 43 percent.[21]

The President's proposals for aid to education in 1958 would have provided $1.6 billion, primarily for the teaching of science, mathematics, and foreign languages. As actually passed, the National Defense Education Act established a $1 billion program designed to improve the teaching of science, mathematics, and foreign languages at all school levels for fiscal 1959–1962. The law authorized the creation of student loan funds for those in colleges and universities, graduate fellowships, grants for the improvement of counseling and testing, the creation of advanced institutes to train public school teachers in the teaching of foreign languages, and monies for the training of skilled technicians.[22]

During the Eisenhower administration, the Public Health Service found it difficult to expand project grants, which are most suitable for aid to local governments and private groups, as a result of opposition from the states and members of the President's staff who disliked "direct" federalism.[23] Nevertheless, by fiscal 1962, two-thirds of all federal grant programs were in the form of project grants.[24]

ORGANIZATIONAL CHANGES IN INTERGOVERNMENTAL RELATIONS

At the same time that changes in the patterns of federal aid were occurring, organizational changes were taking place in the management of intergovernmental relations. Eisenhower became the first Chief Executive to appoint a special assistant to advise him on relationships with state and local government. The assistant, former Governor Howard Pyle of Arizona, was, to be sure, not particularly concerned with the problems of urban America. Moreover, he was denied adequate staff assistance, and he was used primarily to resolve conflicts and misunderstandings that arose with state and local governments. Despite these shortcomings, Pyle's appointment represented an attempt to make more advice on the federal system available to the President.[25]

From the very onset of the administration, plans were initiated to create a new department to consolidate the health, welfare, and educational functions of the federal government. As a result of Reorganization Plan No. 1 of 1953, the Federal Security Agency was elevated to a Cabinet-level Department of Health, Education, and Welfare. Although Eisenhower's recommendation was similar to plans proposed by Truman in 1949–1950, the successful passage of a joint resolution in Congress indicated the desire of the new administration to organize the government in a way that would give greater recognition to issues of important domestic concern.[26]

Before the end of the Eisenhower administration, legislation was enacted to create an Advisory Commission on Intergovernmental Relations (ACIR). In some respects, this was the most important organizational reform during the Eisenhower years which influenced the American federal system. It provided a permanent structure within the executive branch, the basic purpose of which was to study problems of an intergovernmental nature and to make recommendations for their amelioration. Because members of the Commission were to be appointed by the President and by the presiding officers of Congress, and they included state and local as well as federal officials, the ACIR provided a bridge between different branches and levels of government.[27]

THE EISENHOWER ADMINISTRATION AND INTERGOVERNMENTAL RELATIONS: A NEED FOR REASSESSMENT?

The rhetoric and even many of the specific proposals of President Eisenhower did not fully match the actual performance of the administration in providing aid to state and local governments. Eisenhower's remarks and recommendations have sometimes been interpreted as essentially conservative, reflecting the preferences of a President with a "textbook view" of federalism, who thought that functions could be neatly divided between the national and state authorities.[28]

Many of the President's positions, both as a candidate and as Chief Executive, indicated a desire to avoid excessive centralization and, perhaps, a willingness to turn power back to the states. It is not surprising that one who called for the return to the states of offshore oil lands would also favor the reduction of federal influence by limiting grants-in-aid to state and local governments.[29]

Nevertheless, Eisenhower was willing to increase federal aid to those policy areas that had an impact on national security. Thus, he advocated a far-reaching system of interstate highways. He readily admitted the impact of this massive construction project on the economy, but he also added, "And motorists by the millions would read a primary purpose in the signs that would sprout up alongside the pavement: 'In the event of an enemy attack, this road will be closed.' ''[30] The President also supported the National Defense Education Act, which provided for aid both to college students who expressed an interest in mathematics and science and to the states for improvement of guidance and counseling in the secondary schools and for instruction in defense-related fields.[31]

Some will see in the contrast between Eisenhower's rhetoric concerning the dangers of an overly intrusive federal government and the willingness of the administration to support ever increasing amounts of aid to state and local governments an example of what Fred Greenstein refers to as "the hidden-hand presidency."[32] Perhaps Eisenhower's public statements on intergovernmental relations merely indicate an instrumental use of language, a desire to put forward conservative proposals while secretly advancing a mildly liberal agenda.

The conclusion that Eisenhower's public positions on intergovernmental fiscal relations were largely window dressing must be viewed with caution. Scholars who have examined postwar trends in federal aid have generally supported the perception of Eisenhower as a somewhat conservative state-oriented President.[33] Moreover, even after he left office, he continued to warn of the dangers of an overly centralized federal system.[34]

How then can one explain the incongruities between the statements of the President and the actions of the administration which he headed? To understand the reasons for the patterns of aid which developed during the Eisenhower years, it is necessary to recognize the interplay of presidential preferences and environmental factors.

Dwight Eisenhower's views on intergovernmental relations may well have been conservative. He personally expressed little interest in the problems encountered by large American cities as they dealt with the economic and social changes of the postwar period. However, Eisenhower was not a reactionary who sought to reduce massively federal responsibility for economic regulation and social welfare. The thrust of his leadership of the national Republican party was to make it a body that was internationalist in its foreign policy orientations and favorably inclined toward the positivist view of government domestically.[35] He showed no inclination to dismantle the welfare state. Because many of the health and welfare programs that were in place when he became President involved cooperative action between the national and state governments, one would expect him to continue their funding.

During the 1950s, the nation experienced a population growth of over 18 percent. There were significant increases in the number of school-aged children, older Americans, and residents of metropolitan areas. (See Table 8.5.) These social and demographic changes created a momentum for new federal initiatives and encouraged organized interest groups to lobby in behalf of grant-in-aid programs.[36]

For six of the years in which Eisenhower was in office, Congress was under Democratic control. Thus, compromise was a necessity if legislation was to be

Table 8.5 Selected Demographic Changes, 1950 and 1960

	1950	1960	% Increase
Population*	151.3	179.3	18.5
Residents in Standard Metropolitan Statistical Areas*	84.5	112.9	33.6
School Enrollment (Kindergarten - Grade 12)*	28.1	42.7	52.1
Persons Aged 65 and Over*	12.3	16.6	35.0

*All figures except percentages in millions.

Source: U.S. Bureau of the Census, Statistical Abstract of the United States: 1952 and 1961.

enacted. Furthermore, if the President and his chief subordinates failed to promote policies that dealt with critical issues, such as health, education, and transportation, they could be sure that some of the leading Democrats in Congress would propose legislation in these areas. Hence, the final product of any major legislation was the result of several factors—population change, the need to secure bipartisan support, possible pressures from Democratic politicians if no action was taken, and the necessity of presenting some proposals if the Republican party which Eisenhower sought to fashion as a moderately progressive force in American politics was to appeal to a broadly based electorate, including blacks and city dwellers.

It must be remembered that the Eisenhower administration and the President were not synonymous. Despite his attempts to remove some of the more important bureaucrats from civil service protection when he assumed office, most of those who held policymaking positions in the government had been hired by preceding Democratic administrations.[37] As would be expected, many of these persons were sympathetic to an expanding role for the national government. At the very least, they had little to gain from sharp cutbacks in federally funded programs that aided state and local governments. Indeed, the continued implementation of such programs would probably serve to maintain their influence within the bureaucratic structure.

State and local governments were important actors in the making of intergovernmental fiscal policies. If state and local officials could not always obtain the aid they desired from the administration, they could help to block actions desired by the President and assist in the shaping of programs. State officials resisted the recommendations of the Joint Federal-State Action Committee to shift support for vocational education and the construction of waste-treatment facilities to the states.[38] The American Municipal Association and the United States Conference of Mayors fought attempts by the administration to reduce substantially urban renewal funding for fiscal 1958, and some of the Democratic mayors established ties with Democratic chairmen of the housing subcommittees to restore money which the Bureau of the Budget had cut.[39]

The major initiatives of the Eisenhower administration in federal aid tended to favor the development of economic infrastructure. The massive highway construction program and the initiation of urban renewal in American cities were policies that would be beneficial to business interests, real estate developers, some contractors, and construction unions. The Eisenhower presidency, unlike the Johnson and, to a lesser degree, the Kennedy administration, was not characterized by the creation of many new programs in welfare and human services.

In short, the Eisenhower administration's policies concerning intergovernmental relations reflected a mixture of forces. On the one hand, the President's desire for a state-oriented agenda is seen in his appointment of the Commission on Intergovernmental Relations and the Joint Federal-State Action Committee, as well as his reluctance to expand greatly the amount of direct aid to local governments. On the other hand, the essential pragmatism of the administration is illustrated by its willingness to accept continued growth in the amount of federal aid to state and local governments and by Eisenhower's endorsement of programs that had a relationship to national defense. The organizational changes that occurred during the Eisenhower years demonstrate some support for reorganizing the national government to deal more effectively with intergovernmental problems.[40] Rather than seeing the eight years of Eisenhower's presidency as a period of drift and complacency, it may be more accurate to perceive them as a transitional period in American federalism. It was then that the national government did more to aid state and local governments, but it had not yet embarked on the great growth of social programs and new grants-in-aid to cities which were to characterize federal activity for most of the two decades after Eisenhower left office.

NOTES

1. William E. Nelson, ''Federal-City Relations: The Failure of Urban Reform,'' *Urban Affairs Quarterly* 13 (September 1977):118.

2. Roscoe C. Martin, *The Cities and the Federal System* (New York: Atherton Press, 1965), pp. 26–27.

3. A notable exception is Mark I. Gelfand's book, *A Nation of Cities: The Federal Government and Urban America, 1933–1965* (New York: Oxford University Press, 1975). See particularly pp. 157–97.

4. ''Statement by the President Concerning the New Commission on Intergovernmental Relations,'' September 18, 1953, *Public Papers of the Presidents of the United States: Dwight D. Eisenhower, 1953,* pp. 589–90.

5. U.S. Congress, House, *The Commission on Intergovernmental Relations: Message from the President of the United States Transmitting the Final Report of the Commission on Intergovernmental Relations, Pursuant to Public Law 109,* 84th Cong. 1st Sess., 1955:

"Intergovernmental Study Group Endorses Federal Aid to Localities," *American City* 70 (August 1955):24.

6. "Annual Budget Message to the Congress—Fiscal Year 1959," January 13, 1958, *Public Papers of the Presidents of the United States: Dwight D. Eisenhower, 1958* (Washington, D.C.: U.S. Government Printing Office, 1959), pp. 42–43, 46; Edwin L. Dale, Jr., "U.S. Is Urged to Transfer from Programs to States," *New York Times*, December 6, 1957, pp. 1, 24; Bess Truman, "President Proposes Cuts in Health-Welfare Field," *New York Times*, January 14, 1958, pp. 1, 21; Robert H. Connery and Richard H. Leach, *The Federal Government and Metropolitan Areas* (Cambridge, Mass.: Harvard University Press, 1960), pp. 132–33.

7. "Address to the 1957 Governors' Conference," Williamsburg, Virginia, June 14, 1957, *Public Press of the Presidents of the United States: Dwight D. Eisenhower, 1960–61* (Washington, D.C.: U.S. Government Printing Office, 1961), p. 95.

8. "Annual Budget Message to the Congress: Fiscal Year 1961," January 18, 1960, *Public Papers of the Presidents of the United States: Dwight D. Eisenhower, 1960–61* (Washington, D.C.: U.S. Government Printing Office, 1961), p. 95.

9. "The President's News Conference of August 11, 1954," *Public Papers of the Presidents of the United States: Dwight D. Eisenhower, 1954* (Washington, D.C.: Office of the Federal Register, 1960), p. 705.

10. "Special Message to the Congress of the Health Needs of the American People," January 18, 1954, *Public Papers of the Presidents of the United States: Dwight D. Eisenhower, 1954*, pp. 69–77; and "Special Message to the Congress Recommending a Health Program," January 31, 1955, *Public Papers of the Presidents of the United States: Dwight D. Eisenhower, 1955* (Washington, D.C.: Office of the Federal Register, 1959), pp. 216–23.

11. "Special Message to the Congress on Education," January 27, 1958, *Public Papers of the Presidents of the United States: Dwight D. Eisenhower, 1958*, pp. 127–32.

12. "Special Message to the Congress Concerning Federal Assistance in School Construction," February 8, 1955, *Public Papers of the Presidents of the United States: Dwight D. Eisenhower, 1955*, pp. 243–50; "Special Message to the Congress on Education," January 12, 1956, *Public Papers of the Presidents of the United States: Dwight D. Eisenhower, 1956* (Washington, D.C.: U.S. Government Printing Office, 1958), pp. 63–71; and "Special Message to the Congress on Federal Aid to Education," January 18, 1957, *Public Papers of the Presidents of the United States: Dwight D. Eisenhower, 1957*, pp. 89–95.

13. "Special Message to the Congress Regarding a National Highway Program," February 22, 1955, *Public Papers of the Presidents of the United States: Dwight D. Eisenhower, 1955*, pp. 275–80; and Dwight D. Eisenhower, *The White House Years: Mandate for Change, 1953–1956* (New York: New American Library, 1965), pp. 648–50.

14. In a diary entry on June 1, 1953, Eisenhower noted that he disagreed with Senator Taft of Ohio that $10 billion could be cut from the defense budget and that a commensurate reduction in taxes could be enacted. However, he noted," I do believe that we can make sufficient reductions this year to show the American people that we are doing a sensible and sane and efficient job, and win an election next year on a record of economy, efficiency, and effective security. With consistent attention to these matters, I believe that we can cut government expenditures far enough to justify real tax reductions for the fiscal year 1955."

Robert H. Ferrell, ed., *The Eisenhower Diaries* (New York and London: W. W. Norton, 1981), p. 240.

15. Some of Eisenhower's proposed cuts would have had the most adverse effect on major American cities: Gelfand goes so far as to describe federal-city relations during Eisenhower's second term as a "cold war." See particularly his discussion of the 1957 struggle over the funding of urban renewal. Gelfand, *A Nation of Cities*, pp. 184–89.

16. In 1960, for example, only $592 million of the approximately $7 billion of federal payments to state and local governments was allotted to direct payments to local governments. See Martin, *The Cities and the Federal System*, p. 112.

17. Eisenhower did not seek to end public housing or to reduce significantly the number of new units until the last two years of his administration. In 1958, the President in his Budget Message recommended that each state establish an agency for housing, urban development, and metropolitan planning, and that states and localities should be required to assume a larger share of the net costs of urban renewal. In 1959, he requested that no new public housing units be authorized. Although he was not successful in preventing the subsidization of new housing, he was largely able to prevent the authorization of new units in 1960. *Congress and the Nation 1945–1964: A Review of Government and Politics in the Postwar Years* (Washington, D.C.: Congressional Quarterly Service, 1965), pp. 490–94.

18. Urban renewal was in part an extension of the urban redevelopment provisions of the 1949 Housing Act. However, its emphasis was less on slum clearance and housing than on the economic development of cities.

19. Quoted in Gelfand, *A Nation of Cities*, p. 173.

20. Eisenhower, *Mandate for Change*, pp. 649–50. When the Highway Act of 1956 (PL 84–627) was passed, its provisions were somewhat different from those originally proposed by the administration. Nearly $31 billion in federal-state funds were authorized over a thirteen-year period, of which over $26 billion would come from the federal government. A variety of highway taxes and user fees were to be earmarked for the Highway Trust Fund. A number of new or increased taxes were levied on gasoline, diesel, and motor oils; tires and retreads; and trucks, busses, and truck trailers. *Congress and the Nation 1945–1964*, p. 531.

21. Executive Office of the President, Bureau of the Budget, *The Budget for Fiscal Year 1968: Special Analyses* (Washington, D.C.: 1967), p. 147; and Executive Office of the President, Office of Management and Budget, *The Budget for Fiscal Year 1984: Special Analyses* (Washington, D.C.: 1983), p. H–17.

22. The President's original proposal called for 10,000 scholarships a year for four years. The House Education and Labor Committee approved a bill with 23,000 scholarships a year. Ultimately, the House agreed to drop the scholarship provision altogether and to add the $120 million to finance such aid to the student loan fund. The Senate agreed in conference to eliminate the scholarships and accept the House loan provision. *Congress and the Nation 1945–1964*, pp. 1200–1201, 1208.

23. Charles E. Gilbert and David G. Smith, "The Modernization of American Federalism," in Murray S. Stedman, Jr., ed., *Modernizing American Government: The Demands of Social Change* (Englewood Cliffs, N.J.: Prentice-Hall, 1968), p. 145.

24. Advisory Commission of Intergovernmental Relations, *Fiscal Balance in the American Federal System*, Vol. 1 (Washington, D.C.: 1967), p. 151.

25. In appointing Pyle as his special assistant for intergovernmental affairs, Eisenhower accepted the recommendation of the Kestnbaum Commission, which proposed such a

position on the President's staff. Connery and Leach, *The Federal Government and Metropolitan Areas*, pp. 134–37.

26. Republicans and many Southern Democrats had opposed Truman's plans because they feared that Oscar Ewing, the Federal Security Agency (FSA) administrator and a supporter of compulsory national health insurance, would be appointed the first Secretary. Republicans also were concerned that earlier plans would put education and health matters in a welfare-oriented agency. The Eisenhower administration overcame opposition in several ways: by proposing Oveta Culp Hobby, an opponent of national health insurance, as the new Secretary; leaving the functions of the Public Health Service and the Office of Education in these two agencies, which became subordinate units of the new department; creating a new post of special assistant to the Secretary for Health and Medical Affairs, a position to be filled by a person of wide nongovernmental experience in medical and health affairs; and providing for presidential appointment of a Commissioner of Social Security (subject to Senate confirmation), who would carry out duties connected with Social Security and welfare programs under the general direction of the Secretary. Even the American Medical Association, a leading opponent of Truman's plans, endorsed Eisenhower's recommendation. *Congress and the Nation 1945–1964*, p. 1248.

27. For a less generous assessment of the creation of the ACIR, see Connery and Leach, *The Federal Government* and *Metropolitan Areas*, pp. 126, 128, 166. They viewed the Advisory Commission on Intergovernmental Relations as a body that would be concerned primarily with federal-state relations. Hence, they believed it would give little attention to problems of a metropolitan nature.

28. A retired civil servant, who had worked with the Kestnbaum Commission, commented that Eisenhower was not very interested in intergovernmental relations when he first assumed office. He expressed a doubt that the President ever fully understood the work of the Kestnbaum Commission in the same way that he was familiar with the suggestions of the Hoover Commission. He believed that Eisenhower had a fairly good, though "textbookish," view, of federalism. Interview, May 21, 1975.

29. See, for example, Sherman Adams, *Firsthand Report: The Story of the Eisenhower Administration* (New York: Harper and Brothers, 1961), pp. 305–306; and Eisenhower *Mandate for Change*, pp. 256–61 for a discussion of Eisenhower's position on the offshore oil controversy.

30. Eisenhower, *Mandate for Change*, p. 650.

31. "Special message to the Congress on Education," January 27, 1958; and *Congress and the Nation 1945–1964*, pp. 1200–1201, 1208.

32. Fred I. Greenstein, *The Hidden-Hand Presidency: Eisenhower as Leader* (New York: Basic Books, 1982). See Chapter 3 for a discussion of Eisenhower's political strategies.

33. Nelson, "Federal-City Relations"; Martin, *The Cities and the Federal System*. Also see Parris N. Glendenning and Mavis Mann Reeves, *Pragmatic Federalism: An Intergovernmental View of American Government* (Pacific Palisades: Palisades Publishers, 1977), p. 315.

34. See Eisenhower's address before the Fifty-sixth Annual Meeting of the Governor's Conference, June 8, 1964. Reprinted in the article, "State Government and Liberty in America," *State Government* 37 (Summer 1964):138–42. It should be noted that his speech also called on states to adopt organizational reforms, so that their own capacity to deal with problems would be strengthened.

35. Cornelius P. Cotter, "Eisenhower as Party Leader," *Political Science Quarterly* 98 (Summer 1983):255–83. See particularly pp. 257–59.

36. Thus, during most of the years of the Eisenhower administration, the issue of federal aid to education focused on the shortage of classrooms and teachers, which largely resulted from increased school enrollments. James L. Sundquist, *Politics and Policy: The Eisenhower, Kennedy, and Johnson Years* (Washington, D.C.: Brookings Institution, 1968), pp. 155–87; and Philip Meranto, *The Politics of Federal Aid to Education in 1965: A Study in Political Innovation* (Syracuse: Syracuse University Press, 1967), pp. 14–15. A slightly different interpretation of federal aid to education has been offered by Frank J. Junger and Richard F. Fenno, who maintain that the school construction bills of the 1950s were generated by the baby boom and suburban sprawl of that decade. See *National Politics and Federal Aid to Education* (Syracuse, N.Y.: Syracuse University Press, 1962), p. 16.

37. For a discussion of the Eisenhower administration's attempts to exempt certain confidential and policymaking posts from civil service protection, see Herman Miles Somers, "The Federal Bureaucracy and the Change of Administration," *American Political Science Review* 48 (March 1954), particularly pp. 139–47. Apparently, some stalwarts urged Eisenhower to support a proposal that every department should have the authority to discharge 10 percent of its employees without regard to civil service regulations. The President rejected this suggestion. Eisenhower, *Mandate for Change*, p. 160.

38. Sundquist, *Politics and Policy*, pp. 327–28.

39. Gelfand, *A Nation of Cities*, pp. 185–87.

40. Graves argues that Eisenhower took a more active interest than any of his predecessors in intergovernmental relations and refers to three major projects that were designed to improve interlevel and interjurisdictional relations: the Commission on Intergovernmental Relations, the Federal-State Joint Action Committee, and the Advisory Commission on Intergovernmental Relations. W. Brooke Graves, *American Intergovernmental Relations: Their Origins, Historical Development, and Current States* (New York: Charles Scribner's Sons, 1964), p. 178.

9

The Politics of Antitrust: The Eisenhower Era

Theodore Philip Kovaleff

If the charges made during the 1952 presidential campaign had come to pass, a Republican victory would have ushered in vast changes in American society, among which one might have expected to see the Tennessee Valley Authority (TVA) sold or dismantled, Social Security eliminated, and antitrust enforcement cease. Experience proved all of these forebodings unfounded, of course, but the question of antitrust enforcement by the Eisenhower White House took longer than other doubts to be resolved.

When the Eisenhower administration began in early 1953, the climate of opinion was not at all favorable to antitrust enforcement. During the Depression years, President Franklin D. Roosevelt had alternately attempted to use, or not use, antitrust enforcement, or the lack thereof, as a means of restoring prosperity: first, the National Recovery Administration substituted regulation for competition, and then, when that failed, it sought recovery via the Temporary National Economic Committee and a vigorous policy of trade regulation. War-induced activity finally stimulated the economy, but after the advent of peace, people in and out of government feared that the Depression might return. Articles in both scholarly and popular journals and magazines proposed all sorts of remedies, many involving a change of direction in antitrust enforcement.[1]

The way could have been clear then, in 1953, for a holiday from antitrust for the next four, eight, or sixteen years. Indeed, when the former chief of General Motors, Charles Wilson, was incorrectly quoted in his confirmation hearings as saying "What's good for General Motors is good for the country," many interpreted this statement as indicative of Big Business preparing to run the country and as an obvious clue to the shelving of antitrust laws.[2] As shown elsewhere, however, there was no such holiday, for the Eisenhower antitrust policy remained vigorous.[3]

Very broadly stated, antitrust enforcement is based on two statutes, the Sherman Act, which forbids monopolization or attempts thereto, and Section 7 of the Clayton Act, which interdicts actions that may lead to monopoly. The Eisenhower antitrusters were active in enforcing both. To substantiate this claim, one need only examine the timing, conduct, content, and outcome of a number of cases, as will be done in this chapter. In so doing, it becomes clear that not only was the Eisenhower administration active in antitrust enforcement, but also that its enforcement was nonpolitical.

One of the more interesting cases—made the more interesting because of its implications for the recent splitting up of operating companies from American Telephone and Telegraph Corporation (AT&T)—was the case filed in 1949 which had at least three objectives:

1. That Western Electric be divorced from AT&T.
2. That AT&T and the various operating companies be compelled to buy equipment on a competitive-bid basis.
3. That AT&T and Western Electric be required to license their patents to all applicants on a nondiscriminatory and reasonable royalty basis.

Settled by the Eisenhower administration in January 1956, the case at first glance appeared to be a victory for the communications giant because it did not include the divestiture of Western Electric. Nevertheless, there were provisions that precluded expansion into allied fields. These interdictions have been cited as one of the major reasons why AT&T was willing to settle the 1980s suit, which achieved one of the essential goals of the 1949 action. For better or worse, then (and there are those on both ends of the political spectrum who believe the recent AT&T case was either well or poorly settled), the 1984 case did have its roots in the settlement made in the 1950s.

Another case in point concerned the Eastman Kodak Corporation where the Eisenhower administration risked alienating an entire group of consumers by forcing Eastman Kodak to alter its marketing procedures. The antitrusters believed that the Kodak policy of tying the price of processing to the cost of film purchase precluded independents from the processing business. The logic of the argument was sufficient to persuade Kodak to separate the price of film and processing, an action that had the immediate effect of raising the cost of picture taking. In the long term, however, it opened up an entire new industry and resulted in lowered prices. Nevertheless, the case generated scores of excoriating letters attacking the settlement as everything from "antibusiness" to "communistic."[4] According to the chief of the Antitrust Division of the Department of Justice, Stanley Barnes, even "President Eisenhower . . . complained to me . . . about the inconvenience of certain provisions of the . . . decree."[5] Politically, the action gained Eisenhower nothing.

In the areas of interdicting mergers, the Eisenhower administration broke new ground. In 1950, as a response to public clamor over the loopholes in Section

7 of the Clayton Act, Congress passed an amendment to the Clayton Act broadening its coverage considerably. Interestingly, however, the new statute had lain dormant until the Eisenhower antitrusters utilized it in consent decree negotiations halting such mergers as Seabrook Farms with Minute Maid, and Schenley with Park and Tilford Distillers. Everyone realized, however, that a litigated case was necessary to determine the exact parameters of the new law.[6] Again, in an election year, the Eisenhower administration stood firm against a merger of Bethlehem Steel with Youngstown Sheet and Tube, respectively, the second and fifth largest steel companies in the country. Politics would have dictated a less adamant stance. Nevertheless, despite the political power of those involved, the administration was strongly opposed to the merger, with the President even taking part in the deliberations.[7] When the Supreme Court found that the merger violated Section 7 of the Clayton Act, the companies abandoned their plans.[8]

The adversarial relationship between the federal government and E. I. DuPont de Nemours and Company was affected little by the advent of the Republicans to the White House. Ignoring for the sake of time and space the government's vigorous and valiant, but unsuccessful, efforts in the ill-fated Cellophane case, and concentrating instead on the DuPont-General Motors divestiture case, one discovers a lack of partisanship bordering on self-destruction.[9]

The roots of the DuPont-General Motors relationship can be traced to the first quarter of the century, when DuPont was seeking to end its reliance on munitions for its profits. One of the companies in which it invested was General Motors.[10] Without further detailing the background of the DuPont investments in General Motors, it is significant that they were similar to a number of moves, one of which is an interesting historical footnote.

In mid-1927, DuPont purchased 114,000 shares of the United States Steel Corporation.[11] Although the financial community appears to have agreed that this move presaged DuPont involvement with, if not control of, the steel giant,[12] according to Pierre S. DuPont "[the] United States Steel purchase by DP [DuPont] was for temporary investment of surplus cash and was sold when the cash was needed."[13] What actually occurred was that when Colonel William Donovan, the chief of the Antitrust Division of the Department of Justice, wrote to the company asking for information on the relationships between DuPont, United States Steel, and General Motors, DuPont quickly liquidated the purchase.[14]

The DuPont action in question was an outgrowth of an inquiry into the market power and actions of the General Motors Corporation begun in late 1946.[15] As DuPont owned more than a 20 percent equity in General Motors, the investigation was quickly expanded to ascertain the relationship between the two companies, "with particular strength being laid on the control which DuPont exercises over General Motors and the economic and legal results flowing from such control."[16] Then, the inquiry was split so that the action would not interfere with other suits against General Motors. Various members of the Antitrust Division of the Justice Department also feared that, without the differentiation, a "District Court, and perhaps even the Supreme Court, might be reluctant both to dissolve General Motors and divorce it from DuPont in one decree."[17] However, the investigation was hindered by lack of personnel, and it was not until the end of the year that, in order to compel the production of documents, a grand jury investigation of the relationship was initiated, necessitating a criminal action and use of the Sherman Act. Nevertheless, the Division realized that "the type of relief needed to eliminate the abuses arising out of DuPont's . . . control of General Motors" could best be secured by a civil action seeking complete divestiture.[18]

The grand jury empaneled to study the relationships between DuPont, General Motors, United States Rubber Company (now Uniroyal), Ethyl Corporation, Bendix Aviation Corporation, North American Aviation Incorporated, and Kinetic Chemicals Incorporated sent out its first subpoenas on August 20, 1948.[19] The political intent of the original suit, filed within weeks of the 1948 presidential election, was obvious to many observers.[20] Their suspicions were confirmed later by a speech delivered by a former Attorney General, Supreme Court Justice Robert Jackson, in which he admitted that antitrust actions had been initiated for political reasons during his own tenure.[21] Although 1948 was not supposed to be a "Democratic year," two obvious benefits would accrue to the party as a result of the suit. First, it improved the antitrust record of the Truman administration. Second, if the Republicans were victorious, they were likely to drop or lose the case, thus providing the Democrats with an example of the alleged Republican proclivity to satisfy the wishes of big business.

When the government was unable to obtain an indictment from the grand jury, it filed a civil action[22] charging that DuPont's direct and indirect ownership of large blocks of stock in General Motors and United States Rubber gave it *de facto* control of the companies.[23] The resultant reciprocal dealings were in restraint of trade and thus violated Sections 1 and 2 of the Sherman Act and Section 7 of the Clayton Act.

On December 3, 1954, after extensive preparations and a lengthy trial, Judge Walter J. LaBuy of the District Court for the Northern District of Illinois found that the defendants were not guilty. Had the Eisenhower administration been soft on antitrust, as commonly alleged, or politically responsive to its "friends," it would likely have dropped the case and proceeded no further. Instead, it appealed to the U.S. Supreme Court, and on June 3, 1957, an Eisenhower appointee, Justice William J. Brennan, in writing the majority opinion, reversed the lower court and ruled for government in a 4–2 decision.[24] The case was then remanded to the lower court for determination of the necessary remedies.

Many plans were proposed, and once again the Eisenhower administration demonstrated its strong antitrust philosophy and its insusceptibility to political pressure. The government had prayed, first, that DuPont and various family holding companies be required to dispose of their General Motors stock by sale, *not by stock dividends*, to avoid having many shares of General Motors pass to the DuPont family and, second, that the monies received from the sale not remain with DuPont but instead be paid directly to the stockholders. Pending the disposal, the government also requested that DuPont and the family investment companies be enjoined from voting their stock, that General Motors be given the option of purchasing the General Motors stock to be divested, that the defendants be enjoined perpetually from purchasing the stock, that the General Motors-DuPont joint ventures be terminated, and that DuPont be required to divest itself of the business of making tetraethyl lead and other similar products. In addition, the government had prayed that both DuPont and General Motors be required to divest themselves of their respective shares of the Kinetic Corporation, an enterprise they owned jointly.[25] The judgment proposed by the government modified these draconian measures slightly, suggesting that DuPont pay to its shareholders stock dividends in the form of General Motors securities.[26]

DuPont proposed that its shareholders be allowed to vote the General Motors stock held by the company. It stressed that this "pass-through" solution would obviate the disruptiveness of placing 63 million shares of one company's stock on the market, and thereby spare many innocent stockholders a significant financial loss.[27]

Anticipating that some type of stock distribution would be necessary, however, all parties contacted Russell Harrington, the Commissioner of Internal Revenue, requesting a ruling on the tax status of any General Motors shares dispersed as a result of the decision.[28] The Department of Justice had predicated its proposed final judgment[29] on a favorable tax ruling by the Internal Revenue Service (IRS).[30] Everyone's hopes were dashed when, on May 9, 1958, in a lengthy letter, Harrington ruled that the IRS would treat the proposed distribution as a dividend, thus making it taxable.[31] On October 2, 1959, Judge Walter LaBuy made public the lower court ruling, noting that in framing a judgment the court ought to take into account the interests of all the stockholders and that the thirty-year lapse of time between the original acquisition and antitrust action had created a sizable group of shareholders who had purchased DuPont believing that the General Motors holding was legal and proper. He stated that especially since the Clayton Act was not a "penal statute," the government plan without remedial tax arrangements would be "grossly unfair."[32] He ruled that DuPont could keep its investment in General Motors provided that it did not vote the shares itself but allowed its shareholders to vote the General Motors stock as they themselves saw fit. At that point, it was calculated that each DuPont proxy could vote 1.36 shares of General Motors. Among other things, Judge LaBuy ruled that no member of the DuPont family would be allowed to vote his/her or General Motors stock. Finally, he decreed that directors of DuPont or of the holding companies not vote any shares they held in General Motors. With the voting rights of the stock divested, as well as representation on the board of General Motors terminated, the possession of legal title to the stock left DuPont with only three rights:

1. To receive dividends;
2. To share pro rata with other stockholders in the assets of General Motors in the event of liquidation.
3. To dispose of legal title.

Thus, by means of the "pass-through" and other provisions, DuPont's holding in General Motors would be "sterilized," and the symbiotic relationship would no longer exist.[33] To guard further against ties between the two companies, Judge LaBuy included conditions terminating any "requirements contacts, exclusive patent arrangements or arrangements relating to preferential use of discoveries which may exist between DuPont and General Motors." The judgment also enjoined any commercial ventures between the two.[34]

The rationale for LaBuy's decision was that, as they stood, the tax laws made the government's prayer "harsh and punitive."[35] Accepting the DuPont argument, he noted that there had never been a distribution as large as the government had proposed and that smaller ones had had adverse effects on the price of the equity involved in the offering. Besides, if the stock in General Motors were to be distributed as a dividend, under current tax laws it would be likely that a sizable percentage of the 63 million shares of General Motors stock in question would have to be sold to cover the taxes. That would depress the price of General Motors stock and impair the company's ability to negotiate any equity offering it might consider.[36]

The importance of the tax code in this case cannot be overemphasized. It was the ruling of IRS Commissioner Harrington, stating that any distribution of General Motors stock would be treated as a dividend, and hence taxable as ordinary income (at a federal rate of 20 to 91 percent, plus state taxes), that forced LaBuy to reject the government's proposal and to adopt the "pass-through" option. The final judgment did, however, provide that if the tax laws should be changed to lessen the inequities, either party might apply for modification of the judgment.[37]

Judge LaBuy's determination was not the final solution. It was up to the Attorney General to decide whether or not the denouement was satisfactory. If not, the government had the right to appeal the judgment back to the Supreme Court. Since 1960 was a presidential election year and since so many Americans held stock in General Motors and DuPont, there was doubt that the government would remain steadfast in its appeal for complete divestiture. Many expected that the government would be satisfied with the outcome of the lengthy case and would claim a legitimate victory. But that is not what occurred. The financial community was stunned when Robert Bicks, the new acting chief of the Antitrust Division, announced on January 14, 1960, that the relief proposed by the district court was not effective. The government thereupon served notice of its intention to appeal the district court's plan to ask the Supreme Court to rule in favor of outright divestiture.

On May 23, 1960, the Supreme Court replied that it would consider the government's appeal. This entailed the hearing of more testimony from all sides. Most of the material had been covered in either the first trial, the first appeal, or the post-trial hearings and briefs. However, the government stressed that "common ownership of two companies, even if divorced from voting power," is not "effective divestiture," emphasizing that "the exercise of voting rights is but one of the avenues of influence over management.'' It cited instances in which individuals wielded great power over management without the right to vote a single share of stock, and it averred that ''any conscientious management must . . . take into consideration the interests of those investors . . . even if formal power to direct them or fire them is absent.''[38] Therefore, it stated that the only way for relief to be effective would be to remove any possibility of influence by means of a total divestiture of the stock.[39] On the subject of the hardship imposed by the high rate of taxes, the government was very blunt:

We believe that the impact of federal taxes is not a pertinent factor in ordering relief in an antitrust proceeding. What transactions shall be taxed, and how much, is a question of federal tax policy and it is not a proper function of the judiciary to tailor a decree either to add to or to avoid federal taxes. . . . When the court gave such weight to the tax aspects of divestiture it was trespassing on the field reserved for Congress.[40]

After nearly a year, on May 22, 1961, the Court by a 4–3 vote reversed the lower court's plan, stating that the proxy ''pass-through'' procedure was not an effective solution because it did not eliminate the violation of Section 7 of the Clayton Act.[41] The Court, therefore, directed complete divestiture.[42]

The Supreme Court essentially vacated the judgment except for the provisions enjoining DuPont from exercising voting rights in respect to its General Motors stock, and remanded the case back again to the district court for a determination of the equitable relief necessary. The final judgment, written by Judge LaBuy, included provisions that:

1. DuPont dispose of its stock in General Motors.
2. The divestiture be completed within thirty-four months.
3. Until divested, the stock be voted by means of the ''pass-through'' method.
4. Christiana dispose of all its General Motors shares within three years.[43]

After the first Supreme Court decision, several unsuccessful attempts were made to pass legislation alleviating the tax burden in any divestiture of General Motors stock.[44] Since there appeared to be no sense of urgency, the bills never reached a vote in either house of Congress. After the second Supreme Court decision overturning the ''pass-through'' formula and directing total divestiture, the action became more concerted. Apparently without the help of the Treasury and Justice Departments, Republican Senator J. Allen Frear of Delaware and Democratic Senator Harry F. Byrd of Virginia finally obtained passage of a statute (Public Law 87–403) providing that for tax purposes the market value of the General Motors shares received would be treated as a return of capital.[45]

The DuPont-General Motors case assumes its proper significance when viewed in complete perspective. The precedent has not been used for subsequent de-concentration actions, which is a testimonial to the antitrust programs of the subsequent administrations. Even though the Truman administration probably filed the case with partisan intentions and Charles Wilson, the first Secretary of Defense in the Eisenhower administration, had previously been the president of General Motors, and while the final, and extremely unpopular, denouement took place right before the national election of 1960, the Eisenhower administration neither dropped the action nor settled for anything short of total victory.

In terms of media coverage, companies affected, and executives involved, no case or group of cases has ever garnered as much attention as the group of twenty actions collectively known as the Electrical cases. They are significant, not because they broke ground for new legal theory, but rather because of their sheer size and the fact that here, too, the Eisenhower antitrusters took harsh actions without consideration for the possible political effects at election time.

Although the story of the price-fixing conspiracy has been well covered elsewhere, it is instructive to note that the files of the Antitrust Division of the Department of Justice contain material indicating that the Division had been watching various members of the heavy electrical industry for many years.[46] The earliest documents are dated 1902, and file 60–9–0 alone continucs up to 1956 with only a short break for World War II.[47] In addition, during the 1940s several actions were begun; for instance, in April 1941, Thurman Arnold requested authorization for a grand jury investigation of industry practices. The inquiry apparently was dropped in 1942, after General Electric provided evidence that price-fixing had been elminated.[48] In addition, the Federal Trade Commission twice investigated the electrical transformer industry, and in 1949 the Division also launched a special inquiry into the business.

Although by 1951 not enough evidence had been uncovered to support criminal indictments, the action was kept alive in the civil sphere, but records indicate that little further was discovered. As a result, Stanley Barnes terminated the action on November 21, 1953.[49] In mid-1954, another inquiry was begun focusing on the problems of identical bidding and allocation of customers. It studied a total of 1,989 bids and concluded that 1,048 "were identical with one or more companies."[50] But the mere existence of identical bids proves neither price-fixing nor collusion. In certain instances, conscious parallelism in pricing is both explainable and permissible. That nothing was done, however, may well have emboldened the electrical equipment companies, as they inflated their pricing structure to such an extent that it became cheaper to purchase foreign equipment, even after factoring in the cost of shipping and various neo-mercantilist regulations designed to aid domestic manufacturers.[51] The violations became so egregious that Senator Estes Kefauver of Tennessee included the industry as part of his committee's inquiry into "administered prices."[52] Justice Department investigations yielded enough evidence to merit the empaneling of a grand jury, and shortly there were five separate grand juries probing improprieties in the electrical industry.

The various grand juries investigating the electrical industry found twenty separate and distinct conspiracies, and General Electric was involved in all but one. Some of the violations were of long standing, one of them easily traceable to the heyday of the National Recovery Administration,[53] but the Department of

Justice, armed with more than sufficient evidence to secure convictions, concentrated on the most recent data to prove the charges.[54] The violations were blatant, and one group of perpetrators had even formulated a set of rules: (1) minimize phone calls; (2) use plain envelopes if mailing materials; (3) when registering at a hotel, do not include the company's name; (4) endeavor not to travel together; (5) do not eat together; and (6) leave no wastepaper behind after a meeting in a hotel room.[55]

Another group worked out a formula so complicated that it would have delighted an astrologist. Based on the phases of the moon, the scheme determined which company would make which bid. They not only rotated the low bids, but also shuffled the next to lowest bid, and so forth. The plan was so exact, yet so random, that the government was unable to crack it, even with the aid of a cryptographer, until, in return for immunity, a company official provided the information.[56] Bicks felt that the "moon formula" would be most damaging to the companies in court.[57] Although the level of involvement differed, almost every large manufacturer of electrical equipment was cited at least once in at least one of the conspiracies. When the final figures were tabulated, a total of thirty-two corporations were involved as defendants or, to a lesser degree, as "co-conspirators." In addition, forty-eight individual defendants were also named.

Bicks' enthusiasm and vigor were apparent; contrary to tradition, he personally handled large segments of the project. That the government was determined to block an easy escape for the electrical companies was illustrated by its opposition to the court's acceptance of a *nolo contendere* plea. In an unprecedented move, both Bicks and William Rogers, the Attorney General, went before the court and urged Chief Judge J. Cullen Ganey not to accept such pleas. Bicks himself argued that, since the cases included charges that ranked them among the most serious in the entire seventy-year history of the Sherman Act, the acceptance of a *nolo* plea would be highly inappropriate. He also wanted the record to be available so that injured parties could sue to recover treble damages. Finally, he noted that a greater stigma was attached to the plea of guilty than to that of *nolo*.[58] Attorney General Rogers stated by affidavit that each conspirator knew he was violating the law, and that in view of the severity of the crime, acceptance of a *nolo* plea would essentially mean that in the future there could be no other plea.[59] The power of the government's argument was so great that Judge Ganey rejected most of the *nolo* pleas.

Allis-Chalmers then decided to cooperate fully with the government. After conferences, the company agreed to change its plea from *nolo* to guilty, hoping that as a result of its cooperation and previously spotless record of fifty years without any antitrust violations, the government would be lenient. (The government was!)[60] Westinghouse and General Electric were not so quick to alter their stance; rather, they increased their legal staffs.

Bruce Bromley, who had been a member of the Attorney General's National Committee to Study the Antitrust Laws, represented Westinghouse. As the actions progressed, it became obvious that additional aid was necessary. He persuaded his erstwhile superior, former Attorney General Herbert Brownell, to join the Westinghouse team. This was a brilliant coup on Bromley's part, for Brownell and his firm, Lord, Day, and Lord, had an enviable record in antitrust defense actions. Besides, until three years earlier, Brownell had been Attorney General and thus had intimate knowledge of the thought patterns of many in the Antitrust Division. Brownell's acceptance of the position has been attacked as approaching a conflict of interest. He had helped set down strict rules of conduct forbidding anyone, within *two* years of severance from the government payroll, to work for a company having legal dealings with the government.[61] To be fair, Brownell had waited more than the requisite time, and he had requested clearance from the Department of Justice based on his contention that the cases had begun "after I left and I knew about [them]."[62] Because of his background, Brownell quickly became the leader for the defendants and often acted as liaison with the Department of Justice in unsuccessful efforts to obtain a negotiated settlement.[63]

In the end, no companies or executives pleaded not guilty. The burden of recommending sentences then fell on the Department of Justice. This task was complicated by the fact that the Democrats had won the presidential election, and the sentencing was scheduled to be handed down after John F. Kennedy had taken the oath of office. Nevertheless, the personnel at the Antitrust Division did not change that quickly, and they appear to have worked well with the new Attorney General, Robert Kennedy.[64]

What explains the strong even-handed enforcement policy of the Eisenhower administration? Both Eisenhower and his first Attorney General, Herbert Brownell, believed strongly in free enterprise as a way of building a stronger, more productive economy. There is nothing in the record to indicate that William Rogers, Eisenhower's second Attorney General, felt differently. Aware of the irony, they nevertheless initiated antitrust actions as a way of protecting competition, and, in the end, limiting the need of government intervention in the form of regulation. The even-handed enforcement is not surprising either when viewed in the context of the administration record: with but two small exceptions, the record on corruption is pristine. Selective enforcement would not have been "clean as a hound's tooth." There was no "enemies list" in the Eisenhower administration.

NOTES

1. Benjamin Wham, "The Growth of Antitrust Law: A Revision Is Long Overdue," *American Bar Association Journal* 38 (November 1952): 934–35; H. Graham Morrison, "Is the Sherman Act Outdated?," *Journal of Public Law* 1 (Fall 1952): 323–34; John McDonald, "Businessmen and the Sherman Act," *Fortune* 41 (January 1950): 104–14. See also the five-part series by David Lilienthal in *Collier's Weekly* 129 (May 31-June 28, 1952); John McDonald, "Businessmen and the Sherman Act," *Fortune* 41 (January 1950): 104–14; unsigned section of *Fortune* Perspective, "A Note to Mr. Brownell," *Fortune* 51 (February 1953): 107–108. Stanley N. Barnes, "Background and Report of the

Attorney General's Committee,'' *University of Pennsylvania Law Review* 104 (November 1955): 147.

2. He actually said '' . . . what was good for the country was good for General Motors.''

3. *Business and Government During the Eisenhower Administration* (Athens: Ohio University Press, 1980).

4. The papers of the Antitrust Division of the Department of Justice are in storage at the Federal Records Center, Suitland, Maryland. All notes that begin with a company name followed by a file number are from this collection. Antitrust Papers: Kodak Acc. 70A4771, file 60–42–18.

5. Barnes to author, May 7, 1971.

6. ''What the Merger Law Means,'' *Business Week* (October 9, 1954), p. 26, Barnes to author (April 11, 1974).

7. Memorandum of call from the White House, August 3, 1954, Barnes, confidential memorandum of September 2, 1954, in Antitrust Papers: Bethlehem-Youngstown, Acc. 70A4771, file 60 0–37–29. Eisenhower Papers, Central Files: OF–5, Report of the Department of Justice—April 21, 1954–September 30, 1954. The President continued to be very interested in the suit and received regular updates; see for instance, John V. Lindsay to Toner, White House Office, staff research group, records 1956–61, Box 12. The papers of Dwight D. Eisenhower are housed in the Presidential Library, Abilene, Kansas.

8. 168 F. Supp. 576; 1958 Trade Cases per 69, 189.

9. *U.S. v. E. I. DuPont de Nemours and Company*, 351 U.S. 377 (1956) affirming 118 F. Supp. 41 (D. Del. 1953).

10. Alfred D. Chandler and Stephen Salsbury, *Pierre S. DuPont and the Making of the Modern Corporation* (New York: Harper and Row, 1971), paints a good picture of the diversification efforts. P. S. DuPont, rough draft of a speech (undated), Group 10, Papers of P. S. DuPont, file 418: 1917–18, Box 3, folder ''1918: Bonus: End of Wartime Contracts''; Defendant Exhibit 59, ''Proposed Utilization of Excess Plant Capacity'' (memo dated December 30, 1916); Defendant Exhibit 69, ''Completed Recommendations of Excess Plant Utilization Division'' (November 23, 1917). The papers of Pierre S. DuPont are housed in the Eleutherian Mills Historical Library in Greenville, Wilmington, Delaware. The Longwood Manuscripts, Group 10, Papers of P. S. DuPont, Series B. folder 1203–63, ''General Motors,'' pp. 2a, 11.

11. See letter of John Raskob, Acc. 473, file 681, Box 2 of 2, folder: P. S. DuPont. The papers of John J. Raskob are housed in the Eleutherian Mills Historical Library.

12. *New York Evening Post*, July 30, 1927, *New York American* and *New York World*, August 1, 1927, clippings in Raskob Papers.

13. Handwritten note on front cover of Pierre S. DuPont's personal copy of transcript, opening statement.

14. Longwood Manuscripts, Group 10, Papers of P. S. DuPont, file 229, Box 9, folder: Investments: 1903–1948.

15. Memo to Wendell Berge, October 15, 1946, Antitrust Papers: DuPont, file 107–37.

16. Memo to Melville Williams, March 31, 1947, Antitrust Papers: DuPont.

17. Memo to Holmes Baldridge, April 1, 1947, Antitrust Papers: DuPont.

18. Memo to Holmes Baldridge, April 29, 1947, and to John Sonnett, November 6, 1947, Antitrust Papers: DuPont.

19. The reason for the inclusion of the other companies was that, until January 1948, General Motors had owned a substantial interest in Bendix Aviation Corporation. In June

1948, the motor company divested itself of its 29.1 percent equity in North American Aviation. While it is likely that their sales were a result of the antitrust inquiry, they were also part of a redeployment of capital so as to generate funds for postwar expansion. In the same period, General Motors also sold its interest in the Greyhound Corporation. The Ethyl Corporation was the result of a joint venture with the Standard Oil Company of New Jersey. Kinetic Chemicals was jointly owned with DuPont; in December 1949, General Motors sold its interest in the company to DuPont, making the chemical manufacturer the sole owner of Kinetic.

20. See E. I. DuPont de Nemours & Co. Papers, Series II, Part 2, Ac1054, *DuPont-General Motors Scrapbook*, Vol. 1. The company papers on the suit are housed in the Eleutherian Mills Historical Library.

21. Speech to the New York State Bar Association delivered January 30, 1951, at the Harvard Club, New York City, noted by Ray Tucker, February 1, 1951, in his nationally syndicated column, "National Whirligig." A copy of the column is included in the *DuPont-General Motors Scrapbook*, Vol 1, 88. Although the papers of Supreme Court Justice Robert Jackson contain several letters asking for copies of the speech, the requests appear to have gone unanswered, and there are no notes or text of the speech in the files. The Jackson papers are in the possession of his son, William Jackson.

22. *Quick Magazine*, July 11, 1949. (Included in *DuPont-General Motors Scrapbook*, Vol. 1, 22.)

23. Complaint at 26; Pretrial Brief for Plaintiff at *United States* v. *DuPont et al.*, 126 F. Supp. 235. Copies of all court papers are located in the Eleutherian Mills Historical Library as well as in the Federal Records Center, Suitland, Maryland. See also background memo to Newell A. Clapp (Acting Assistant Attorney General in charge of the Antitrust Division of the Justice Department), December 17, 1952, Antitrust Papers: DuPont.

24. *United States* v. *E. I. DuPont de Nemours and Company et al.*, 353 U.S. 586 (1957). Those justices voting with the majority were Justices William Brennan, Hugo Black, William Douglas, and Chief Justice Earl Warren. Those dissenting were Justices Harold Burton and Felix Frankfurter. Justices Tom Clark, John Marshall Harlan, and Charles E. Whittaker took no part in the consideration of or decision on the case. Clark had been the Attorney General when the case was filed; Harlan had helped form the defense for DuPont; and Whittaker was appointed to the bench after much of the work on the case was already finished.

25. Transcript of Record, Vol. 1 at 256–60, *United States* v. *E. I. duPont de Nemours*, 353 U.S. 586.

26. *Proposed Final Judgment for Plaintiff* at 5.

27. See "Memorandum (by Victor Hansen, Assistant Attorney General in charge of the Antitrust Division) for the Attorney General," April 1, 1958, Attachment, "The Adverse Effects of the Government's Plan," 19; see also memo to George Reycraft, April 2, 1958, Antitrust Papers; DuPont.

28. Letter dated December 16, 1957, to Russell Harrington from Daniel Gribbon, attorney for DuPont de Nemours and Company; letter dated January 16, 1958, to Russell Harrington from Leo Tierney, attorney for General Motors. These and other letters are found in the DuPont-General Motors Case material at the Eleutherian Mills Historical Library and in Antitrust Papers: DuPont.

29. A copy of the proposed decree is in the Rogers Papers, Box 29, A67–6, "Antitrust Division," Eisenhower Library.

30. Victor Hansen to Harrington, December 18, 1957, Antitrust Papers: DuPont.

31. Harrington to Gribbon, May 9, 1958, Antitrust Papers: DuPont.

32. Opinion of Judge Walter J. LaBuy at 21–23, 26 (October 2, 1959).

33. Ibid., 73–76.

34. Ibid., 82–83.

35. Ibid., 99.

36. Ibid., 97–101. For the DuPont position, see numerous press releases of the Public Relations Department, especially a thirty-page memo dated May 31, 1962, by the director, Harold Brayman, Records of the DuPont Company: Public Relations Department, Acc. 1111, Box 51, "Press Analysis, Reports, and Clippings," Eleutherian Mills Historical Library.

37. Final Judgment at 13 (November 17, 1959).

38. Brief for Plaintiff at 43–45, 54 (October 1960).

39. Ibid., 45.

40. Ibid., 59–61.

41. The majority decision was written by Justice Brennan with Warren, Black, and Douglas concurring; Justices Frankfurter, Whittaker, and Stewart dissented; and Justices Clark and Harlan abstained.

42. 366 U.S. 316, 331.

43. Final Judgment at 4–23 (Mimeographed copy). Also see section in *DuPont-General Motors Scrapbook*, Vol. 8. Letter to the stockholders from Crawford H. Greenewalt, president of DuPont (May 31, 1962), Scudder File, Watson Library of Business and Economics, Columbia University, New York City.

44. See, for example, memorandum for the Attorney General written by Victor Hansen discussing a conference between the staff of the Antitrust Division and the Under-Secretary of the Treasury, Fred Scribner, June 26, 1958. Staff Files: Papers of William Rogers, Box 29, Eisenhower Library.

45. *DuPont-General Motors Scrapbook*, Vols. 8 and 9.

46. Charles A. Bane, *The Electrical Equipment Conspiracies* (New York: Federal Legal Publications, 1973); John Herling, *The Great Price Conspiracy* (Washington, D.C.: R. B. Luce, 1962).

47. Antitrust Papers: Electrical, file 60–9–0, Section 1.

48. Antitrust Papers: Electrical, July 29, 1948.

49. Barnes memo dated November 21, 1953, Antitrust Papers: Electrical.

50. Barnes memo to files dated July 22, 1954; and Victor Hansen memo to J. Edgar Hoover dated July 18, 1957. Antitrust Papers: Electrical, file 60–230–27. (Hansen replaced Barnes as chief of the Antitrust Division in 1956.)

51. A non-American manufacturer had to pay 15 percent customs duty; 50 percent of the machinery had to be delivered in high-cost American ships. In addition, a 20-percent differential was allowable (6 percent for Buy American, 6 percent for a contract to a company located in areas of high unemployment, and 8 percent "to cover the cost of sending men to make a general factory inspection"). Testimony of Alan Barraclough of English Electric, Ltd., before Grand Jury #4 empaneled April 21, 1960, *in re* Electrical Suppliers Industry, located in Antitrust Papers: Electrical, file 60–230–45.

52. U.S. Senate, Subcommittee on Antitrust and Monopoly, Committee on the Judiciary, 87th Cong., 1st Sess., *Administered Prices: Hearings*, in 28 pts. (Washington, D.C.: 1969), Pt. 13.

53. "A Theory for Computing Damages Sustained by the United States and Tennessee

Valley Authority in the Direct Purchase of Power Transformers,'' 2 (a memorandum dated July 25, 1961), Antitrust Papers: Electrical, file 60–230–55.

54. Bicks to William Maher (chief of the Philadelphia office, which was the headquarters for the investigation), April 30, 1960, Antitrust Papers: Electrical, file 60–230–29.

55. U.S. Senate, *Administered Prices: Hearings*, Pt. 28, 17, 394–17, 396.

56. Baddhis Rashid to author, July 8, 1971.

57. Memorandum for the Attorney General from Bicks, dated June 2, 1960, Antitrust Papers: Electrical, file 60–230–30.

58. Bicks to Rashid, March 17, 1960, Antitrust Papers: Electrical, file 60–230–29.

59. Rogers to author, October 22, 1974. Also in Bane, *The Electrical Equipment Conspiracies,* pp. 1–22. Attorney General Rogers' affidavit is reprinted in James Clabault and John Burton, *Sherman Act Indictments: 1955–1965* (New York: Federal Legal Publications, 1966), pp. 58–62.

60. W. Wallace Kirkpatrick to Robert Kennedy, January 27, 1961, but formulated by Bicks; and Government's Recommendations for Sentences, Antitrust Papers: Electrical.

61. Herling, *The Great Price Conspiracy*, pp. 267–68; Eisenhower Papers, Central Files, OF–5, Department of Justice release dated March 27, 1957, citing the rule from an April 1956 "handbook for employees" which set forth standards of conduct; see also "Post-Employment Conflict of Interest Regulations," Staff Files: Rogers, Box 32, Eisenhower Library.

62. Brownell to author, April 11, 1974.

63. See, for example, Bicks memo to files dated July 7, 1960, Antitrust Papers: Electrical, file 60–230–29.

64. See, for example, the memorandum for the Attorney General dated January 27, 1961, written by W. Wallace Kirkpatrick, who had been Bicks' first assistant. Antitrust Papers: Electrical, file 60–230–29. At the sentencing, fines of nearly $2 million were imposed on the companies and then on responsible executives. In addition, seven individuals were sentenced to jail for thirty days. Others were more fortunate, receiving suspended sentences and long probations that were canceled in December 1961.

10

The Philosophy Underlying Eisenhower's Economic Policies

Raymond J. Saulnier

It is sometimes difficult to identify a philosophy or ideology underlying a President's or an administration's policies other than to say that they are motivated by pragmatic considerations. It has been said of pragmatism, however, that it is less a philosophy than a method of doing without one, and to say that President Dwight D. Eisenhower was a pragmatist not only says little that would distinguish him from anyone else in the presidency of the United States, but also misses completely any notion of the deeply held convictions that underlay the strong positions he took on crucial questions of economic strategy. For in Eisenhower's case, economic questions were approached from a definite philosophy to which pragmatic considerations were then attached. It is useful to separate the two aspects in order to better appreciate their interplay.

First, the philosophy was individualism, in the American style. At its center was a concept of the individual as independent and self-reliant, with a whole battery of inherent rights enjoyed in conjunction with equally formidable responsibilities. There was no room in this for governmental paternalism; much less was there room in it for socialism or any other species of collectivism.

Second, in matters of government, Eisenhower was decentralist. Armed with the secret ballot and adequately informed, citizens could take care of themselves in exercising their voting franchise. Again, with the proviso that they were adequately informed, they could be relied on to resolve questions sensibly and constructively. Thus, in a whole host of areas, the government best positioned to act constructively was the government closest to the people. Foreign policy was the business of the central government, as were defense policy and policies in a number of other key areas. But in many areas, such as education, the Eisenhower administration maintained that responsibility should rest mainly on local government. Local administration would avoid that absentee control over policy which was considered a danger wherever there was "centralization of power and authority." If federal aid was to be extended to essentially local projects, it should be so devised as not to invite that danger; wherever possible, local as well as federal funds should be involved in the financing.

Third was Eisenhower's perception of the enterprise system. He did not see it, as so many had, as a system suffering from some kind of malaise, needing to be resuscitated more or less continuously by infusions of federal funds. He perceived it as a system with enormous internal dynamism, with a built-in capability, by dint of competitive markets, for allocating resources in close keeping with consumer demand. And, providing it was not hamstrung by government regulation or overburdened by taxes, he believed it capable of economic achievement far greater than collectivism in any form.

Finally, there was Eisenhower's belief in the relationship between freedoms. As he put it many times, freedoms come in a bundle: political freedom is one of them and economic freedom another. One cannot pick and choose among them; rather, one must take the whole bundle, including a market-directed enterprise system with its institutions of private property and individual responsibility, or one ultimately loses the struggle to collectivism, with political freedom an early and certain victim. A society that denies economic freedom, he believed, will sooner or later deny political freedom as well.

This philosophical stance led to programmatic implications that were crucial to Eisenhower's economic policies.

First, a central objective of his strategy was to check the rising weight of government in the economy. The ratio of government spending to national income had increased from 12 percent in 1929 to 23 percent in 1940 and stood at 33 percent when Eisenhower came to the White House. "Time for a Change," the Republican slogan in the 1952 presidential campaign, meant among other things that this trend would be challenged. But Eisenhower was a gradualist in most matters, and his object was not to reverse the trend abruptly. As he put it much later: "the government cost curve cannot be abruptly turned down; it has to be gradually bent." And so it was. When he left the White House, the ratio of government spending to national income had been stabilized for eight years at 33 percent. Moreover, the federal component of total government spending had dropped from 76 percent to 60 percent. Government would do whatever needed to be done and couldn't be done by the individual or by private groups, but the ideal was limited government, not big government becoming increasingly bigger.

Second, it followed from his philosophical stance that the economy had to be kept as vigorously competitive as possible. It was not easy for Eisenhower's critics to understand how strongly he felt on this point. Typically, they viewed him as a champion of big business, if not its captive. Because they perceived big business as generally monopolistic, or something approaching that, it followed that there would be no bearing-down on anticompetitive business practices. How wrong they were. Vigorous enforcement of the antitrust laws, and their strengthening where necessary, was a major thrust of administration policy from the beginning. Given Eisenhower's philosophical convictions, it couldn't be any other way.

Accompanying this feeling about antitrust enforcement was an essentially deregulationist approach to many questions involving the relation of government to business, but in the 1950s the idea of deregulation was only beginning to take shape. As can be seen in Sherman Adams' volume of memoirs entitled *First Hand Report, the Story of the Eisenhower Administration* (New York: Harper, 1961), Eisenhower had a good deal less difficulty than some in his Cabinet in understanding that quick termination of the wage and price controls carried over from the Truman administration would benefit the economy. Nor did he delay in supporting termination of the Reconstruction Finance Corporation (RFC), which was already under a cloud for having misused its lending authority. But 1952 offered only a hint of the deregulation that was to come. Eisenhower would probably not have moved into it with the speed that others brought to it, if his instincts and convictions had not been strongly on the deregulationist side.

Finally, it derived from Eisenhower's philosophy and from the confidence he had in the individual that the task of government was not to plan the economy but first to establish an environment in which the enterprise system could be expected to work effectively, and then to let it work. Establishing such an environment was no easy task. For one thing, it meant that the economy had to be free of inflation. For another, it meant that the economy's tendency to fluctuate widely had to be significantly reduced. It also meant that there should be reasonable protection for the individual and for the family—through public means where necessary, through private effort where possible—against the economic and federal risks encountered in an urbanized, industrialized system operating on the enterprise model.

If the economic program which this stance suggests seems to be unarguable (as its traditionalist qualities may make it appear to be), it was far from unarguable as Eisenhower sought to apply it. For one thing, it was a total and jarring challenge to the advocates of big government. It was similarly anathema to advocates of central economic planning. It was the utter dismay of paternalists. To some, its fear of inflation was fetishism, and for those who knew, or were sure they knew, that federal budget deficits mattered little or not at all, it was unenlightened economics.

Fiscal responsibility was the issue on which argument tended to concentrate. For a while, everyone knew better than Eisenhower. But if the experience of the last twenty years has anything to do with establishing the difference between right and wrong in theorizing about the economy, we have to be more respectful of what was implied by Eisenhower's insistence on fiscal responsibility and on the importance he attached to a reasonable match between budget income and outgo and a low inflation rate.

Eisenhower's philosophy and its programmatic implications collided head on with much of what was mainstream thinking at the time. But there was a more general complaint in which one could join without benefit of particular economic learning. This was that Eisenhower stood for a style of government that was insufficiently activist. The indictment was totally mistaken. What was at issue was not activism *versus* nonactivism. It was simply that the activism which Eisenhower's programs called for was not the kind of activism his critics would like to have seen.

Any number of illustrations can be cited to demonstrate this idea. Breathing life into the wage and price controls that were dying when Eisenhower came to the White House would probably have qualified, to some, as a thoroughly bold and activist initiative. Seeing to it that the whole apparatus was eliminated, with as little discomfort as possible, and seeing to it that there was no need for it to be revived, did not qualify as activism, but it took all kinds of action to accomplish it. Not many in 1953, even among the Democrats in Congress, wanted to continue the RFC, but the Eisenhower administration's activist image was not helped when it moved to liquidate that troubled agency. Nor did activism in antitrust count for much with Eisenhower's critics. His image as an activist was also not enhanced when he stated that once conditions of stability and balance had been established in the economy, the inherent dynamism of the enterprise system could be depended on to produce long-term growth and improvement, even though it took no end of government effort to establish those conditions of stability and balance.

It was similarly a vain hope, at least in the 1950s that Eisenhower's reliance on money policy to control inflation and to help stabilize the economy could gain him or his administration any credit as activist. Money policy was the business of the independent Federal Reserve System, not that of the President. More important, money policy did its work in ways that were indirect and basically rather arcane. Few understood money policy then, even fewer than do now.

Finally, in the innocence of the times, the bottom-line test of activism in economic policy was for the President to propose and somehow manage to obtain a cut in taxes, with a place close to the top of the list of true activist measures for a tax cut that would prevent that greatest of all disasters, a swing in the budget from deficit to surplus!

Since the 1950s, the United States has had a good deal of experience with cutting taxes, and some of Eisenhower's critics on this subject have subsequently revised their views and have done so in praiseworthy fashion. But it was long throught to have been grievously inactivist not to have cut taxes in 1958; and if not to have cut taxes then, at least to have cut them in 1959; and if not in 1959, then surely in 1960.

It would require an account far longer than can be undertaken here to deal adequately with the pros and cons of tax reduction as they were faced in each of those three years. Suffice it to say that the reasons for doing what was done had absolutely nothing to do with activism *versus* inactivism. There was, of course, a good deal of action on the tax front under Eisenhower. Both an excess profits tax and a surtax on personal income that had been enacted to help finance the Korean Conflict were terminated as previously scheduled in January 1954, but a large tax cut in 1954 under new legislation sponsored by the Eisenhower administration was designed to remove a long list of inequities from the tax code and make it less obstructive of economic growth. Other reductions and reforms that Eisenhower was anxious to make were deferred year after year because it was deemed fiscally irresponsible to propose them. Although Eisenhower did not rule out tax reduction as a measure to help conteract recession, he was not easily drawn to its support. And certainly not when cutting taxes at such times would be to enter a tug-of-war, as he put it, with a money policy that could properly be less restrictive. Eisenhower was too much the strategist and tactician to deploy the forces of government in a wasteful and inconsistent manner. As the *January 1961 Economic Report* stated, it was "important that the full benefits of tax revision . . . not be jeopardized by the hasty improvisation of reductions in the hope of countering cyclical downturns in economic activity."[1] At stake was the opportunity to make significant reductions and reforms in taxes within the context of a budget in structural balance. This meant a budget in which income and outgo would be matched under all conditions other than recession and emergency such as war. In short, although Eisenhower would not shrink from countercyclical tax reduction if circumstances warranted, his basic belief was that the budget should be in structural balance before significant tax reduction was undertaken.

Unfortunately, structural balance and the opportunity it afforded to propose large-scale tax reduction did not arrive until January 1960. Eisenhower refrained from proposing it on the ground that proposing it should be left to the next administration and to the next Congress. As the January 1960 budget message stated:

If expenditures are held to the levels I am proposing for 1961 and reasonable restraint is exercised in the future, higher revenues in later years will give the next administration and the next congress the choice they should rightly have in deciding between reductions in the public debt and lightening of the tax burden, or both. Soundly conceived tax revision can then be approached on a comprehensive and orderly basis, rather than by haphazard piecemeal changes, and can be accomplished within a setting of economic and fiscal stability.[2]

There is no reason to believe that Eisenhower was thinking of a Democratic administration in the White House when he made that statement, but even if he had been his attitude toward tax reduction in 1960 would likely have been the same.

In many ways, politically as well as economically, things did not turn out in 1960 as Eisenhower expected and hoped they would. Among the disappointments was the economic slump in the closing months of that year. It was a mild recession, explained entirely by a shift in inventory policy by American business, and by December 1960 the Eisenhower administration correctly judged it to be close to its trough. It was a recession all the same and untimely in the extreme. Still, the conditions of stability and balance that were needed if the economy was to work effectively had been established.

The budget was in structural balance. Inflation was under control. Labor cost increases were so matched with productivity improvement as to favor keeping it under control. There was still a troublesome outflow of gold, but the Federal Reserve System was so positioned for the conduct of money policy that the monetary stimulus needed at that point could be had without undue risk.

As the administration ended, these conditions were summed up in the *January 1960 Economic Report of the President*:

As expansion is resumed, there is a good chance to realize more fully our economy's potential for growth. The basis for advance has been laid in recent years in the enlargement and improvement of our productive capacity and in policies that have brought the forces of inflation under control. Some temporary acceleration of growth might have been achieved if expectations of price increases had been allowed to persist and to become firmly rooted. But the unsustainable nature of such growth would now be confronting the economy with the need for far-reaching and painful correction. Because action to maintain stability and balance and to consolidate gains were taken in good time, the economy can now look forward, provided public and private policies are favorable, to a period of sound growth from a firm base.[3]

The achievement involved in establishing conditions of stability and balance should have been apparent to all, but, not surprisingly, it was little appreciated at the time. Eisenhower, however, never worried greatly about instant commentaries on his record. When he was asked in one of his presidential news conferences how he thought his place in history would be affected by certain foreign policy reverses that had just afflicted him, his quick response was that "my place in history will be decided by historians."[4]

NOTES

1. *January 1961 Economic Report of the President* (Washington, D.C.: Government Printing Office, p. 59).

2. *The Budget of the United States for the Fiscal Year 1961* (Washington, D.C.: Government Printing Office).

3. *January 1960 Economic Report of the President* (Washington, D.C.: Government Printing Office, p. 44).

4. *Public Papers of the President 1960–1961* (Washington, D.C.: Government Printing Office, p. 553).

11

Eisenhower, Constitutional Practice, and the Twenty-fifth Amendment

Gerard F. Giannattasio and Linda R. Giannattasio

A major feature that distinguished the United States among nations is the smoothness of its leadership transitions.[1] The framers of the Constitution created a supple instrument that contains as one of its principal strongpoints provision for an amendatory process. In 1787, the Constitution was not viewed as a plan for all time—unchangeable—but one by which future generations as well as the one then present might live.[2] In Article 2, Section 1, of the Constitution, provision is made for presidential succession as follows:

In Case of the Removal of the President from Office, or of his Death, Resignation, or Inability to discharge the Powers and Duties of the said Office, the same shall devolve on the Vice President, and the Congress may by law provide for the Case of Removal, Death, Resignation or Inability, both of the President and Vice President, declaring what Officer shall then act as President, and such Officer shall act accordingly, until the Disability be removed, or a President shall be elected.

This chapter investigates Dwight David Eisenhower's contribution to the implementation of this constitutional provision for the transition of presidential powers.

The constitutional Succession Clause was first used in 1841 when President William Henry Harrison died in office. At that time, the single sentence in the Constitution, quoted above, served as the only available guide.[3] The lack of a more detailed statement can be traced to the Convention of 1787 which had been conducted in secrecy.[4] James Madison's *Papers*, published the year before, provided only a partial picture of the events,[5] and Max Farrand's definitive compilation of the proceedings did not appear until 1911.[6] These and other records have been the chief means by which modern scholarship has probed the intent of the framers of the Constitution. In 1841, however, John Tyler struck out "Acting" before the word "President" in documents presented to him for signing, and, despite an unsuccessful attempt to impeach him, a precedent, followed since on eight occasions, was set.[7] This Tyler Precedent, as it is known, stated that a President who died in office was succeeded by the Vice-President who then served out the unexpired term.

To understand the specific nature of the succession problem faced by Dwight Eisenhower during his presidency, it is necessary to briefly sketch the controversy, fueled by the Tyler Precedent, which came to surround the Succession Clause in the Constitution.[8] When debate closed at the Constitutional Convention, the mass of acceptable provisions was referred to the Committee on Style for consolidation and codification by subject. The Committee took two separate succession provisions and returned one sentence of four clauses.[9] Much debate has since turned on the grammatical construction of the sentence minted by the Committee. The objective of this analysis, which has excercised some of the best legal minds in the periods during which debate peaked, was to discover the antecedent of the phrase "the same." If the antecedent were "powers and duties," then a Vice-President became acting President during a time of presidential inability. If the antecedent were "the office," then a Vice-President actually became President and worked permanent ouster of the ill, disabled, captured, or otherwise incapable incumbent.[10]

The establishment of the Tyler Precedent in the political life of the country complicated constitutional analysis. Strong evidence now indicates that the framers of the Constitution wanted the Vice-President to exercise presidential power only until a special election for President could be held or a presidential inability, if not the result of death or otherwise permanent, should cease.[11] This original design was unknown, and acceptance of the Tyler Precedent voided such an intent.[12] Indeed, the Tyler Precedent became an important source of authority for the proposition that the replacement of a disabled President by a Vice-President effected permanent ouster in favor of the Vice-President regardless of how temporary the nature of the inability.[13]

The problem posed for a Chief Executive is acute. Despite unearthed historical evidence and even a certain logical inconsistency to the argument for permanent ouster,[14] no President could allow and few counselors would advise a temporary surrender of power and duties in favor of a Vice-President as long as ouster was a possibility, however remote.[15] Understandably, Vice-Presidents developed a tradition of admirable reticence. As President James Garfield lay dying for eighty days, Chester A. Arthur refused entreaties that he assume the powers and duties of the first office.[16] During the time of Woodrow Wilson's major stroke, Thomas R. Marshall of Indiana steadfastly ignored the summons of administration and congressional leaders to seize the helm of state.[17] Eisenhower's experience with the vice-presidency was no less fortunate. Richard Milhous Nixon, in whose personal integrity and political wisdom Eisenhower often reiterated his complete confidence,[18] behaved in every way with total probity during Eisenhower's two periods of inability.[19]

Not all Presidents were as open with either the public or their seconds in command as was Eisenhower. Woodrow Wilson's condition was a topic of intense mystery at the time and, to some extent, remains so.[20] The case of Grover Cleveland is even more to the point. By all accounts, President Cleveland enjoyed a strong relationship with his Vice-President, Adlai Ewing Stevenson.[21] Nevertheless, Cleveland's operation for mouth cancer in July 1893 took place without Stevenson's knowledge[22] and remained shrouded in secrecy for twenty-four years until the *Saturday Evening Post* "scooped" the story in 1917.[23]

As Eisenhower took office in 1953, the presidential inability problem remained at an impasse. If a President died in office, it was settled constitutional doctrine, (thanks to Tyler) that the Vice-President succeeded to the office for the unexpired term.[24] If that same President became unable to discharge his or her duties for whatever reason, it was established political wisdom that neither President nor Vice-President would act for fear of working a permanent ouster.[25] Popular and scholarly discussion occurred at every episode of presidential inability or vice-presidential succession, after which public debate would cease and the literature would remain quiescent until the next such event.[26]

Analysis of these national episodes reveals three stumbling blocks to permanent solution. First, despite some shutdown of the executive branch, nothing immediately perceivable as truly catastrophic ever occurred.[27] Second, a natural inertia combined with a desire on the part of politicians to avoid a solution that might generate an advantage for an opposing political faction.[28] Lastly, there arose a consensus that, even if any replacement of the President by the Vice-President did not work an ouster, in the face of the Tyler Precedent, it would be unwise in the extreme to force the issue.[29]

Dwight David Eisenhower confronted presidential inability in an environment much changed from that which had previously surrounded the problem. He took over leadership not only of the United States, but also of the free world. Advances in transportation and communication, in weapons technology and delivery, speeded the tempo of international exchange and increased the penalties attending a failure of nerve.[30] To offset these additional pressures, President Eisenhower had certain advantages when he faced the problem posed by the country's lack of a workable presidential inability policy. Chief among these were his professional training and experience, his concept of the vice-presidency, and the man whom he had chosen to fill the second slot.

Eisenhower graduated from the United States Military Academy in the class of 1915.[31] West Point alumni are commissioned as company grade officers in the regular army with the expectation that the majority will remain as career professionals.[32] To further this mission of national defense, the U.S. military early instituted programs of continuing education.[33] An officer of general grade would have acquired the equivalent of a terminal graduate degree with the learning periods scattered over many years.[34] Eisenhower was no exception.[35] It was his graduation in 1926 from Command and General Staff School, standing first in a class of 275, which first marked him as an officer of exceptional potential and earned him a position on Douglas MacArthur's staff.[36]

As a former career military officer, President Eisenhower was well versed in both the principles of war and the staff concept.[37] Among the chief principles of war was one clearly violated by the nation's presidential inability policy in 1953: the doctrine of unity of command. Briefly put, this formalization of martial common sense states only that someone is in charge and everyone knows who is in charge.[38] To continue to grossly oversimplify, the staff concept posits that a commander is assisted in the exercise of command by a group of officers who are thoroughly familiar with both the commander's policies and the organization charged with carrying them out.[39] A number of management authorities have described the correspondence that exists between organizational staff in business and in the military.[40] A similar correspondence exists as well between the military and government.[41]

The Cabinet, responsible for the major functions of government, corresponds to a general or coordinating staff group.[42] Most non-Cabinet members of the National Security Council, whose agencies provide technical, administrative, and logistical support to further major governmental functions, correspond to the special staff group.[43] The Vice-President, as that office had begun to develop before Eisenhower, as it was used by Eisenhower, and as it continued to develop with greater impetus after Eisenhower,[44] corresponds to the personal staff group, which performs duties largely prescribed by the chief, to whom it reports.[45]

The Constitution had created the office of the vice-presidency with duties in both executive and legislative branches.[46] As midcentury approached, the thrust of vice-presidential activities shifted from the legislative to the executive.[47] The change represented the vice-presidency's response to the increasing complexity of the U.S. government as it rose to the challenges of the modern world. In addition, the second office matured as an executive institution in response to the increasing need of the President for a personal envoy and troubleshooter of recognized position and prestige.[48] Eisenhower continued these executive trends and increased them with the full cooperation of Vice-President Nixon.[49]

These were the pieces of Eisenhower's solution to the inability problem. The problem itself sorted out as follows: constitutional expectations in the event of inability were clear to a point. The Vice-President took over from an ill, comatose, captured, hostage, lost, or otherwise disabled chief. All other circumstances surrounding such a transition had been hopelessly muddled by the grammatical tidying up engaged in by the Committee on Style, combined with the precedent set by John Tyler upon the death of President Harrison.[50] Given contemporary weapons technology, world crisis potential, and the failure of geographic isolation through improvements in transportation and communication, it was obvious to a former military leader of General Eisenhower's stature and accomplishment that the total lack of presidential inability policy in 1953 was suicidal folly.[51]

After his heart attack in September 1955, Eisenhower explored the possibility of amending the Constitution or seeking other legislation that would clarify the Succession Clause.[52] Broaching the subject in a special presidential message to Congress was considered politically impossible. Influential politicans of both parties feared that public confidence in Eisenhower's health would be undermined with disastrous consequences at home and for U.S. initiatives abroad.[53] Bowing to practical necessity, Attorney General Herbert Brownell, Jr., in January 1957 presented the administration proposal in the form of a constitutional amendment in testimony before a special subcommittee of the House Judiciary Committee.[54]

The Eisenhower proposal, as Brownell referred to it afterwards, first pragmatically adopted the proven and accepted Tyler Precedent.[55] The remaining three sections provided that (1) if the President declared in writing that he or she was unable to fulfill his or her duties, the Vice-President would take over temporarily, (2) should the President not so request in writing, the Vice-President, if satisfied that an inability existed, might temporarily assume the powers and duties of the first office upon approval in writing of a majority of the Cabinet, and (3) in either event the President would resume his or her duties upon stating in writing that the inability had ceased.[56]

The plan was clearly one of presidential initiative. The Vice-President was to serve only in a temporary capacity, and ability to terminate the arrangement was vested definitely and exclusively in the President. In the event of a President unable or unwilling to declare a state of inability, responsibility remained within the executive branch.[57]

The only process for arbitrating a dispute between President and Vice-President was impeachment.[58] Criticism of this feature of the Eisenhower proposal was met in 1958 when Attorney General William P. Rogers presented a revised final section to the Subcommittee on Constitutional Amendments of the Senate Judiciary Committee. In the event that the Vice-President and a majority of the Cabinet did not agree with the President that an inability had ceased, both houses of Congress would vote to decide the matter.[59] With minor additions reflecting the legislature's desire to participate more fully in the inability process, this Eisenhower proposal was practically identical to the Bayh-Celler proposal which eventually became the Twenty-fifth Amendment.[60] Section 3 of the Bayh-Celler proposal deals with vice-presidential vacancy, a subject not covered by Eisenhower. However, the former President's agreement with this provision now in force was expressed in a 1964 letter to Senator Birch Bayh's Subcommittee on Constitutional Amendments.[61]

Accepting political and diplomatic constraints on the amendatory process as a solution to the inability problem, Eisenhower reaffirmed in writing his previous oral agreement with Vice-President Nixon. Under the provisions of this memorandum dated March 3, 1958, the Vice-President would serve as acting President during an inability. Should the President be unable to inform the Vice-President of an inability, the Vice-President would take over after ''such consultation as seems to him appropriate.'' In any case, the President would decide when the inability terminated.[62]

This agreement was intended solely to hold between Eisenhower and Nixon and was morally rather than legally binding.[63] In an attempt to address the legal side of the question, Attorney General Robert Kennedy analyzed the inability problem at the request of his brother, President John F. Kennedy. In an opinion dated

August 2, 1961, Robert Kennedy recommended to the President that the Eisenhower-Nixon agreement be continued in the new administration.[64] In view of the vice-presidency's recent growth as a national executive office, the agreement was an especially desirable precedent and was, as Robert Kennedy stated, "clearly constitutional [and] as close to spelling out a practical solution to the problem as is possible."[65] This precedent was continued by President Lyndon Baines Johnson and Speaker John McCormack and by Johnson and Vice-President Hubert Horatio Humphrey.[66] On February 10, 1967, the Twenty-fifth Amendment became valid, and the Eisenhower Precedent, as well as the Tyler Precedent, became enshrined in the Constitution.[67]

Eisenhower's role as architect of the United States' current presidential inability policy and his contribution to the Constitution in the Twenty-fifth Amendment have never been properly recognized. He perceived the true scope of the inability problem and proposed a constitutional amendment as the preferred solution. When this suggestion proved politically infeasible, he implemented a precedent-setting extralegal agreement that was followed by subsequent administrations until tragic events made the preferred constitutional amendment solution possible. The present amendment, as it now stands, contains four sections, the first of which is the Tyler Precedent, and the second, that which pertains to the vice-presidential vacancy. The remaining two sections are the gift of Dwight David Eisenhower and his administration to U.S. constitutional history and practice.

NOTES

1. See, for example, Zentner, "A Typology of American Presidential Transitions," *Duquesne Review* 16 (1971): 101, 101–103; cf. Jordanes, *Gothic History*, 2d ed. (C. Mierow, 1915; reprint, 1960) pp. 87–88 (failure of Ermanarich's united Gothic kingdom); T. Manteuffel, *The Formation of the Polish State*, A. Gorski, trans. (1982), pp. 77–104 (central power fails in Poland as the Piast dynasty proves unable to establish orderly succession); I. Nicholson, *The Liberators* (1969), pp. 224–27 (Bolivar dies fearing anarchy will be his country's heritage).

2. U.S. Constitution, art. V.

3. Herbert Brownell, "Presidential Inability: The Need for a Constitutional Amendment," *Yale Law Journal 68* (1958): 189, 193.

4. Ibid., p. 192.

5. *The Papers of James Madison* (Washington, D.C.: 1840).

6. Max Farrand, *Records of the Constitutional Convention of 1787* (1911).

7. J. Goldstein, *The Modern American Vice Presidency,* Table 1.1 p. 10; I. Irving, *The Rise of the Vice Presidency* (1956), p. 50; Brownell, "Presidential Inability," p. 193.

8. Brownell, "Presidential Inability," p. 193.

9. For example, 42 Op. Att'y Gen. 69, 74 (1961); Brownell, "Presidential Inability," p. 191.

10. For example, "Presidential Inability," *North American Review 133* (1881): 29 (four-part symposium, Garfield inability); Kerney, "Government by Proxy," *Century* 111

(1926): 481 (Wilson inability); Smith, "If a President Collapses . . . ," *Saturday Evening Post* (March 23, 1957), p. 20 (Eisenhower inabilities); Birch Bayh, "Our Greatest National Danger," *Look* (April 7, 1964), p. 74 (Kennedy assassination). See generally R. Silva, *Presidential Succession* (1951): 52–111 (intellectual history, collects citations); D. Jensen and L. Norris, *The 25th Amendment to the United States Constitution*, (rev. ed., 1982) (selective annotated bibliography); *Selected Material on Preisdential Inability*, 12 Rec. A.B. City N.Y. (1957): 462 (cites older literature, items 19 and 22 are identical, disregard item 26).

11. For example, E. Corwin, *The President: Office and Powers* (1957), p. 57; Brownell, "Presidential Inability," p. 192; Silva, "Presidential Inability," *Univ. Det. Law Journal* 35 (1957): 139, 150–151; see also Christopher, *A Special Election to Fill a Presidential Vacancy*, 30 Rec. A.B. City N.Y. (1975): 47, 49–50 (advocating a return to original intent); Arthur Schlesinger, "On the Presidential Succession," *Political Science Quarterly* 89 (1974): 475, 502–505 (calling for special elections and abolition of the vice presidency). *But* see Kirby, "The Making of a President: The Thinking in 1787," *A.B.A. Journal* 60 (1974): 1357, 1358, 1361–62 (advocating return to an original intent of legislative selection of Chief Executive); Sindler, "Completing a Presidential Term with a Successor of Presidential Caliber," *Policy Studies Journal* 2 (1974): 284, 288 (importance of automatic succession procedure to regime stability).

12. Brownell, "Presidential Inability," pp. 193–94, 205; Silva, "Presidential Inability," pp. 151–52.

13. E.g., 42 Op. Att'y Gen. 69, 85 (1961); Brownell, "Presidential Inability," pp. 192–95; Silva, "Presidential Succession and Disability," *Law and Contemporary Problems* 21 (1956): 646, 648–51. *Contra* 42 Op. Att'y Gen. (1961): 69, 85–88 (citing Corwin, *The President*, p. 54, and Brownell, "Presidential Inability," pp. 196, 202–203).

14. 42 Op. Att'y Gen. 69, 85 (1961); Brownell, "Presidential Inability," pp. 192–93.

15. R. Hansen, *The Year We Had No President* (1962), pp. 26–27, 36–40, 46–48; Butler, "Presidential Inability," *North American Review* 133 (1881): 428, 431; Silva, "Presidential Succession," p. 52; see 42 Op. Att'y Gen. 69 (1961): 83–86; Brownell, "Presidential Inability," pp. 193–98; Letter from Chief Justice Earl Warren to Kenneth B. Keating (January 20, 1950) (noting likelihood of litigation before the Supreme Court should controversy occur), reprinted in Brownell, "Presidential Inability," p. 199.

16. J. Doenecke, *The Presidencies of James A. Garfield and Chester A. Arthur* (University Press of Kansas, 1981), p. 53. But see A. Peskin, *Garfield* (1978): 599.

17. Hansen, *The Year We Had No President*, pp. 40–41; T. Marshall, *Recollections of Thomas R. Marshall* (1925): 367; D. Young, *American Roulette* (1965): 125–44; Kerney, "Government by Proxy," p. 482.

18. For example, News Conference (March 14, 1956), in 1956 Public Papers, ¶56, p. 302; News Conference (January 25, 1956), ¶20, p. 182; see News Conference (April 2, 1958), in 1958 Public Papers, ¶63, pp. 268–69; Television Broadcast, "The People Ask the President" (October 12, 1956), in 1956 Public Papers, ¶241, p. 904; *Remarks at the Republican Campaign Picnic at the President's Gettysburg Farm* (September 12, 1956), ¶206, pp. 767–68. See generally J. Hart, *When the Going Was Good! American Life in the Fifties* (New York: Crown, 1982), pp. 58–62 (outlining the personal and political relationship); M. Natoli, "The Vice Presidency Since World War II" (Ph.D. diss., Tufts University, 1975), ch. 20 (available from University Microfilms International, order number 76–19455) (outlining the working relationship).

19. For example, Telephone conversation between Arthur Krock of the *New York Times* and Vice-President Richard M. Nixon (September 26, 1955), in A. Krock, *Memoirs* (1968), pp. 304–305; Young, *American Roulette*, pp. 263–66, 269–74; David, "The Vice Presidency," J. Pcl. 29 (1967): 721, 738, see Pear, "The American Presidency Under Eisenhower," *Political Science Quarterly* 28 (1957): 5, 12.

20. Silva, "Presidential Succession," pp. 652–53. See generally Kerney, "Government by Proxy" (for a sense of the alienation which struck policymakers during the Wilson inability).

21. Schlup, "Presidential Disability: The Case of Cleveland and Stevenson," *Presidential Studies Quarterly* 9 (1979): 303, 306–307.

22. Ibid., p. 304.

23. Keen, "The Surgical Operations on President Cleveland in 1893," *Saturday Evening Post* (September 22, 1917), p. 24.

24. 42 Op. Att'y Gen. 69, 85 (1961); Brownell, "Presidential Inability," pp. 193–95.

25. For example, Richard M. Nixon, *Six Crises* (1962): pp. 178–80; Brownell, "Presidential Inability," pp. 196–98.

26. See sources cited in note 10 above.

27. For example, J. Doenecke, *The Presidencies of Garfield and Arthur*, p. 53; Schlup, *Presidential Disability*, pp. 304, 308–309; Silva, "Presidential Inability," pp. 140–43, 147–48; "President Scores Report He'll Quit," *New York Times* (April 4, 1957), p. 1, col. 7. *Contra* Kerney, "Government by Proxy," pp. 485–86; Laukhuff, "The Price of Woodrow Wilson's Illness," *Virginia Quarterly Review* 32 (1956): 599, 610; Feis, "When Roosevelt Died," *Virginia Quarterly Review* 46 (1970): 576, 587–89; Rogers, "Presidential Inability," *Review* 2 (1920): 481, 482; *see generally* Brodie, "The Political Hero in America, *Virginia Quarterly Review* 46 (1970): 46, 53–56 (discussing Wilsonian psychohistorical revisionism).

28. For example, Brownell, "Presidential Inability," pp. 194, 196; Silva, "Presidential Inability," pp. 141–42. See generally Kirby, "A Breakthrough on Presidential Inability," *Vanderbilt Law Review* 17 (1964): 463, 464, 478 (spurred by the John F. Kennedy assassination, an American Bar Association sponsored Special Conference works toward consensus); Wildavsky, "Choosing the Lesser Evil," *Parliamentary Aff.* 13 (1959–1960): 25, 36–37 (early analysis of inability problem from the policymaker's perspective).

29. See sources cited above in note 14. But see Letter from John Brooks Leavitt to Editor (January 31, 1922), *American Bar Association Journal* 8 (1922): 189, 190.

30. For example, Eulogy by President Nixon, State Funeral of Dwight David Eisenhower (March 30, 1969), in H. R. Doc. No. 195, 91st Cong., 1st Sess., xiv, xv-xvi (1970); Hart, *When the Going Was Good*, pp. 68–80; David "The Vice President," pp. 721–22; F. Greenstein, *The Hidden-Hand Presidency* (1982): 3–54 passim; Branyan, "Eisenhower the Politician," *American Chronicle* 1 (1972): 43–46; Griffith, "Dwight D. Eisenhower and the Corporate Commonwealth," *American History Review* (1982): 87, 94–96, 110–16; Immerman, "Eisenhower and Dulles," *Political Psychology* 1 (1979): 21, 27–31, 34–37.

31. *Official Army Register* 1 (1946): 205 [hereinafter cited as *Army Reg.*, 1946].

32. S. Ambrose, *Duty, Honor, Country: A History of West Point* (1966): 36, 253–55, 261–83, 324, 330–32; F. Todd, *Cadet Gray* (1955): 8–9, 56–57, 81–87; T. Williams, *Americans at War*, rev. ed. (1962): 42–43, 57–59.

33. J. Masland and L. Radway, *Soldiers and Scholars* (1957): 76–99 passim.

34. H. Clark and H. Sloan, *Classrooms in the Military* (1964): 63.

35. *Army Reg.*, 1946, p. 205.

36. Greenstein, *The Hidden-Hand Presidency*, p. 11.

37. News Conference (August 24, 1960), in 1960–1961 Published Papers ¶268, p. 653. Compare Foreword by Dwight D. Eisenhower with Ambrose, *Duty, Honor, Country*, pp. vii-ix with J. Alger, *The Quest for Victory* (1982): xi-xiii (front matter reminiscences of two West Pointers illustrating the timelessness of the basic course of instruction). But cf. Griffith, "Dwight D. Eisenhower," p. 88 (Eisenhower as representative of a generic managerial class nonspecific to a particular profession).

38. Alger, *The Quest for Victory*, pp. xi-xiii, 183, 248–49, 259, 261. See generally H. Eccles, *Military Concepts and Philosophy* (1965): 110–11 (brief explanation of principles of war).

39. J. Beishline, *Military Management for National Defense* (1950): 168.

40. Ibid., pp. 70–71; E. Harrison, *Management and Organizations* (1978): 549–52, 598–600; G. Terry, *Principles of Management* (1968): 360–61, 374.

41. See Eccles, *Military Concepts and Philosophy*, pp. 152–54.

42. See Beishline, *Military Management for National Defense*, p. 170.

43. Ibid., pp. 169–70.

44. For example, News Conference (July 22, 1959), in 1959 Published Papers ¶167, p. 541; News Conference (November 5, 1958), in 1958 Published Papers ¶310, pp. 829–30; News Conference (April 2, 1958), ¶63, pp. 268–69; News Conference (June 5, 1957), in 1957 Published Papers ¶105, pp. 433–37; News Conference (February 6, 1957), ¶28, 132–33; News Conference (June 30, 1954) in 1954 Published Papers ¶157, at 610–11; Goldstein, *The Modern American Vice Presidency*, pp. 134–50; "Nixon's Own Story of 7 Years in the Vice Presidency," *U.S. News and World Report* (March 16, 1960), p. 98, passim; H. Maxon, "Political Practice in the Vice Presidency" (Ph.D. diss., Brown University 1974) (available from University Microfilms International, order number 75-09206); Natoli, "The Vice Presidency Since World War II," chs. 9 & 20.

45. Beishline, *Military Management for National Defense*, pp. 169–70; Humphrey, "Changes in the Vice Presidency," *Current History* (August 1974): 58, 59; Natoli, "The Vice Presidency Since World War II," ch. 20.

46. U.S. Constitution, Art. I, §3, cl. 4; Art. III, §1, cl. 6.

47. See sources cited above in note 44.

48. For example, David, "The Vice Presidency," pp. 721–22 and passim; Humphrey, "Changes in the Vice Presidency," p. 59; Light, "The Institutional Vice Presidency," *Presidential Studies Quarterly* 13 (1983): 198, 198–201 and passim.

49. For example, David, "The Vice Presidency," pp. 727–28, 731–32; Williams, "The American Vice Presidency and Foreign Affairs," *World Affairs* (September 1957: 38, 40–41; "Nixon's Own Story of 7 Years in the Vice Presidency," pp. 100–103, 105–106; Natoli, "The Vice Presidency Since World War II," pp. 418–19, 421–22.

50. For example, Brownell, "Presidential Inability," pp. 193–95.

51. See sources cited above in note 48.

52. Brownell, "Presidential Inability," p. 196.

53. Sherman Adams, *Firsthand Report: The Story of the Eisenhower Administration* (New York: Harper and Brothers, 1961), pp. 198–201.

54. Brownell, "Presidential Inability," p. 196.

55. Ibid., p. 201.

56. Ibid., p. 197.

57. Ibid., pp. 196–97.

58. Ibid., p. 197.

59. Ibid., pp. 201–202.

60. Compare Brownell, "Presidential Inability," pp. 197, 201–2 with Feerick, "Proposed Amendment on Presidential Inability and Vice-Presidential Vacancy," *A.B.A. Journal* 51 (1965): 915–16 (the latter quotes what was to become U.S. Constitution, Amend. 25).

61. Birch Bayh, *One Heartbeat Away* (1968): 75–76; see generally, for example, Schlesinger, "On The Presidential Succession," pp. 475–76 and passim (eloquent denouncement of the most controversial section of this amendment).

62. For example, *Agreement Between the President and the Vice President as to Procedures in the Event of Presidential Inability* (March 3, 1958), in 1958 Published Papers ¶40; 42 Op. Att'y Gen. 69 (1961): 92–94; Nixon, *Six Crises*, pp. 178–80; Brownell, "Presidential Inability," pp. 203–205; Stathis, "Presidential Disability Agreements Prior to the 25th Amendment," *Presidential Studies Quarterly* 12 (1982): 208, 209–10; Dale, "Eisenhower Disability Pact Calls for 'Acting President,' " *New York Times* (March 4, 1958), p. 1, col. 2.

63. For example, 42 Op. Att'y Gen. 69 (1961): 92–93.

64. Ibid., pp. 94–95.

65. Ibid., p. 95.

66. For example, Stathis, "Presidential Disability Agreements," pp. 211–12; Mohr, "Johnson Reaches Disability Accord," *New York Times* (January 28, 1965), p. 13, col. 1; "Johnson Provides for a Disability," *New York Times* (December 6, 1963), p. 1, col. 8.

67. J. Feerick, *The Twenty-fifth Amendment* (1976): 111–13. The amendment was one of many pieces of legislation facilitated by President Johnson as a memorial to his slain running mate; see. B. Caton, "Presidential Transitions: Vice Presidential Succession" (Ph.D. diss., University of Virginia, 1978) (available from University Microfilms International, order number 79–16291). Popular and scholarly debate was informed by a sustained sense of urgency new to the traditionally relaxed treatment of the inability problem; see, for example, Blackman, "Presidential Disability and the Bayh Amendment," *W. Political Quarterly* (1967): 440, 444–45; Feerick, "Presidential Inability: A Constitutional Amendment is Needed Now," *A.B.A. Journal* 50 (1964): 59, 62; Kirby, "A Breakthrough on Presidential Inability," p. 464; Kury, "The Crises in the Law of Presidential Succession," Pa. B.A.Q. 36 (1965): 301, 307–308; Powell, "The Risk of Having No President," *Oklahoma B.A. Journal* 36 (1965): 354, 358–59.

THE PRESIDENT: FOREIGN POLICY

12

Dwight D. Eisenhower and the Foreign Policymaking Process

J. Philipp Rosenberg

During the past few years, there has been a reevaluation of the Eisenhower presidency. Led by Fred Greenstein, scholars have discovered a new, more active Eisenhower whose activism had been concealed from public view by his "hidden-handed" style of leadership.[1] This reevaluation has touched on Eisenhower's foreign as well as domestic policy, shattering the image of a domineering John Foster Dulles making foreign policy with the acquiescence of a deferential Eisenhower.[2] As a result of this process, scholars are looking more closely at Eisenhower's foreign policy beliefs in attempts to link them to foreign policy results. This chapter is an attempt to do just that. But first, a few words about beliefs.

Beliefs do *not* determine actions. A comprehensive knowledge of Eisenhower's belief system is not sufficient to explain his foreign policy actions. Beliefs do, however, affect the process by acting as a filter through which incoming information is processed, so that certain aspects of the informational flow are emphasized at the expense of others. Thus, beliefs can be viewed as guiding the discussion of a given situation by highlighting the salient aspects of the situation, as perceived by the decision-maker. This, in turn, will affect the generation and viability of the various possible solutions to the problem.[3]

BELIEF SYSTEM: ITS CONCEPTUALIZATION

Numerous attempts have been made to conceptualize the structure of the belief system. One of the most valid conceptualizations of a belief system, that by Milton Rokeach, is composed of three concentric circles.[4] According to this conceptualization, beliefs are distributed along a central-peripheral dimension in which the less centralized beliefs are derived from the more central ones, lending continuity to the belief system. Indeed, one is therefore able to view the belief system as an intricate spider's web with the core beliefs in the center of the web and all others spreading out from the center, but each connected to the strand closer to the center and all ultimately emanating from the center.[5]

With this conceptualization structure as a model, this chapter will use a framework that focuses on four specific belief sets, varying from central to peripheral. The first of these belief sets is the *Weltanschauung* which can be defined as a philosophy of life containing beliefs about oneself and the nature of the individual. It is from this set that the total belief system orginates. The second is the political set that contains all the individual's beliefs concerning the political process. These beliefs are derived from the *Weltanschauung* and are less central to the belief system as is the third set, political role beliefs. This set contains the individual's beliefs toward the proper occupation of political roles and is, in reality, a subset of the political set when it is restricted, as it is here, to political roles. The last belief set is the least central of the sets examined and contains those beliefs associated with whatever subject matter is under consideration at any given time. For the purposes of this chapter, it consists of Eisenhower's foreign policy beliefs. The methodology used is the qualitative content analysis of Eisenhower's writings and statements, with special emphasis placed on private letters, diary entries, and memos of conversations. These are emphasized because they were not meant to become public knowledge at the time of issuance and therefore would be more respresentative of Eisenhower's true beliefs.

EISENHOWER'S *WELTANSCHAUUNG*

Central to an individual's *Weltanschauung* are beliefs about the nature of human beings. To Eisenhower, this nature revolved around two relationships: the relationship between the individual and God and the relationship between the individual and his or her fellows. Although Eisenhower was not an overtly religious man, he viewed the individual as a "spiritual thing."[6] He regarded devotion to principle as one of humankind's two most priceless possessions.[7] Eisenhower believed that this spiritual nature was America's greatest strength,[8] one which he chose to emphasize in his inaugural address for fear that the nation was becoming too secular.[9]

This belief in God was combined with a belief in individual initiative as contained in the Protestant work ethic. Those who shirked their responsibilities were condemned.[10] This explains Eisenhower's fondness for a quote attributed to Prime Minister Harold Macmillan that stated "Better to go down fighting than helplessly to await starvation."[11] This reflects Eisenhower's belief that human beings had the capability to act and therefore must act or risk shirking their responsibilities not only toward God but also toward their fellows. However, the capability for action was not enough given what Eisenhower perceived to be the individual's selfish nature.

According to Eisenhower, "the instinct for self-preservation leads us into short-sightedness, and self-centered actions, often at the expense of our fellows.''[12] How do individuals discharge their God-given responsibilities given their selfish nature? The answer was provided ten-year-old Dwight by his mother: ''He that conquereth his own soul is greater than he who taketh a city.''[13] Self-discipline was the key that his mother believed in deeply and preached constantly. ''According to her, each of us should behave properly not because of fear of punishment but because it was the right thing to do.''[14] This emphasis on the necessity for self-control and mechanisms to augment it accounts for Eisenhower's fondness for the Patton quote, ''Talking tough may not give me more courage but at least it insures that my sense of shame will prevent my running from a battle.''[15] Sometimes one had to paint oneself into a corner in order to assure the correct behavior. Thus, having mastered one's selfish nature, one could proceed to discharge one's responsibilities.

But what were those responsibilities? According to Eisenhower, they were to follow the Golden Rule with the implied emphasis on conduct benefiting all instead of just oneself. Thus, people were judged on how well they applied this moral principle. General George C. Marshall was held in high esteem because ''I have never known a man so selfless as Marshall.''[16] When asked how he had acquired this philosophy, Eisenhower alluded to the influence of his mother, a woman whose philosophy was best illustrated by the fact that her last words before death were directed to the comfort of the woman caring for her.[17] On the other hand, Eisenhower could not stand people who had not mastered their selfish behavior. As he wrote to Marshall during World War II, ''I get weary of people that have no other thought but 'me.' ''[18] This emphasis on fulfilling one's moral responsibilities toward the betterment of others led to his belief in a concept that has been closely identified with him, the concept of duty.

To Eisenhower, doing one's duty entailed discharging one's responsibility to the best of one's ability. In letters to his wife during World War II, Eisenhower continually emphasized the uncertainty of the war's outcome but the certainty that he was doing his duty as dictated by his conscience:

No man can always be right. So the struggle is to do one's best, to keep the brain and conscience clear; never to be swayed by unworthy motives or inconsequential reasons, but to strive to unearth the basic factors involved and then do one's duty. . . . When you remember me in your prayers, that's the special thing I want—always to do my duty to the extreme limit of my ability.[19]

Duty, as perceived by Eisenhower, was a universal concept. When King Edward VIII abdicated, Eisenhower criticized him for losing sight of his duty.[20] Commenting on the role of the teacher in American society, Eisenhower emphasized what needed to be taught to the young generation. He cited the teaching of obligations as well as the privileges of American citizenship, the virtue of old-fashioned patriotism and ''the necessity for earnest devotion to duty'' as things that had to be taught to the children "if we are to survive as a sturdy nation."[21]

To summarize, Eisenhower's *Weltanschauung* included a deep faith in the existence of God and in the individual's obligation to live up to having been created in God's image. This entailed controlling one's selfish nature and discharging one's duty to one's fellow by acting always for the betterment of humankind. This one could do because God had given people the capability of individual initiative which they therefore had the obligation to use.

POLITICAL BELIEFS

Eisenhower's political beliefs can be traced back to his *Weltanschauung*. The foundation of government, he maintained, was a firm belief in God:

When our forefathers attempted to express themselves and their ideas of government to the world, they were compelled to say, "we hold that all men are endowed by their Creator with certain rights." The point is that except for his equality of right, a gift from the Almighty, there was no sense, logic or reason in free government. I think that any American contemplating the whole history of the writing of our Declaration and the establishment of our Constitution must conclude that an essential foundation stone of free government is this sincere religious faith.[22]

This moral foundation of government meant that the function of government must be interpreted in terms of helping the individual discharge his or her moral responsibilities. This entailed establishing a system that "recognizes and protects the rights of the individual and that ascribes to the individual a dignity accruing to him because of his creation in the image of a supreme being."[23]

It also meant that government had a second function. "But the very fact that man is a spiritual thing makes it impossible for any durable governmental system to ignore hordes of people who through no fault of their own suddenly find themselves poverty stricken, and, far from being able to maintain their families at decent levels, cannot even provide sustenance."[24] How did the government know where to draw the line between noninterference with individual liberties and helping those who could not help themselves? Eisenhower's solution was to follow the advice of a former President, Abraham Lincoln. "The legitimate object of government is to do for a community of people whatever they need to have done but cannot do at all, or cannot so well do for themselves—in their separate and individual capacities. In all that the people can individually do as well for themselves, government ought not to interfere."[25]

Eisenhower's perception of the distinction between government and politics was based on this understanding of the function of government. To him, there was only one correct solution to any problem. If there was opposition, it was either because those who opposed him did not have all the facts or because they were engaged in politics, which Eisenhower defined as the pursuit of selfish interests at the expense of the national interest.[26] The selfish interests permeating politics were totally unacceptable to him. Thus, we have the interesting assumption that government can and should be run without politics. In its stead, government should be run by a general consensus of principle.

POLITICAL ROLE BELIEFS

Another essential set of beliefs important in the decision-making process is the set revolving around the concept of political role. This set establishes self-imposed boundaries of action within that role. It dictates not only what is perceived as the limits of the authority of office but also the prescriptions of office.

One recurring theme in Eisenhower's *Weltanschauung* is the belief that one must work toward the benefit of all instead of oneself. As stated above, this notion was at the root of his dislike for politics. It also was at the root of his perception of public service roles. Eisenhower viewed the Cabinet as a group of people who should represent the entire government, not just the interests of the department they headed. Thus, Eisenhower's first Secretary of Labor was fired because he "could not free himself of the feeling that he was placed on the Cabinet to be a 'trade unionist.' "[27] This, in Eisenhower's view, was a violation of role prescription that could not be tolerated. To Eisenhower, all public service roles, especially the presidency, had to be as apolitical as military positions, such as the one he occupied as Commander of SHAPE.[28]

Eisenhower believed that the President was President of all the people. This statement, by itself, is not novel since all Presidents hold similar views. What is different is the implication Eisenhower drew from the belief. When he stated that the President was President of all the people, he meant that the President must remain above politics. Therefore, a President like Truman was constantly violating the prescriptions of the office by being too political. "I know that there is nothing that Mr. Truman did that shocked my senses of the fitting and the appropriate as did his barnstorming activities while he was actually President of the United States."[29] In barnstorming, Truman had violated one of Eisenhower's central beliefs about the presidency, that is, not to engage in partisan politics. Indeed, in reference to the 1956 election campaign Eisenhower stated that "It was agreed that the whole idea was to get across the idea that the President was President of all the people—that the words 'Democrat' and 'Republican' would not be mentioned. In this connection, the President said, 'I doubt I shall make any "political" speeches.' "[30]

Only a concept so central to his belief system as the idea of duty could have forced Eisenhower to accept the presidency and run for reelection. Had it not been for this sense of duty, his moral code would have predisposed him to reject the position. For example, in a diary entry Eisenhower discusses filling the position of Governor of Hawaii which, at that time, was an appointive office. There were two candidates for the position, each actively seeking the appointment, complete with pressure groups behind him. Eisenhower's reaction reflects his feelings toward those who *pursue* public office:

Such an approach to a public service position violates every instinct I have. To seek such a post is, to me, clear evidence of unsuitability. I feel that anyone who can, without great personal sacrifice, come to Washington to accept an important governmental post, is not fit to hold that post.[31]

To summarize, Eisenhower perceived the public servant as one who represents all the people, and he believed that one must not seek public office but rather accept it out of a strong sense of moral obligation to the society. This is especially true of the presidency which Eisenhower saw as a role that should be above the selfish interests of partisan politics and that must be filled by an individual with a strong sense of duty to his or her fellows.

FOREIGN POLICY BELIEFS

According to Eisenhower, foreign policy was no different from domestic policy. The major problem in international relations was the same short-sighted selfishness that plagued domestic politics. The solution, as Eisenhower saw it, was the same. It was to "find a way to bring men and nations to a point where they will give to the long-term promise the same value that they give to immediate and individual gains."[32] The danger, as Eisenhower saw it, was that "unconsciously, we were guilty of one of the greatest errors that ignorance can make—we assume that our standard of values is shared by all other humans in the world."[33]

This was even true of other Western democracies. When France differed from the United States in its perception of international relations, Eisenhower attributed this difference to a lack of "spiritual guidance" in France.[34] How much more so was it true of nations that did not share America's Judeo-Christian heritage? Thus, Eisenhower perceived international relations in terms of "a moral fight as well as a diplomatic maneuver."[35] The main opposition in this moral fight was, of course, the Soviet Union.

The most important fact of international life, according to Eisenhower, was the existence of an "irreconcilable conflict between the theories of Communist dictatorship and the basic principles of free world existence."[36] This conflict was irreconcilable because the communists lacked the morality which, to Eisenhower, represented the essence of being human. Consequently, communists were "liars and cheats."[37] They were "fanatical" individuals possessed of greed and "lust for power."[38] Soviet leaders were perceived as individuals who would resort to bribery, corruption, subversion, and threat of force to achieve their goals.[39] Thus, the problem in international relations was

Truth, honor, justice, consideration of others, liberty for all—the problem is how to preserve them, nurture them, and keep the peace—if this last is possible—when we are opposed by people who scorn to give any validity whatsoever to these values.[40]

Eisenhower linked the Soviet problem with the problem that had been presented by Hitler, and he saw the solution as necessarily the same. The United States had to meet the situation "exactly as our Grand Alliance of the 40's met our enemies and vanquished them."[41] This link to Hitler also made the memory of Munich more salient to him and therefore cautioned him against the dangers of appeasement.[42] This was especially true of U.S. foreign policy toward the Third World, the area Eisenhower saw as most vulnerable to Soviet exploitation.

The problem in the Third World, as Eisenhower viewed it, was that "Nationalism is on the march and world Communism is taking advantage of that spirit of nationalism to cause dissention in the free world."[43] This situation was further complicated by the colonial powers' refusal to recognize that the independence of these areas was inevitable.[44] This attitude, in turn, caused resentment toward the colonial powers and the West in general in these areas.[45] As a result, these new nations were blinded to the real choice before them: between "slavery, preceded by a momentary independence, as in the case of Czechoslovakia," on the one hand, and "orderly progress toward independence," on the other.[46] Instead, they looked at the West with suspicion as if the West wanted to reimpose its domination over these nations. This Third World perception interfered with Eisenhower's attempt to save them from communism because it was his position that a nation helped must provide the bulk of the defense against communist penetration attempts. "If the heart is right, other nations can help; if not, that particular nation is doomed."[47]

To summarize, Eisenhower perceived an international system dominated by a struggle between communist slavery and American freedom. This struggle was being fought in the Third World, an area dominated by the concept of nationalism. Communism was taking advantage of this spirit of nationalism by attempting to separate the Third World from the West, thus insuring the enslavement of those nations in which the attempt succeeded. Further complicating this struggle was the blindness of America's Western European allies to the fact that they could not retain their empires in light of this nationalism. This made it extremely difficult for the United States to protect these areas since the Third World nations, wary of U.S. allies, were suspicious of U.S. motives. Most importantly, Eisenhower believed that the United States had a moral obligation to protect these nations just as the U.S. government had a moral obligation to protect the individual liberties of its own citizens. The function of government was the same in both instances: to do for others what they could not do for themselves under the obligation of individual initiative. But how were these related to foreign policy outcomes? Three examples should suffice to illustrate this relationship.

INDOCHINA, 1954

Indochina placed Eisenhower in a moral quandary. On the one hand, he was sympathetic to the regional aspirations for independence. On the other, he recognized that nationalism in Indochina was being exploited by the communists. The real battle, according to Eisenhower, was "to defeat Communism in the region and to give to the natives their freedom."[48] This was not easy to do because of France's differing perception of the problem.

Eisenhower repeatedly tried to convince the French that they could succeed only if they promised to grant the region its independence.[49] The French, however, insisted on viewing the situation as a rebellion against French authority, a perception which, according to Eisenhower, doomed them to failure.[50] To Eisenhower, the only way the United States should intervene in the area would be as part of a concert of nations, some of whom had to be Asiatic, with the sole purpose of combatting communism, because "to contemplate anything else is to lay ourselves open to the charge of imperialism and colonialism or—at the very least—of objectionable paternalism."[51] This the French were not ready to do, nor were the British. Thus, lacking the moral justification to intervene, Eisenhower refused to militarily aid the French at Dienbienphu.[52] However, his decision did not indicate a failure to recognize the importance of the situation. What it did reflect was Eisenhower's perception that, given the French attitude, intervention did not conform to his idea of the moral path the United States should follow in international relations.[53] Intervention for the moral purpose of saving the region from communism would have been justified in his view, but intervention for the selfish purpose of perpetuating French rule was not.

Others have maintained that Eisenhower's main objection to Dienbienphu was military and that, therefore, he would not have intervened had he been President in the 1960s under the same conditions under which Johnson ordered American intervention into Vietnam.[54] What these people fail to understand however, is that the existence of a free and independent South Vietnam would have changed Eisenhower's reluctance to intervene. In 1965, those conditions which Eisenhower had set up for intervention would have been fulfilled. In 1965, he could have intervened in a concert of nations, some of whom were Asiatic, with the express purpose of stopping communism, since the independence issue that plagued him in 1954 had, by 1965, been removed. An indication that this would have been the case is provided by the third example to be cited, Lebanon, 1958. Before turning our attention to Lebanon, however, let us first discuss a crisis in the same region which occurred two years earlier—Suez, 1956.

SUEZ, 1956

The British, French, and Israeli attempt to topple Egypt's Colonel Gamal Abdel Nasser put Eisenhower in another moral quandary. On the one hand, Eisenhower shared the British and French opinion of Nasser, seeing him as an "evil influence'' in the region.[55] He also saw the Soviet Union manipulating Nasser and the Pan Arab movement for its benefit.[56] Early in October 1956, after the nationalization of the canal but prior to the Israeli invasion, Eisenhower was informed that discussions on how to topple Nasser were already taking place. Because he viewed Nasser's removal as a necessary step toward saving the region from communism, Eisenhower did not object to the nature of these discussions, only to the timing.[57] However, once the Israelis invaded, he told the British that ''he felt it was incumbent upon both of us to redeem our word supporting any victim of aggression'' and that he would not ''betray the good word of the United States.''[58] In a meeting with his advisers, he stated that he did not like helping Egypt but that the word of the United States must be made good.[59] Only if the Soviets intervened would Eisenhower consider aiding his two closest allies.[60] Lacking Soviet intervention, Eisenhower was forced to side with a man who was the chief obstacle to American interests in the region, and against the United States' two closest allies. Why was this the case? Simply because his belief system had predisposed him against aiding the British and French because of the immorality of their action. But lacking any moral grounds of his own for intervention, Eisenhower decided to go against what would have been in the short-term interest of the United States in order to be true to what he perceived as in the nation's long-term interest, the pursuit of morality in international relations.

In both of the above examples, Eisenhower was forced to do something he did not want to do. In both instances, he felt compelled to deny the requests of his closest allies because he felt they were acting in an immoral manner. This prevented him from doing what he perceived had to be done in order to defeat the major challenge to a moral world order. In each instance, he accepted a short-term defeat in order to pursue his long-term goal. The third example presents an example of Eisenhower's willingness to combine short-term with long-term goals when no moral obstacles were present to prevent such action.

LEBANON, 1958

Events in Lebanon concerned Eisenhower greatly because he saw them as a prime example of communist aggression in the Third World. In a conversation he had with the Lebanese foreign minister in 1957, Eisenhower stated his agreement with the statement of the President of Lebanon that ''there was a great struggle going on in the world between those that supported independence, freedom and progress and those who were guilty of intolerence, distrust and greed.''[61] In the same conversation, he expressed U.S. concern about the ''threat of international Communist aggression and subversion in the region,''[62] and he lamented the fact that area leaders like King Saud of Saudi Arabia ''did not seem to realize the extent to which the Communists were gaining greater and greater control in Syria and Egypt.''[63]

To Eisenhower, the biggest threat to Lebanon were the communists, aided by Arab money and Egyptian influence.[64] In private letters written during the first stages of the Lebanese crisis, May and June 1958, Eisenhower explained the situation in Lebanon in terms of "a great internal campaign of subversion and deceit, possibly communistic in origin."[65] Although he had previously resisted Lebanese requests for intervention because he felt the United Nations should handle the matter, a coup in Iraq on July 14, 1958, changed his mind and he immediately ordered in the Marines. Why did he do so? What made this situation different from the two previous situations discussed? The answer can, in part, be found in the way in which Eisenhower perceived the situation.

Eisenhower did *not* perceive the situation in Lebanon as a civil war; rather, he saw the rebellion as orchestrated by Nasser.[66] Nasser, in turn, appeared to Eisenhower to be a Russian puppet, whether or not Nasser knew it.[67] Thus, in Eisenhower's mind, what seemed to be a civil war was instead a Soviet penetration attempt. This changed the stakes of the game considerably and also meant that the Eisenhower Doctrine could apply.

In justifying the invasion, Eisenhower stated, "it was better if we took a long strong position rather than a Munich-type position, if we are to avoid the crumbling of our whole security structure."[68] This was especially true because the intervention was the right thing to do "as long as the action rests on moral grounds."[69] He continued that, if the only argument for intervention had been economic, it would have been different and inferior to the purpose which the United States was pursuing: the right to govern by consent of the governed. He reiterated this point in his speech to the nation announcing the intervention in which he drew parallels between Lebanon and past attempts to contain communist aggression.[70]

In the Lebanese situation, Eisenhower finally found an opportunity to blend short-term and long-term interests. He had the request of the nation being victimized; he had support for the intervention by other countries in the region; he had support from his Western European allies, especially the British who were themselves intervening in Jordan; and most importantly, he was intervening for the right reasons, the preservation of a democratic government which was the victim of a communist penetration attempt. Thus, he could act in accordance with his belief system, in terms of both action and purpose.

CONCLUSION

In the past, two generally accepted generalizations were made about foreign policy during the Eisenhower years. One was that it was a product of Dulles the moralist tempered occasionally by Eisenhower the pragmatist. The second was that it was a product of Dulles the Cold Warrior tempered occasionally by Eisenhower the Peacemaker. These generalizations created a picture of a Russian-baiting Dulles being restrained by an Eisenhower who looked for peaceful coexistence with the Soviets. While partially true, recently declassified documents show a more complex picture.

Dulles was indeed a moralist but so was Eisenhower, and it was their shared beliefs in a moral world order which constituted the key to their successful relationship. Dulles was indeed a Cold Warrior but so was Eisenhower. If Eisenhower appeared to be more conciliatory, it was only because he hoped the Soviets would see the light, not because he had changed his mind about the basic Russian objectives.

Eisenhower was a man guided by a set of moral principles embedded in his *Weltanschauung*. The three examples provided here have shown the nature of the relationship between this set of moral principles and foreign policy decisions taken during his administration. Dienbienphu, Suez, and Lebanon presented Eisenhower with difficult foreign policy decisions. All were decided within a common framework built around the beliefs contained in Eisenhower's *Weltanschauung*. All were guided by Eisenhower's perception of American long-term objectives which were, in turn, affected by Eisenhower's beliefs about the nature of the individual and the nature of the political process.

The French in Indochina and in Suez were motivated by what Eisenhower perceived to be selfish and therefore unacceptable motives. The French were merely interested in retaining the glory of their empire. The British chose an unacceptable method in solving their dispute with Nasser. Just as in domestic politics, selfish motives and immoral methods were unacceptable. On the other hand, Eisenhower perceived the Christians in Lebanon as being motivated by moral principles, not selfish interests. Therefore, they not only could be, but also deserved to be supported.

Eisenhower's belief system did not necessarily determine these actions. Rather, his belief system oriented him in a direction that made the selection of certain alternative courses of action more acceptable than other alternatives.

NOTES

1. Fred I. Greenstein, *The Hidden-Handed Presidency: Eisenhower as Leader* (New York: Basic Books, 1982).

2. For an example of this reevaluation of the Eisenhower–Dulles relationship, see Richard Immerman, "Eisenhower and Dulles: Who Made the Decisions?," *Political Psychology* 1, no. 2 (Autumn 1979).

3. For an excellent summary of the issue, see Ole Holsti, "Cognitive Process Approaches to Decision-making," *American Behavioral Scientist*, 20, no. 1 (October 1976).

4. Milton Rokeach, *Beliefs, Attitudes and Value* (San Francisco: Jossey-Bass, 1968), p. 3.

5. For a similar discussion, see J. Philipp Rosenberg, "The Belief System of Harry S Truman and Its Effect on Foreign Policy Decision-Making During His Administration," *Presidential Studies Quarterly* 12, no. 2 (Spring 1982).

6. Dwight David Eisenhower (hereafter DDE) to General G. Chynoweth, July 20, 1954, Ann C. Whitman (hereafter ACW Files, DDE Diary "January-November 1954," Dwight David Eisenhower Library (hereafter DDEL). Also quoted in DDE, *The White House Years: Mandate for Change, 1953–1956* (Garden City, N.Y.: Doubleday and Co., 1963), p. 442.

7. DDE, *The White House Years: Waging Peace, 1956–1961* (Garden City, N.Y.: Doubleday and Co., 1965), p. 261.

8. Speech Outline, April 13, 1954, ACW Files, DDE Diary, "April 1954."

9. DDE, *Mandate for Change*, p. 100.

10. DDE, *At Ease: Stories I Tell to Friends* (Garden City, N.Y.: Doubleday and Co., 1967), p. 349 and p. 79.

11. DDE, Handwritten list of quotations by acquaintances, ACW Name File, DDE Personal (2).

12. Diary Entry, July 31, 1953, DDE, *Mandate for Change*, p. 203.

13. DDE, *At Ease*, p. 52. This "Halloween Incident" is also discussed in Stephen Ambrose, *Ike: Abilene to Berlin* (New York: Harper and Row, 1973), pp. 18–19.

14. DDE, *At Ease*, p. 32.

15. George S. Patton, quoted in DDE, list of quotations, ACW name file, DDE Personal (2).

16. Conversation between DDE and Senator Styles Bridges, May 21, 1957, p. 7, ACW Diary, "May 1957(1)." For another example of selflessness, see DDE, *Mandate for Change*, p. 313.

17. Diary entry, May 2, 1955, ACW Diary, "May 1955(7)."

18. DDE to General George C. Marshall, January 9, 1942, as quoted in Joseph P. Hobbs, ed., *Dear General* (Baltimore: Johns Hopkins University Press, 1971), p. 88.

19. DDE to Mamie Eisenhower, February 15, 1943, as quoted in John S. D. Eisenhower, ed., *Letters to Mamie* (Garden City, N.Y.: Doubleday and Co., 1977), p. 95. See also letters dated October 30, 1942, and October 31, 1942, pp. 51 and 53.

20. Kay Summersby Morgan, *Past Forgetting* (New York: Simon and Schuster, 1976), p. 137.

21. DDE to Hazlett, October 20, 1943, ACW Name File, "Capt. Swede Hazlett 1941–49(1)." The correspondence between DDE and Hazlett is the most revealing of all DDE correspondence.

22. DDE to General A. F. Lorenzen, Rtd., September 9, 1953, ACW Files, DDE Diary, "August-September 1953." See also diary entry July 2, 1953, ACW Files, DDE Diaries, 1935 et al., "December 52-August 19, 1953 (2)."

23. DDE to Hazlett, Julyu 19, 1947, ACW Name Files, "Capt. Swede Hazlett, 1941–49(4)." See also DDE to Hazlett, June 4, 1955, p. 3, "Hazlett, Swede, 1951(1), and Notes dictated by DDE to be included in Future Farmers speech, October 6, 1953, ACW Files, DDE Diary, "October 1953(2)."

24. DDE to Chynoweth, July 20, 1954, p. 3. For an example of this in regard to agricultural policy, see "Notes taken during President's conversation with Governor Adams," October 12, 1955, ACW Diary, "October 1955(6)."

25. Ann C. Whitman to Rosemary Chwatal, November 3, 1956, PPF 1-A–18. In this letter, Whitman writes that Eisenhower frequently used this quote which "contains the essence of his philosophy of government."

26. DDE, *Mandate for Change*, p. 212 and Diary entry, July 14, 1955, p. 4, ACW Diary, "July 1955(3)." See also DDE to Hazlett, February 26, 1958, p. 2–3, ACW Name File, "Hazlett, Swede, January 1956-November 1958 (3)"; Conversation with Merriman Smith, November 23, 1954, p. 1, ACW Diary, "November 1954(2)," DDE to Paul Hoffman, June 23, 1958, p. 8, ACW Administrative File, "Hoffman, Paul (1)," DDE to Joel Carlson, April 5, 1956, p. 1, ACW Files, DDE Diary, "April 56, Misc. (3)" and DDE, *Mandate for Change*, p. 14.

27. Diary Entry, January 18, 1954, p. 2, ACW Files, DDE Diary, "Personal diary January-November 1954."

28. For his beliefs on partisan politics as Commander of SHAPE, see DDE to Hazlett, November 14, 1951, p. 5.

29. DDE to Thomas Dewey, October 8, 1954, p. 1, ACW Files, DDE Diary, "October 1954."

30. Memorandum of Appointment, September, 2, 1955, ACW Diary, "September 1955 (6)."

31. Diary entry, January 5, 1953, as quoted in DDE, *Mandate for Change*, p. 98.

32. Diary entry, July 2, 1953, p. 6. See also Memorandum of appointment DDE-Larmon, et al., September 2, 1955, p. 3, DDE to Nixon, September 3, 1957, p. 2, ACW Files, DDE Diary "September 57-DDE Dict." and Diary entry, January 22, 1952, p. 1, ACW Files, DDE Diaries 1935 et al., "1/1/50–2/28/52(3)."

33. DDE, handwritten notes, February 7, 1954.

34. I. Jack Martin to Ann C. Whitman, November 5, 1953, ACW Diary, "November-December 1953(4)."

35. I. Jack Martin to Ann C. Whitman, June 13, 1955, ACW Diary, "June 1955(4)."

36. DDE to General A. M. Gruenther, February 1, 1955, ACW Files, DDE Diary, "February 1955."

37. DDE to the Attorney General, November 4, 1953, p. 1, ACW Files, DDE Diary, "November 1953."

38. DDE to Mrs. Marie Green, June 14, 1954, ibid., "June 1954."

39. DDE to William S. Paley, January 16, 1956, p. 1, ibid., "January 56 Misc. (2)."

40. DDE to L. W. Douglas, March 29, 1955, pp. 2–3, ibid., "March 1955."

41. DDE to Winston Churchill, March 29, 1955, p. 5, ibid. See also DDE to Gruenther, February 1, 1955, p. 3 and DDE to Churchill, April 4, 1954, as quoted in DDE, *Mandate for Change*, p. 347.

42. DDE to Churchill, March 29, 1955, p. 5, and DDE to Churchill, February 19, 1955, as quoted in DDE, *Mandate for Change*, p. 473.

43. Diary entry, January 6, 1953, ACW Files, DDE Diaries 1935 et al., "12/52–8/19/53(2)."

44. See DDE to Paul Hoffman, June 23, 1958, pp. 1 and 3 and DDE to Gruenther, November 30, 1954, ACW Files, DDE Diary "November 1954," for examples of this belief.

45. For examples involving Nehru and India, see DDE to Malcolm Muir, May 25, 1955, ACW Diary, "May 1955(2)" and DDE, *Waging Peace*, p. 114.

46. Diary entry, January 6, 1953.

47. DDE to Hazlett, June 21, 1951, p. 2, ACW Name File, "Capt. Swede Hazlett 1951(2)."

48. DDE to Hazlett, April 27, 1954, p. 2, ibid., "1954(2)."

49. DDE to Gruenther, June 8, 1954, ACW File, DDE Diary, "June 1954."

50. DDE to Paul Hoffman, June 23, 1958, pp. 4–5.

51. DDE to Gruenther, April 26, 1954, p. 1, ACW Files, DDE Diary, "Personal Diary January-November 1954." This excerpt is also quoted in DDE, *Mandate for Change*, p. 352.

52. DDE to Hazlett, October 23, 1954, ACW Name File, "Hazlett, Swede 1954(1)."

53. See DDE, *Mandate for Change*, p. 373–74, for the best post hoc analysis of why he decided to intervene.

54. Richard Immerman, "The Anatomy of the Decision Not to Fight: Multiple Advocacy or Presidential Choice," Paper delivered at Presidency Research Panel, American Political Science Association Meeting, Denver, 1982.

55. DDE to Dulles, December 12, 1956, p. 1, ACW Files, DDE Diary, "December 56 Misc."

56. Meeting with congressional leaders, January 1, 1957, p. 3, ibid., "January 57 Misc. (3)."

57. Memorandum of Conference, DDE-Hoover, October 8, 1956, p. 2, ibid., "October 56 Diary-Staff Memos."

58. Memorandum of Conference, DDE-Dulles-Coulson, October 19, 1956, pp. 1–2, ibid.

59. Ibid., p. 4.

60. DDE-Allen Dulles et al., November 6, 1956, ibid., "November 56 Diary-Staff notes."

61. Memorandum of Conversation, February 6, 1957, pp. 1–2, International Series, "Lebanon (3)."

62. Ibid., p. 2.

63. Ibid.

64. Summary of Phone Call, DDE-Dulles, February 6, 1957, p. 4, ACW Files, DDE Diary, "February 1957 Phone Calls."

65. DDE to Paul Hoffman, June 2, 1958, ACW Administrative Files, "Hoffman, Paul (1)."

66. Memorandum of Conference with the President, July 15, 1958, p. 1 and 4, ACW Files, DDE Diary, "Staff Memos-July 1958(2)."

67. Memorandum of Conference with the President, July 15, 1958, p. 1, ibid.

68. Memorandum of Conference, July 14, 1958, p. 3.

69. Memorandum of Conference, July 15, 1958, p. 1.

70. DDE, *Waging Peace*, p. 174–75. See also DDE to Dr. Edward Elson, July 31, 1958, p. 5, ibid., "DDE Dict. July 1958."

13

Eisenhower as Commander in Chief

James D. Weaver

I am Commander in Chief of the armed services as well as President, and there is no important question involving military policy in which I am not involved, in which I do not intervene; of course, I must.
—Press Conference, May 23, 1956

An analysis of the Eisenhower style as Commander in Chief requires a few introductory comments on the post-World War II presidency. The Constitution designates the President as supreme civilian commander of the armed forces, and, therefore, he possesses the constitutional authority and political responsibility to manage and direct—to command and control—the defense forces of the nation. Since World War II in particular, the modern Commanders in Chief have upheld civilian control through the development of command and control "systems" or "machinery" required for effective presidential direction of military and other national security forces. Thus, modern Commanders in Chief have utilized and expanded their constitutional authority to develop new policymaking dimensions—as in the emergence of war powers, crisis emergency powers, or "national security" powers.

In addition, more presidential "war powers" normally are invoked within one or several categories or conditions in national policymaking: declared wars, undeclared wars, power projections/force deployments ("war measures"), diplomacy (treaties and agreements), and national security affairs (domestic or international). The President's exercise of his defense, war, and emergency powers within these circumstances, whether at home or abroad, therefore dramatizes the Commander in Chief's presumed constitutional and political prerogatives to invoke "emergency powers" and, when necessary, to take extraordinary military or paramilitary measures to safeguard the national security. As "keeper of the sword," the modern Commander in Chief legitimately commands and controls U.S. armed forces as well as all other national security forces through war and emergency policy planning and operations. On matters of war-making, therefore, the President, as Commander in Chief, can engage in a variety of policy actions based on "national security" while he may prepare for, initiate, conduct, or terminate wars.

WAR POWERS: POLICIES AND STRATEGIES

This description of presidential power in defense and national security affairs accurately portrays a fundamental post-World War II national policy condition in the United States. Once labeled by E. R. Corwin the "forgotton clause" in the Constitution, the power of the Commander in Chief has acquired, since 1945, significant unprecedented dimensions for the modern presidency. As the second postwar Chief Executive, President Dwight D. Eisenhower well understood the impact of past presidential actions and other legal, political, and strategic factors on the evolution of the powers of the Commander in Chief. Eisenhower recognized the importance of expanded presidential power in post–1945 defense and national security affairs; as he stated in a press conference: "The President, by the Constitution, is the Commander in Chief, and what he decides to do in these things, in the forms—in the form and the way that you arm and organize and command your forces—must be carried out."[1]

No aspect of the Commander in Chief's power is more well known or controversial than the President's exercise of his military and emergency powers—clustered as "war powers." The Eisenhower presidency was involved primarily in the three previously cited classifications of "power projections/force deployments," "diplomacy," and "national security affairs." There were no declared wars in which the United States was involved, nor were there any protracted undeclared wars to which Eisenhower committed U.S. armed forces. In addition, he had always maintained that only Congress held the constitutional prerogative to authorize war: "I will never be guilty of any kind of action that can be interpreted as war until the Congress, which has the constitutional authority, says so."[2] The Eisenhower administration claimed, moreover, that the size and mission of U.S. armed forces was proscribed during the 1958 Lebanon invasion and the 1955 commitment to defend Formosa and the Pescadores. These two examples of power projections/force deployments, therefore, did *not* evolve into protracted presidential wars, even though Marines in Lebanon exceeded short-of-war parameters and engaged in short-term, "qualified hostilities."

As Commander in Chief, then, Eisenhower presided over the formulation and execution of military and security doctrines and strategies that were directly concerned with the readiness and use of armed forces in diplomatic and national security affairs. His administration was committed to the fundamental policy assumption and objective to avoid direct U.S. involvement in declared or undeclared wars. Several of these policy achievements deserve brief attention.

Under the "power projections/force deployments" category, for example, Eisenhower's position, that he recognized congressional war powers, must also be measured by his commitment to uphold presidential war powers—particularly to deploy military and other security forces. As Sherman Adams explained the administration's request for congressional support in the 1955 Formosa Resolution, "Eisenhower did not want Congress to assume that he was signing over to the legislators the constitutional right of the President to use Armed Forces on his own responsibility."[3]

Power projections in Asia, Central America, Europe, and the Middle East, whether conventional military or paramilitary activities or nuclear threats, were viewed as proper and necessary exercises of executive prerogatives to protect U.S. interests in defense and foreign affairs. The deployment of U.S. paratroopers into Little Rock, Arkansas, to enforce the desegregation decision, was a similar illustration of the Commander in Chief's military powers—at home in this instance—invoked to "faithfully execute the laws."

At the same time, the development of global defense and national security doctrines/strategies by Eisenhower and his "senior team"—namely, "New Look," "Massive Retaliation," and the construction of an extensive international collective security and basing alliance network unprecedented in U.S. diplomacy—set guidelines for a new defense posture and commitment in the conduct of U.S. foreign relations. According to R.G. Hoxie, Dulles' global alliance complex was formidable: "Between NATO, SEATO, CENTO and bilateral arrangements, including those with Formosa and South Korea, the Soviet-Communist Chinese land mass had virtually been encircled by alliances."[4] Furthermore, the New Look policy initiated both organizational and conceptual changes in defense and national security policymaking: the 1953 and 1958 Department of Defense (DOD) reorganizations were designed to streamline, centralize, and strengthen the Office of Secretary of Defense (OSD) civilian control, and to include fiscal-budgetary considerations as priorities in national security decisions, and established a new commitment to modernize and utilize, if necessary, nuclear forces as a primary strategy in U.S. and Western self-defense. The New Look policy was thus coupled with the Massive Retaliation strategy, and Eisenhower and Dulles could practice their Containment and "brinkmanship" in foreign relations to shore up the Western alliance by threatening a nuclear response to communist aggression while significantly reducing military spending. Regarding nuclear weapons, it is quite clear that Eisenhower and his security advisers seriously considered and would have authorized the use of nuclear weapons against an enemy's military forces if U.S. national interests warranted it (for example, against the North Koreans or the People's Republic of China if the Korean War continued or an armistice was breached, or against the Soviets if NATO forces were endangered). In fact, Eisenhower stated, "I see no reason why the [atomic weapons] shouldn't be used just exactly as you would use a bullet or anything else."[5]

To Eisenhower, then, the New Look was "simply an attempt by intelligent people to keep abreast of the times ('security with solvency')."[6] Massive Retaliation, as the military twin of New Look, illustrated the nuclear supremacy and capability of the United States as well as the cost-efficient benefits of this new strategic doctrine ("more bang for the buck"). Secretary Dulles sponsored Massive Retaliation as a critical link to his worldwide alliance network, and, in effect, it was pieced together by Eisenhower and the Chairman of the Joint Chiefs of Staff, Admiral Arthur Radford.[7] In short, the "team" of Eisenhower-Dulles-Wilson-Radford and Humphrey constructed a new and different national security program that claimed to coordinate, if not integrate, key military, foreign, and economic interests and policies in the form of a balanced, "grand strategy."

Finally, several other achievements in diplomacy and national security should be noted as significant supplements to Eisenhower's defense doctrines. His determination to end the Korean War and virtually to mandate a cease-fire among the British-French-Israeli forces in the 1956 Suez Crisis illustrated his competency as the allied leader to terminate hostilities and negotiate settlements (by coercion if necessary). The 1957 Eisenhower Doctrine and the 1955 Formosan Resolution signaled a diplomatic and security commitment to U.S. allies and global spheres of interests. Although Eisenhower did *not* propose a military commitment to South Vietnam, he did sign the Manila Pact which established SEATO, and he did propose the "domino theory" for Southeast Asia: "For the fall of Laos to Communism would mean the subsequent fall—like a tumbling row of dominoes—of its still free neighbors, Cambodia and South Vietnam, and in all probability Thailand and Burma."[8]

The 1953 Atoms for Peace and the 1955 Open Skies proposals were two significant diplomatic options which represented a step toward accommodation with the USSR since they proposed bilateral and multilateral pacts on arms control and the "peaceful" uses of scientific (nuclear) knowledge. In Eisenhower's words, "it was an opportunity to demonstrate to the world . . . the dedication of the United States to world peace and disarmament."[9]

All of these additional examples, then, reinforce the proposition that Eisenhower as Commander in Chief was very active and skillful in the exercise of his war powers in foreign affairs. The frequency and degree of success, of course, was measured by the effectiveness of the machinery created to invoke these prerogatives.

POLICY MACHINERY

President Eisenhower had already earned a reputation as the capable Supreme Allied Commander in Europe in World War II, in particular through his display of organizational and diplomatic skills in command decisions. As President and Commander in Chief, he set out to develop a dependable, elaborate, and routinized command structure for defense and national security affairs over which he, as President and Commander in Chief, would preside.[10] His approach to civilian command and control over the organization, preparedness, and utilization of defense and national security forces was to construct a "Civilian High Command" based on (1) his personal supervision and intervention, when necessary, as Commander in Chief, and (2) a policy process "fully staffed out" which institutionalized overall defense and national security policymaking.

Figure 13.1 diagrams Eisenhower's command and control machinery over defense and national security forces. This attempt to integrate both personal and staff-departmental approaches, therefore, represented Eisenhower's perceptions and basic objectives regarding the management of policy planning and operations in civil-military affairs.[11] Relations with and two reorganizations of the DOD in 1953 and 1958, and the development of a "National Security Council (NSC) system" meant that the Commander in Chief could rely on two distinct, yet interrelated, policy structures and lines of command subject to presidential authority and jurisdiction. Thus, a "unity of command" could be ensured—originating with the President as Commander in Chief through the DOD and as chairman of the NSC through the key national security departments and agencies.

Eisenhower's interpretation and application of presidential authority and obligations, as Chief Executive and Commander in Chief, may be described as follows:

1. To develop the presidency as a "modified stewardship."[12] This would emphasize the "Administrator-Coordinator" role of the office, maintain Eisenhower's personal command, and remain compatible with his accustomed staff concept of administration; and be accompanied by a "team spirit" instilled in Eisenhower's immediate executive subordinates delegated to oversee national security policy (a "Civilian High Command" with ample authority and "fully staffed out").

2. To restore a high priority to fiscal-budgetary needs and considerations as essential guidelines and components in national security decision-making.[13] (Treasury Secretary George Humphrey was a regular participant at NCS meetings.)

3. To reorganize the DOD toward more centralized and integrated, if not unified, civilian command and control in the OSD over all planning and operations. In addition, to strengthen the chairman of the CJCS and designate the JCS as the Secretary's military staff over the operational commands.

4. To complete a major institutionalization and codification of national security machinery—superintended by a White House-NSC System. Since the 1947 National Security Act, dispersed control over national security policy through various layers of civilian policymakers in national security affairs had formed numerous and overlapping centers of power in need of coordination.

These four features of Eisenhower as President and as Commander in Chief restructured and realigned civilian command and control. A coordinated "Civilian High Command" through OSD and an NSC System was made directly responsible to Eisenhower as Commander in Chief. Concurrently, a complementary command relationship was reinforced between the Commander in Chief and

Figure 13.1 The Eisenhower Command and Control Machinery*

I.   COMMANDER IN CHIEF
II. DEPARTMENT OF DEFENSE: CIVILIAN
III. DEPARTMENT OF DEFENSE: MILITARY
IV. OTHER NATIONAL SECURITY ORGANS

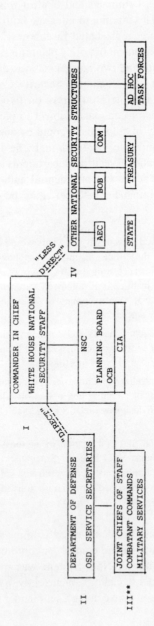

* (1) The Commander in Chief's command over defense and security forces is transformed into his authority and jurisdiction over the areas of organization (composition and shape), development (level of preparedness) and utilization (crisis decision-making, force commitments and weapons control) over these forces. "Planning and operations", therefore, are regarded as related, separate - but - equal functions in each area.

  (2) Each of these areas favors or excludes certain civilian command and control structures, but, in some instances, an overlap of command and control structures may occur (for example, the BOB plays a small role in "utilization" but a large role in "organization" and "development", or the CIA has little interest in "organization" but major interests in "development" and "utilization").

** Since the 1958 Reorganization two distinct military structures emerged:

  (1) The 8 Combatant Commands (Unified and Specified) functioning as the operational forces under the direct command and control of the Secretary of Defense and/or the Commander in Chief (via the Joint Chiefs of Staff).

  (2) The three services functioning as the "provide and support" structures to the Combatant Commands (to administer the organizing, training, logistics and supplies for the Combatant Commands).

his senior military advisers/planners (CJCS and JCS). In this way, Eisenhower could direct and control the chief personnel (civilian and military alike) who administered national security policy and "what, when, where, and how" to organize, prepare, and utilize U.S. defense and other security forces. From Eisenhower's vantage point, the Commander in Chief's reliance on and access to civilian and military decision-makers was crucial:

Every Chief of Staff and every Secretary has been invited to come to my office . . . there is no one that is barred from seeing me;[14]

and,

A President needs this kind of organized advice (on national security affairs) far more than a war-time theatre commander . . . this was accomplished in the 1950's through the NSC and its supporting bodies.[15]

With regard to the "direct line" of command to DOD, in 1953 and 1958, the Eisenhower administration initiated two major renovations toward more centralized and unified civilian control. The 1947 National Security Act had established a confederation of the Services called the National Military Establishment directed by a Secretary of Defense (SecDef) who attempted to coordinate the Services designated as separate Executive Departments; and the 1949 Amendments increased the authority of the SecDef over a federative organization renamed the Department of Defense, and a Chairman of the Joint Chiefs was authorized. Eisenhower's New Look, however, prompted further changes in 1953 because it reevaluated and "streamlined" the defense establishment and proposed several new assumptions: (1) separate ground, sea, and air forces as combat commands were obsolete, (2) victory in nuclear war was impossible but a credible nuclear deterrent was indispensable, (3) conventional limited wars were undesirable and unnecessary costs to the United States and its "antimilitarist" tradition, and (4) Research and Development and production of weapons systems must be coordinated, simplified, and more efficiently managed ("get more security with less money"). The 1953 Plan did revise the organization of the DOD, increase the authority of civilian policymakers, and alter and modernize the roles and missions of the Services and the responsibilities of the JCS.

The 1958 reorganization was proposed to reaffirm and implement the 1953 goals and principles—to "finalize" DOD's centralized civilian authority and jurisdiction through OSD over all military planning and operations, and organization preparedness and utilization. The 1958 Reorganization Plan 1 sought to correct most of the deficiencies of the 1953 Plan. Eisenhower personally worked on the various drafts of the Plan before submission to Congress: "Between November 1957 and April 1958, I spent many hours working on details of reorganization plan."[16]

The major changes were as follows:

• A single chain of command from the Commander in Chief and/or SecDef through the

JCS to the combatant commands was established. (Commanders were given full operational command over forces.) The JCS would serve as the SecDef's military staff.

- Service Secretaries were removed from the chain of command and were charged to administer their Services in their "provide and support" functions to the operational commands.

- OSD increased its fiscal powers and jurisdiction: a Director of R&D was authorized; and the Defense Intelligence Agency, the Defense Advanced Research Projects Agency, and the Defense Communications Agency were all established to strengthen OSD control over intelligence, research, and communications.

Above all, the 1958 reorganization confirmed the command powers of the Commander in Chief and established the foundations for executive command authority that would be considerably enlarged by Eisenhower's successors. After the 1958 reorganization, strengthened civilian control was in effect (including command powers for the Secretary of Defense), operational commands were established; and the senior military leaders began to function as corporate-team advisers subordinate to the senior civilian leadership (Secretary of Defense Thomas Gates, for example, initiated the practice of attending the weekly JCS meetings), and the CJCS was strengthened and became a functional military "Deputy Commander in Chief." Eisenhower introduced a significantly "healthier balance" in civil-military relations than his immediate successors, however, because he did not encourage civilian "overcontrol" that would impair effective command and control. As Thomas Gates indicated, the 1953 and 1958 reorganizations did not increase the SecDef's authority because "it was always there." However, the reorganization made available for him and his deputies "information channels" that were formerly unstructured or displaced, and "they clarified the legal position of the Secretary versus the Congress."[17] In addition, a corporate JCS was formed and made loyal to the administration.[18]

Finally, the NSC System provided new policy machinery which executed the new responsibilities and power of the Commander in Chief (his new military and war powers—national security powers. It has been established that Eisenhower's style and method as Commander in Chief emphasized several decision-making principles and practices: his own surety of command as professional military expert in defense organization, the exercise of power projections and force deployments, a focus on direct and intimate White House DOD relations, a respect for the privileged autonomy of selective administration officials in national security affairs to whom Eisenhower delegated extraordinary policy authority, and a reliance on presidential *ad hoc* task forces "outside the system" to analyze and make recommendations on security issues. The NSC System under Eisenhower, however, represented an enlargement of the Commander in Chief's total command and control machinery since it was designated a "policy guidance" mechanism at the presidential level to shape a national Grand Strategy ("Basic National Security Policy"). The NSC itself *is* the Commander in Chief's advisory   council,   and   during   the   Eisenhower   years   was   appropriately called the "Super Cabinet" or "Supreme High Command" for national and international security affairs.

The national security components of the White House staff, namely, the Special Assistant for National Security Affairs and Staff Secretary to the President and the NSC Staff, collectively formed the President's highest policy level to determine national security interests and policies. The Special Assistant supervised the entire operation of the "system": set NSC agendas, chaired Planning Board meetings which selected policy papers for NSC decisions, presented papers, and led discussions of NSC meetings.[19] The Staff Secretary (General Andrew J. Goodpaster from 1954 to 1961) coordinated the paper work to and from Eisenhower, served as a "principal military assistant" or "sergeant-major" to the Commander in Chief, and monitored and reported on daily security operations (NSC-approved programs). The Staff Secretary and Special Assistant, therefore, directed two separate but related White House-centered staff channels within the national security machinery; both Executive Assistants effectively coordinated and complemented their work.[20] Essentially, Goodpaster managed the flow of national security information and monitored security operations, and the Special Assistant focused on major security issues and developed policy recommendations on the Planning Board of NSC approval and Operations Control Board (OCB) followup.

In sum, the NSC System was one of Eisenhower's most formally organized command and control instruments and channels. As a semi-White House-centered system, it should have routinely provided the Commander in Chief with consistently complete and analyzed policy proposals, and reliable, superior policy performance. The Council itself met 366 times between 1953 and 1961, and Eisenhower clearly intended to develop it (through the Special Assistants) as another permanent corporate advisory body serving the Commander in Chief on national security affairs. It correlated and often integrated defense, economic, and diplomatic interests, and even incorporated psychological and internal security matters in policy developments. Finally, Eisenhower's Special Assistants never presumed or exhibited the amount of policy authority or jurisdiction that their successors accumulated in later administrations. (Gordon Gray remarked on Henry Kissinger, for example, that "Eisenhower never would have sent me to China").[21] The Special Assistant functioned as the senior staff officer to the Commander in Chief for national security affairs, and was not expected to exceed his coordinator-staff role as an individual policymaker.

In conclusion, Eisenhower was the first post-World War II President to institutionalize supreme civilian control over the organization, preparedness, and utilization of defense and other security forces. It is ironic and distinctive, of course, that a professional soldier was the individual motivated and delegated to expose the necessity, desirability, and capabilities of executive command and control. President Eisenhower invoked and extended the 1947 National Security Act beyond its original ambitions and initiated an innovative, comprehensive civilian command and control system. His strategy to institutionalize operative civilian control by the subordination and incorporation of the "military factor" in national security affairs through two major defense reorganizations and the formation of a White House-directed policy network for security affairs was unique and formidable.

As Commander in Chief, Eisenhower recognized that he possessed authority and powers to manage and direct military and other defense forces, that the modern Commander in Chief may exercise "constitutional dictator" powers in the interests of national security, and that "providing for the common defense" means more than provisions for armed forces and requires the construction of broad command and control machinery to consider and assess *all* major security interests. The exercise of this presidential power—as Commander in Chief—indicates that the "proper balance" in discerning and governing the course of national security was finally realized in the Eisenhower presidency.

NOTES

1. Press Conference, May 23, 1956. Eisenhower's personal intervention in military decisions is confirmed, for example, by Sherman Adams' biography *Firsthand Report, The Story of the Eisenhower Administration* (New York: Harper and Bros., 1961), and by an interview with former Secretary of Defense, Thomas S. Gates, Jr. (June 1971).

2. Press Conference, April 4, 1956. Similar remarks were made at other press conferences: March 10, 1954, April 29, 1954, September 11, 1956, August 12, 1959. The credibility of "massive retaliation," therefore, was in doubt since that doctrine would be diluted if a congressional authorization of war must precede the President's conduct of war and/or taking war measures.

3. Adams, *Firsthand Report*, pp. 120–30.

4. R. G. Hoxie, "Eisenhower and Presidential Leadership," *Presidential Studies Quarterly* 13, no. 4, (Fall 1983): 600.

5. Press Conference, March 16, 1955. Numerous other references to the utilization of nuclear weapons can be cited. In his article, "Eisenhower and Presidential Leadership" (p. 595), R. G. Hoxie comments on Eisenhower's meeting with General Douglas Mac-Arthur at Columbia University: "whatever the two old soldiers talked about, it comprised of unleashing nuclear weapons." Bernard Gwertzman (*New York Times* article, July 13, 1983) states that Secretary Dulles' Memoranda record Eisenhower's commitment to use nuclear weapons in the defense of Europe and against North Korea if the armistice was breached: "we would expect to strike back with atomic weapons" (Eisenhower to Churchill in Bermuda, December 4, 1953). See also, Eisenhower's letter to General Lemnitzer (January 2, 1961) in *The White House Years: Waging Peace, 1956–1961* (Garden City, N.Y.: Doubleday, 1965), p. 611.

6. Eisenhower quoted in *Washington Post and Times Herald*, March 20, 1954.

7. See Walter Millis, Harvey Mansfield, and Harold Stein, *Arms and the State: Civil-Military Elements in National Policy* (New York: 20th Century Fund, 1958), pp. 397–98. In an interview with General Maxwell Taylor (June 1971), Taylor indicated that Dulles had served as spokesman for the concept of "massive retaliation," and Eisenhower and Radford "worked it out." Keith Clark and Laurence Legere point out the close relations between Eisenhower and Radford (*The President and the Management of*

National Security [New York: Praeger, 1969], p. 206). Regarding Dulles, Gordon Gray has stated that Eisenhower and Dulles were "substantially as attuned to the same objectives and the way to reach them. . . . He [Dulles] never took a position without knowing what the President's view was" (Gordon Gray, *Oral History Statement*, Columbia University Collection). In an interview with Admiral Radford, he indicated that "massive retaliation" was not a new concept anyway, and preferred to call it "maximum deterrence."

8. Eisenhower, *Waging Peace*, p. 607.

9. Eisenhower, *The White House Years: Mandate for Change*, 1953–1956, (Garden City, N.Y.: Doubleday, 1963), p. 630.

10. As Keith Clark and Laurence Legere have noted, "Eisenhower was almost unavoidably his own Secretary of Defense." See *The President and the Management of National Security*, p. 175. Most of the biographies, memoirs, congressional hearings, and interviews conducted with key executives in the Eisenhower administration overwhelmingly confirm the view that Eisenhower was a very self-confident, self-assured, and activist Commander in Chief—a man to whom command decisions were inbred. His command stature is perhaps verified in his trust and dependency on civilian and military subordinates.

11. Several government and nongovernment studies proposed major reorganizations in defense and national security planning and operations, and founded, directly or indirectly, the 1953 and 1958 Reorganization Plans for DOD. For example, the Rockefeller Committee (1953), Second Hoover Commission (1955) Task Force on the Defense Department ("Hook Committee"), Gaither Report (1957), Advisory Committee on Government Operations (1953), "Coolidge Committee" (1957 advisory committee to Secretary of Defense McElroy), "Kissinger Committee" (1958 Rockefeller Brothers Fund project on military aspects of security, chaired by Henry Kissinger).

12. A term used by Arthur Krock in an interview (June 1971). See the recent article by R. G. Hoxie on Eisenhower's leadership qualities which emphasizes his command abilities (Hoxie, "Eisenhower and Presidential Leadership").

13. See the 1953 State of the Union Message. Fiscal priorities were also determined by the Bureau of the Budget and the Comptroller in DOD.

14. Press Conference, May 23, 1956.

15. Eisenhower, in his article "The Central Role of the President in the Conduct of Security Affairs," in A. A. Jordan, *Issues of National Security in the 1970's* (New York: Praeger 1967), p. 211.

16. Eisenhower, *Waging Peace*, p. 240. See also Emmet J. Hughes, *The Ordeal of Power: A Political Memoir of the Eisenhower Years* (New York: Atheneum, 1963), pp. 260–61. General Andrew Goodpaster has confirmed that "I had occasion to work with him (Eisenhower) at length on this project (1958 Plan) together with Bruce Harlow" (Letter to James Weaver, November 3, 1971). In addition, in a press conference on April 9, 1958, Eisenhower remarked: "I don't care just who is against this thing (1958 reorganization). It just happens I have got a little bit more experience in military organization and the direction of unified forces than anyone else on the active list."

17. Interview with Thomas S. Gates, Jr. (June 1971).

18. In a press conference held March 30, 1955, Eisenhower remarked on the opinions of the JCS: "He cannot utter them properly, in my opinion, if he is going to create difficulty for his Administration, his Commander in Chief . . . then he doesn't belong as a member of the team."

19. There were four Special Assistants under Eisenhower: Robert Cutler (1953-April

1955 and January 1957-July 1958); Dillon Anderson (April 1955-September 1956); William Jackson (September 1956-January 1957); and Gordon Gray (July 1958–1961).

20. For example, General Goodpaster has stated that "Gordon Gray and I worked very intimately" on coordinating operations with policy making (Letter to James Weaver, November 3, 1971). Gordon Gray confirmed that his relationship with Goodpaster "was a happy one and never in disagreement" (Interview, September 1971).

21. Interview with Gordon Gray (September 1971).

14

Eisenhower's New Look Reexamined: The View from Three Decades

Duane Windsor

In the protracted conflict of Cold War with the Soviet Union, national security policy is necessarily a fundamental dimension of every presidency. A major hallmark of the Eisenhower years was the relative emphasis on foreign and defense policy, as distinct from civilian expenditure programs—an emphasis to which we have apparently returned full circle in the Reagan administration. It is now three decades since the formulation of the Eisenhower administration's "New Look" at American defense policy in 1953. Since 1961, we have proceeded more than two decades into Soviet-American conflict under both Democratic (Kennedy, Johnson, Carter) and Republican (Nixon, Ford, Reagan) administrations. There may well be basic lessons and principles, or at least fundamental and continuing issues, of defense policy to be gleaned even at this date from comparing the 1953 New Look's formulation and implementation to the United States' subsequent defense policy.

This study is based on the premise that the role and impact of the New Look still have not been fully appreciated by historians or defense specialists. Because the New Look was widely criticized at the time and then replaced by the flexible response strategy of the Kennedy-Johnson administrations, the prevailing view has been that the New Look was a strategic failure. It was followed by a massive buildup of both American nuclear weapons and conventional forces—a reversal of the New Look posture. It is argued here that, contrary to this conventional wisdom, the New Look created the strategic weapons and organizational foundations for its successor flexible response and set the basic pattern of U.S. Cold War policy. This conclusion is drawn from a wide-ranging reexamination of defense strategy, organization, management, budgeting, and politics as closely interrelated aspects of national security policy in the Eisenhower New Look.

The Eisenhower era has been underrated in the defense area because the New

Look has been narrowly defined and misidentified with a particular force structure—one heavy on nuclear retaliation doctrine, but limited in nuclear weapons
deployment and weak in conventional forces. This New Look force posture
should be separated from a wider conception of Cold War strategy which will be
termed the Eisenhower Doctrine here. That doctrine became a particular force
posture under specific fiscal, political, and Cold War conditions as interpreted by
the Eisenhower administration—a force structure altered by subsequent administrations. Critics of the New Look have tended not to distinguish force posture
from the Eisenhower Doctrine, largely because debate has focused on the specific
decisions of 1953 without tracing the subsequent evolution of Eisenhower's
defense policy.

ELEMENTS OF A REEXAMINATION

While this force structure and the accompanying reduction in defense spending
flowed from the New Look philosophy, force structure is always a temporary
solution for a specific set of circumstances. The New Look was partly a response
to an unbalanced force structure generated by the Korean War; it shifted defense
strategy from that posture (one committed to "perimeter defense") to one that set
the foundations for the Kennedy-Johnson era of large-scale nuclear weapons
deployment. The decision was made to focus on nuclear weapons in order to
develop American technological superiority while conventional forces were
viewed as an unnecessary financial drain. Concentration of effort was desired,
while a "long haul" expectation led to fiscal conservation. The later simultaneous
expansion of conventional forces was predicated on a change in willingness to
engage in ground wars—a change that helped lead to the Vietnam War.

Reexamined from this perspective, the New Look was much broader in conception and more decisive for Cold War strategy than pictured by the conventional
view—hence the use of the wider term "Eisenhower Doctrine" to explain that
conception. The Vietnam War jerked American defense policy back in the direction of the Eisenhower Doctrine's basic strategic tenets, although not necessarily
to the particular force structure of the New Look because specific circumstances
have evolved over three decades. Thus, the Eisenhower Doctrine is not so much
a discarded policy (its specific force structure, designed for certain assumptions
and circumstances, was discarded), as a template for the recurrent pull between
the principle of flexible response and potential overcommitment to ground war in
Korea, Vietnam, and possibly in the future in Central America. In this sense, the
Eisenhower Doctrine is still quite alive. Consider the following aspects of a
reexamination of the New Look over the years 1953–1961:

1. While Eisenhower was not the only professional military man to occupy the
White House in the postwar era (Jimmy Carter was a Naval Academy graduate),
he was by far the most highly qualified military professional to have become
President during the Cold War. Having served as Chief of Planning and Operations for the War Department (February-May 1942) and European Theatre Com-

mander (June 1942-May 1945) in World War II, as well as Army Chief of Staff (November 1945-May 1948), Chairman of the Joint Chiefs of Staff (February-August 1949), and NATO Supreme Commander (January 1951-June 1952) in the postwar period, General of the Army Eisenhower possessed unique credentials in the national security arena of the 1950s. These credentials gave him an unusual position vis-à-vis defense policy, the Joint Chiefs of Staff, and the Congress (which was controlled by Republicans in only two of the eight years of the Eisenhower administration). Eisenhower thus brought a personal prestige and popularity to national security affairs not likely to be duplicated in the future. Even so, his approach to, techniques for, and skill at the bureaucratic and legislative politics of defense should be a fertile field for study.

2. The long prevailing view of Eisenhower as a congenial and popular President who allowed powerful subordinates like John Foster Dulles and Sherman Adams to direct the executive branch while he played golf is being rapidly dispelled. As European Theatre Commander, Eisenhower had worked closely with Churchill, Roosevelt, and Marshall at one level, and with Montgomery and Patton at another. The general who took the gamble to invade Normandy under adverse weather conditions was unlikely to be a passive observer of his own presidency. But Eisenhower had learned to operate as an allied commander by indirection. The revisionist view of the Eisenhower presidency portrays an activist, policy-oriented leadership played out behind closed doors as a "hidden-hand presidency."[1] That revisionist view has been adopted in major works on Eisenhower's defense policy by John L. Gaddis, Arnold Kanter, Douglas Kinnard, and Lawrence J. Korb.[2] Kanter and Korb focus on a comparison of the Eisenhower and Robert McNamara methods for control of defense policy through domination of the budgetary process for resource allocation. It has been argued that whereas Eisenhower, with his military background, could successfully "politicize" the defense management process by simply overruling military recommendations based on his expertise, McNamara turned to analytical techniques (cost-effectiveness and program budgeting) as a partial substitute for such technical expertise. Kinnard states this revisionist interpretation as follows:

. . . contrary to the conventional picture of him as a passive president, Eisenhower was a skilled practitioner of bureaucratic politics who dominated and frequently manipulated a powerful set of political and military appointees. In managing the strategic policy and defense budget processes, he was personally involved and remarkably effective.[3]

3. The Eisenhower administration was the first administration to confront the basic issues of American military strategy for the Cold War. This is not meant to downplay the very important role of the Truman administration's NSC–68 and NSC–141 (National Security Council) plans, to which flexible response was only something of a return. But those recommendations were effectively derailed for NSC–68 and driven for NSC–141 by the conventional buildup necessitated by the Korean War. Soviet nuclear capability fundamentally altered Soviet-American

relations. NSC–68 and NSC–141 were more in the nature of planning exercises which highlighted the defense issues confronted in the New Look. Judgment of this question should not be carried out too finely, however. NSC–68 and NSC–141 were clearly first steps to the Eisenhower Doctrine. More critically, the New Look eventually embraced issues of organization, management, and politics—as well as strategy and budget—which NSC–68 and NSC–141 did not envision. The New Look of 1953 was thus not a return in any vital sense to the pre-Korean War defense policy of the Truman administration (although both policies were based on the strategy of containment and fiscal ceiling for defense spending adopted by the Truman administration in 1947–1949). On the contrary, whereas the 1950 NSC–68 plan—the policy statement literally overwhelmed by Korean War rearmament—aimed at a projected crisis year (1954 when the Soviet nuclear threat was expected to occur) and proposed a "crash buildup"[4] of American nuclear and conventional forces, the New Look focused on what was termed the "long haul" of protracted conflict. The New Look foresaw protracted conflict rather than a short period of crisis—a better description of the Cold War's subsequent history. At the same time, the New Look cut defense expenditures from the level recommended in the Truman administration's 1953 NSC–141 policy statement. More importantly it grappled with a new set of interrelated strategic, organizational, managerial, budgetary, and political issues generated by the Cold War.

In the evolution of the Cold War, we have continually had to confront new sets of such issues: the rapid evolution of weapons technology (MIRV, cruise missiles, smart weapons, stealth aircraft, and "Star Wars" devices to name a few) which may be accelerating; rapprochement between the United States and the People's Republic of China which fought directly in the Korean War and indirectly in the Vietnam War; the Middle East cauldron and its impact on international terrorism; the use of Cuban forces as Soviet surrogates in Africa; and communist penetration in Central America and the Caribbean. The New Look was the first cut at a comprehensive military and diplomatic strategy for conduct of the Cold War, which (as suggested in Eisenhower's "long haul" expectation) is still being waged at probably a hotter and more dangerous level of conflict after thirty years, despite détente and several rounds of arms control negotiations. We have now come full circle to another "new look" at military strategy by the Reagan administration, although that term has not been used. The United States stopped the SALT (Strategic Arms Limitation Talks) process; the substitute START (Strategic Arms Reduction Talks) and INF (Intermediate-range Nuclear Forces) processes have been halted by the Soviets over issues of fundamental moment. Since 1981, the Reagan administration has consistently recommended modernization, rearmament, and expansion of U.S. military forces, even at the cost of unprecedented budget deficits in the face of large tax cuts.

4. Because of Eisenhower's unique position as a military hero, his skills as a practical bureaucratic politician, and the circumstance that the Eisenhower Doctrine was the first comprehensive attempt at Cold War strategy, the New Look

tended in several dimensions to determine the foundations of present defense policy. Despite the continuing evolution of strategic doctrine and specific defense issues, the New Look established the basic tenets of post-Korean War defense strategy and military organization. Even the modifications subsequently made have occurred largely within the framework of the issues identified in the New Look decisions or in the flexible response options rejected despite NSC–68 and NSC–141. It is here that the least has been done to reexamine the origins and effects of the New Look. Much of what is today viewed as the basic framework of the United States' present defense policy developed from the New Look and its subsequent evolution during the Eisenhower administration: the strategic triad, continental air defense, emphasis on reserve forces and airlift/sealift capability, the NATO trip-wire and ladder of escalation strategy, civilian control of defense policy, the National Security Council machinery, and so on. It was the New Look which produced the Minuteman ICBM and the Polaris missile submarine. The flexible response policy of the Kennedy-Johnson years was a return to NSC–141 recommendations in some ways. But we may conclude that the Eisenhower Doctrine was not a deviation from, but rather the foundation of, Cold War strategy for the United States. The Vietnam War, détente, and the SALT experience—together with accelerating weapons technology evolution—have tended to obscure this reality.

THE NEW LOOK IN STRATEGY

In 1949, Soviet achievement of an operational atomic weapon altered the postwar strategic situation facing the United States as the Cold War began to unfold. The emergence of bipolar nuclear confrontation kicked off the search for a new national security policy (interrupted temporarily by the Korean War) that resulted in the New Look of 1953. In that year, the Soviets achieved hydrogen bomb capability. The original Truman strategy was based on the containment policy which was predicated in turn on a U.S. monopoly of nuclear weapons. This policy was implemented through the Truman Doctrine (1947) of economic and military assistance, the Marshall Plan for the reconstruction of Western Europe, the Berlin airlift (1948–1949), and the formation of NATO (1949).

NSC–68 was an overall review of foreign and defense policy adopted in 1950 just before the Korean War.[5] This policy statement envisioned a stronger U.S. military commitment to enforce the containment policy; it was swept aside by Korean War rearmament which placed a necessarily heavy emphasis on buildup of active conventional forces. The defense budget jumped from $15 to $40 billion. NSC–68 anticipated that 1954 would be a crisis year in which Soviet nuclear capability would emerge as a serious threat.

In 1952, NSC–141 was adopted for the guidance of post-Korean War strategy. This policy statement (supported by the State and Defense Departments, the Mutual Security Agency, and the Joint Chiefs of Staff) called for substantial defense budget increased *beyond* Korean War-level spending. Although the

Truman administration's goals included an air force of 143 wings for FY 1955, NSC–141 envisioned relatively balanced nuclear and conventional forces. The term "flexible response" had not yet been developed. NSC–141 was based on the premise of balanced forces for perimeter defense.[6] The necessary financial resources would be generated through sustained economic growth.

The hallmark of the New Look (a term introduced in December 1953 by Admiral Arthur Radford, Chairman of the Joint Chiefs of Staff) was that it reoriented defense strategy while reducing the defense budget. It thereby constituted a highly innovative approach to the problem of a clearly developing bipolar nuclear capability. It is all but certain, based on the studies by Kinnard and Korb, that this strategic conception was developed and implemented by Eisenhower himself. The Eisenhower Doctrine was considerably broader in scope than the conventional view of the New Look as a specific force posture.

The essence of the New Look was that it substituted firepower and airpower for manpower at both the strategic and tactical levels, and that it emphasized massive retaliation by nuclear weapons as a deterrent to both general and limited war. To achieve these objectives, the New Look attempted to create a central strategic reserve of highly mobile forces in which manpower requirements would be minimized by technology. The Eisenhower administration also argued that a sound economy, a balanced budget, and strategic stockpiling were important ingredients in long-term strategy through building potential for defense mobilization. Hence, strict controls on military spending were necessary.[7] The principal elements of the New Look were, in the author's view, more diverse than has been typically acknowledged:[8]

1. Soviet aggression anywhere in any guise would be met by selective (rather than flexible) response up to massive retaliation. The United States would create a nuclear umbrella for itself *and* its allies, particularly NATO, through a policy of nuclear deterrence; but it eschewed preventive war or preemptive strike options. The New Look's central thrust was, of course, the development of strategic nuclear retaliation capability *and* continental air defense. It is important to grasp the notion that massive retaliation and continental defense are two sides of the same coin. The New Look resulted in DEW and NORAD, as well as the Minuteman and Polaris missile systems and the B–47, B–52, and B–58 bomber systems. Much of the United States subsequent strategic weapons technology—both offensive and defensive—flowed from Eisenhower administration initiatives.

2. The Eisenhower Doctrine focused on the "long haul" of protracted conflict with the Soviets rather than rapid rearmament (a "crash buildup") for a particular crisis year (1954 as anticipated by the Truman administration). American defense expenditures would be paced out over time to avoid any unnecessary damage to the U.S. economy, which was regarded as the free world's "first line of defense." Economic strength should be safeguarded through reduced defense budgets, since the strategic problem was one of managing a long haul, rather than one of immediate crisis management. Budget reductions would insure "security with solvency." Eisenhower stated this philosophy in terms of what he called the "great equation" which incorporated

adequate defense, domestic requirements, and budget/tax reductions. The National Defense Education Act was passed following Sputnik; the National Defense (now the Interstate) Highway System was begun. This "great equation" is again at issue in the Reagan administration.

3. The United States would not become involved in conventional local wars like Korea (or Vietnam). Eisenhower was elected on the specific platform pledge of a negotiated settlement in the Korean War. The United States would rely on psychological warfare and covert action supported by the nuclear umbrella. This policy of nonintervention lasted until the lesson was bitterly relearned in Vietnam.[9]

4. The United States' principal allies would handle such local conflicts. Thus, primary emphasis could be placed on allied land forces around the Soviet periphery. The United States would supply the nuclear umbrella, reserve forces, and economic backbone of the free world. A worldwide system of mutual security alliances was created, modeled in principle, although not in substance, on NATO to which West Germany was admitted in 1954. These alliances included SEATO (1954), the Baghdad Pact (1955), and the Central Treaty Organization (1959). Bilateral treaties were signed with South Korea and Taiwan. Allies would be supported with economic and military assistance to operate under the U.S. nuclear umbrella. Flexible response teeters on the edge of substituting U.S. for allied manpower.

5. NATO land forces would serve a trip-wire function for the U.S. nuclear umbrella. Their goal was not to defend Western Europe with conventional weapons alone but to provide a convincing first step on the ladder of escalation to nuclear retaliation. As a result, the United States need not invest in conventional defense at the level necessitated by the Korean War. A peculiarity of that war was that U.S. technological superiority was not a decisive factor because of limitations on air and seapower, the relative inability to use armored forces in the mountainous terrain, and the decision not to employ nuclear weapons (lessons rediscovered in Vietnam). Chinese (and later Vietnamese) manpower was sufficient to just offset the U.S. effort resulting in strategic stalemate.

6. The United States *and* its NATO allies would, to the largest degree feasible, substitute science and technology (nuclear and nonnuclear) for manpower. This approach led, of course, to the still prevailing emphasis on tactical nuclear weapons for NATO defense. This philosophy was further reflected in the appointment of a Special Assistant for Science and Technology (1957) after Sputnik and the creation of NASA (1958). Smart conventional weapons are a continuation of this theme.

7. The U.S. conventional role would focus on air and sea control, rather than provision of large-scale ground forces. Air and sea control, supported by nuclear options, would emphasize technology rather than manpower.

8. Army policy would emphasize the buildup of mobile ready reserves rather than the maintenance of a large active force. In case of general war, these reserves would be mobilized and moved overseas by air and sea forces. Allied land forces on the periphery of the Soviet Union, supported by the nuclear deterrent, would hold the Russians until U.S. reserves could be deployed.

9. American defense policy, immediately after the Korean War and in light of these planning assumptions, would involve substantial force reductions as a basis for budget cuts. For example, the Air Force goal would be cut from Truman's recommended 143

wings for FY 1955 to 120 wings (subsequently revised upward to 137 wings), and the Army by three divisions to seventeen active divisions. A modest reduction in the Navy was anticipated.

10. Defense policy would involve major reallocations of resources among the basic military missions of strategic retaliation, continental air defense, sea control, reserves, and overseas conventional forces (focused on the immediate defense of NATO and South Korea). Annual spending for continental air defense was increased by more than $1 billion despite the overall budget cut.

11. It is not usually emphasized that a central tenet of the Eisenhower Doctrine emphasized arms control initiatives. Thus, President Eisenhower made his 1953 "Atoms for Peace" proposal (for a U.N. International Atomic Energy Agency) and invited the Soviet Union to negotiate a nuclear test ban treaty (a step concluded in 1963 by the Kennedy administration as the real starting point of détente and the subsequent SALT, START, and INF processes).

EVALUATING THE NEW LOOK

The basic planning assumption undergirding NSC 162/2 (adopted October 29, 1953) was the emphasis on deployment of nuclear weapons as the principal defense strategy for the United States. Coupled with the twin philosophies of economic mobilization and no ground intervention in local wars (beyond the use of air- and seapower), that assumption led to the other principles of the New Look surveyed above. In judging the sophistication of this New Look, it is important to remember three basic considerations: (1) the only use of nuclear weapons (against selected urban targets in Japan) had been convincingly devastating and had rapidly precipitated surrender by a military dictatorship prepared for last-ditch defense of the home islands; (2) the United States had a decisive lead in nuclear weapons over the Soviet Union, while tensions between the two countries had clearly eased following Stalin's death and the end of the Korean War; and (3) Eisenhower sincerely believed in the conservative fiscal policy embraced by his administration.[10]

The key element of the New Look was technology investment within a reduced defense budget. The strategic implications of the New Look were straightforward: (1) strategic deterrence *and* continental air defense, together with air and sea control, for selective response rather than fully balanced forces for perimeter defense; (2) development of economic mobilization capacity and sustainable military capability over the long haul; (3) selective nuclear response rather than conventional intervention; (4) emphasis on allied conventional military forces within the same balancing of economic and military factors; and (5) arms control efforts, given reduced tensions with the Soviet Union following the Korean War.

Evolution of the New Look

The history of this New Look strategy can be briefly summarized. In early 1953, the new Eisenhower administration quickly reduced Truman's proposed FY

1954 defense budget by about $6 billion from $41.2 to $35.8 billion, particularly cutting Air Force spending, on grounds of efficiency and economy through proposed management improvements. The final budget approved by Congress was $39.7 billion. The FY 1954 budget was not based on a New Look, but rather reflected the negotiated end of the Korean War interpreted through conservative fiscal lenses. Eisenhower saw no reason for massive military investment in peacetime. The New Look was born with the FY 1955 budget, in which the administration proposed a further reduction to $30.9 billion. It was at this stage that the Army's role in particular was reassessed. The final budget approved by Congress was $34.9 billion. Kinnard concludes that force reduction through strategic innovation was unavoidable in order to achieve lower defense spending.[11] The search for strategic innovation was thus driven by fiscal conservatism.

The "Operation Solarium" planning exercise (conducted by the Naval War College at the administration's request) took place in the summer of 1953. (Named for the White House solarium where the decision for conducting the exercise was made, the "operation" eventually set up four study groups which evaluated strategic options.) In July 1953, when Eisenhower met with the new Joint Chiefs of Staff, he emphasized that he wanted them to draw up a single defense policy paper defining post-Korean War strategy. The JCS agreed on such a paper but left their FY 1955 budget estimates at $42 billion (the FY 1954 level proposed by Truman). It has been recorded that the Treasury Secretary and the Budget Director were "horrified"; they had expected a major defense budget reduction.

NSC 162/2 was the result of this policy confrontation; its function was to justify a major budget reduction by stating a new basis for defense strategy. It appears that Admiral Radford, the JCS Chairman and a supporter of Eisenhower's position, proposed the New Look solution of primary reliance on nuclear weapons in an NSC meeting on October 13, 1953. Secretary of Defense Charles Wilson obtained qualified agreement on NSC–162/2 from Army Chief of Staff Matthew Ridgway and Chief of Naval Operations Robert B. Carney. The Air Force would, of course, be assigned the major role in the New Look. In a speech to the Council of Foreign Relations on January 12, 1954, Secretary of State Dulles enunciated the doctrine of massive retaliation (he did not actually use that term), largely as a means of justifying the FY 1955 defense budget.[12] In December 1954, NATO approved MC 48, which accepted the basic planning assumption of atomic weapons for the defense of Europe against a Soviet conventional attack.

The Eisenhower administration implemented the New Look in the FY 1955 through 1957 budgets as a smaller and less expensive force structure was created. The main outlines of this change in force structure can be seen in a comparison of the personnel and budget allocations by service for FY 1954 (essentially a modification of the Truman NSC–141 recommendations, although prepared by the Eisenhower administration) and FY 1955 (the actual first budget year of the Eisenhower New Look). Between October 1954 and January 1955, planned manpower fell from 3.48 to 2.84 million. The Army was cut 37.5 percent

(600,000 personnel) from 1.6 to one million, and the Navy and Marine Corps 13 percent (130,000 personnel) from 920,00 to 870,000. The Air Force was modestly increased from 960,000 to 970,000. Roughly corresponding to these personnel figures, the FY 1955 Army budget dropped 31.8 percent (from $15.6 to $16.4 billion) to accommodate the new SAC B–46 and B–52 jet fleet and continental air defense. The total defense budget fell from $39.7 to $34.9 billion (12.1 percent). The percentage allocation of personnel and budget among the services was rapidly shifted. The Navy remained roughly constant at 30 percent personnel and 28 percent budget. The reallocation was largely from the Army (dropping from 46 to 35.2 percent in personnel and from 32.5 to 25.2 percent in budget) to the Air Force (rising from 27.5 percent to 34.2 percent in personnel and from 39.3 to 47 percent in budget). These personnel and budget proportions then remained roughly constant during the Eisenhower era.[13]

During 1955–1960, the Eisenhower administration continued a buildup in nuclear strategic and continental air defense forces. The evolution of the New Look debate during that period focused on three major strategic issues. The first concerned continued nuclear superiority over the Soviets and the invulnerability of U.S. retaliatory forces to a Soviet first strike. The secret 1957 Gaither Report predicted a possible missile gap[14] (a prediction repeated in an unclassified version that surfaced as part of the 1958 Rockefeller Brothers Fund report on defense policy).[15] This report led to deployment of the Minuteman ICBM and Polaris submarine missile forces. Nevertheless, John Kennedy made the alleged missile gap a major campaign issue in 1960. For all practical purposes, the Kennedy administration continued this deployment program at a greatly upgraded level. Many more weapons were produced and deployed, but the ICBM systems were Eisenhower administration initiatives. The second and third issues concerned flexible response, a strategic doctrine subsequently adopted by the Kennedy administration. On the one hand, some argued the case for use of tactical nuclear weapons in Europe, creating what has come to be called the "ladder of escalation" in nuclear strategy.[16] On the other hand, both the armed services (the Army in particular) and the Congress called for a heavier emphasis on conventional forces. The basic argument was that sole reliance on a nuclear umbrella reduced U.S. flexibility to act. Revolutionary wars in particular seemed to fall below the threshold of nuclear retaliation. The United States did not intervene at Dienbienphu in the first Indochinese War because it would not bring itself to use conventional airpower, much less nuclear weapons. The Eisenhower administration strongly resisted this second aspect of the flexible response strategy because nuclear and conventional buildup could not be handled simultaneously within the fiscal ceiling imposed on defense spending by the New Look doctrine.

Strategic Issues of the Cold War

Morton Halperin classifies strategic options into arms control, general nuclear war, theatre nuclear war, local (conventional) war, and revolutionary war.[17]

Another category would be the emerging category of international terrorism, which theoretically can eventually expand from a conventional to a nuclear threat. Over the last three decades, the United States has developed a complex force structure for flexible response capabilities: strategic nuclear forces (the traditional term "strategic triad" is somewhat obsolete, given the obvious role of tactical aircraft and intermediate-range ballistic missiles stationed on the Soviet periphery); continental air defense forces; tactical nuclear forces of a wide variety; and various conventional forces (for global movement, theatre defense, and special warfare missions). The New Look focused on the general nuclear war option and a force structure built around strategic nuclear and continental air defense forces. It was subsequently extended to incorporate theatre nuclear war and tactical nuclear forces as an analogous technological solution. The role of weapons technology has steadily accelerated in the post-New Look era. Such technological evolution is occurring both in nuclear weapons at the strategic (MIRV, stealth) and tactical (Pershing II, cruise missiles) levels, and in conventional weapons down to terrorism (car bombs). Conventional armies are now heavily armed with extremely destructive automatic, antitank, antiaircraft, and increasingly "smart" weapons.[18]

Other developments over the last three decades can be summarized briefly. First, the Soviet Union (apparently propelled by the humiliation of the October 1962 Cuban missile crisis) has achieved at least strategic parity with the United States across the board. Second, it too has adopted a policy of flexible response through rapid expansion of its conventional theatre forces (on the NATO and Chinese frontiers) with heavy tank, artillery, antitank, antiaircraft, tactical air, and biological-chemical warfare equipment, in addition to massive manpower; large blue-water naval forces including marines, a limited aircraft carrier ship type, many submarines and ship-killing missile weapons; and large-scale airborne forces with increasing airlift capability. The Soviet Union may be involved in a strategy of consolidation of military and naval bases around its periphery. It is deeply involved in revolutionary wars ("wars of national liberation"), using the Cubans as modern-day mercenaries in Africa and Latin America. Strategic parity and the aggressive tone of Soviet behavior may have made arms control negotiations more difficult. It is patently clear that the Soviets are aiming the INF process at the political breakdown of NATO. Strategic doctrine has moved far beyond the New Look of 1953 in three decades. But the main elements of strategic evolution were laid down in the Eisenhower era. The subsequent fate of strategic doctrine has been propelled weapons technology, the Soviet buildup, and the spread of revolutionary conflicts around the globe.

THE NEW LOOK IN DEFENSE MANAGEMENT

Following the conclusion of the Korean War, the Eisenhower administration achieved considerable control over defense policy through use of a formal budget ceiling. Each service was also in effect assigned relatively fixed allocations.

During 1954–1961, the Air Force received about 47 percent, the Navy 29 percent, and the Army 24 percent of the defense budget.[19] Internal allocation of funds was generally left to the services. This approach was again adopted in the Nixon administration.

In evaluating the New Look, it has been widely ignored that the Eisenhower administration also fundamentally restructured the defense decision-making machinery. To a substantial degree, Eisenhower created the United States' present organizational structure for national security policy. He carried out two reorganizations of the Defense Department designed to increase the formal authority of the Secretary of Defense. The President believed strongly that civilian control of defense policy must be ensured. He viewed the Joint Chiefs of Staff not as a unified command system but as a committee still dependent on voluntary cooperation as in World War II. Whereas defense policy is essentially political in nature, the JCS is a military body composed of professional technicians protecting purely service interests.[20] The military department secretaries are inevitably civilian partisans of the same views. Only the Secretary of Defense can ensure both civilian control and a strategic perspective above service interests. To these ends, the Secretary required greater control over both policy formulation and operations.

In addition, a unified strategic planning system was necessary for protracted conflict in an increasingly technological world. World War II revealed the need for a unified military command in place of interservice rivalry; economies through consolidated administration and supply; and centralized control of military planning, intelligence, and operations. The war had been fought by unified (interservice) theatre commands under the informal JCS arrangement which operated on a unanimous consent principle. The problem of unification and coordination of the postwar national military establishment was exacerbated by the creation of the Air Force and the escalation of interservice competition for reduced missions and funds. Until the development of nuclear weapons, each service had a single primary mission. Rapid advances in military technology blurred traditional service lines; the Army role was particularly threatened by nuclear weaponry.

Both the Navy and War departments advanced different plans for postwar unification. In December 1945 (with Eisenhower serving as Army Chief of Staff), President Truman proposed a unified Department of National Defense with each military service to be placed under an Assistant Secretary of Defense along the lines of the Army scheme. The objectives as stated by President Truman were to unite ''strategy, program, and budget'' and to achieve economy through central supply and service functions. This administration approach was strongly opposed by the Navy and its congressional allies. The basic organizational issue was whether the new Department of National Defense should be a loose confederation of highly independent military services or a unified force of combined arms. The limited coordination plan advocated by Navy Secretary James Forrestal was in fact adopted over Truman's opposition. The Forrestal plan was less far-reaching than the War Department proposal for a department of defense and effected only a partial unification of the military services.[21]

The Truman Machinery

Based on the Forrestal coordination plan, the National Security Act of 1947[22] created three distinct levels of defense agencies.[23] Forrestal, the first Secretary of Defense, soon became convinced that his own scheme was unworkable. The period between World War II and the Korean War (June 1950) was one of severe budget retrenchment, marked largely by a long struggle between the Navy and the Air Force over air missions, and weapons, in the face of a rapidly deteriorating Cold War with the Soviet Union. The struggle over the strategic bombing role of proposed super carriers and B–36 bombers led to the so-called revolt of the admirals and a congressional inquiry into the B–36 program.[24] Before the Korean War, a chief of naval operations was dismissed and all three service secretaries had resigned. The 1948 report of the Task Force on National Security Organization of the First Hoover Commission adopted Forrestal's recommendations for a fundamental restructuring of the national military establishment into a true Department of Defense.

In 1949, President Truman proposed amendments to the National Security Act on this basis.[25] The 1947 act had failed to provide the Secretary of Defense with either a department or a staff; the 1949 amendments corrected this situation. An executive Department of Defense was created. The Army, Navy, and Air Force were downgraded to military departments responsible for training, supply, and administration; the service secretaries were removed from the Cabinet and the NSC. The military departments, however, were authorized to make recommendations to Congress and the President after informing the Secretary of Defense. The retitled JCS Chairman was made the primary military adviser to the Secretary of Defense. By law, the JCS were the military advisers for both Congress and the President; their Joint Staff was more than doubled. The Vice-President was named to the NSC, for whom the JCS Chairman and CIA Director served as advisers. The Office of the Secretary of Defense (OSD) was reorganized with a deputy and three assistant secretaries of defense. In addition, the previous limitation of the Secretary's powers to specified authority was eliminated; the term "general" was dropped from in front of "direction, authority, and control" of defense policy. However, the executive branch could not change the combat functions of the services, and Congress had to be informed of any other consolidations.

The 1949 amendments specifically sought to enhance the policy influence of the Secretary of Defense by giving him full authority over the budgetary process, exercised through the new position of the Defense Comptroller, ranking as an Assistant Secretary of Defense. Prior to 1949, the service budgets had been developed, not by the service secretaries, but by each of the bureaus or technical services within the military departments. The budget was now identified as the principal management tool of the Defense Secretary.[26] Title IV created comptrollers in each of the military departments, and specified uniform budgeting and financial procedures. The Defense Comptroller was now responsible for development of the defense budget.[27] Working capital and management funds were also authorized. The military comptrollers were responsible for budgets, accounts, and financial reports. In the Eisenhower era, a performance-budgeting approach was implemented, and a 1956 statute required cost-based budgeting and accrual accounting.

The 1953 Reorganization

The 1953 changes were implemented by executive order under general reorganization authority granted to the President by Congress (Reorganization Plan No. 6, June 30, 1953).[28] The reorganization plan was recommended by Rockefeller Committee report (issued April 1953) functioning as part of the Second Hoover Commission. The Munitions Board, Research and Development Board, and other staff agencies were abolished as unwieldy committee devices. The Secretary was authorized to have an additional six assistant secretaries (in order to exercise greater budget and administrative control), and to appoint a general counsel (ranking as an assistant secretary) as chief legal officer of the department (for a total of ten assistant secretaries). The service secretaries were instructed to act as "operating managers" and "principal advisers" of the Secretary, rather than as heads of "separately administered" departments. The Secretary was explicitly identified as part of the formal chain of command between President and JCS.

The JCS Chairman was given additional administrative responsibilities, including clearance of all Joint Staff appointments. Unified commands were channeled through the service secretaries rather than the service chiefs, who became responsible for military advice and planning. In principle, the service secretaries were restricted to policy execution rather than policy formulation. The assistant secretaries of defense became "staff executives" in charge of major functions. (A Director of Installations and a Defense Supply Management Agency had been created by statute in 1952.) The 1953 effort was nevertheless hampered by the limited scope of the President's reorganization authority. Moreover, Congress retained control over assignment of combat missions and the internal structure of the military departments. (In 1952, the Marine Corps was given a floor for authorized personnel strength, and its Commandant was placed on the JCS for matters affecting the Corps.)

The 1958 Reorganization

President Eisenhower subsequently submitted legislation to Congress which became the Defense Reorganization Act of 1958.[29] In November 1957, the President's (Rockefeller) Committee on Governmental Organization issued a report that reached roughly the same conclusion as an advisory group on organizational matters in the Defense Department chaired by Charles A. Coolidge. On April 3, 1958, Eisenhower sent a special message to Congress asking for statutory reorganization of the Defense Department. He requested that Congress: (1) repeal any statutory authority for conduct of military operations except through the Secretary of Defense; (2) allow the service chiefs to delegate their service responsibilities to the vice chiefs; (3) provide the Secretary of Defense with greater appropriations flexibility; and (4) eliminate separate administration of the military departments. He also advised Congress that he would directly create more emphasis on unified commands, give the Secretary greater budgetary authority, and eliminate the Joint Staff committee system. The objectives of this proposal package were to recognize and strengthen the Secretary's authority over policy formulation, budgeting, and military operations; focus the service chiefs on their JCS responsibilities; and provide the JCS Chairman with a vote. Congress was strongly opposed to either service unification or a general staff concept. A bipartisan group of centralization opponents drafted their own bill which would have put the service secretaries back on the NSC; limited assistant defense secretaries to four; held the OSD civilian staff to 600, or one-third of its then present size; and reduced the authority of the Defense Comptroller.

Under the compromise act finally passed, the Secretary of Defense was given direct control over assignment of functions and combat missions, subject to a sixty-day legislative veto by either house through simple resolution (the President was empowered to act in an emergency). However, he could not abolish, create, or merge bureaus and offices; the National Guard, Marine Corps, and naval aviation were specifically exempted from his assignment authority. A unified chain of command from the President through the Secretary of Defense to the JCS and military departments was codified. The President could establish unified or specified commands and assign forces under JCS control. He was given authority to assign common service and support activities. The JCS were authorized to operate a national military command post, while daily service operations could be delegated to the vice chiefs. The JCS were authorized to direct unified commands. Unified and specified commanders were given "full operational control" over assigned forces. The Joint Staff was again nearly doubled (from 210 to 400).

The JCS were specifically prohibited from functioning as a general staff with direct authority over field commanders or military departments. Service chiefs were authorized to define "major combatant function" and (with the service secretaries) could go directly to Congress. JCS Joint Staff service was limited to three years. The Joint Staff "shall not operate or be organized as an over-all Armed Forces General Staff and shall have no executive authority." A Directorate of Defense Research and Engineering was established to conduct weapons development. A Defense Communications Agency was created in the spring of 1960, followed by a Joint Strategic Target Agency. Nearly 200 of 300 Joint Staff committees were abolished, to be replaced by a unified staff system of seven directorates. President Eisenhower, though strongly opposed to a statutory National Guard and service access to Congress, signed the bill. His own proposal had already dropped the request for appropriations flexibility owing to congressional opposition on this sensitive point.

The Eisenhower Machinery

The 1953 and 1958 reorganizations strengthened the operational direction of the national military establishment by the Secretary of Defense. The military departments had been removed from the chain of command; restricted to training, supply, and administration functions; and explicitly instructed to act as "separately organized" but not "separately administered." The unified and specified commands reported to the Secretary of Defense through the JCS, although a general staff role was forbidden. The JCS served as principal military advisers by law to the President, Secretary of Defense, NSC, and Congress; provided a military operations staff for the Secretary of Defense; and conducted military planning and operations. These reforms implemented President Eisenhower's view that: "It is . . . mandatory that the initiative for . . . planning and direction rest not with the separate services but directly with the Secretary of Defense and his operational advisers, the Joint Chiefs of Staff, assisted by such staff organizations as they deem necessary."[30]

The reforms of the 1947–1961 period had established an OSD staff, a unified budgeting system for the Department of Defense, and the legal authority by which the Secretary of Defense could manage defense policy. A dual organization had been created in the Defense Department through OSD and the military services. Mission execution was assignable by the Secretary of Defense to unified and specified commands. The JCS were responsible for military strategy and force planning, the Defense Comptroller for budgeting and financial management, and the Director of Defense Research and Engineering for weapons development. The military departments functioned as support, not operational, agencies. In July 1970, a Blue Ribbon Defense Panel report recommended that the JCS be relieved of operational responsibility in order to focus on planning, that the Defense Department be reorganized a long functional (rather than service) lines, and that the major combat commands be restructured.

Nevertheless, major defects in the military planning system remained.[31] First, the legal authority of the Secretary of Defense to act was hampered by various restrictions and inadequate means. He still essentially functioned as a "referee" for the JCS and service secretaries. The national military establishment was still characterized by interservice rivalry, committee decision-making, and traditional service missions. By law, the military departments were "separately organized" and could not be merged; congressional approval of changes in statutory functions was required, except for new weapons and common supply or services; and the JCS and service secretaries were permitted direct access to Congress and the President. The Secretary still lacked OSD staff assistance for military requirements planning, which was conducted by the JCS Joint Staff.[32] Second, there was no coordinated military planning. The Basic National Security Policy (BNSP) developed by the NSC was so general as to be operationally meaningless; the Joint Strategic Objectives Plan (JSOP) developed by the JCS pursuant to the BNSP as a basis for force requirements was simply a compilation, not an integration, of separate service plans. The BNSP stated general military strategy and national objectives, formulated in light of the expected budget ceiling; the JSOP stated threat assessment and military force structure without regard to this ceiling. Third, as a result, military planning and defense budgeting were, for all practical purposes, completely separated at both the NSC and OSD levels. The specified and unified commands had only operational, not budgetary or planning, responsibility—budgeting was handled through the military departments. The JCS had planning and operational, but not budgetary, responsibility. Military planning occurred through the JSOP which more or less pasted together service plans approved by JCS unanimity.

Annual budgeting was conducted by the service secretaries and military comptrollers based largely on the fiscal ceiling and fixed service allocations imposed by the Eisenhower administration as the main techniques for implementing its New Look. Military planning was fiscally unrealistic. One effect was that the services competed for new weapons systems and were reluctant to fund new programs out of the existing allocation. Each service regarded the existing budget as a fixed entitlement; new weapons required additional funding. The Navy focused on missile submarines and aircraft carriers, the Air Force on long-range bombers and intercontinental missiles, and the Army on air defense. Conventional forces were neglected by all services. Considerable research and development duplication occurred. Budgeting on an annual basis, combined with service rivalry, led to underestimates of total costs for new weapons. The revolution in military technology made this problem increasingly important. Finally, there were no quantitative standards by which force adequacy could be determined. The JSOP depended more or less on military intuition rather than analysis.[33]

Critics of the pre-1961 planning system focused particularly on the budgeting and financial management tools as the best way to implement the Secretary of Defense's legal authority to direct defense policy. "The defense budget was far from the vital policy instrument it should have been. Rather than a mechanism for integrating strategy, forces, and costs, it was essentially a book-keeping device for dividing funds between Services and accounts and a blunt instrument for keeping a lid on defense spending."[34] The comptroller system created in 1949 provided unified financial management in the Department of Defense, but failed to handle interservice missions or full costing of weapons systems. The costs of both functions were scattered across traditional appropriation categories. Financial management was on an annual basis with no distinction drawn between investment and operating expenses. The Defense Department budget simply consolidated the three service budgets—established through negotiations among the military departments, Defense Comptroller, and the Bureau of the Budget. Target budget ceilings were the principal device for constraining military spending decisions. It is instructive to note, however, that these criticisms concern use of the civilian budgetary authority in defense. The McNamara revolution was built on budgetary authority developed, and recognized as vitally important, by the New Look.

THE McNAMARA REVOLUTION

Robert McNamara secured from President Kennedy a commitment that the Secretary of Defense would direct national security policy, which would not be subject (at least formally) to the "arbitrary" budget ceilings of the Truman-Eisenhower eras. The 1960 election campaign had featured an attack on the New Look. First, it was alleged that a serious "missile gap" existed between the United States and the Soviet Union. A major weapons expansion was undertaken, although McNamara's own postelection investigation disproved the gap. A second criticism was that the emphasis on massive retaliation had seriously limited the nation's military capabilities to deal with situations other than nuclear confrontation. The Kennedy administration adopted a new policy of flexible response, aimed at creating a wider range of options for dealing with conventional and counterinsurgency situations—while also substantially strengthening nuclear deterrence and continental air defense forces.[35]

These adjustments in the force structure of our military Services were carried out in accordance with the President's directive that military requirements should be considered without regard to arbitrary budget ceilings, but that major emphasis should be placed at the same time on operating the forces found to be essential at the lowest possible cost.[36]

Elements of the Revolution

The McNamara revolution occurred along three major dimensions. The first, already alluded to, was McNamara's philosophy of active leadership in defense policy by the Secretary of Defense. The Secretary was responsible for the review of all major budgetary and program proposals, with operational control of unified and specified commands exercised through the JCS, serving as military advisers to the Secretary. The second was the creation of a coherent defense strategy through an integrated system of military planning and coordination. The basic objective was to create unified longer range planning for a national military establishment that would produce an integrated defense plan rather than simply an aggregation of separate service plans. Flexible response was the essential thrust of this planning. Strategic nuclear forces were expanded to achieve both second-strike "assured destruction" and first-strike "damage limitation."[37] In 1961, McNamara proposed doubling the Polaris program from five to ten missile submarines per year, and acceleration of the longer range Polaris A–3 missile program. The land-based Minuteman missile program was also accelerated. "The most significant aspect of Defense policy in fiscal year 1962 was the emphasis given to the creation of a more flexible deterrent for the United States."[38] In addition to generating additional and more flexible retaliatory power, the McNamara strategy also aimed at a balanced and strengthened force structure. The Army was expanded from eleven to sixteen divisions, and was provided with more tactical air support, airlift, and counterinsurgency capabilities. The formation of Strike Command (STRICOM) was announced in September 1961 to combine Army units with air support and airlift for rapid deployment.

The third dimension involved a number of related management reforms. A civilian staff with analytical capability was created in OSD. Initially, this staff (the System Analysis Office, or SAO, under Alain C. Enthoven from the Rand Corporation) reported to the Defense Comptroller (Charles J. Hitch, formerly head of the Economics Department at Rand). In 1965, Hitch was succeeded by Robert N. Anthony, an accountant from the Harvard Business School. At that time, Enthoven was made the first Assistant Secretary of Defense for Systems Analysis. The OSD civilian staff in the comptroller and systems analysis areas was made the primary channel for policy control in the Department.[39] The comptroller reviewed budget proposals and the SAO program weapons proposals. A Five-Year Cost Reduction Program (fiscal years 1962–1967) was implemented in logistics management, with estimated savings of over $14 billion. Thereafter, the program was placed on an annual basis.[40] Revolving stock and industrial funds were expanded. A number of functions were centralized at the Defense Department level in the areas of procurement, supply, intelligence, and communications.[41] The military departments remained responsible for the training, supply, and administration of forces assigned to unified and specified commands.

The central thrust of the McNamara reforms was to have the Department of Defense operate as "the largest business in the world,"[42] with the military personnel serving as technical specialists rather than policymakers. The critical role of financial management tools in the McNamara revolution—centered on Planning-Programming-Budgeting Systems (PPBS), and systems (or cost-effectiveness) analysis was that "the new planning system allowed us to achieve a true unification of effort within the Department without having to undergo a drastic upheaval of the entire organizational structure."[43] The goal of PPBS in McNamara's strategy was to change program control from a service to a mission basis, so that the military services would compete for missions rather than weapons systems. PPBS placed military planning in longer range (multiyear costing) and output terms (missions, forces, and weapons systems), rather than in input (traditional appropriation) terms. The annual budget could then be treated as an increment within a longer range plan. The SAO put decision information together for OSD review of program proposals. Systems analysis aimed at a quantitative assessment of alternative proposals for mission achievement. The combination of PPBS and cost-effectiveness studies resulted in accounting by program elements on a full cost basis rather than by an annual object-of-expenditure basis. This information was intended to permit a comparison of tradeoff opportunities. Beginning in 1965, the new comptroller Anthony focused on Project PRIME, which emphasized introduction of responsibility center accounting for full cost measurement; systems analysis was made a separate function at the assistant secretary level.[44]

The Post-McNamara Retreat

To a larger degree than in other policy arenas, budgeting and financial management are crucial in determining military policy. Secretary McNamara grasped the essential point of defense management that "policy decisions must sooner or later be expressed in the form of budget decisions on where to spend and how much."[45] Budget decisions finalize weaponry, personnel, logistics, training, and force structure. The basic mission of the Department of Defense is combat readiness. Defense policy may be divided into four phases: plans, budgeting, procurement, and operations.[46] The revolution in military technology—with its technical complexity, long lead times for development and production, and high costs—has steadily made planning and procurement through budgeting, rather than operations, the most important functions in defense policy. The same revolution has placed a high premium on both economy and interservice coordination. The New Look emphasized a fiscal ceiling and fixed service allocations, but officially left weapons and force structure decisions to the military services. The McNamara revolution moved further to increase civilian control over such specific decisions.[47]

President Nixon's first Secretary of Defense was former Congressman Melvin Laird, who had served as a member of the House Military Appropriations Subcommittee. Laird was faced with the principal task of military reduction and withdrawal from the Vietnam War. He was convinced that McNamara's approach had resulted in overcentralization of policymaking in OSD and an insufficient role for the military services. Laird announced what he termed a new philosophy of "participatory management."[48] The Deputy Secretary of Defense negotiated in 1969 what was in effect a "treaty" with the JCS and the service secretaries. Systems analysis was relegated to a purely review and evaluation role; all military proposals would come solely from the JCS. Contrary to the practice under McNamara, the systems analysis staff would no longer originate independent proposals. In exchange, the JCS agreed to return to the formal budget ceiling method of the Eisenhower era.

It would not be accurate to characterize Laird's method as a surrender of OSD authority to the military.[49] Rather, the JCS was given a larger role in what Laird regarded as basically military decisions. Under the participatory management philosophy, the service secretaries were also assigned increased duties and stature.[50] The more crucial feature was recognition of a formal ceiling on defense budgets; the Laird period (1969–1973) was characterized by extensive budget cuts from Vietnam levels reminiscent of the New Look era. The NSC was revitalized by President Nixon, and greater reliance was placed on National Security Study Memoranda, which constituted something of a return to the BNSP of the Eisenhower era.

There was a significant return to defense organization issues in the 1986 report of the Packard Commission (headed by David Packard, chairman of Hewlett-Packard Company, and Deputy Secretary of Defense under President Nixon) to President Reagan. The report recommended substantially upgrading the role of the Chairman of the JCS by making him the chief military adviser to the President and the Secretary of Defense, providing him with a staff, and authorizing him to draw up five-year plans for all military weapons systems and personnel. Those plans would go directly to the President and upon approval become guidelines for service planning activities. The report also proposed centralizing defense procurement under a new Undersecretary of Defense and providing regional military commanders with more authority over combined forces under their command. Another recommendation was for adoption of two-year budgets in the Defense Department. These proposals may be interpreted as a rejection of the more decentralized management procedures introduced by Laird and subsequently continued by Caspar Weinberger under the Reagan administration.

THE NEW LOOK IN POLITICS

Like all policy arenas, "Military or defense policy making is essentially a political process."[51] A major criticism of the New Look was that it provoked intense interservice competition along two dimensions.[52] First, the imposition of a fiscal ceiling forced the services to battle over a fixed pie, misdirecting their attention from strategic issues. The Kennedy administration's solution was to expand weapons and forces. Second, that competition led to a focus on duplication of effort in nuclear and air defense weapons systems, because funds were restricted for any other purpose. The Army, Air Force, and Navy/Marine Corps struggled over weapons systems, roles, and mission assignments as a means of obtaining additional resources. The budget became the focus of this competition. Thus, Eisenhower's New Look was said to have "politicized" the defense policy arena. More recent analysts such as Kanter, Kinnard, and Korb have assigned higher marks to Eisenhower as a "skilled political practitioner" who outmaneuvered the Joint Chiefs of Staff to centralize defense decision-making in the White House.[53]

This political maneuvering was evident in several dimensions. First, Eisenhower selected business managers as Secretary of Defense. Charles E. Wilson (January 1953-October 1957) had served as president of General Motors; Neil H. McElroy (October 1957-December 1959) as president of Proctor and Gamble and chairman of the National Industrial Conference Board; and Thomas S. Gates, Jr. (December 1959-January 1961), who subsequently became president and chairman of Morgan Guaranty Trust. Gates had previously served as Undersecretary of the Navy (1956–1957). It is significant that in July 1957 Treasury Secretary Humphrey was succeeded by Robert B. Anderson, who had served as Secretary of the Navy and Deputy Secretary of Defense. These selections suggest that Eisenhower viewed the Defense Secretary as a business manager (Robert McNamara came from a similar background), and took a fiscal approach to defense planning.

Second, Eisenhower did not hesitate to replace his service chiefs when they opposed his policy. He placed the JCS chairmanship in the hands of Navy and Air Force supporters of the New Look until late 1960. The JCS chairmen were Arthur Radford (1953–1957) who was a supporter of the New Look, and former Air Force chief Nathan F. Twining (1957–1960) who was its principal beneficiary. In

1953, a new Joint Chiefs of Staff was appointed. Eisenhower told the JCS that he wanted "unanimous decisions" from them. Whereas Twining remained in office until selected for the JCS chairmanship, the Army and Navy chiefs were replaced in 1955 for their opposition to the New Look. The next Air Force chief Thomas D. White had been Twining's vice-chief for four years. Army chief Maxwell Taylor (1955–1959) continued to be a strong proponent of flexible response and was appointed JCS Chairman in the Kennedy administration, and then Ambassador to South Vietnam.

Eisenhower's basic method of operation may be seen in his handling of the NSC. Reflecting his military experience, Eisenhower converted the NSC into a highly structured staff system for defense planning and coordination at the presidential level. The Special Assistant for National Security Affairs ran the NSC process. Reflecting the fiscal ceiling approach, the Treasury Secretary and Budget Director were added to the NSC. Prior to each meeting (the NSC met weekly in 1953 and 1954 chaired by Eisenhower) a formal agenda and policy papers were circulated. The NSC was expected to function as a central planning body for defense policy above the level of the JCS. The "Senior Staff" became an NSC Planning Board, essentially an interagency committee at the assistant secretary level and chaired by the Special Assistant for National Security Affairs, to develop policy papers (often including a financial impact appendix). An Operations Coordinating Board, essentially an interagency committee at the undersecretary level chaired by the Undersecretary of State, was created to transmit NSC decisions to departments and receive progress reports from them. Kinnard concludes, however, that the NSC was basically a coordinating body with critical decisions made by Eisenhower in small informal meetings at the White House or through his special assistants.[54] Kinnard further argues that Eisenhower designed a process that separated policy and budget issues: "he operated separate organizational channels for strategic policy and for the defense budget."[55] Policy went through the JCS to the military services, but the budget went through the Secretary of Defense. Integration was achieved only at the presidential level.

SUMMARY AND CONCLUSIONS

This reexamination of the New Look has emphasized several points. First, Eisenhower brought unique skills and credentials to the first cut at U.S. military strategy for the Cold War. Second, despite the obvious changes in defense strategy toward flexible response and acceleration of weapons technology, the essential outlines of U.S. strategy (strategic triad, continental defense, allied land forces in Europe and South Korea, arms control initiatives) were established in that first cut. As a result of the disaster in Vietnam, the United States has drawn back somewhat from conventional intervention in local wars precisely as occurred following Korea. Third, the New Look in the 1953 and 1958 reorganizations established the basic institutional framework by which the United States still operates its defense forces. Eisenhower strongly emphasized civilian control and removal of policymaking (as distinct from operational planning) from the JCS to the Secretary of Defense and the NSC. Finally, the New Look stimulated the essential features of defense politics.

Even after three decades, the New Look of 1953 appears distinctly peculiar. Consider that it was General of the Army Eisenhower who: (1) cut the defense budget despite the NSC–141 recommendations (by which he could have justified more funding); (2) substantially reduced the size and role of the Army; (3) greatly strengthened the position of the civilian Secretary of Defense; and (4) removed defense policy from the purview of the JCS committee system. His farewell address warned the nation about the dangers of the military-industrial complex engendered by the arms race. Generally, the New Look is attributed to Eisenhower's genuine fiscal conservatism, and clearly a very strong element of this conservatism is present in the policy.

Most analysts have overlooked the equally important factor that a close reading of Eisenhower's military career begins to predict the New Look particularly as shaped by the Korean War experience. In the first place, fiscal conservatism and civilian control were long established principles in the prewar Army. As one historian observes, in World War II, "with few exceptions Eisenhower did not try to set policy. He believed that his function was to carry out the policies created by his superiors."[56] Despite the undoubtedly positive experience of serving under Marshall, Eisenhower must have gotten a bellyful of military prima donnas before and during World War II. He studied "dramatic acting" as special assistant to Chief of Staff Douglas MacArthur (1933–1935) and in the Philippines (1935–1939). Eisenhower may well have had a poor view of Montgomery, and found George Patton a problem child.

As European Theatre Commander, Eisenhower was intimately involved in the whole process by which Roosevelt and Churchill directed the war, as well as the policy differences within and between the U.S. Joint Chiefs of Staff and the British Chiefs of Staff. The British traditionally operated by committee, the Americans by unified command. He would have developed definite views on this choice. He undoubtedly learned about the political character of policymaking and the particularistic interests of military services. The requirements of the European Theatre made him a skilled bureaucratic politician. Eisenhower (as did Marshall) viewed the Torch landing in North Africa as a purely political decision by Roosevelt. In the Normandy invasion planning, he had to threaten resignation to obtain control over strategic bombers for a transportation bombing effort.

As Army Chief of Staff after World War II, Eisenhower strongly supported universal military training and service unification (the Army proposal rejected in the 1947 National Security Act). He was recalled in 1949 to serve temporarily as JCS Chairman to oversee implementation of the National Security Act amendments. As NATO Supreme Commander, he was intimately involved with planning for European defense at a time when the Truman administration felt the Korean War might be a feint for a Soviet move against Europe. Eisenhower would have come into the White House with strong views on defense strategy, organization, management, budgeting, and politics after having served twice as a unified theatre commander in Europe, service chief, and JCS Chairman.

Even his views on economic mobilization and Army strength may have been shaped in World War II. The United States made a conscious decision to gamble on a ninety-division Army in order to provide personnel for the "arsenal of democracy" and the air/sea control absolutely vital in both the European and Pacific theatres. It has been said that "the decision for 90 divisions . . . was one of the greatest gambles taken by the Washington high command in World War II."[57] Mobilization, not an active Army, was the traditional U.S. policy.[58] The manpower strategy of the United States in World War II, relative to total mobilization, was very similar to that adopted in the New Look. The United States decided to minimize its ground forces in favor of air and naval forces, as well as war production for the supply of Britain and Russia. Stress was placed on technology and mobility.[59]

It is unlikely that policymakers suddenly develop new views upon taking office. Eisenhower did not "invent" the New Look; rather, he brought it with him in the sense that his fiscal conservatism and service experiences had prepared him for a specific reaction to the Truman administration's NSC–141. The essential elements of the New Look flowed naturally from Eisenhower's whole career and the situation posed by the end of the Korean War. Henry Kissinger observes that "It is an illusion to believe that leaders gain in profundity while they gain experience . . . the convictions that leaders have formed before reaching high office are the intellectual capital they will consume as long as they continue in office."[60] Alexander L. George states this same conclusion in a concept he calls the "operational code" of political leaders. This operational code is a set of assumptions formed early in one's career which governs response to decision situations.[61] From this point of view, the question of whether the New Look reflected Eisenhower's military "genius" (or lack of it depending on one's appraisal) is nearly irrelevant.[62] Eisenhower was a skilled political decision-maker; the success or failure of the New Look as defense policy is a wholly different question. Flexible response failed in Vietnam; it is not clear whether détente has retarded or accelerated the arms race and the Cold War. The Kennedy-Johnson and Reagan arms buildups may not have improved our security.

The New Look was fully consistent with Eisenhower's biases and experiences. Other policymakers will behave differently without necessarily achieving better or worse policy outcomes. It may be an overstatement to argue that the New Look of 1953 was a translation of Eisenhower's views on World War II's Allied grand strategy for global warfare into a post-Korean War environment. But it may be proper to assert more strongly than has been done previously how Eisenhower's service experiences must have shaped his views on strategy and organization for the Cold War. Economic mobilization, air- and seapower, and technology were the keys to U.S. victory in global warfare. It was perhaps an easy psychological adjustment from Nazi Germany to Soviet Russia as an opponent for global domination. At the same time, Eisenhower drew fundamental lessons (strengthened no doubt by his postwar military services) about the JCS, service interests, and defense politics. In many respects, this confluence of historical factors substantially informed the New Look of 1953. What is fascinating is that three decades later the U.S. defense posture is still fundamentally shaped by that original Eisenhower framework for protracted conflict in the Cold War. It is easier to delineate and appreciate this contribution once we separate the broader Eisenhower Doctrine from the particular force posture of the New Look. History will have to judge whether flexible response—despite its considerable merits—is a more suitable force posture. But flexible response was not a substitute for the Eisenhower Doctrine.

NOTES

1. Fred I. Greenstein, *The Hidden-Hand Presidency: Eisenhower as Leader* (New York: Basic Books, 1982); and "Eisenhower as an Activist President: A New Look at the Evidence," *Political Science Quarterly* 94 (Winter 1979–1980): 575–99. See also Gary W. Reichard, "Eisenhower as President: The Changing View," *South Atlantic Quarterly* 77 (Summer 1978): 265–81; Douglas Yates, Jr., *The Politics of Management: Exploring the Inner Workings of Public and Private Organizations* (San Francisco: Jossey-Bass, 1985), ch. 7, "Conflict Management in Practice: Case Studies," pp. 166–98.

2. John L. Gaddis, *Strategies of Containment: A Critical Appraisal of Postwar American National Security Policy* (New York: Oxford University Press, 1982); Arnold Kanter, *Defense Politics: A Budgetary Perspective* (Chicago: University of Chicago Press, 1979); Douglas Kinnard, *President Eisenhower and Strategy Management: A Study in Defense Politics* (Lexington: University Press of Kentucky, 1977); Lawrence J. Korb, *The Joint Chiefs of Staff: The First Twenty-five Years* (Bloomington: Indiana University Press, 1976) and "The Budget Process in the Department of Defense: The Strengths and Weaknesses of Three Systems," *Public Administration Review* 37 (July-August 1977): 334–46.

3. Douglas Kinnard, *The Secretary of Defense* (Lexington: University Press of Kentucky, 1980), p. 71.

4. Gaddis, *Strategies of Containment*, p. 185.

5. Available in *Naval War College Review* (May-June 1975). Gaddis' *Strategies of Containment*, p. ix, argues that postwar defense policy is divisible into five "strategic" or "geopolitical" codes: (1) the 1947–1949 strategy of containment implemented by the Truman administration; (2) the 1950 NSC–68 implemented by happenstance in the Korean War (1950–1953); (3) the 1953–1960 Eisenhower New Look; (4) the 1961–1969 Kennedy-Johnson flexible response strategy; and (5) the 1970–1979 Nixon-Kissinger détente policy continued by the Ford-Carter administrations. The Reagan administration has returned not so much to flexible response—now a basic principle of U.S. policy—but to a major arms buildup. Containment has remained a fundamental element of the U.S. Cold War doctrine. The policy debate has been over cost, force structure, and U.S. aggressiveness.

6. See Gaddis, *Strategies of Containment*, ch. 4, "NSC–68 and the Korean War," pp. 89–126; Paul Y. Hammond, "NSC–68: Prologue to Rearmament," in Warner R. Schilling, Paul Y. Hammond, and Glenn H. Snyder, *Strategy, Politics and Defense Budgets* (New York: Columbia University Press, 1962), pp. 267–378; Samuel F. Wells,

Jr., "Sounding the Tocsin: NSC 68 and the Soviet Threat," *International Security* 4 (Fall 1979): 116–38.

7. The New Look is examined in: Martin C. Fregus, "The Massive Retaliation Doctrine," *Public Policy* 17 (1968): 231–57; Gaddis, *Strategies of Containment*, ch. 5, "Eisenhower, Dulles, and the New Look," pp. 127–63, and ch. 6, "Implementing the New Look," pp. 164–97; Kinnard, *President Eisenhower and Strategy Management*, ch. 1, "How the New Look Came to Be," pp. 1–36; Korb, *The Joint Chiefs of Staff*, "The Eisenhower Administration," pp. 103–11; Clark A. Murdock, *Defense Policy Formation: A Comparative Analysis of the McNamara Era* (Albany: State University of New York Press, 1974), ch. 1, "Defense Policy Formation and Weapons Innovation Under Eisenhower," pp. 7–43; Charles Murphy, "Eisenhower's Most Critical Defense Budget," *Fortune* 54 (December 1956): 112 ff.; Glenn H. Snyder, "The New Look of 1953," in Schilling, Hammond, and Snyder, *Strategy, Politics, and Defense Budgets*, pp. 379–524. See also Robert A. Divine, *Eisenhower and the Cold War* (New York: Oxford University Press, 1981).

8. Gaddis, *Strategies of Containment*, p. 148, focuses on nuclear retaliation, alliance systems, psychological warfare, covert action, and arms negotiations.

9. Gaddis argues that Vietnam was a test of the flexible response doctrine; see *Strategies of Containment*, ch. 8, "Implementing Flexible Response: Vietnam as a Test Case," pp. 237–73. A somewhat similar view is offered in Gregory Palmer, *The McNamara Strategy and the Vietnam War: Program Budgeting in the Pentagon, 1960–1968* (Westport, Conn.: Greenwood Press, 1978).

10. Kinnard, *The Secretary of Defense*, p. 44.

11. Kinnard, *President Eisenhower and Strategy Management*, p. 6.

12. John Foster Dulles, "Policy for Security and Peace," *Foreign Affairs* 32 (April 1954): 353–64.

13. Dwight D. Eisenhower, *The White House Years, 1953–1956: Mandate for Change* (Garden City, N.Y.: Doubleday, 1963), p. 452 n.7.

14. Morton H. Halperin, *National Security Policy-Making: Analyses, Cases and Proposals* (Lexington, Mass.: Lexington Books, 1975), ch. 4, "The Gaither Committee and the Policy Process," pp. 47–110.

15. Rockefeller Brothers Fund, *International Security: The Military Aspect* (Garden City, N.Y.: Doubleday, 1958).

16. Seymour J. Deitchman, *Limited War and American Defense Policy* (Cambridge, Mass.: MIT Press, 1964); Henry A. Kissinger, *Nuclear Weapons and Foreign Policy* (New York: Harper, 1957); Robert E. Osgood, *Limited War: The Challenge to American Strategy* (Chicago: University of Chicago Press, 1957).

17. Morton Halperin, *Contemporary Military Strategy* (Boston: Little, Brown, 1967), ch. 4, "The Evolution of American Military Strategy," pp. 43–55.

18. It has been suggested that the U.S. Marine Corps is not properly armed for the modern conventional battlefield in which the amphibious mission may become virtually impossible. Martin Binkin and Jeffrey Record, *Where Does the Marine Corps Go from Here* (Washington, D.C.: Brookings Institution, 1976).

19. Alain C. Enthoven and Wayne K. Smith, *How Much Is Enough? Shaping the Defense Program, 1961–1969* (New York: Harper and Row, 1971), p. 14.

20. Halperin, *National Security Policy-Making*, ch. 1, "Why Bureaucrats Play Games," pp. 3–16.

21. Charles J. Hitch, *Decision-Making for Defense* (Berkeley: University of California

Press, 1965), ch. 1, "1769–1960," pp. 3–18; William R. Kintner, *Forging a New Sword: A Study of the Department of Defense* (New York: Harper, 1958); John C. Ries, *The Management of Defense: Organization and Control of the U.S. Armed Services* (Baltimore: Johns Hopkins University Press, 1964).

22. C. W. Borklund, *The Department of Defense* (New York: Praeger, 1968), Appendix IV, "National Security Act of 1947," pp. 317–33; Demetrios Caraley, *The Politics of Military Unification: A Study of Conflict and the Policy Process* (New York: Columbia University Press, 1966); Hoxie, *Command Decision and the Presidency*, ch. 5, "James V. Forrestal and the National Security Act of 1947," pp. 129–52; Elias Huzar, *The Purse and the Sword: Control of the Army through Military Appropriations, 1933–1950* (Ithaca, N.Y.: Cornell University Press, 1950), pp. 29–314; Ries, *The Management of Defense*, ch. 6, "The National Security Act of 1947," pp. 88–106.

23. The Army, Navy, and Air Force were made coequal executive departments with Cabinet status. These service departments were responsible, through their chiefs of staff, for the military direction of specified (single service) and unified (interservice) field commands. The act specified permanent continuation of the Marine Corps and naval aviation as part of the Navy Department. Above the service departments was created a "national military establishment," not a Department of Defense, under a Secretary of Defense to whom reported the now formally established JCS (the three service chiefs for Army, Navy, and Air Force) under a "Chief of Staff to the Commander in Chief" (not a chairman), a War Council (later Armed Forces Policy Council), a Research and Development Board, and a Munitions Board. Committee decision-making rather than unified command was retained in all these devices. The Secretary was given three special assistants. The JCS were given a Joint Staff. The national military establishment was a loose confederation of the military services. The service secretaries and JCS were given free access to the President and Congress. At the Cabinet level of the government were created a National Security Council (NSC) and a National Security Resources Board (NSRB, which in 1953 became part of the Office of Defense Mobilization). The NSC consisted of the President, the secretaries of Defense and State, the NSRB Chairman, and the three service secretaries. A Central Intelligence Agency (CIA) was formed, reporting to the NSC. The NSRB consisted of those Cabinet officers involved in defense mobilization; its chairman was given Cabinet rank.

24. Paul Y. Hammond, "Super Carriers and B–36 Bombers: Appropriations, Strategy, and Politics" (Indianapolis: Bobbs-Merrill, 1963), ICP Case No. 97.

25. Hoxie, *Command Decision and the Presidency*, ch. 6, "The Admirals' Revolt and the 1949 Amendments," pp. 153–68; Ries, *The Management of Defense*, ch. 8, "The 1949 Amendments to the National Security Act," pp. 125–46.

26. William W. Kaufman, *The McNamara Strategy* (New York: Harper and Row, 1964), ch. 1. The position of Defense Comptroller was held by William H. McNeil during the years 1949–1959, a fact that helped to institutionalize the new comptrollership system.

27. Frederick C. Mosher, *Program Budgeting: Theory and Practice with Particular Reference to the U.S. Department of the Army* (Chicago: Public Administration Service, 1954), ch. 2, "The Setting of Military Budgeting," pp. 19–46, and ch. 6, "Military Comptrollers and the Budget," pp. 191–229; David Novick, "The Role of the Military Comptroller in Defense Management" (Santa Monica, Calif.: Rand Corp., June 6, 1961), p. 2236.

28. Borklund, *The Department of Defense*, "Reorganization Plan, 1953," pp. 65–67;

Ries, *The Management of Defense*, ch. 9, "Defense Reorganization of 1953," pp. 147–66.

29. Borklund, *The Department of Defense*, "Reorganization Act of 1958," pp. 70–77; Joseph P. Harris, *Congressional Control of Administration* (Washington, D.C.: Brookings Institution, 1964), "The Defense Reorganization Act of 1958," pp. 25–31; Ries, *The Management of Defense*, "The Reorganization of 1958," pp. 167–92.

30. "Special Message to the Congress on Reorganization of the Defense Establishment, April 3, 1958," *Public Papers of the President, Dwight D. Eisenhower, 1958* (Washington, D.C.: U.S. Government Printing Office), pp. 178 ff.

31. Enthoven and Smith, *How Much Is Enough?*, ch. 1, "Unfinished Business," pp. 1–30; General Maxwell D. Taylor, *The Uncertain Trumpet* (New York: Harper, 1959), ch. 5, "The Making of Our Military Strategy Theory," pp. 80–87, and ch. 7, "The Failure of Decision-Making: How Military Strategy Is Formulated in Fact," pp. 115–29.

32. The Committee on the Defense Establishment report (December 1960) recommended that the service secretaries be replaced by three undersecretaries of defense with centralized OSD administration; and that its Chairman replace the JCS in the chain of command with the assistance of a "military advisory council," relegating the chiefs of staff to purely service heads.

33. Enthoven and Smith, *How Much Is Enough?*, pp. 11–21.

34. Ibid., p. 11. See also Arthur Smithies, *The Budgetary Process in the United States* (New York: McGraw-Hill, 1955), pp. 357–77.

35. Robert S. McNamara, *The Essence of Security: Reflections in Office* (New York: Harper and Row, 1968), ch. 6, "Managing for Defense," pp. 87–104; Taylor, *The Uncertain Trumpet*, ch. 8, "Flexible Response—A New National Military Program," pp. 130–64.

36. *Annual Report of the Secretary of Defense,* in *Department of Defense Annual Report for Fiscal Year 1962* (Washington, D.C.: U.S. Government Printing Office, 1963), p. 3. Kanter, *Defense Politics: A Budgetary Perspective*, p. 77, challenges this view. He concludes that the Kennedy and Johnson administrations were just as driven by "fiscal pressures." During fiscal years 1963 through 1966, the defense budget was within 1 percent of $46 billion, or about the same level as under Eisenhower. The budget was split about 17 percent Army, 32 percent Navy, and 41 percent Air Force. James M. Roherty, *Decisions of Robert S. McNamara: A Study of the Role of the Secretary of Defense* (Coral Gables, Fla.: University of Miami Press, 1970), p. 76. The same conclusion is reached in John P. Crecine, "Defense Budgeting: Organizational Adaptation to External Constraints," in R. F. Byrne et al., eds., *Studies in Budgeting* (Amsterdam: North-Holland, 1971), pp. 210–61. The Vietnam War costs were added to the existing defense budget as an increment (Kanter, p. 112).

37. McNamara, *The Essence of Security*, ch. 4, "Mutual Deterrence," pp. 51–67; Enthoven and Smith, *How Much Is Enough?*, ch. 5, "Nuclear Strategy and Forces," pp. 165–96.

38. *Annual Report of the Secretary of Defense*, p. 3.

39. This aspect of the McNamara revolution created the most friction between OSD and the military services. In the eyes of most professional military men, PPBS and systems analysis were essentially devices for substituting social science techniques for military experience and transferring the making of strategy from the military to inexperienced civilians. Korb, *The Joint Chiefs of Staff*, p. 17. A case can be made that military officers are trained and experienced principally in operations and tactics, not in national strategy

formulation or weapons procurement. Enthoven and Smith, *How Much Is Enough?*, ch. 3, "Why Independent Analysts," pp. 73–116. General Maxwell Taylor endorsed the view that OSD might be better at weapons selection in *The Uncertain Trumpet*, pp. 119–20.

40. *Annual Report of the Secretary of Defense*, "Logistics," pp. 40–48.

41. The Defense Atomic Support (later Nuclear) Agency had been created in 1959, the Director (now Undersecretary) of Defense Research and Engineering in 1958. The Defense Communications Agency was formed in March 1961, and the Defense Intelligence Agency and Defense Supply (later Logistics) Agency in August 1961. Subsequently, the Defense Contract Audit Agency was added in 1965. As of fiscal year 1981, there were twelve such defense agencies, including the Defense Investigative Agency, Defense Security Assistance Agency, Defense Mapping Agency, Defense Advanced Research Projects Agency, Defense Audit Agency, and the National Security Agency. For an opposing view, see former Secretary of Defense Harold Brown, "Managing the Defense Department: Why It Can't Be Done," *Dividend: The Magazine of the Graduate School of Business, University of Michigan* 12 (Spring 1981): 10–14.

42. Hitch, *Decision-Making for Defense*, p. 39.

43. McNamara, *The Essence of Security*, p. 95.

44. Steven Lazarus, "Planning-Programming-Budgeting Systems and Project PRIME," in Fremont J. Lyden and Ernest G. Miller, eds., *Planning Programming Budgeting: A Systems Approach to Management* (Chicago: Markham, 1968), pp. 358–70.

45. Enthoven and Smith, *How Much Is Enough?*, p. 35.

46. Korb, *The Joint Chiefs of Staff*, p. 94.

47. Bernard Brodie, "The McNamara Phenomenon," *World Politics* 17 (July 1965): 672–86; Keith C. Clark and Laurence J. Legere, eds., *The President and the Management of National Security* (New York: Praeger, 1969), ch. 8, "A Decade of Change in the Department of Defense," pp. 173–205; Malcolm W. Hoag, "What New Look in Defense?," *World Politics* 22 (October 1969): 1–28.

48. Ralph Sanders, *The Politics of Defense Analysis* (New York: Dunellen, 1973), ch. 4, "Analysis under Laird," pp. 93–129.

49. The final ceilings for the total and service budgets were negotiated by the Defense Program Review Committee (chaired by the President's Special Assistant for National Security Affairs and composed of the Secretary of Defense, Undersecretary of State, JCS Chairman, Office of Management and Budget Director, CIA Director; and Chairman of the Council of Economic Advisers), created in October 1969 for fiscal year 1971. This committee, however, could give only limited attention to the defense budget.

50. This trend was picked up again in the Reagan administration under Secretary Caspar Weinberger. More program responsibility has been delegated to the service secretaries, who have been members together with the JCS Chairman and OSD officials of the Defense Resources Board, chaired by the Deputy Secretary of Defense. This board currently controls the entire planning and budgeting process. The amount of documentation which OSD can request from the services has been cut in half and restricted to oversight and coordination purposes. Donald D. Holt, "Cap Weinberger's Pentagon Revolution," *Fortune* 103 (May 18, 1981): 79–82. In 1977, under the Carter administration, zero-base budgeting (ZBB) was introduced. PPBS was retained; PPBS and ZBB were, therefore, handled separately. The basic PPB cycles were still in place and formed the foundation for the ZBB exercise. Lawrence J. Korb, "The Process and Problems of Linking Policy and Force Through the Defense Budget Process," in Robert Harkavy and Edward A. Kolodziej, eds., *American Security Policy and Policy-Making: The Dilemmas of Using and Controlling Military Force* (Lexington, Mass.: Lexington Books, 1980), pp. 181–92.

51. Korb, *The Joint Chiefs of Staff*, p. 94.

52. Samuel P. Huntington, "Interservice Competition and the Political Roles of the Armed Services," *American Political Science Review* 55 (March 1961): 40–52.

53. Kinnard, *President Eisenhower and Strategy Management*, p. ix.

54. Ibid., p. 17.

55. Ibid., p. 127.

56. Stephen Ambrose, *The Supreme Commander: The War Years of General Dwight D. Eisenhower* (Garden City, N.Y.: Doubleday, 1970), p. v.

57. Maurice Matloff, ed., *American Military History* (Washington, D.C.: Office of the Chief of Military History, U.S. Army, 1969), p. 466.

58. Ibid., p. 539.

59. Maurice Matloff, "The 90-Division Gamble," in Kent Greenfield, *Command Decisions* (Washington, D.C.: U.S. Department of the Army, 1960), pp. 365–81.

60. Henry A. Kissinger, *White House Years* (Boston: Houghton Mifflin, 1979), p. 54.

61. Alexander L. George, "The 'Operational Code': A Neglected Approach to the Study of Political Deision-Making," *International Studies Quarterly* 12 (June 1969): 190–222.

62. George H. Quester, "Was Eisenhower a Genius?," *International Security* 4 (Fall 1979): 159–79.

15

Eisenhower, Churchill, and the "Balance of Terror"

John Kentleton

In June 1954, in his eightieth year, Winston Churchill visited the United States for the last time as British Prime Minister for talks with President Eisenhower. His doctor had no doubts as to what drove him: "To hold off the threat of war until it is no longer worth while for anyone to break the peace—that is the only thing left to him now, his one consuming purpose. Without it there is little meaning in life. In his heart he has a great fear: he dreads another war, for he does not believe that England could survive." As Churchill himself confided to Lord Moran, "My thoughts are almost entirely thermonuclear. I spend a lot of time thinking over deterrents."[1]

Eisenhower and Churchill had first met briefly in the White House at the time of the so-called Second Washington Conference in June 1942 and, if their subsequent written accounts are to be believed, both men were immediately taken with each other.[2] While Eisenhower had been a relatively obscure Army officer until the coming of the war, Churchill, of course, had been a world figure for more than a quarter of a century. Indeed, in his casual reminiscences published during his retirement, *At Ease*, subtitled "Stories I Tell to Friends," Eisenhower claims to have heard about Churchill from two British officers in 1918 while Commandant of an Army camp at Gettysburg, receiving delivery of some tanks, a weapon Churchill had had a hand in producing: "he sounded like a good chap."[3] Genuine intimacy had developed in the course of the war, both in North Africa and especially in London. In one of his last letters to President Roosevelt, Churchill had paid a glowing tribute: "I wish to place on record the complete confidence felt by His Majesty's Government in General Eisenhower, our pleasure that our armies are serving under his command, and our admiration of the great and shining qualities of character and personality which he has proved himself to possess in all the difficulties of handling an Alliance command."[4] For his part, in the first volume of his memoirs *Mandate for Change*, Eisenhower, in listing his qualifications for the presidency, cited his chance to observe and work with Churchill, describing their friendly relationship and the pleasure he gained from their conferences. He particularly recalled Churchill's far-seeing attitude regarding the Soviet Union, his distrust of the Soviet leaders, and his frequent reminders that he was "suspicious of the Bear."[5] When at the end of 1950 it was learned that Eisenhower was to be NATO's military commander, Churchill, who was then out of office, publicly welcomed the appointment in the House of Commons. Eisenhower's time at SHAPE included Churchill's return to Downing Street in October 1951, until his own resignation effective June 1952, in order to seek the Republican presidential nomination.[6] At the beginning of that year, learning that Eisenhower might be nominated by the Republican party it is recorded that Churchill's "face lit up."[7]

The American presidency has generally been regarded as a very personal office, the fortunes of each administration largely determined by the character and abilities of the occupant in the White House. In contrast, a parliamentary system as in Britain, which requires a meaningful Cabinet taking collective responsibility for decisions and where the Prime Minister is at best *primus inter pares*, seems above all to place a premium on teamwork. Yet between October 1951 and April 1955, perhaps for the last time in British politics, the rules of ordinary political conduct were suspended; at the head of the government stood a man who was in one sense irreplaceable, in another immovable, yet in a third living on borrowed time dependent on the actions of a foreign statesman to provide a *raison d'être*. That statesman was the American President, Dwight D. Eisenhower. It is a fascinating example of the interplay of personality in politics, the role of chance, the nourishing of unrealized hopes, and the enduring realities of international relations.

The most recent writer on the subject has characterized it as "Churchill's Indian Summer."[8] It is a kind verdict, but it is not an entirely accurate one. The judgment of Anthony Eden, the British Foreign Secretary, was discerning, "They say to him exactly what they said to Neville Chamberlain, that he is the only man who can save the situation. And the people who are saying this to Winston are the same who said it to Neville."[9] Yet, for that role to be realized required another's cooperation. With an American mother, born in Brooklyn, and maternal grandparents from Rochester, New York; with an ancestor on their side who had fought in Washington's army, Churchill was in little doubt what this necessitated. In his third address to a joint session of Congress in January 1952, he concluded by reminding his audience that Bismarck had once said that the supreme fact of the nineteenth century was that Britain and the United States spoke the same language. He urged them to make sure that the supreme fact of the twentieth century would be that they "tread the same path."[10]

Yet 1952, as Churchill fully realized, was a presidential election year; if he were to inspire a meaningful initiative, everything would depend on whom Truman's successor—once Truman had declared himself a noncandidate—would be. Time was short. Britain, Dean Acheson once said, had lost an Empire but had not yet found a role; in this respect, as the authoritative historian of the British conservative party has suggested, Churchill's resignation marked the end of an era. Britain may have ceased to be a world power in 1945, but for another ten years the country could believe it was one. Perhaps Churchill's presence fed the illusion. In any event, it vanished within two years of his departure from the scene, to be interred at Suez.[11]

If one event was both cause and effect of this ambiguous status, it was the American Atomic Energy or MacMahon Act of 1946, passed in violation of the loosely worded Quebec agreement between Roosevelt and Churchill, not out of malice but out of ignorance.[12] It hurt Churchill deeply, and it was not the least of his resentments against British Prime Minister Clement Atlee that he had acquiesced in its passage. Unaware that notwithstanding the curtailment of information, the then Labour government had secretly decided to work on a British atomic bomb, he had applauded Atlee's urgent trip to the United States in December 1950 on possible American use of the bomb in the Korean War; "The Prime Minister's visit to Washington has done nothing but good. The question we all have to consider—is how much good."[13] But, as the foregoing reservation might suggest, within three months of his own return to Downing Street, he was in Washington seeking formal and public agreement on its use from American bases in East Anglia. Later that year, in October, Britain was to explode its own first atomic bomb, but, it might be argued, this seemed a paltry achievement when on November 1, two days before the presidential election, America conducted its first thermonuclear explosion. (It was not strictly a hydrogen bomb, as it was nondeliverable.) Britain, too, decided it must have an H-bomb, though with somewhat less soul-searching, it must be added, than America had undergone within its most secret councils in 1949. Churchill, however, had no illusions as to its consequences; "There is an immense gulf between the atomic and hydrogen bomb," he later admitted to Parliament. The atomic bomb, terrible a weapon though it was, still lay within the scope of human control, but with the invention of the hydrogen bomb, he direfully warned his hearers, "the entire foundation of human affairs was revolutionized, and mankind placed in a situation both measureless and laden with doom."[14] It was his last great speech in the House of Commons where, in a packed Chamber, he was listened to with deep respect and almost total silence (a rare occurrence in the rowdy debates common to that body). Yet his March 1955 swansong concealed a heartache.

Churchill had dreamed of a summit meeting on the lines of the wartime gatherings at Teheran, Yalta, and Potsdam in which the great issues between the Soviet Union and the West might be settled. He had first aired the idea in the British General Election campaign of February 1950 which had narrowly returned Atlee's Labour government for another eighteen months.[15] Ernest Bevin, the British Foreign Secretary, had dismissed the idea as a stunt proposal; his successor, Anthony Eden, was long doubtful of its value. Yet Churchill, perhaps half romantically, half in deadly earnest, believed in its efficacy. Once when asked what was his biggest mistake in the war, he replied at once, ''Not going to meet Truman after Roosevelt's death. During the next three months tremendous decisions were made, and I had a feeling that they were being made by a man I did not know.'' He added ''It wasn't my fault. I wanted to cross the Atlantic. But Anthony [Eden] put me off. He telegraphed from Washington that they did not want me.''[16]

Now surely with the election of Eisenhower they would want him. When, within two months of the inauguration, Stalin died, Churchill believed that as the last survivor of the wartime Big Three he could play the peacemaker. It would be his legacy to posterity. Moreover, the taunt of warmonger, often thrown at him in domestic British politics, hurt him deeply. In the 1951 General Election, Britain's most popular daily newspaper, *The Daily Mirror*, had rhetorically asked its readership, Whose finger did they want on the trigger? The implication for Churchill was not flattering. Now if he could get Eisenhower to the conference table with the new Russian leadership, of whom George M. Malenkov seemed to be the strongest, he could justify his seeking reelection and his unwillingness to retire. It might provide a way out of a situation, in Churchill's own words, where ''safety will be the sturdy child of terror, and survival the twin brother of annihilation.''[17]

Eisenhower himself was perhaps not unwilling. Less than ten days before Stalin died, he had expressed a willingness to meet him if there was any chance that it would do any good and if it suited what the American people expected of their President. Such an attitude perhaps reflected Eisenhower's instinctive belief in the value of face-to-face settlement of issues that had worked so well in wartime; it even accorded with advice he had received from so unlikely a quarter as General MacArthur. Then, on Stalin's death, he issued a statement of goodwill to the Russian people. Just over a month later on April 16, in an address to the American Society of Newspaper Editors, he invited the new Soviet leaders to take the opportunity to demonstrate their good intentions. He instanced an Austrian treaty and then went on to offer specifically ''universal disarmament.''[18] On May 11, Churchill added his weight, calling for ''a conference on the highest level'' and wisely urging that little should be required as evidence of good faith before such a meeting.[19] John Foster Dulles, however, was less than enthusiastic; perhaps as a new President, Eisenhower felt bound to pay attention to the fears of the State Department. In any case, fate soon intervened to strengthen his hand. Before any meeting with the Russians a Western get-together of the U.S., Britain, and France was an obvious prerequisite, and it was agreed that the three governments should met in Bermuda in June 1953, near enough for Eisenhower but where Churchill might act as host. In May, however, the French government fell yet again, and for five weeks France had no leader; by the time the crisis was resolved, Churchill had had a stroke, though the illness was deliberately underplayed. His doctor recalls him in bed remarking,

I don't feel like managing the world, and yet never have they looked more like offering me it. I feel—I could do something that no one else can do—I have stretched out a hand to grasp the paw of the Russian bear. Great things seemed within my grasp. Not perhaps world peace, but world easement. I feel I could have changed the bias of the world. America is very powerful, but very clumsy—I could have made her more sensible.[20]

The Bermuda meeting was not rescheduled until December. Eisenhower, as his subsequent account suggests, did not think such informal talks of great significance. Perhaps, as it was his first international conference, he was still feeling his way; a less explicit reason was his doubt as to Churchill's physical and mental abilities. In the end he was pleasantly surprised. Eisenhower had shown Churchill a draft of his "Atoms for Peace" speech which he delivered to the United Nations immediately after their meeting and was gratified by the enthusiasm with which Churchill and Eden responded. Both men conceded to Dulles that in atomic matters American thinking, compared to that of the British, was "evidently years ahead."[21]

Perhaps with the ending of the Korean War some perceptible thaw in the Cold War was possible. Ironically, both Eisenhower's and Churchill's defense programs made it at once more urgent, though perhaps more difficult. Both were economy minded. Churchill in 1952 had backed a Global Strategy Paper which would allow a cutback of conventional forces (Britain at the time had a severe balance-of-payments deficit) and place reliance on nuclear bombs. Clearly, however, such a policy involved not just Britain but the Western Alliance; initially, Washington treated it politely but unenthusiastically. When Eisenhower took office, bent on a "New Look", however, it was urged as a reason for the American defense review that ultimately cut the defense budget from $42 million in 1953 to $29 million in 1954. However, there was another price to be paid: the concept of massive retaliation enunciated by Dulles in a speech to the Council on Foreign Relations in New York on January 12, 1954. The policy may have been open to misinterpretation, but it was less than entirely credible, if America's atomic monopoly or even vast superiority was being challenged by the very nation against whom it would presumably be implemented. As Representative George Mahon was later to say succinctly in Congress: "Massive retaliation is rapidly becoming a two-way street."[22]

Dulles had not shared those wartime experiences of joint cooperation which created so much camaraderie a decade later among many in the highest reaches of the American and British governments; hence, Churchill's last trip, with which this chapter began, to his old time associate. Yet increasingly he was welcomed more as Winston Churchill and less as British Prime Minister; it was a distinction he found hard to grasp. Perhaps nothing better displays the ambiguity of his position than his own confused response to the European Defense Community (EDC) which he had partly inspired and then doubted. To Churchill, the Anglo-American partnership was more important than Europe; to Washington, he was increasingly another European Prime Minister, and for the future a Germany and an Adenauer might be just as valuable. When on August 30, 1954, the French National Assembly rejected the EDC, the formation of which was a necessary prelude to any negotiations with the Soviets since the Western Alliance could not go to a summit divided, Churchill's hopes were dashed. Six months later, with the fall of Malenkov came the *coup de grace*. Churchill had outlived his usefulness. On April 5, 1955, he resigned.

Yet the importunings belatedly bore fruit. His successor, Eden, perhaps anxious to insure an election victory in May, called for a summit during the campaign. The Western European Union was now a face, and Germany had entered NATO. More significantly, an Austrian State Treaty had been signed. For two years Eisenhower had had a stock answer to the persistent questions from the press about a possible summit: that he would not go merely because of friendly words and plausible promises but required actual evidence of Soviet willingness to enter into negotiations. Now he agreed to such a meeting at Geneva beginning on July 18, 1955.[23]

To some extent, Eisenhower's caution was justified; the ultimate value of the Geneva Conference in terms of hard substance can be disputed. Yet perhaps he sensed that his own image needed some refurbishment. Something of the hopes and expectations of 1952 had been dimmed as the President struggled to contain and then outflank the danger of a Senator McCarthy or the recalcitrance of members of his own party. In the public mind at least, however inaccurately, too often it looked as if the President was led by his Secretary of State. It was not true, but the unfortunate effect of this seeming influence of the ponderous, even grim Dulles in curbing Eisenhower's natural sunniness may perhaps be construed from Dulles' advice to the President before the summit: the President should minimize any Russian exploitation of the event for propaganda purposes by eschewing social contact with the Russian leaders, lest he be photographed, and, where photographs were inevitable, he should maintain "an austere countenance."[24]

In one respect, this lack of enthusiasm was to work to Eisenhower's advantage. If summitry had its risks such as at Teheran, Yalta, and Potsdam where Eisenhower later argued, "Every agreement the Soviets entered into—was ruthlessly broken, save for those palpably to their advantage," then these kinds of private meetings were to be eschewed. The Geneva Conference would be far larger and more formal; there would be a strict agenda limited to the main causes of tension, thereby preventing Russian attempts to discuss any issue they cared to raise. Moreover, as the only one present who was both head of state and head of government, Eisenhower was able to take the chairmanship of the first meeting and set the tone in a speech of undemonstrative sincerity, aiming at creating a new spirit in superpower relationships.[25]

This "spirit of Geneva," as it came to be called, was the Conference's main achievement, reflecting Eisenhower's own optimism and willingness to conciliate. Of course, one may argue that such an outcome was largely chimerical and did not survive the cold dose of reality of Soviet obstructionism. By the October Foreign Ministers' Conference held in the same room as the summit conference, the Russians repudiated every measure to which they had agreed in July. Even

Eisenhower's greatest triumph, the dramatic "Open Skies" proposal, was stalled. Détente as such had proved illusory.[26]

In another sense, however, attitudes had been changed. It was the first time for ten years since Potsdam that such a meeting had occurred; if it did not end the Cold War, perhaps it allowed the transition to a Cold Peace. The West and Russia had actually met and spoken; the danger of war had surely receded when both sides had talked over their differences in face-to-face discussions. Somehow their mutual problems appeared not quite so intractable, even if immediately incapable of solution. If nothing of substance had been achieved and the goodwill gradually evaporated, an indefinable softening of tension had taken place. Even the ranks of Tuscany could scarce forbear to cheer. Senator McCarthy paid Eisenhower an unintentional backhanded compliment: Did he not detect, he asked the Senate, "appeasement in the air."[27]

In the face of the American President's manifest sincerity and willingness to accommodate, it was the Russians who now appeared inflexible. The propaganda battle was going against them. In return, soon first Nikolai Bulganin and Nikita Khrushchev, and then just Khrushchev would embark on a series of journeys, sometimes mildly comic, occasionally threatening, which yet all in all must have helped relax tension by substituting acquaintance with the West for fear and ignorance. The Russian leader's visit to the United States in 1959 would have been unthinkable ten years earlier when Stalin was alive.

Churchill, too, was gone from the scene. A visitor to Chartwell, his country home in Kent, at the time of the Conference, recalled the old man's inability to suppress great emotion as he contemplated the meeting he had hoped would round off his premiership in a great bid for peace, his pale blue eyes welling with tears at the thought of his ill-time resignation. "I could not erase the memory of the sad face and the blinking eyes, watching history—at long last—move pitilessly past, to leave him behind to gape." Realizing how much it meant to be at last excluded, Eisenhower with great kindness had written to Churchill, regretting his absence at Geneva, signing the letter "Your old friend."[28]

Eisenhower had inherited Churchill's mantle as the world's elder statesman. He sensed his uniqueness. Geneva had taught him that he enjoyed a relationship with Bulganin, Khrushchev, and his old wartime associate Zhukov which no other American shared. Even if the Russians still had not abandoned their long-term objectives, even if they would continue to be petty, obstructionist, and intransigent, still Eisenhower believed he could get through to them and his ability to communicate might be vital. Moreover, he had established links with other European statesmen who looked to him for leadership and did not particularly relish starting anew with another American President. Indeed, it had been partly to help Eden out and forestall the need to work with a Labour government that Eisenhower had concurred with Eden's suggestion during the British election campaign of 1955 to have a summit. Was it wise now to waste such capital? Such thoughts may not have been decisive, but clearly it was one factor—and an important one—urging him to seek a second term when his age, his September 1955 heart attack, and his natural inclination after forty years of public service led him to think of the possibility of retirement to his farm in Gettysburg. To the historian there is a pleasing irony in that the summit which Churchill had desired as a means of vindication, but which he missed by three months, should have become for the initially unenthusiastic Eisenhower a factor justifying his continuance in office.[29]

NOTES

Acknowledgments are due to A. D. Peters and Company, Ltd., and Barrie and Jenkins for permission to quote from Francis L. Loewenheim, Harold D. Langley, and Manfred Jonas, eds., *Roosevelt and Churchill: Their Secret Wartime Correspondence*, and to Constable and Company, Ltd. for permission to quote from Lord Moran, *Winston Churchill, The Struggle for Survival 1940–1965*.

1. Lord Moran, *Winston Churchill, The Struggle for Survival 1940–1965* (London: Constable and Co., 1966), pp. 562–63.

2. Dwight D. Eisenhower, *Crusade in Europe* (London: William Heinemann, 1948), p. 58; Winston S. Churchill, *The Second World War*, Vol. 4, *The Hinge of Fate* (London: Cassell and Co., 1951), p. 345.

3. Dwight D. Eisenhower, *At Ease: Stories I Tell to Friends* (London: Robert Hale, 1967), p. 147.

4. Francis L. Loewenheim, Harold D. Langley, and Manfred Jones, eds., *Roosevelt and Churchill: Their Secret Wartime Correspondence* (London: Barrie and Jenkins, 1975), p. 698. See also Warren F. Kimball, ed., *Churchill & Roosevelt. The Complete Correspondence*, 3 vols. (Princeton, N.J.: Princeton University Press, 1984).

5. Dwight D. Eisenhower, *The White House Years: Mandate for Change, 1953–1956* (London: William Heinemann, 1963), p. 31. See also Eisenhower, *Crusade in Europe*, pp. 69–70; Stephen E. Ambrose, *The Supreme Commander: The War Years of General Dwight D. Eisenhower* (London: Cassell and Co., 1971), p. 93. In contrast, Eisenhower's views on the Russians were less developed. See, for example, Eisenhower, *Crusade in Europe*, pp. 502–21; Stephen E. Ambrose, *Eisenhower*, Vol. 1, *Soldier, General of the Army, President-Elect 1890–1952*) (New York: Simon and Schuster, 1983), pp. 447–52.

6. Robert Rhodes James, ed., *Winston S. Churchill: His Complete Speeches*, Vol. 8, *1950–1963* (New York and London: Chelsea House Publishers in association with R. R. Bowker Co., 1974), p. 8142.

7. Moran, *Winston Churchill*, p. 358. For Eisenhower's ambiguity to the nomination, see Ambrose, *Eisenhower*, Vol. 1, p. 518: "What it came down to was that Eisenhower wanted to be nominated by acclamation" and passim. Churchill, the old pro, summed it up more pithily: "Ike has not only to be wooed but raped."

8. Anthony Seldon, *Churchill's Indian Summer: The Conservative Government 1951–1955* (London: Hodder and Stoughton, 1981).

9. Moran, *Churchill*, p. 501.

10. Churchill, *Speeches*, p. 8329. Churchill's Anglo-Saxon obsessions could be unhelpful. See, for example, Ambrose, *Eisenhower*, Vol. 2, *The President 1952–1969*, p. 174.

11. Robert Blake, *The Conservative Party from Peel to Churchill* (London: Eyre and Spottiswoode, 1970), p. xi.

12. Dean Acheson, *Present at the Creation: My Years in the State Department* (New York: W. W. Norton and Co., 1969), pp. 164–68, 314–21; Churchill, *Speeches*, p. 8343.

13. Churchill, *Speeches*, p. 8140.

14. Ibid., p. 8626.

15. Ibid., p. 7944.

16. Allan Bullock, *The Life and Times of Ernest Bevin*, Vol. 3, *Foreign Secretary 1945–51* (London: William Heinemann, 1983), p. 755; Anthony Eden, *Memoirs*, Vol. 3, *Full Circle* (London: Cassell and Co., 1960), pp. 9, 50–51; Moran, *Churchill*, p. 347.

17. Churchill, *Speeches*, p. 8629.

18. Eisenhower, *Mandate for Change*, pp. 143–46; Ambrose, *Eisenhower*, Vol. 1, pp. 402–403; Vol. 2, p. 34.

19. Churchill, *Speeches*, pp. 8483–85.

20. Moran, *Churchill*, pp. 409–10.

21. Eisenhower, *Mandate for Change*, pp. 242–55; Ambrose, *Eisenhower*, Vol. 2, pp. 146–47.

22. Norman Moss, *Men Who Play God: The Story of the Hydrogen Bomb* (London: Victor Gollanez, 1968), pp. 105–11. The phrase "massive retaliation" is, of course, strictly a misnomer, juxtaposing a word Dulles used elsewhere in his speech.

23. Eisenhower, *Mandate for Change*, pp. 505–507.

24. Townsend Hoopes, *The Devil and John Foster Dulles* (London: Andre Deutsch, 1974), p. 295.

25. Eisenhower, *Mandate for Change*, p. 504 passim.

26. Ibid, pp. 520–30.

27. Richard Goold-Adams, *The Time of Power: A Reappraisal of John Foster Dulles* (London: Weidenfeld and Nicolson, 1962), p. 193 passim.

28. Emmet S. Hughes, *The Ordeal of Power: A Political Memoir of the Eisenhower Years* (London: Macmillan Co., 1963), pp. 167–68. Moran, *Churchill*, p. 679.

29. Eisenhower, *Mandate for Change*, pp. 530–31, 566–73; Robert J. Donovan, *Eisenhower: The Inside Story* (London: Hamish Hamilton, 1956), pp. 396–407.

16

Lifting the American Iron Curtain: Cultural Exchange with the Soviet Union and National Security, 1955–1956

J. Gerrit Gantvoort

After the death of Joseph Stalin in March 1953, the new Russian leadership launched a full-scale cultural offensive, recognizing that cultural diplomacy could be employed to demonstrate the superiority of the Soviet system and to win friends for Moscow in many parts of the world.[1] This ambitious policy immediately called attention to the fact that the attitude of the United States toward cultural exchange was one of indifference and neglect. In January 1954, *New York Times* Associate Art Editor Aline Louchheim lamented that Congress and the State Department shunned participation in international exhibitions: "It reinforces the accusation that we are cultural barbarians, interested only in dollars and materialism . . . and emphasizes the impression that we believe we can 'buy' friendship and alliances."[2] George Kennan, in an address delivered at the University of Notre Dame, suggested that the Eisenhower administration had no cultural exchange policy because it was being held hostage by "diffuse" forces, linked by the conviction that any exchange program would be exploited by the communists to further their cause. Consequently, Kennan continued

. . . we begin to draw about ourselves a cultural curtain similar in some respects to the Iron Curtain of our adversaries. In doing so, we tend to inflict upon ourselves a species of cultural isolationism and provincialism wholly out of accord with the traditions of our nation.[3]

Wounded by such criticisms, the Eisenhower administration announced a stepped-up United States Information Agency effort to "tighten cultural ties with people all over the world."[4] Despite this effort, lifting the "American Iron Curtain" high enough to permit cultural relations with the U.S.S.R. was an entirely different matter. The record demonstrates that, although President Eisenhower always believed in the efficacy of East-West contacts, his views were not shared by Secretary of State, John Foster Dulles. Hence, the issue was contentious and divisive. The first limited postwar commitment to cultural exchange with the U.S.S.R., in March 1955, did not reflect any resolution of the problem. It was prompted by the knowledge that Moscow was effectively calling attention to the contradiction between American claims of a free society and American actions which seemed to limit such claims. Eisenhower attempted to circumvent Dulles, convincing the Western powers to place discussion contacts on the agenda of the July 1955 Geneva Summit Conference. But failure at Geneva led to a conservative political assault on existing exchanges, causing a major rift within the administration. The June 1956 decision to proceed took place only when Dulles, for reasons entirely different from those of the President, endorsed East-West exchanges. Eisenhower then accepted the Dulles position.

Lauren Soth of the *Des Moines Register* triggered the debate over the merits of cultural exchange with the U.S.S.R. On February 10, 1955, he proposed that Soviet farmers come to Iowa to study corn and hog agriculture. Reporters asked the President what he thought of the idea during his March 2 press conference. Eisenhower responded with enthusiasm, while cautioning that certain legal difficulties had to be resolved before the visit could occur.[5] The problems to which he referred were caused by the provisions of the Immigration and Nationality Act of 1952 (McCarran-Walter Act). The McCarran Act excluded all nonofficial Soviet visitors from the United States unless the Attorney General granted a specific waiver. Visitors then had to be fingerprinted. Even such a dedicated anticommunist as publisher William Randolph Hearst, who had been quickly admitted to the Soviet Union in 1955, found U.S. travel restrictions difficult to accept:

One of the best ways I can think of to promote mutual understanding is to encourage the youth and common people of each other's countries to visit this nation and see what we have to offer. The Russian people have no conception of how much better life is in the U.S. The Soviets appear willing to let some of their people, and especially their youth, come and see. Why I don't quite know. But I can't understand the policy of not allowing them to come.[6]

Such restrictions had caused Secretary Khrushchev to complain to visiting American attorney Marshall MacDuffie, who later relayed those concerns to the President with obvious sympathy.[7]

Khrushchev, however, could not have been desperately unhappy with the handiwork of Senator McCarran, which afforded the Soviets an opportunity to conduct a propaganda campaign attacking the "American Iron Curtain." The fingerprinting requirement of the McCarran Act became a vivid symbol of a closed society.[8] The strategy worked. In March 1955, the National Security Council met and expressed alarm over mounting worldwide criticism of American cultural isolationism:

Despite its traditional policy favoring freedom of travel and its record of having favored a liberal exchange of persons with the U.S.S.R., the U.S. is being accused of maintaining an ''Iron Curtain''; and these accusations are being made not only by representatives of international communism, but also by otherwise friendly persons in the free world. This situation is causing damage, and may cause further damage to U.S. prestige and the U.S. reputation for liberal world leadership.[9]

The effectiveness of Soviet political rhetoric in demonstrating the very real weakness of the American position was what caused the United States to develop a postwar cultural exchange policy. Eisenhower authorized short visits by Soviet citizens for ''participation in bona fide cultural, educational, religious, scientific, professional, or athletic activities'' provided that such exchanges were reciprocal.[10] The president's decision caused concern in some quarters. The Interdepartmental Intelligence Conference (IIC) and Interdepartmental Committee on Internal Security (ICIS) had previously gone on record as opposing all Soviet exchanges, citing deficiencies in U.S. internal security controls.[11] (Consequently, the National Security Council [NSC] decided that such controls had to be tightened still further.)[12] The members of the NSC collectively expressed the fear that cultural exchange might cause the American people to believe that Moscow desired only friendly coexistence, and U.S. vigilance toward the communist menace might slacken.[13] Although the views of individual participants remain classified, this argument reflected the influence of Secretary Dulles whose speeches during this period were replete with warnings to Americans not to ''let down their guard'' in the struggle against communism. His fears about our vulnerability were real, but perhaps Dulles also remembered the price that the Democrats had paid for collaboration with the Soviet Union during the wartime alliance.[14]

In conclusion, one must stress that the NSC did not regard limited exchanges as a first step toward a full-fledged cultural exchange with the U.S.S.R. This had been considered and quickly rejected. Although such a program would result in a greatly enhanced U.S. opportunity to collect strategic intelligence, it would create correspondingly great internal security problems. Furthermore, such a course of action must have been less than attractive because the question of how large-scale exchanges might help achieve the broader aims of American foreign policy was never addressed.[15]

Ironically, a decision made largely to alleviate criticism caused even more of it. The United States hoped quietly and unceremoniously to accommodate further Soviet requests, thereby assuring that the propaganda campaign would lose its impact without anyone having to admit that a decision had been made to fraternize with communists. The ''rub'' was that the fingerprinting provision of the McCarran Act (which Congress was not about to repeal) became an even more effective Soviet weapon as the number of prospective Russian visitors increased. In the case of the Russian farm delegation, the State Department avoided controversy by declaring members Soviet officials. But when Russian student editors applied for admission there was little justification for such a ploy. The Soviet press had a field day.[16]

The "American Iron Curtain" campaign became less effective only when discussion of increased contacts between East and West became the final agenda item at the July 1955 Geneva Summit Conference. A *New York Times* editorial ascribed this proposal to Eisenhower, not to Dulles.[17] The record confirms that opinion. In his 1954 address to the American Publishers Association, the President had expressed his firm conviction that cultural exchanges could facilitate mutual understanding:

If increased knowledge and understanding are necessary to promote the unity of our people, they are equally necessary to the development of international cooperation. At this juncture in world affairs, ignorance of each other's capacities, hopes, prejudices, beliefs, and intentions can destroy cooperation and breed war.

Even the most rabid Marxist, the most ruthless worshiper of force, will in a moment of sanity admit that. International understanding, however, like domestic unity, depends in large part on the free flow of information and its balanced presentation.[18]

This attitude toward East-West contacts engendered very basic differences with Dulles about how to approach the Soviet Union at Geneva. In the words of Paul C. Davies, the President,

Tending to reduce politics to the problems of human personality and not overly informed about Marxism . . . was ready to accord universal human attributes, notably essential goodness, to his adversaries.

[Dulles] believed not at all in Soviet sincerity; his religion was no bland belief in people-to-people togetherness, but a stern distrust of the sinner, combined with the lawyer's zeal to outwit him.[19]

Eisenhower's idealism, however, was always tempered with pragmatism, and this was certainly true in the case of cultural exchange.[20] Although the President spoke of an almost ethereal relationship between increased contacts and friendly understanding in his opening statement at Geneva, he hoped that such an appeal would enable him to "break the ice" with the Russians and generate the momentum necessary to resolve other questions.

There is no indication that Dulles vigorously resisted discussion of cultural exchanges. Perhaps distrust of the Soviet Union caused him to reason that Moscow, interested only in milking the last drop of propaganda from the uproar over the "American Iron Curtain," would manage not to agree to anything concrete. Hence, although obligated loyally to represent his chief at the summit, he may have regarded the inclusion of the "Contacts" question on the Geneva agenda as a moot point.[21] The evidence does suggest a subtle campaign on Dulles' part to reassure conservative leaders of groups like the American Legion and American Federation of Labor that he still had reservations about exchanges with the U.S.S.R. But when reporters tried to pin him down about conversations in which he had allegedly expressed such views, the Secretary usually avoided answering the question.[22]

The President's personal interest in exploring the possibility of expanded contacts between East and West was further reinforced by recommendations submitted by Nelson Rockefeller, Eisenhower's Special Assistant for Cold War Planning, on June 10, 1955. Rockefeller had assembled a group of "experts" at the Quantico, Virginia, Marine base, whose task had been to develop a more flexible summit strategy than the one advocated by Dulles. The Quantico Report suggested that raising the "Contacts" issue at the summit could only strengthen the U.S. position vis-à-vis the Soviet Union:

If the Soviets reject all of these proposals, it will be possible for us to make abundantly clear where the responsibility for restrictions on free movement of people, goods, and ideas really lies. If they accept any of these proposals, we will be credited with important steps forward in lifting the Iron Curtain.[23]

Finally, it is apparent that Eisenhower could afford to endorse cultural exchange because of surprisingly strong congressional support. In Early July, Senator Karl Mundt (co-author of the Smith-Mundt Educational Exchanges Act of 1948) asked him to discuss international exchanges of persons at Geneva: "When people meet," Mundt observed, "tensions are lessened."[24] Application of such a philosophy to the Soviet Union by a diehard conservative on internal security questions must have allayed presidential fears of a right-wing backlash. Mundt's suggestion quickly received the support of a bipartisan group of House liberals, for whom New Jersey Democrat Frank Thompson acted as spokesman.[25] Thompson subsequently urged Congress to increase appropriations for cultural exchanges. While arguing that additional resources were needed to support a Soviet-American exchange program, he was politically astute enough to stress that the money could be used to support a "soft [cultural] war" against Moscow if there was no agreement.[26]

Eisenhower presented the details of his "Contacts" proposal to the Sixth Plenary Session at Geneva. He called on the Soviet Union, Great Britain, France, and the United States:

1. To lower barriers that now impede the interchange of information and ideas between our peoples.
2. To lower the barriers that now impede opportunities for people to travel anywhere in the world for peaceful and friendly purposes so that we will all have a chance to know each other face to face.
3. To create conditions that will encourage all nations to the exchange of peaceful goods.[27]

When the Foreign Ministers convened the next day to discuss his proposal, an impasse quickly developed. Assistant Secretary Livingston Merchant described the meeting as one in which "a sense of deadlock hung in the air and the discussion of East-West contacts that followed was close to perfunctory."[28] Hopes that the Russians would accept this, or any other Western proposal, quickly faded. Eisenhower finally did secure Soviet agreement concerning the desirability of "increased visits by citizens of one country to the territory of the other." This one tangible manifestation of the elusive "Spirit of Geneva" reinforced the President's battered idealism when he addressed the American people on the failure of the conference.

The final directive of the Heads of State to their Foreign Ministers mandated continued study of the "Contacts" question "by means of experts." After considerable delay, on September 17, Secretary Dulles appointed William H. Jackson to coordinate the shaping of an American position and to serve as negotiator when the Foreign Ministers met again in November. When the *New York Times* interviewed Jackson two weeks later, he voiced concerns about cultural exchange that were remarkably similar to those of Dulles.[29] Jackson cautioned that, if the United States did reach an agreement with the Soviet Union, others might follow our lead. This possibility deeply troubled the Secretary: a large infusion of Soviet visitors, which the United States could tolerate, would be "poisonous" to Third World nations. Moscow might be handed an opportunity to seize control of those countries from within.[30] Jackson even expressed skepticism as to whether friendly contacts between Soviet and American leaders would really "create an atmosphere in which East-West political problems could be worked out," confessing that he was casting doubt on one of the President's fundamental assumptions at the summit. Here he echoed the reservation of a Secretary of State who had so little use for such personal interaction that he frowned on all visible contacts between Soviet and American officials, because such meetings set a bad example for others.[31]

Jackson's letter of appointment, however, called on him to develop a "Contacts" policy only after consulting all interested departments and individuals. The philosophy behind his final recommendations was clearly that of Nelson Rockefeller with whom Jackson had shared earlier policymaking decisions. In 1953, Jackson had chaired the President's Committee of International Information Activities, one of whose tasks was to sculpt an American psychological warfare offensive against the Soviet Union. Rockefeller, as Special Assistant to the President for Cold War Planning, was directly responsible for further development of that policy. In January 1955, Eisenhower had approved NSC policy paper 5505/1 (which remains fully classified after a 1982 review). This document, in Rockefeller's words, set forth:

. . . the advantages to our own future security interest of attaining steadily wider and deeper contacts with the middle and upper echelons of Soviet leadership: technicians, industrial managers, scientists, and other groups of potential future leaders of the Soviet political structure, . . . [Material deleted by the NSC.] Sustained contacts with people behind the Curtain who will one day wield power is a principal path towards that goal.

Their attitudes and convictions can only be changed—gradually—if we can reach them on something approaching a normal, human basis.[32]

On September 22, 1955, Rockefeller wrote to Jackson suggesting that cultural exchange could help him fulfill his mission to implement NSC 5505/1. The eventual goal was to "redemocratize" Russia by flooding the country with information and ideas. Stefan Possony, a participant in Rockefeller's post-summit Quantico strategy session, elaborated:

It is therefore necessary to provide the Russian intelligentsia (in the broadest meaning of the term, which includes political leaders, industrialists, officers, etc.) with the necessary wherewithal in this field—to do their thinking for them or at least work up the required documentation.[33]

The final Western "Contacts" proposal at the October-November Foreign Ministers' Meeting was designed to realize those objectives. Of the seventeen points, five dealt with removal of barriers that interfered with free communications—jamming, restrictions on diplomatic movements, lack of direct air service, censorship of books, and censorship of press dispatches. The remaining twelve points had to do with expanded exchanges of people (through tourism, scientific exchanges, and cultural exchanges) and of information (through books, films, and radio broadcasts).[34] In addition, Dulles announced that U.S. passports would henceforth be valid for travel in the U.S.S.R. and that only moderate revision of the McCarran Act would be required.[35]

Moscow's first priority was to remove restrictions on East-West trade. The Soviet proposal did not touch on the question of barriers. It did, in general terms, endorse expanded exchanges of people and information.[36]

The unusually detailed published record of the Foreign Ministers' deliberations need not be recapitulated here. Suffice it to say that neither they nor their "experts" could reconcile the Soviet and Western views of the "Contacts" question. Moscow branded the Western proposal on removal of barriers a transparent excuse for interference in Soviet internal affairs. The West declared Soviet trade proposals outside the scope of the directive because they dealt with strategic trade, rather than trade in "peaceful goods." The delegations could not agree on specific procedures for exchanges of people and information.[37] Secretary Dulles captured the tenor of the discussions in a dispatch to the President:

There seems to be no willingness at all on the Soviet side to make any concessions in the way of freer flow of information through exchanges of broadcasts, information centers, and the like.

After session relatively calm at the beginning [sic] matters became heated largely as a result of [French Foreign Minister] Pinay's presentation and Molotov made a harsh Bolshevik-type statement to effect [sic] that Bourgeoise powers representing special class interests should never be allowed to see their wares in the Soviet Union. . . . This was said with cold finality which obviously Molotov as an old Bolshevik enjoyed.[38]

As was the case at the summit, Dulles carried out the President's wishes to the best of his ability but was not much perturbed by the final deadlock. He cabled Vice-President Nixon that there probably would not and *should* not be an agreement.[39] Given a choice, he preferred that specific and highly desirable exchanges first be proposed by the United States. Proceeding from general principles toward specifics during the course of international negotiations gave wily Moscow too great a role in shaping policy. Dulles, however, did not want to make such a choice at all. Jealous of Rockefeller's influence with the President and still very concerned about the liabilities of cultural exchange, he was not about to take the initiative.

This became obvious when the State Department had to accept or reject numerous pending exchange proposals from private American groups and organizations. The State Department had pigeonholed every one of these before the Foreign Ministers' meeting, hoping to strengthen the Secretary's bargaining position. On November 10, when failure at Geneva was already evident, a new request to allow Soviet agricultural experts to visit this country was held up. A spokesman confessed that the exchange policy was still "in flux" and that it was necessary to develop more orderly procedures. The seed industry group that had invited the Russians promptly and vigorously protested.[40] Faced with the possibility that such tactics would revive charges of an "American Iron Curtain,"[41] Dulles had to make a decision. On November 14, Ambassador Charles Bohlen handed the Soviet Foreign Office a memorandum suggesting that both sides go ahead with reciprocal exchanges in several areas, particularly medicine and agriculture. This initiative was not made public because the State Department again found itself between Scylla and Charybdis on cultural exchange. *Pravda* finally revealed the contents of the memorandum on February 3, 1956, when Moscow announced acceptance of its terms. The timing of the *Pravda* article was significant. Failure at the Foreign Ministers' conference had strengthened opposition to exchanges, causing a full-fledged controversy within the Eisenhower administration. Moscow apparently decided to intervene in favor of those who supported broadened exchanges by accepting the November 14 proposal.[42]

Marguerite Higgins disclosed the new imbroglio in an exclusive *New York Herald Tribune* article on January 23, 1956. She described efforts by Under Secretary Herbert Hoover, Jr., certain officials of the Department of Commerce, the FBI, and the Pentagon to persuade the President to halt existing exchanges with the U.S.S.R. Hoover feared that U.S.-Soviet fraternization would cause U.S. allies to reduce defense expenditures. The Commerce Department worried about a technology drain, warning that the United States "would give away technological secrets and get nothing in return." The FBI felt powerless to deal with increased Soviet espionage. The Pentagon reasoned that reduction of tensions would "give Secretary of the Treasury Humphrey just the argument he needed to reduce the military budget still further."[43]

Those who supported exchanges (identified by Higgins only as the "majority of the Department of State," with no mention of Dulles) appeared to be on the defensive. While they did respond convincingly to the disturbing questions asked by their opponents, they built no strong case of their own. Perhaps this was because they could not agree on a single justification for cultural exchanges. Optimists hoped to promote coexistence with a regime that pessimists yearned to subvert; some, like the President, could not view the problem in such simple, "either-or" terms. But faced with a major and now public rift, Eisenhower must have been under pressure to act decisively.

A showdown apparently took place during the National Security Council sessions of February 27 and March 1, 1956. (Minutes of both sessions remain classified.) The President accepted a recommendation calling for "selective expansion of free-world Communist bloc contacts," thereby effectively bloodying the noses of the opposition.[44] Nonetheless, the triumph must have been less than satisfying. The muddled rationale for exchanges conceded by the NSC could, and was perhaps intended to, mean all thing to all the victors. Hence, it probably pleased no one: "[Cultural Exchange,] if accepted, would favor evolution of the Soviet society and economy toward peaceful development, or if rejected, would expose the persistence of expansionism behind the facade of Soviet tactics and propaganda."[45] This statement was followed by the obligatory Dulles caveat concerning the impact of such a decision on allies and Third World nations. With the departure of Rockefeller (who resigned in December 1955), and Khrushchev's speech to the Twentieth Party Congress, which caused him to question long-held beliefs about the stability of the Soviet regime, the Secretary must have been more sanguine about the possibility that the benefits of cultural exchange would more than outweigh the disadvantages.

Eisenhower ordered a study of how this decision might be implemented. The process was tortuously slow. During his May 9 press conference, the President told James Reston that he had not made a detailed analysis of the question recently and knew of no progress.[46] Apparently, there had been none because Dulles, whose department was most directly involved, had not made his position clear. Shortly afterwards, William Jackson paid the Secretary a visit, lamenting that the issue "had been batted around for two months and that the time had come to reach a decision."[47] Warned by Jackson that the matter might be settled without his participation, Dulles almost immediately drafted a detailed statement on cultural exchange policy.

In his May 12 memorandum, Dulles not only decisively endorsed large-scale exchanges, but also sided with those who would employ them to subvert the Soviet regime. He did so because he was finally convinced that "for the first time since the end of World War II" internal pressures were forcing liberalization of the Soviet system and promoting independence in Eastern Europe.[48] Because he believed that communism would succumb to a combination of internal pressure accentuated by external pressure,[49] Dulles concluded that the time had come for the United States to

promote within Soviet Russia evolution toward a regime which will abandon predatory policies, which will seek to promote the aspirations of the Russian people rather than the global ambitions of International Communism and which will increasingly rest upon the consent of the governed rather than upon despotic police power.[50]

At first glance, this strategy appeared to differ from that of Nelson Rockefeller only in shrillness of expression. There was a crucial distinction, however. Rockefeller placed great faith in an intellectual appeal to future Russian leaders, urging them to initiate reform from above. He assumed that such people could be approached on a "normal, human basis." Dulles, who made an absolute distinction between the essential goodness of the Russian people and the evil nature of international communism, would set one against the other, initiating reform from below. Hence, the objectives of his program were really quite different:

(a) To increase the knowledge of the Soviet people as to the outer world so that their judgements will be based upon facts and not Communist fiction.
(b) To encourage freedom of thought by bringing to the Soviet people challenging ideas and demonstrating to Soviet intellectuals the scope of intellectual freedom which is encouraged in the United States.
(c) To stimulate the demand of Soviet citizens for greater personal security by bringing home to them the degree of personal security which is afforded by our constitutional and legal systems.
(d) To stimulate their desire for more consumer's [sic] goods by bringing them to realize how rich are the fruits of free labor and how much they themselves could gain from a government which primarily sought their well being and not conquest.
(e) To stimulate nationalism within the satellite countries by reviving the historic traditions of these peoples and suggesting the great benefits which can be derived from a courageous policy of defiance of Moscow such as Tito exhibited.[51]

Dulles proposed that the United States adopt the seventeen-point Geneva proposal on contacts between East and West as a guide for bilateral negotiations with Moscow. He further recommended that a new Assistant Secretary be appointed to implement the new policy.

The Operations Coordinating Board (OCB) and National Security Council discussed the matter at meetings on May 31 and June 29, respectively. The OCB minutes are too cursory to be informative, and the NSC minutes remain classified.[52] Fortunately, this does not present an insurmountable problem to the researcher, since the Dulles memorandum was approved and accepted as U.S. policy by the NSC and the President *word for word*.[53]

On June 29, 1956, the President's Press Secretary, James Hagerty, announced Eisenhower's acceptance of the National Security Council's recommendation that the United States seek to expand exchanges of people and information with the Soviet Union and Eastern Europe. Of course, the real rationale for the decision was not stated. Moscow could hardly be expected to rush into cultural relations with a government that openly proclaimed its resolve to undermine the Soviet system. Hagerty spoke only of the President's belief that such a program "may now contribute to the better understanding of the peoples of the world, that must be the foundation of peace."[54] But in reality the "American Iron Curtain" had been lifted for the same reason that it had descended several years earlier. Cultural exchange policy had consistently reflected the assumption that U.S. national security depended on defeating international communism, not learning how to coexist with it.

President Eisenhower's conviction that exchanges of people and information could enhance mutual understanding and preserve peace did not shape American policy during 1955–1956. The National Security Council endorsed limited exchanges with the U.S.S.R. in March 1955 only because of widespread fear that Moscow might reap immense benefits by demonstrating that the Iron Curtain had been both invented and erected in America. Western proposals for expansion of East-West contacts at both Geneva conferences fell on deaf ears, and conservatives seized on Soviet rejection of the President's initiative as proof that all exchanges should be terminated. Eisenhower refused to accept their advice in early 1956, but could not secure approval of large-scale exchanges without the support of his Secretary of State. Dulles offered that support in May 1956. His fears of communist subversion were finally tempered by the hope that exchanges might encourage an incipient rejection of communism by the peoples of Russia and Eastern Europe. Eisenhower finally obtained the ringing endorsement of cultural exchange with the Soviet Union that he had so long desired, but the cost of that endorsement was an acceptance of Dulles' cultural exchange policy.[55]

NOTES

1. Frederick C. Barghoorn, *The Soviet Cultural Offensive* (Princeton, N.J.: Princeton University Press, 1960).

2. Aline B. Louchheim, "Cultural Diplomacy: An Art We Neglect," *New York Times Magazine*, January 3, 1954, p. 36.

3. *New York Times*, May 15, 1953.

4. *New York Times*, July 5, 1954.

5. "The President's News Conference of March 2, 1955," *Public Papers of the Presidents of the United States: Dwight D. Eisenhower* (Washington, D.C.: Government Printing Office, 1955), p. 47.

6. "Notes from W. R. Hearst on Russian Visit," *Dwight D. Eisenhower, Papers as President of the United States* (Whitman File), International Meetings Series, USSR, 1953–55 (2), Box 45.

7. "Marshall MacDuffie Meeting with Khrushchev in Moscow, February 1, 1955," *Eisenhower Papers* (Whitman File), International Meetings Series, USSR, 1953–55 (1), Box 45.

8. D. Zaslavsky, "Iron Curtain U.S.A.," *Pravda*, January 20, 1955. Complete translation in *Current Digest of the Soviet Press* No. 3 (1955). Numerous articles on this same theme appeared in the Soviet press during the first six months of 1955.

9. "Admission to the U.S. of Certain European Non-Official Temporary Visitors Excludable under Existing Law, NSC 5508/1," *Eisenhower Papers* (Whitman File), NSC Series, Box 1, pp. 1–2.

10. NSC 5508/1, p. 11.

11. Hoover to Lay, Yeagley to Lay, NSC 5508/1, pp. 14–17. These were committees within the National Security Council. The IIC included the Director of the FBI, as well as the directors of Army, Air Force, and Naval Intelligence. The ICIS included representatives from the Department of State, Justice, Treasury, and from the military. See Athan Theoharis, *Spying on Americans* (Philadelphia: Temple University Press, 1978), p. 78.

12. NSC 5508/1, pp. 6–7.

13. NSC 5508/1, p. 7.

14. Townsend Hoopes, *The Devil and John Foster Dulles: The Diplomacy of the Eisenhower Era* (Boston: Little, Brown, 1973), p. 161.

15. NSC 5508/1, pp. 8–9.

16. *New York Times*, April 16, 1955. Harrison Salisbury commented on the effectiveness of Soviet propaganda in the *New York Times*, May 7, 1955, more than a month after the new policy was in place.

17. *New York Times*, July 23, 1955.

18. Dwight D. Eisenhower, "Propaganda and Truth," in *Peace and Justice* (New York: Columbia University Press, 1961), p. 72.

19. Paul D. Davies, "The New Diplomacy: The 1955 Geneva Summit Meeting," in Roger Hilsman and Robert C. Good, eds., *Foreign Policy in the Sixties* (Baltimore: Johns Hopkins University Press, 1965), pp. 165–67.

20. Dulles referred to the President's pragmatism regarding cultural exchange in "Telephone Conversation with Attorney General Brownell," *John Foster Dulles Papers, 1952–59, Telephone Calls Series, Telephone Conversations, General, Sept. 1-Dec. 30, 1955* (4), Box 4.

21. It is difficult to document Dulles' views on cultural exchange before the summit. Compare "Dulles to Eisenhower, June 18, 1955" (a statement of thoughts on the Geneva agenda which does not mention cultural exchange) with "U.S. Goals at Geneva," dated July 1, 1955 (where the issue finally surfaces), *John Foster Dulles Papers* (Mudd Library, Princeton), *Selected Correspondence and Related Materials, F-G: Geneva "Big Four Conference, July, 1955*. The problem is further complicated by the fact that NSC policy paper 5524/1, approved on July 12 for the purpose of providing policy guidance to Dulles on agenda items, does not even mention cultural exchange. See "Basic U.S. Policy in Relation to Four Power Negotiations, NSC 5524/1," *Eisenhower Papers* (Whitman File), NSC Series, Four Power Negotiations (1).

22. Examples of such evasive responses may be found in Dulles' exchanges with reporters during his press conferences of July 26, 1955, and October 18, 1955, in *Press Conferences of American Secretarys of State* (Wilmington, Del.: Scholarly Resources, 1978).

23. "Report of the Quantico Vulnerabilities Panel, June 10, 1955." Published in *Declassified Documents Retrospective Collection* (Washington, D.C.: Carrolton Press, 1975), 1984, 000435, Appendix B, p. 6.

24. Mundt to Eisenhower, *Eisenhower Papers* (Whitman File), Ann Whitman Diary, Geneva, 1955 (4), Box 6.

25. Thompson to Eisenhower, *Congressional Record Appendix*, July 14, 1955, A–5157-A5159.

26. *New York Times*, October 24, 1955.

27. *Meeting of the Heads of Government of France, United Kingdom, Soviet Union, and United States, Geneva, 1955* (Washington, D.C.: Department of State, 1955), p. 63.

28. Livingstone Merchant, *Recollections of the Summit, Geneva, 1955, Written for Circulation to Members of the Delegation* in *Dulles Papers* (Mudd Library, Princeton), *Selected Correspondence and Related Materials, 1955: F-G, Geneva "Big Four" Conference, July, 1955*, p. 44.

29. *New York Times*, October 2, 1955.

30. Dulles expressed this view both publicly and privately. See his press conference of April 24, 1956, and his crucial May 12 memorandum on cultural exchange cited in note 48.

31. Charles Bohlen, *Witness to History* (New York: W. W. Norton, 1973), pp. 343–44.

32. Rockefeller to Jackson, September 22, 1955, *Eisenhower Papers* (Confidential File), Rockefeller, Nelson (1), Box 61.

33. Stefan Possony, "The Purpose, Requirements, and Structure of an American Ideological Program," a component paper in: Quantico Vulnerabilities Panel, *Psychological Aspects of U.S. Strategy*, published in *Declassified Documents Retrospective Collection, 1977* (Washington, D.C.: Carrolton Press, 1975), A–269, p. 219.

34. *Geneva Meeting of Foreign Ministers, October 27–November 16, 1955* (Washington, D.C.: Department of State, 1955), pp. 245–48.

35. *New York Times*, November 6, 1955.

36. *Geneva Meeting of Foreign Ministers*, pp. 238–40.

37. Ibid., pp. 279–83.

38. Dulles to Eisenhower, November 14, 1955, *Eisenhower Papers* (Whitman File), Dulles-Herter Series, Hon. Foster Dulles, November 1955 (1).

39. Dulles to Nixon, *Dulles Papers* (Mudd Library, Princeton), *Selected Correspondence and Related Materials, 1955: H-J, Hoover, Herbert, Jr.*

40. *New York Times*, November 11 and 12, 1955.

41. This possibility had never been totally dismissed. See the *New York Times*, September 19, 1955.

42. *Pravda*, February 3, 1956.

43. *New York Herald Tribune*, January 23, 1956. Under Secretary Hoover's position is more clearly stated in the *New York Times* of June 4, 1956. The Pentagon quotation reflects columnist Drew Pearson's conversations with several high Pentagon officials. It appeared in his column of November 26, 1955. All of these articles may also be found in the FBI unclassified file "East-West Exchanges," file number 105–42300-A. Other FBI sources remain classified after a 1982 review.

44. "Basic National Security Policy, NSC 5602/1," *Eisenhower Papers* (Whitman File), NSC Series, Box 4.

45. NSC 5602/1, p. 13.

46. "The President's News Conference of May 9, 1956," *Eisenhower Public Papers, 1956*, p. 472.

47. "Memorandum of a Conversation with William Jackson, 11 A.M.," *Dulles*

Papers, General Correspondence and Memoranda Series, Memoranda of Conversations, General, J-K (1), Box 1.

48. "East-West Exchanges (Draft 2)," *Dulles Papers, Subject Series, East-West Contacts, 1956*, Box 4, p. 2.

49. Rudolph Holsti, "The Belief System and National Images: John Foster Dulles and the Soviet Union," Ph.D. diss., Stanford University, 1962, p. 206.

50. "East-West Exchanges (Draft 2)," p. 2.

51. Ibid., pp. 5–6.

52. "OCB Meeting of 5/31/56 re. East-West Exchanges," *Eisenhower Papers* (Whitman File), NSC Series, OCB Minutes of Meetings, 1956 (3), Box 3. According to Fred I. Greenstein, the mission of the Operations Co-ordinating Board was "to see that decisions did not just go into the files in the form of re-edited policy papers, but actually resulted in plans for carrying out the decided policies." Fred I. Greenstein, *The Hidden-Hand Presidency* (New York: Basic Books, 1982), p. 133.

53. "East-West Exchanges, NSC 5607," *Eisenhower Papers* (Whitman File), NSC Series, Box 17.

54. *New York Times*, June 30, 1956.

55. Eisenhower first accepted Dulles' position in a cryptic note to Herbert Hoover, Jr. See Eisenhower to Herbert Hoover, Jr., May 30, 1956, *Eisenhower Papers* (Whitman File), Dulles-Herter Series, Dulles, Foster, May 1956, Box 5. The President did not give any reason for accepting Dulles' view. Until the minutes of the NSC session of June 28 are declassified, this must remain the subject of speculation.*

*The minutes of the National Security Council sessions of June 28, 1956, and March 24, 1955 (see discussion in text preceding note 14) were declassified in 1986, as this chapter was going to press. While providing a wealth of new detail, they substantially confirm the conclusions reached here. President Eisenhower's position regarding NSC 5607 is, unfortunately, not explicitly stated.

17

The Specter of Neutralism: Eisenhower, India, and the Problem of Nonalignment

Henry William Brands, Jr.

As fighting in Korea sputtered to a close in the early 1950s, a change in the nature of the Cold War was becoming evident. The development of deliverable nuclear weapons predisposed both American and Soviet strategists to shift the struggle for world influence from the military to the political and economic realms. Coinciding as it did with the emergence of new nations in Asia and Africa, this shift resulted in heightened competition for support among the newly independent peoples.

To many Americans, recently won over to the doctrine of collective security, support was often interpreted as implying formal alliance. With the enthusiasm of the converted, American officials, especially in the Eisenhower administration, spread the message of concerted resistance to communism across Asia from the Mediterranean to the Pacific, with some success. Among the new nations, however, were several that had no desire to limit their hard-won independence by a pact with the United States—or, for that matter, with any country. Within this consciously distant group there developed the postwar concept of nonalignment, or neutralism. The most influential of the neutralists was India. (Although the terms ''nonalignment'' and ''neutralism'' seem to carry somewhat different connotations—neutralism implying an active promotion common to most ''isms''—the two words, along with ''neutrality,'' were used interchangeably within the Eisenhower administration. As will be seen, American officials clearly recognized the difference between a passive nonalignment and an active neutralism. In writing and speech, however, the terminological distinction was not usually made. No confusion will arise here from following contemporary usage.)

Neutralism represented a potential problem to the Eisenhower administration. American security, it seemed, rested on American alliances, and while nonalignment itself might be unobjectionable, to the extent that it drew would-be allies away from the United States, neutralism posed a threat to American security. Thus, neutralist tendencies had to be discouraged. However, the issue was complex—as most diplomatic questions are—and competing interests had to be balanced.

This chapter examines some evidence regarding the attitude of the Eisenhower administration toward neutralism generally and toward Indian neutralism in particular. The focus is on American reactions to India because they so well elucidate the complexities involved in the neutralism issue. American planners considered India to be of vital importance to the future of the free world in Asia, but India's advocacy of nonalignment created special difficulties for the United States.

The Eisenhower administration's most-noticed statement on the subject of neutralism was made by Secretary of State John Foster Dulles in the spring of 1956. In a speech at Ames College, Dulles declared that the postwar period was the age of collective security. Neutrality, he said, had become outmoded; it was "an increasingly obsolete conception." Furthermore, he continued, it was, except under very special circumstances, "an immoral and short-sighted conception."[1]

As Dulles must have expected, an announcement by the American Secretary of State that nonalignment was "immoral" immediately caught the attention of observers in the United States and abroad. Even coming from one who was commonly thought to consider the dispensation of hellfire and damnation as part of his official duties, this was strong talk. Questions at once arose as to whether Dulles was speaking *ex cathedra* in denouncing neutralism or was merely exercising his talent for provocative phrase-making.

A good deal of confusion clouded the matter, for only a few days before Dulles' address, President Eisenhower had offered some comments at a news conference that could be taken either to support or to contradict the Secretary's statement, depending on how they were interpreted. On one side of the issue, Eisenhower had gone out of his way to publicize Dulles' speech, and he had specifically directed reporters' attention to the remarks the Secretary would be making regarding neutralism. More than this, the President said that Dulles would be speaking "not only with my approval but really with my great support." On the other hand, moments before this enthusiastic buildup of Dulles' statement on nonalignment, Eisenhower had taken a considerably softer line than the one the Secretary would pronounce. Eisenhower reminded those present that the United States had been a neutral for 150 years, and he suggested that nonalignment might be less an ethical choice than a political and military one. Furthermore, he indicated that he himself could understand how, under certain circumstances, the national self-interest of a particular country might prescribe a neutral stance between the two great power blocs.[2]

Reporters trying to resolve the question of which of the President's and Secretary's statements on neutralism represented official American policy did not make much progress a couple of days later when they attempted to pin Dulles down.

Was there any discrepancy between the positions of the White House and the State Department, they asked. Of course not, replied Dulles. What *was* the administration's attitude, then, they pressed. Dulles responded by saying that, as usual, the President's remarks represented government policy; if there appeared to be any divergence between his own statements on neutralism and certain statements by the President, such difference was entirely a matter of semantics. When a correspondent asked Dulles to expand on the type of circumstances that might justify—in the opinion of the administration—a neutral position for a country, the Secretary declined to elaborate.[3]

Students of American politics at the time were left wondering what the Eisenhower administration really thought about neutralism, and for students of American history today, the question remains. A number of answers are possible. One that would have met general acceptance several years ago but seems less tenable in light of recent scholarship is that, since Dulles was the prime mover of American foreign policy, the Secretary's statement on "immoral" neutralism was the operative one. If the White House and the State Department seemed to be saying differing things, it was because Dulles was given more or less free rein to decide where the government stood on diplomatic issues. In any event, his was the voice to listen to. A variation of this explanation would have Dulles on a shorter leash, with Eisenhower more firmly in control but with the Secretary trying to tug the President in the direction of a tougher approach to what appeared to be a proliferation of agnosticism between democracy and communism. In this version, Dulles would not have had policymaking carte blanche, but rather a checking account with limited overdraft protection supplied by Eisenhower's trust in the Secretary's judgment.

A third explanation for the evident split between Eisenhower and Dulles on nonalignment is that the administration was engaged in some deliberate obfuscation. Adherents of the Eisenhower-as-activist school might find this interpretation appealing; by keeping the world guessing, the President kept open as many alternatives as possible. A variant of this approach would invoke the old "tough-cop-nice-cop routine," with Dulles in the role of ideological brinksman—and sentry on the administration's domestic right flank—and Eisenhower as peacemaker. In either variation of this explanation, the discrepancy between the confrontational attitude and the conciliatory was by design. A fourth possibility is that, on the issue of neutralism, the administration could not make up its collective mind; the seeming ambivalence and confusion were genuine—the consequences of a lack of a clearly thought-out policy.

There is, undoubtedly, some truth in each of these explanations, and the interpretation offered here, though different from each, will borrow features from more than one of the above. Specifically, the present argument is that, on the issue of neutralism, the Eisenhower administration *did* have a fairly coherent policy; that the discrepancy between the publicly stated views of the President and the Secretary *was* by design; and that this discrepancy did *not* represent an attempt to sow uncertainty as much as it reflected a perception that neutralism was a multifaceted issue requiring a flexible set of responses. To the Eisenhower administration, it would seem, there was neutralism, and neutralism.

With regard to the opinion of Eisenhower himself on the various issues wrapped up in neutralism, the clearest expression appears in a letter which the President wrote to his brother Edgar in the late winter of 1956. In this letter, Eisenhower distinguished between what could be termed ideological-ethical neutralism and military-political neutralism. He also pointed out that American resources were not unlimited; he argued that these limitations dictated a certain flexibility in approaching the issue of nonalignment; and he stressed the importance of world opinion regarding the matter. Wrote the President:

You and I, of course, know that there is no neutral position as between honesty and falsehood, or, indeed, as between any moral value and its opposite. However, the concept of neutrality for a nation does not necessarily mean that that nation is trying to occupy a position midway between right and wrong. In the ordinary sense, neutrality applies to military combinations.

Now it is very true that we want every nation we can reach to stand with us in support of the basic principles of free government. But for a long time, I have held that it is a very grave error to ask some of these nations to announce themselves as being on our side in the event of a possible conflict. Such a statement on the part of a weak nation like Burma, or even India, would at once make them our all-out ally and we would have the impossible task of helping them arm for defense.

Moreover, if a country would declare itself our military ally, then any attack made upon it by Communist groups would be viewed in most areas of the world as a more or less logical consequence. Since so much of the world thinks of the existing *ideological* struggle as a *power* struggle, the reaction to the kind of conflict I talk about would be, ''Well, they asked for it.''

On the other hand, if the Soviets attacked an avowed neutral, world opinion would be outraged.[4]

Eisenhower repeated much of the argument expressed in this letter at the June 1956 press conference previously mentioned. Here again he emphasized the significance of world opinion, especially the way in which the peoples of the world viewed the contest between the United States and the Soviet Union. Flexibility, too, was stressed—as it was again in some remarks made to presidential assistant Sherman Adams at about the same time. ''Neutralism is not necessarily an evil,'' Eisenhower told Adams. Rather, if the administration played its cards right, neutralism might, at times, be of positive benefit to the United States. As an example, Eisenhower cited the rift between the Soviet Union and Yugoslavia, and he said that he regarded Tito ''as one of the greatest assets we have in dealing with the satellite states of Europe.''[5]

Pragmatic though he was on the neutralism issue, Eisenhower was no liberal. His flexibility must not be ignored, but neither should it be overplayed. Eisenhower was no less firm in his anticommunism and no less committed to the doctrine of collective security than was the more outspoken Dulles, and the

President's acceptance of nonalignment in particular cases did not imply endorsement of nonalignment as a general policy. American interests might benefit from the existence of communist neutrals like Yugoslavia; American security might not be incompatible with a few democratic neutrals like Burma or India; but if neutralism should spread as a third force among the emerging nations of Asia and Africa, it might erode the alliance system on which the administration placed so much weight. It was for this reason that Eisenhower and his advisers were very attentive to the role of India and its Prime Minister Jawaharlal Nehru as active advocates of nonalignment.

Because of its size and location alone, American planners would have regarded India as the key to the underdeveloped world. Intelligence analysts underlined the potential economic and military value of the subcontinent to the security of the United States.[6] In the summer of 1953, Eisenhower noted that one of the reasons why the United States had to worry about French problems in Indochina was that Indochina guarded the approaches to India. Were a communist victory in Indochina allowed to occur, he said, "India would be outflanked."[7]

But India's importance transcended military and economic considerations. Following the triumph of communist forces in China, India had become a symbol of the hopes of Americans for the future of Asia. China had fallen to the communists; India was the last great democracy among the newly independent nations, and it must not fall. Eisenhower captured this sentiment when he told a visitor, "India is a vast continent of 350 million people. If they are ever added to the great populations that the Communists now control, the free world will be up against it, not only in the East but throughout Asia."[8]

India's symbolic significance was heightened by a perception that India was competing with China for the destiny of the developing world. According to American strategists, the competition centered not on armaments but on the ability of the governments of India and China to attain the economic expansion required to meet the basic needs of their growing populations. China, by the methods of communism, seemed to be making progress in this direction. The question was, could India deliver the goods by democratic means? The authors of a 1954 study for the National Security Council were not entirely optimistic. Reporting a general disappointment within the subcontinent at the region's slow rate of growth, the authors concluded that if democracy did not improve its economic performance, "an increasing number of South Asians may become susceptible to Communist argument that the only alternative is the adoption of methods employed in communist countries, especially Communist China."[9]

To some observers in and near the Eisenhower administration, the solution to the problem of matching the communists in raising living standards lay in American economic aid. This solution gained some support from an apparent decision by Soviet leaders, after the death of Stalin, to mount an "economic offensive" in Asia and Africa. The arguments of the proponents of aid were not lost on Eisenhower. At one point in 1955, the President spoke of forming an economic alliance system similar to the network of military alliances that the United States had built.[10] By his second term in office, Eisenhower had become convinced that the United States must respond to the new Soviet challenge.[11]

An economic counteroffensive was slow to materialize, however, especially in the direction of India. Congress was parsimonious enough when it came to appropriating funds for declared American allies; in the case of neutralists like India, the purse snapped nearly shut. Opponents of aid argued that tax dollars spent on countries clearly on the side of the free world would yield greater returns than dollars offered to countries that appeared to be playing the United States off against the Soviet Union. Republican right-wingers declared that subsidizing India would seem to be rewarding neutralism, with a consequent demoralizing effect on America's allies.[12]

Thus, Indian neutralism confronted the Eisenhower administration with a perplexing problem. India had to be saved for the free world, but this could be accomplished only by economic development. Economic development along democratic lines seemed to require American aid, but India's deliberate aloofness made it politically impossible to provide aid at the level required. So the question became, could India be weaned from its neutralist ways?

The answer to this question, as everyone in the administration recognized, depended on the often inscrutable Pandit Nehru. The Indian Prime Minister, for reasons both of personality and politics, was a source of endless fascination to American officials. Eisenhower got along quite well with Nehru but found his character difficult to fathom. "Nehru was not easy to understand," the President wrote; "few people are, but his was a personality of unusual contradictions." Eisenhower judged Nehru to be sadly naive in his belief that Western imperialism and Soviet expansionism were evils of a similar order. Stating that the passive resistance techniques that had been successful in achieving India's independence from Britain had worked because Britain had a conscience, Eisenhower remarked, "Should Nehru try passive resistance against the Communists, I am sure he would get a rude awakening."[13]

The President puzzled over Nehru's reliability and wondered about the dependability of Indian officials generally. "I don't know about these Indians," he commented to Press Secretary James Hagerty. "They are funny people and I don't know how far we can actually trust them."[14] Eisenhower believed that Nehru often responded to events more emotionally than rationally, and he told Dulles, "Nehru seems to be often more swayed by personality than by logical argument. He seems to be intensely personal in his whole approach."[15]

It was this personal aspect, Eisenhower felt, that lay behind Nehru's neutralism—behind his aversion to forming close ties with the West and his equanimity in the face of clear evidence of Soviet aggressiveness. Part of the explanation, Eisenhower admitted, was that it was the West—that is, Britain—that had dominated Nehru's country for centuries. He added:

But I think the answer goes deeper than that; as an Asian from a less-developed nation, it is possible that Mr. Nehru felt more resentment of an intangible Western condescension toward his people than he felt toward any specific act of violence that either East or West might commit. Life, after all, is cheaper in the Orient, or so it would appear; recognition as equals by the "white" race is not. Perhaps Mr. Nehru, despite his excellent Western education and flawless English, was able to identify with the Soviets at times as "fellow Asians," a point that came out continually in his hope that the West could do something to make the Soviets feel they "were not being looked down upon."[16]

Whatever the source of Nehru's neutralist feelings might have been, Eisenhower and other administration officials realized there was little hope of enticing India into the Western camp. Matters were not helped by the fact that Nehru seemed to be getting much of his advice about the West from Krishna Menon, the Indian Foreign Minister who was generally considered within the Eisenhower administration to be an apologist for the communists. "A menace and a boor," Eisenhower labeled Menon.[17] However, Nehru's advisers were of secondary importance; the Prime Minister was the key to India's foreign policy. A 1956 intelligence estimate summarized the American view of Nehru: "He *is* India—since Independence, no Indian policy, domestic or foreign, has had any other author."[18] Moreover, Nehru's attachment to neutralism was unshakable; nonalignment was the foundation stone of his diplomatic philosophy.[19]

Thus, any attempt to turn India away from neutralism was bound to fail. The administration might as well recognize this fact and put the best face on it. This, no doubt, was what Eisenhower was doing when he spoke of neutralism as being something less than a sin. The administration ought not to rail publicly against that which it could not change—or at least the President should not. Especially after the Geneva Summit Conference, Eisenhower had a reputation to maintain as a broadminded man of peace.

Neutralism in India was one thing, but Nehru was in the business of exporting neutralism—of actively promoting nonalignment in Asia and Africa as an alternative to the American doctrine of collective security. To the extent that Nehru's sales pitch succeeded, the system of alliances on which the administration considered the safety of the United States to rest would be put at risk. This rationale was evidently what Dulles had in mind when he denounced neutralism as a form of immorality. While a committed and relatively powerful neutralist like India might be immune to American persuasion, other nations were not. American allies and clients in Asia had to be reminded that any softening of support for the United States would be viewed with disapproving eyes.

Nor were the reminders merely rhetorical. Before the 1955 Bandung Conference of Asian and African countries, for example—an affair which American leaders considered a test of Nehru's stature as the number-one neutralist in the developing world—the administration put pressure on Pakistan, Turkey, Iran, and other "friendly Asian nations" to counter Nehru's influence. Dulles, for one, was pleased with the results. Bandung, he reported to Eisenhower, "was a severe reverse for Mr. Nehru and a great loss of prestige for him."[20] After the conference, the administration continued the attempts to neutralize Indian neutralism.

Dulles went so far as to lay plans for what he called a "Bandung Conference in reverse."

Although this antineutralist gathering of American allies never took place—the trial balloons Dulles lofted were shot down over Suez in the autumn of 1956—the fact that it was contemplated was significant.[21] A rollback of neutralism might not be possible, but its containment *was* possible and seemed necessary. Nehru might be beyond the reach of the United States, but would-be emulators would be warned against following Nehru's example. If the diplomatic leverage which the administration could bring to bear had to be supplemented with the language of the pulpit—well, Dulles was hardly the person to shirk such a duty.

The Eisenhower administration's two-track policy toward neutralism—a policy of acquiescence where neutralism could not be prevented, but of opposition to its extension—was a rather sophisticated response to a tricky problem. To hold the American alliance system together in the face of India's neutralist challenge, without having the whole administration sound like warmongers, was not a simple task. To say that the response was sophisticated, however, is not to say that it was appropriate, nor that it worked. Whether it was, whether it did—these questions deserve more attention than can be given here; to each, the answer is, Yes and No. For the moment, let two observations suffice.

First, on the positive side: The attempts to deal with neutralism, whether or not successful, at least had the commendable quality that they were relatively pacific. No B–52s had their engines revved up; no marines were landed; no governments were overthrown. In light of the activities of the Eisenhower administration elsewhere in the world, this is no small consideration.

Second, on the negative side: For all its subtlety, administration policy toward neutralist nations was rather shallow. The attitudes of Eisenhower, Dulles, and other top officials toward neutralism were informed by the same unquestioning anticommunism that inspired most American foreign policy during the 1950s. Neutralism was perceived to be a threat because communism was a threat; indeed, problems with India and other nonaligned states were seen not as problems with those countries but as problems with the Russians. The nations of Asia were judged to be little more than pawns—or dominoes—in a larger game. The Eisenhower administration managed to escape most of the consequences of playing dominoes in Asia, but later administrations—and the people of the United States—did not.

NOTES

1. *Department of State Bulletin*, June 18, 1956, pp. 999–1000.
2. *Public Papers of the Presidents: Dwight D. Eisenhower, 1956* (Washington, D.C.: U.S. Government Printing Office, 1958), pp. 554–56.
3. *Department of State Bulletin*, June 25, 1956, pp. 1064–65.
4. Eisenhower to Edgar Eisenhower, February 27, 1956, Box 13, DDE Diary Series,

Eisenhower Papers as President (Whitman File), Eisenhower Library, Abilene, Kansas. (All archival references below are to the Eisenhower Library.)

5. *Public Papers, 1956*, pp. 554–56. Pre-press conference notes, June 6, 1956, Box 5, Press Conference Series, Whitman File.

6. See, for example, National Intelligence Estimate (NIE–79), "Probable Developments in South Asia," June 30, 1963, *Foreign Relations of the United States, 1952–1954* 11 (Washington, D.C.: U.S. Government Printing Office, 1983), p. 1074.

7. *Public Papers, 1953*, p. 541.

8. James C. Hagerty diary, February 24, 1955, Box 1a, Hagerty Papers.

9. NSC 5409, "United States Policy Toward South Asia," undated (c. March 1954), *Foreign Relations, 1952–1954*, 11, pp. 1096–1117. See also Progress Report on NSC 5409, July 28, 1954, Box 9, Office of the Special Assistant for National Security Affairs Series, White House Records; and Draft NSC 5617, December 7, 1956, Box 19, ibid.

10. Eisenhower to Dulles, December 5, 1955, Box 3, Dulles Papers.

11. Changing attitudes within the Eisenhower administration on the merits of economic aid are well documented in Burton I. Kaufman, *Trade and Aid: Eisenhower's Foreign Economic Policy, 1953–1961* (Baltimore: Johns Hopkins University Press, 1982).

12. Kaufman, *Trade and Aid*, see especially ch. 4.

13. Eisenhower, *The White House Years: Waging Peace, 1956–1961* (Garden City, N.Y.: Doubleday, 1965), pp. 107–14.

14. Hagerty diary, March 15, 1955, Box 1a, Hagerty Papers.

15. Eisenhower to Dulles, March 23, 1955, Box 4, Dulles-Herter Series, Whitman File.

16. Eisenhower, *Waging Peace*, pp. 113–14.

17. Eisenhower diary, July 14, 1955, Box 11, DDE Diary Series, Whitman File.

18. Richard Collins, Deputy Director for Intelligence, Joint Chiefs of Staff, to JCS, September 11, 1956, *Declassified Documents References System* (Washington, D.C.: Carrollton Press, 1981), p. 460B.

19. See Draft NSC 5617, December 7, 1956, Box 19, Office of the Special Assistant for National Security Affairs Series, White House Office Records; NSC 5409, undated, *Foreign Relations, 1952–1954*, vol. 11, pp. 1100–1101; NIE–79, June 30, 1953, ibid., pp. 1074–76; W. Norman Brown, *The United States and India, Pakistan, and Bangladesh*, 3d ed. (Cambridge, Mass.: Harvard University Press, 1972), p. 387.

20. Cabinet minutes, April 19, 1955, Box 5, Cabinet Series, Whitman File.

21. On the proposed counter-Bandung conference, consult the Dulles Papers: for instance, Dulles to Hoover, November 23, 1955, Box 3; Dulles memcon with Lange, October 27, 1955, Box 6; Dulles telcon with Rusk, November 21, 1955, Box 4; Dulles memcon with Harold Macmillan, November 16, 1955, Box 6; Dulles to Macmillan, January 6, 1956, Box 6; and Warren I. Cohen, *Dean Rusk* (Totowa, N.J.: Cooper Square Publishers, 1980), pp. 82–83.

18

The Eisenhower Administration, Castro, and Cuba, 1959–1961

James M. Keagle

The story of the Cuban Revolution, as it was played out from 1959 to 1961, remains important to scholars, policymakers, and laypersons alike—important beyond the historical interest in drawing accurate inferences about U.S. policy and motivations or placing certain responsibilities on the Eisenhower administration for the abortive Bay of Pigs fiasco.[1]

Ever since 1961, a cornerstone of U.S. policy in the Western Hemisphere has been the isolation of Cuba, the prevention of another Cuba in this hemisphere, the containment of communism to Cuba, and an underlying hope that a democratic government would return to Cuba. Such objectives were made law in 1962 (Public Law 87–733) and reconfirmed in 1965.[2] In a more contemporary context, the Reagan administration has apparently chosen to view the development in Nicaragua and El Salvador by emphasizing the Cuban and Soviet connections. Secretary of Defense Caspar Weinberger has argued for the relevance of the Monroe Doctrine in response to questions about Cuban and Soviet involvement in the unrest in Central America. In November 1981, Secretary of State Alexander Haig was quoted as characterizing the Nicaraguan army under the Sandinista government as a "force for aggression and expansion of Marxist-Leninist policy in the hemisphere."[3] For that reason, he has refused to rule out a naval blockade against Nicaragua, and he has said there was a danger that the country could develop into "another Cuba in this hemisphere."

President Reagan has refused to rule out a blockade of Cuba. Early in 1982, he referred to the recent Soviet military buildup in Cuba as the largest since 1962; he called Cuba a "stooge" or "puppet" of the U.S.S.R., stating, "If Cuba were smart, they would rethink their position on rejoining the Western Hemisphere."[4] Most recently, the United States has responded to the crisis in the Caribbean by deploying carrier and battleship task forces to the region and exercising 5,000

Army troops in joint maneuvers with Honduras. The purpose, many believe, is to demonstrate U.S. resolve to meet the challenge posed by the Nicaraguan-Cuban-Soviet axis' fueling of Marxist, revolutionary insurgencies.

A better understanding of the U.S. response to the Cuban Revolution could conceivably contribute to a more informed, if not enlightened, U.S.-Latin American policy in the 1980s. By using some sources of information not previously available to or emphasized by researchers (recently declassified materials, public political communications such as news conferences, statements, and press releases, news reports and editorials at the time, and personal interviews with prominent and knowledgeable members of the Eisenhower staff), it has been possible to piece together more accurately than has been done before exactly what the evolution of President Eisenhower's policy was and why.

Although many specific questions remain to be answered, in part because many of the pieces of the puzzle remain classified or otherwise unavailable, the broad outlines are clear. Fidel Castro, as perceived by the United States, pursued a course inimical to the United States and eventually maneuvered himself into an alignment with the Soviet Union. In the U.S. view such an arrangement demonstrated the subservience of Castro and the Cuban government to the revolutionary aims of international communism and Soviet imperialism. This satellite status posed a grave threat to the security of the Western Hemisphere.

Ever since colonial times, many Americans had uniquely defined and perceived their national security interests in the Western Hemisphere. They viewed the hemisphere as a refuge for freedom and democracy. Above all, the Western Hemisphere represented a second chance for humankind. To achieve success in this new Garden of Eden, the contagion and disease of the rest of the world had to be denied entrance; once granted a foothold, this contamination could quickly spread—to the very borders of the United States. U.S. territorial, political, and economic expansion, as well as Eisenhower's response to the Cuban Revolution, can be explained in part by these perceived security needs.

In the Cold War atmosphere that dominated the late 1950s and early 1960s, "international communism" and "Soviet imperialism" were extracontinental threats. In the views of American policymakers, they threatened not only the principles of democracy, but also the very integrity and fabric of the inter-American system that had been cultivated by recent administrations. A communist, Soviet-dominated Cuba could not be tolerated, for it represented a beachhead from which communism and the Soviet Union could penetrate the rest of Latin America.

What made this threat even more ominous was Eisenhower's awareness that social, economic, and political change was on the immediate horizon for Latin American nations. Advisers such as John Moors Cabot, Assistant Secretary of State for Latin American Affairs, and the President's brother, Milton Eisenhower, had stressed the importance of this dawning era.[5] Drastic changes in the socioeconomic class structure and political leadership were inevitable. In these turbulent times, the United States could and should encourage the changes to take place via peaceful social evolution. Excessive resistance to the dynamics of change would only increase the likelihood that changes would be accomplished by violent social revolutions. Moreover, the United States was not alone in its attempt to influence the process of modernization. The Soviet Union and international communism were also competing to capture the lead and exercise a guiding force in Latin America. Thus, what was at stake in Cuba was more than just the personal leadership of the Cuban Revolution. Rather, in the minds of the Eisenhower administration, Cuba had become a battleground for U.S. and U.S.S.R. policies that were designed to meet the challenge of this new era of change.[6]

The perceptions that drove the U.S. decision-makers to authorize the abortive Bay of Pigs invasion in April 1961 were clearly articulated in the U.S. Department of State White Paper on Cuba, released just prior to the attack.[7] While attempting to place the United States on the side of economic and social reform, the Kennedy administration condemned Castro and the course of the Cuban Revolution, and stressed the grave and urgent challenge that Cuba posed to the inter-American system and Western Hemisphere. Specifically, the Kennedy administration argued that:

1. Castro had betrayed the Cuban Revolution by moving away from social reform and constitutional, democratic government dedicated to social and economic justice toward totalitarianism.

2. Castro's totalitarianism had sold itself to the ruthless discipline of communism.

3. Castro's subservience to the communists had resulted in an alliance between Cuba and the Soviet Union in which the U.S.S.R. was the dominant partner.

4. Castro, communism, and the U.S.S.R. in Cuba were a threat to the entire hemisphere—a staging base for revolutionary activity against the hemisphere (as demonstrated by Cuban aid and support for the armed aggression in Panama, Nicaragua, the Dominican Republic, and Haiti in 1959 and Castro's articulated rejection of the Organization of American States (OAS).

This argument will be tested by ascertaining when and why Eisenhower reached these conclusions which precipitated U.S. policy changes; by identifying patterns and shifts in the Eisenhower administration's public and private communications; and by demonstrating how the administration's policies and actions were affected by its (changing) perception of the course of the Cuban Revolution and constrained by other factors such as OAS and world support, and U.S. domestic politics.

A POLICY SHIFT

Between January 1959 and January 1961, the Eisenhower administration's policy toward Castro and the Cuban Revolution changed dramatically from a policy of wait and see to a policy designed to overthrow the Castro regime and reorient the direction of the Cuban Revolution. The shift did not come suddenly.

The initial period after Castro's takeover, January–June 1959, was dominated by doubt as to his ideological orientation and the direction in which he would lead the Cuban Revolution. The consensus was that he was a radical without either a real ideology or program aside from the ouster of Batista. Castro's links with communism and the Kremlin were unclear. Conflicting evidence (moderates in the newly appointed government, the background of the Che Guevara and Raul Castro, executions, postponement of elections, democratic promises, anti-American rhetoric, land reform) led the United States into a policy that has often been categorized as "wait and see."

During the second six months of 1959, however, new evidence began to pile up on one side of the scales, evidence that led to drastic and fundamental changes in U.S. perceptions and policies. For a variety of reasons, key figures in the Eisenhower administration, including the President, concluded as early as November/December 1959 that the Castro regime was inimical to U.S. interests and that its continued existence would have serious adverse effects on the United States. Among these reasons were the case of Diaz Lanz, Urrutia, and Huber Matos, the virulent anti-American campaign, the exportation of revolution, increasing evidence of communist penetration of the Cuban government and Society, resumption of executions, reports of Castro's waning popular support within Cuba, anticipated expropriations of U.S. property without compensation, and CIA assessments of the Party Congress held in Moscow in early 1959. Eisenhower now began to give serious study to the development of a strategy to change the orientation of the Cuban government, including Castro's removal. Castro was perceived as a power-hungry fanatic. He was either a full-fledged communist or convinced that he could use communists for his purpose and then discard them. Even if he did discard them, the result would be the same—without positive U.S. action, there would eventually be a communist government in Cuba—something Eisenhower would not tolerate. Because of his sensitivity to the problem of U.S. intervention and the lack of an immediate, severe threat to U.S. security interests, Eisenhower proceeded carefully in developing and implementing the means to deal with Castro.

Eisenhower pursued various strategies in the next period, the first six months of 1960. In January, he publicly left the door open for a reconciliation between Cuba and the United States. The emphasis was on U.S. patience, restraint, and a commitment to nonintervention. At the same time, he gave his go-ahead for the development of a program of covert activities against the Castro regime, a program he formally approved on March 17, 1960. The essentials of this strategy are clear. The United States was to pursue an all-out propaganda offensive aimed at the Castro opposition within Cuba, Latin America as a whole, and the world. The desired outcomes were three: first, that the opposition against Castro in Cuba would eventually (with perhaps a push from the United States) rise up; second, that the OAS would recognize the extent of communist penetration in Cuba and its threat to the Western Hemisphere and declare a "holy war" on Castro;[8] third, that the world would support the U.S. position, at least to the point that the United

Nations would permit the OAS to be the forum to discuss and resolve U.S.-Cuban difficulties. In order to help realize the first hope, the U.S. push consisted of training guerrillas for use in a possible uprising against Castro as well as in sabotage. An additional element of U.S. strategy involved the use of economic sanctions for either of two reasons: Castro would see the economic facts of life and terminate his Soviet ties, or economic conditions would deteriorate and lend fuel to the already smoldering fire of opposition within Cuba.

The variable that is most crucial to understanding the March 1960 decision and the policy choices leading to it is timing. A careful reading of the Church Committee report (1975) leaves the strong impression that timing was critical.[9] An immediate move in March 1960 against Castro was not the Eisenhower administration's preferred course of action, because the CIA estimated that it would take six months to train and equip a guerrilla force and because the anti-Castro forces were leaderless and formless. A viable alternative (government-in-exile) was necessary not only to lend cover and legitimacy to any subsequent U.S. involvement in Castro's removal, but also to ensure that a leadership vacuum, which would precipitate bold moves by the communists in Cuba, did not develop. Furthermore, time was needed to win the world over to the U.S. position. Specifically, time was needed so that the Latin Americans would become convinced either from the effects of the U.S. propaganda offensive, from the inevitable unfolding of events, or from a Castro mistake, that communism had deeply penetrated Cuba and threatened the hemisphere. Time was no longer needed to see if Castro could be moderated, however; by March 1960, Eisenhower had given up hope of this possibility.

In the remaining six months of 1960, the United States did not reap many fruits from its policy. In spite of what the Eisenhower administration perceived as ever increasing evidence of the Moscow connection, the OAS responded at San José in August with only a lukewarm condemnation of the extracontinental threat posed by Sino-Soviet activity in the hemisphere. There was no economic collapse, nor was there an organized opposition within Cuba. Castro had yet to mend his ways. Eisenhower was seemingly faced with a choice between two alternatives, neither of which was very palatable. Either he could accept the Cuban situation as a *fait accompli* or intervene more forcefully, i.e., militarily, on a unilateral basis. Eisenhower had tried to avoid making a choice since late 1959. Domestic politics had pressured him (William H. Jackson's subcommittee on the effectiveness of his National Security Council machinery, Truman's and Kennedy's calls for stronger action against Castro, the 1960 presidential election), but the President had stood firm. Until the end of 1960, all other avenues were not yet closed, nor was the military option ready. But by late November/December 1960, the day of reckoning had arrived; it was time to choose. Nothing else had worked. The OAS would be no help. All prognoses pointed to further consolidations of Castro's control over the island and communist control over Castro. Only a direct U.S. effort could reverse that development.

Determining *exactly* when shifts in thinking occurred remains difficult, not

only because of the classified (and otherwise unavailable) nature of much of the
evidence, but also because of the President's operating style. Eisenhower made
extensive use of small, informal meetings of his closest advisers to assist him in
reaching his decisions—decisions that are not easily decipherable from the written
record. That written record is replete with expressions that disguise the extent of
the President's involvement and the nature of his decision, if any ("The President
noted the report;" "I briefed the President;" "elimination"). Even so, it is
abundantly clear that Eisenhower accepted the basic thrust of Secretary of State
Christian Herter's proposed policy guidance regarding Cuba in early November
1959. By that time, the Castro regime had demonstrated to the President, beyond
any shadow of doubt, that its orientation was inimical to the United States.
Positive U.S. action was essential in order to redirect the Cuban government and
the Cuban Revolution.

The evidence does suggest the possibility that Eisenhower still perceived the
door as open, however slightly, for a moderation of Castro rather than for his
replacement. Specific policy intended to "effect a change in government" was in
its formative stages. Many alternatives were discussed: some were developed,
others discarded, some employed, and others kept in abeyance—assets to be
utilized when the circumstances so dictated. Eisenhower's reaction to developments during the first quarter of 1960, however, indicates that he closed the door
on any remaining hopes to moderate Castro. In private political communications
in late January (following Castro's personal, verbal attacks on Eisenhower and
Nixon, among others), the President labels Castro a "wild man" and a "madman."

By March 1960, following another series of verbal harangues by Castro denouncing the U.S. government's and Cuba's commitment to the OAS/Rio Pact,
Eisenhower approved of a program specifically intended to bring a new government to power. The President's strategy to overthrow Castro included *much* more
than the development of a paramilitary force outside of Cuba for possible future
guerrilla action. An analogy (strategy—timetable) is most helpful in understanding Eisenhower's policy as it developed and was implemented during the remaining months of his administration. Economic sanctions, sabotage,
propaganda, and U.S. assistance to Castro's opposition within and outside of
Cuba all had vital roles to play in Castro's overthrow, as the Eisenhower administration anticipated developments to unfold. The emphasis was also on
gaining OAS support for any U.S.-inspired move against Castro.

Eisenhower's sensitivity to the problem of U.S. intervention in the hemisphere
and his desire for OAS support cannot be overestimated. Still, he remained
flexible enough both in his public comments and in the development of contingency plans to be prepared and able to offer justification for an overt U.S. move
against Castro without OAS approval.

WHY DID THE POLICY CHANGE?

The United States had long sought to "affect the situation" in Latin America by encouraging friendly, stable governments. Cuba, being strategically located in the Caribbean, geographically proximate to the United States, and economically intertwined with the United States, had almost always been particularly important to U.S. policymakers. During the period January 1959 to January 1961, the Eisenhower administration perceived developments in Cuba as necessitating a direct U.S. effort to change the leadership and course of the Cuban Revolution. Why?

The thrust of the present study supports the second of two contentions offered by William Appleman Williams in *The United States, Cuba and Castro*, that U.S. policy toward Cuba "appears to have grounded . . . on the axiom that the U.S. could not continue to exist as a democratic and prosperous capitalist nation if any major European power challenged or blocked or decreased its existing power in . . . areas and countries along its frontiers."[10] Eisenhower perceived Castro and the Cuban Revolution as an opportunity for Sino-Soviet communist penetration not only of Cuba, but also of the entire hemisphere—an opportunity that had to be denied.

It was extremely difficult for Eisenhower to reach any firm conclusions about Castro's ideological orientation early on. The crucial decision he eventually reached was not that Castro was (or was not) a communist. Rather, what he concluded was that given Castro's personality (a "wild man," a "madman," a man who thought he could use the communists for his purposes and then discard them at his convenience), communist control of Cuba was inevitable. Once in control of Cuba, Sino-Soviet communism would attempt to export its revolution throughout the hemisphere.

That was the security threat that Eisenhower perceived. That was the message he tried to convey to the Latin Americans, emphasizing Sino-Soviet penetration of the hemisphere and the Cuban Revolution, especially after March 1960. Castro's greatest sin (at least as charged during the period January 1959 to January 1961) was not that he was a communist, a totalitarian, an antidemocrat, or an economic statist, though he was charged with being all of these. Rather, he was accused of opening the door to the Sino-Soviet communists (maneuvering himself into an alignment with the Sino-Soviet bloc)—a door he could not close even if he wanted to.

Eisenhower chose not to embrace Castro with open arms, and U.S. economic support, in 1959. Instead, he elected to wait until Castro's ideological orientation and the direction of the Cuban Revolution became clearer. As Eisenhower watched and waited in 1959, he increasingly perceived Castro as leading Cuba toward Soviet control. Eisenhower acted in 1960 to prevent such an eventuality. Although his policies were not successful, he should not be criticized for pushing Castro into the arms of the Soviet communists unless one is prepared to argue that the "open arms/bank account" approach in 1959 or 1960 would have produced a decidedly different Castro/Cuba. Edward Gonzalez argues that in spite of the nationalistic impulses of Castro's ideology (*fidelismo*) that placed defiant opposition to the United States as the core of the Cuban Revolution, the evidence at least suggests the possibility that "Fidel may initially have been receptive to U.S. [economic] overtures [until about October 1959]."[11] Eisenhower, to his credit, was patient for almost one year while he and his team sifted through the information available to them and assessed Castro. Then, in late 1959, faced once again with the choice of doing nothing, opting for the stick , or offering the carrot, Eisenhower chose the stick. In actuality, he chose to develop a bundle of sticks (options) that he could pick and choose from as his assessment of the circumstances dictated.

LESSONS FOR THE 1980s

Uniquely perceived American security interests have significantly shaped American policy toward the Western Hemisphere for two hundred years. Right or wrong, most American policymakers have expressed great fears about extracontinental presences in the hemisphere. (El Salvador as America's "front yard" is an expression frequently employed by President Reagan.) They have attempted to justify American policies toward the "New World" from the formative days of the Union through territorial and economic expansion and Good Neighborism to the post-World War II, nuclear age, Cold War environment by playing on the ideology-rooted security fears of foreign "contamination" and presence in this hemisphere.

Today, the Reagan administration is using similar tactics in presenting its justification to the American people and Latin America for U.S. assistance to the El Salvador government in its civil war. According to the Reagan administration, the rebels are armed and supported by Cuba, Nicaragua, and the U.S.S.R. and represent another example of the Soviet Union's efforts to export revolution to this Hemisphere, undermine the solidarity of regional defense agreements, and threaten the physical security of every country on the American continents.

The United States lacks the practical means by which it can arrest political violence or direct the immediate course of social change. Eisenhower's policy toward Castro and the Cuban Revolution is only one in a series of dramatic examples that support this view. That is not to say, however, that America should remain indifferent to the scale of political violence and nature of social change throughout Latin America. Aside from its security interests, the United States has a moral responsibility to reduce the level of such violence and affect the course of social development in Latin America. These are long-term goals, to be achieved by long-range policies. Developmental economic aid such as Eisenhower's forerunner to Kennedy's Alliance for Progress and the power of the American example remain relevant means to be employed in the 1980s to realize such objectives. President Reagan's recently announced program of U.S. economic assistance to the Caribbean Basin appears to be following this course.

A relevant distinction needs to be made regarding U.S. policy toward political violence and certain types of social change in this hemisphere. The crucial question American policymakers must ask themselves is, does a country that is cultivating the violence and change have a desire and willingness to export them? A "no" answer should tell American policymakers that the United States has no quarrel with that country—its domestic politics are its own business. On the other hand, should the answer be "yes," then American policymakers have reason to act, particularly when the violence and change are being cultivated by a brand of revolutionary Marxism-Leninism.

This is the problem with which Eisenhower wrestled. Was the Cuban Revolution a matter of Cuban domestic politics, or was it something much more? When Eisenhower became convinced that without U.S. action the inevitable result in Cuba would be a Sino-Soviet-sponsored communist government, he initiated policy to prevent such a development. If anything, Eisenhower waited too long to move against Castro. Because of Eisenhower's sensitivity to the problems posed by the history of U.S. intervention in the hemisphere, he actively sought an OAS endorsement for any U.S. action—action he felt justified by the Sino-Soviet threat. He also desired a government-in-exile to further legitimate any U.S. moves against Castro as well as to avoid a power vacuum following Castro's overthrow. Eisenhower got neither, and in that sense his policy was a failure. In addition, by taking the time he did seeking OAS support and an alternative government, Eisenhower lost whatever cover existed regarding U.S.-directed military action against Castro and contributed to the overall problem of the history of U.S. intervention in Latin America. Not only did Eisenhower lose the cloak, but he also gave Castro ammunition (Yankee menace) to aid his manipulation of revolutionary fervor. The world media exposed the U.S. government's covert training operations with regard to Castro and shifted attention away from the problem of Soviet communist penetration of the hemisphere and toward the problem of U.S. intervention in the affairs of other American nations.

The perception of threat, a multilateralized Monroe Doctrine (in the form of inter-American solidarity–OAS support, bringing the Rio Pact into play), the timing of U.S. actions, and cover or justification for U.S. unilateral acts remain today, as they were in 1960, important variables in any U.S. policy equation vis-à-vis Latin America. Understanding the relationships among them can lead the United States to a more successful Latin American policy in the 1980s.

The 1980s are not the 1960s, however. For one, most of today's analysts regard international communism as something other than a monolithic structure. Even so, what happened in 1959/1960 could occur again. Beyond the ideologically rooted security threat Cuba poses by exporting violence and revolution lies the possibility that the Soviet Union may make a second attempt to introduce nuclear missiles to the Western Hemisphere, as Soviet President Leonid Brezhnev threatened to do on March 16, 1982.[12] The political and military value of such weapons is enormous, not only to the host country, but also to the Soviet Union.[13]

The best policy means by which to deal with such a potentiality is debatable. Blockade, particularly to arrest all arms movements into and within the Caribbean, seems to be the best option available to the United States, just as it was in 1962 and would have been in 1960. At least one highly respected political analyst, William F. Buckley, Jr., has advocated that very policy choice.[14]

American and hemispheric security requirements in 1983 are not the same as they were in 1783, 1883, 1933, or even 1962. A Soviet-sponsored or communist government in El Salvador or Nicaragua does not pose the same security threat to the United States that it might have forty years ago. U.S. policymakers must be aware of the changing strategic context and pursue policies that can effectively meet the ideological, economic, as well as security threats, demands, and challenges posed by social change, unrest, revolution, and modernization in Latin America. A "New World"—the last great chance for humankind, as President Reagan calls it—remains a dream worth reaching for. But it requires pragmatic and long-range policies suited to a changed, and changing, environment.

NOTES

1. See Stephen Ambrose, *Ike's Spies* (Garden City, N.Y.: Doubleday and Co., 1981) for discussions about a plan's momentum; compare the findings and conclusions in the State Department White Paper of April 1961 with the findings and conclusions in the U.S. Memorandum to the Inter-American Peace Commission, August 1960.

2. See U.S. Congress, House of Representatives, Committee of Foreign Affairs, Subcommittee on Inter-American Affairs, 91st Cong., 2nd Sess., 1970 for a full text of House Resolution 560 and Public Law 87–733 as well as a detailed discussion of their relevance to the events in 1970.

3. *New York Times*, November 13, 1981.

4. Interview of President Ronald Reagan by Dan Rather, CBS Television, January 27, 1982.

5. Personal interview with Milton Eisenhower, Baltimore, Md., July 16, 1981.

6. Personal interview with General Andrew Goodpaster, Staff Secretary for the President, Washington, D.C., November 10, 1981; personal interview with John S. D. Eisenhower, Assistant Staff Secretary to and son of Dwight D. Eisenhower, Valley Forge, Pa., July 28, 1981. Note also that the term "administration" is used loosely in this chapter to refer to the foreign policymaking team that debated, discussed, and ultimately determined the U.S. response to the Cuban Revolution. It was a team that General Goodpaster, in this cited interview, referred to as "a close knit group that saw things pretty much the same." "Effect a change in government" and "affect the situation" are also used loosely in this text. They are used in the Church Report (1975), which is cited later, with regard to his investigation of discussions by the Eisenhower team from December 1959 to March 1960 to bring another government to power in Cuba.

7. *Department of State Publication 7171*, "Cuba," April 1961.

8. Personal interview with John S. D. Eisenhower, Valley Forge, Pa., July 28, 1981.

9. *Church Committee Report*, U.S. Congressional Senate Select Committee with respect to intelligence activities, 94th Congress, 2nd Sess. (Washington, D.C.: U.S. Government Printing Office, 1975).

10. William A. Williams, *The United States, Cuba and Castro* (New York: Monthly Review Press, 1962), pp. 142–43.

11. Edward Gonzalez, *Cuba Under Castro: The Limits of Charisma* (Boston: Houghton Mifflin, 1974), pp. 53–68.

12. Walter Pincus, "Missile Crisis: The Cuban Connection," *Washington Post* Service as reported in *The Philadelphia Inquirer*, March 21, 1982. Interestingly, this Soviet threat to deploy missiles, much like the 1962 plan, appears to be linked directly to American missile deployment in Europe. In 1962, Khrushchev was responding to American intermediate-range Thor and Jupiter missiles in Turkey. In 1982, Brezhnev appeared to be responding to the proposed American deployment of Pershing 2 intermediate-range ballistic missiles. Events in Europe do seem to affect the Western Hemisphere.

13. NATO chose the Pershing 2, a land-based system, because of the greater military and political value of land-based systems over sea-based systems. Furthermore, Soviet weapons in a Central American country (Nicaragua?) could serve as a guarantee of that nation's security. The parallels between Nicaragua, 1982, and Cuba, 1960–1962, are striking. Recently, before the United Nations, the Nicaraguan government claimed that an invasion of its country was "imminent."

During the week of March 21, 1982, the American press and television reported evidence suggesting that the Reagan administration had approved a CIA-directed paramilitary operation for use in Central America. From the Soviet perspective, the missiles would allow Moscow to play its role as defender of international communist movements and to balance new American missiles in Europe, both in terms of capability and world visibility.

In addition, top Kremlin spokesmen have challenged what they feel are American perceptions of invulnerability and isolation in much the same way that Khrushchev declared the Monroe Doctrine anachronistic in 1960. Stated General Nikolai Chervov, Chief of the general staff of the Soviet armed forces, "In the U.S.A. they probably entertain illusions that they are invulnerable, separated by two oceans. At present, however, distances must be evaluated differently in the sense that by moving a threat closer to others, the U.S.A. is in the same manner bringing it closer to itself." Stated in the context of the U.S. and NATO's decision to deploy Pershing 2 and cruise missiles in Europe, which Valin Falen, First Deputy Chief of the Communist party Central Committee's International Information Department, has labeled a "grievous error," Chervov's remarks are "the clearest indication yet that Soviet missiles might be deployed in Cuba or Nicaragua." As reported and analyzed by the Associated Press, in the *Trenton Times*, "Soviets Issue Warning to U.S.," March 18, 1982.

14. William F. Buckley, Jr., "Cuba Is the Real Problem . . . ," *The Philadelphia Inquirer*, March 21, 1982.

19

Reform, Yes; Communism, No! Eisenhower's Policy on Latin American Revolutions

Loretta Sharon Wyatt

Evaluation of President Dwight D. Eisenhower's foreign policy toward Latin America has concentrated on his administration's negative relationships with the revolutionary governments of Jacobo Arbenz Guzman in Guatemala and of Fidel Castro in Cuba. The impression that has resulted is that American foreign policy during this era consistently opposed Latin American revolutions. However, Eisenhower and his advisers were not inevitably antagonistic to revolutions in that area, as American relations with Bolivia and Venezuela prove. In fact, American actions were guided by a policy that was more complex in one way and simpler in another than is generally thought.

The Eisenhower policy regarding Latin America can be criticized for the same reason that all preceding and subsequent official American attitudes toward the nations in this hemisphere can be criticized: they are ignored, neglected, or taken for granted unless and until there is a crisis in one of them which Washington perceives as potentially inimical to the best interests of the United States. On pragmatic grounds any country can be expected to conduct its foreign policy in such a way as to protect its interests and concerns. What is unfortunate is that the United States has consistently been far more interested in other areas of the world than in its own hemisphere, an attitude that may not ultimately be in its best interests. This is not to say that American leaders have not known better. Eisenhower recognized that "a region of the world of vital importance to the United States is Latin America, . . . whose weight in the scales of the balance of power has become steadily more important."[1] He and his two major advisers on Latin American matters, his brother Milton and the Secretary of State John Foster Dulles, were well aware that Latin Americans resented "what seemed to them to be our preoccupation with other areas of the world."[2] Unfortunately, in practice the Eisenhower administration repeated the same pattern.

Eisenhower regarded revolutions as either good or bad. "Bad" ones, whatever they promised, primarily brought ambitious dictators to power, the worst of whom were communistic, totalitarian dictators. In contrast, "good" revolutions did not just talk about reforms to improve the lives of their people but actually tried to follow through with constructive programs. Eisenhower was fully prepared to accept and even to support and to underwrite the efforts of revolutionary governments to attain political, social, and economic changes and reforms, as long as the proposed changes did not include the introduction of a communist regime in the Americas.

Eisenhower believed in being flexible and in responding to the particular set of circumstances:

I earnestly try to avoid becoming arbitrary in personal opinions as to what is best for America in her relations with other countries. . . . What I have tried to do . . . is to promote understanding of our basic position, the principal factors of which are that America cannot live alone, and that her form of life is threatened by the Communistic dictatorship. These facts give rise to the problems we have in developing general policies applicable to the situation. All of these policies much conform to the yardstick of our own enlightened self-interest.[3]

This meant that Eisenhower was not to pursue an active policy with Latin Americans. Rather, he *reacted* to the aggressive policies devised by the Latin Americans and to the attitudes they expressed toward the United States. The President and his administration tended to be benign unless the Latin American attitude was manifestly hostile to the United States. To use his own military analogy, he did not intend to permit the Soviets to attain their first beachhead in the Americas, but he would wait for positive proof of their involvement before acting. As long as he and his advisers tailored the American response to the particular circumstances and events in each country, this proved a reasonably satisfactory procedure, at least from the President's point of view. But it was vital to remember that Latin American countries differed from each other and that what might work in one instance would fail miserably in another.

GUATEMALA

In 1953, Eisenhower inherited two trouble spots, Bolivia and Guatemala, which had long since become areas of concern to the outgoing Truman administration.

The Guatemalan revolutionary government had been in power since 1944, but had achieved only minor tangible results as far as the people there were concerned. Although some advances had been made in such areas as social security and labor legislation, what was most apparent was not progressive programs to improve peoples' lives, but rather the tremendous power being attained by the relatively small Communist party over a populace that was not communist. This was particularly obvious after the inauguration of President Jacobo Arbenz Guzman in 1951.[4] Arbenz' closest political adviser, José Manuel Fortuny, was the Secretary-General of the newly legalized Communist party. Many of the leading people employed in the Arbenz administration, especially in education, the social security program, and the evolving agrarian reform project, were communists. Furthermore, the major labor unions and the official press and radio were all controlled by communists. Analysts for the Eisenhower administration concluded that "[t]he Arbenz government, beyond any question, was controlled and dominated by Communists. These Communists were directed from Moscow. . . . And the Communist conspiracy in Guatemala did represent a real and very serious menace to the security of the United States."[5] The Guatemalan government was also accused of infiltrating and subverting its Central American neighbors which, given the past practices and relations of these countries, was extremely likely.

The Arbenz regime in its turn mounted a strident propaganda offensive against the United States, not so much on political issues as on economic, nationalistic grounds. As specific proof of their charges, Guatemalan attacks concentrated on criticizing the enormous influence exerted within that country by the United Fruit Company. Arbenz justified his assault on the American company by citing a need for land to distribute to individual poor and landless farmers. In February 1953, perhaps in a test of the will of the newly inaugurated Eisenhower to resist, Arbenz finally began implementing an agrarian reform bill passed in 1952, which had been promised in his own inaugural address in 1951 and which was the only reasonably constructive policy he ever promoted. Arbenz decreed the expropriation of several hundreds of thousands of acres of uncultivated lands owned by an American firm, the United Fruit Company, for distribution. Most of the land, however, ended up in cooperatives, not in the promised and intensely desired private farms.[6]

The United Fruit Company issue put into sharp focus the differences between the United States and Guatemala. The basic problem was not expropriation, little though Eisenhower cared for it. Rather, the problem was the political ideology motivating this particular action. Eisenhower pursued what was to be his usual procedure: he accepted a government's legal right to expropriate property, but he always insisted on just compensation for the lost property, a reiteration of American policy which had become the standard since the time of Woodrow Wilson's trouble with Mexico. This policy (coupled with the fact that several members of Eisenhower's administration, including Dulles, had previously worked for United Fruit) supplied Arbenz' Office of Publicity and Propaganda with most of its ammunition.

Now Eisenhower perceived that American foreign policy could not narrowly focus on merely protecting American companies in an updated version of dollar diplomacy. On several occasions, he expressed the view that if the United States did not accommodate the nationalistic and economic aspirations of other countries, these countries might well turn to the communists for inspiration and support. On the other hand, until a country actually did have a communist government, the possibility existed for accommodation and mutual understanding between it and the United States.[7] An indemnity was the litmus test for Eisenhower of a government's true intentions and ideology. On this score as on other counts, Arbenz failed.

Yet, what could the United States do? It could make its own position clear through diplomatic channels, though to no avail. It could monitor the Arbenz government's statements and actions to determine the opposition's ultimate intent. But could the Eisenhower administration do anything practically to counter what was believed to be a dangerous government, dangerous to its own country as well as to the United States? Many of the President's policymakers advised against armed intervention except as a last resort because of the inevitably adverse Latin American reaction. They proposed as a feasible alternative supporting an opposition group based in a neighboring state, and on this basis Eisenhower authorized the Central Intelligence Agency in mid–1953 to formulate a contingency plan for aiding and abetting any Guatemalan effort to overthrow the Arbenz regime. As it happened, by this time not only were a number of Guatemalans within the country unhappy with Arbenz, but a group of rebels was joining forces outside the country. Subsequently, Colonel Carlos Castillo Armas received American money for an Honduran base to train an army of disaffected Guatemalans.[8]

Such training camps are never especially secret. By early 1954, a nervous Arbenz had increased the anti-American barrage of words and had resorted to measures designed to intimidate internal opponents by suppressing civil rights and summarily arresting or ordering assassinated anyone suspected of antigovernment activities.

While his internal problems increased, the United States was taking steps to isolate the Arbenz government at the Tenth Inter-American Conference of the Organization of American States held at Caracas in March 1954. Dulles went to the meeting with the specific purposes of denouncing communism as "alien intrigue and treachery" and of persuading the delegates to adopt a carefully worded resolution:

Domination or control of the political institutions of an American state by the international Communist movement constitutes a threat to the sovereignty and independence of the American states, endangers the peace, and calls for the adoption of appropriate action in accordance with existing treaties.

Although Latin Americans were extremely sensitive to anything suggesting intervention in their internal affairs, they also recognized the acuteness of the United States' sensibilities on this issue and ratified the resolution despite Guatemalan opposition.

Nevertheless, there was as yet no clearcut evidence of direct tangible Soviet aid to the Guatemalan government until May 17, 1954, when 2,000 tons of Czech small arms, ammunition, and light artillery pieces arrived in Guatemala. The American government interpreted this situation as an infringement of the Monroe Doctrine and the Caracas Resolution. Dulles knew that communist misinformation would try to twist and distort the American reaction, so he confronted the issue straight on and declared: "If the United Fruit matter were settled, . . . the problem would remain just as it is today as far as the presence of Communist infiltration in Guatemala is concerned. That is the problem, not United Fruit."[9]

Ultimately, the tense situation ended in mid-June with the invasion of Guatemala by Castillo Armas and his forces of perhaps 100 to 150 Guatemalans, a sufficiently large enough army to severely threaten Arbenz and to precipitate a minor civil war. Actually, this was more a war of nerves where most Guatemalans, including the military, were spectators, not participants. It is possible that Arbenz may have considered using the Czech arms to outfit a worker-farmer militia, but if so he hesitated to trust them any more than he would the Army. Americans did help to jam the Guatemalan communications systems; on June 22, they guaranteed the replacement of Nicaraguan planes damaged on strafing flights over Guatemala. Since Arbenz was isolated without army or mass support, he surrendered at the end of June, resigned, and went into exile. In recent years, liberals and communists (who seem to have relied on Arbenz's propaganda rather than on facts) have attempted to portray the Arbenz era as a lost utopian chance to establish democracy in Guatemala. Though less effective than most of Guatemala's leaders, Arbenz conforms to the national tradition of petty dictators (in this instance a dictator of the far left).

Eisenhower always regarded the Guatemalan action as one of his administration's major successes.[10] Certainly, the Guatemalan events fit well within the President's perception of what was necessary to counter communist aggression: "free nations must maintain countervailing military power." At the same time, "we must also frustrate the efforts of Communists to gain their goals by subversion."[11] That was why "to refuse to cooperate in providing indirect support to a strictly anti-Communist faction in this struggle would be contrary to the letter and spirit of the Caracas resolution."[12]

BOLIVIA

The Eisenhower administration focused on Guatemala probably because of the high drama implicit in the events. Yet compared with the concurrent situation in Bolivia, the emphasis was wrong, for it was in Bolivia that genuine and far-reaching reforms were instituted—with the help of the United States—which significantly modified the country for the better.

Such aid was not to be automatically expected in 1953. The Revolution of 1952 had been led by the National Revolutionary party (MNR), which was influenced by Marxism and, in times past, accused first of fascist and then of communist leanings, though always ultranationalist in its policies. In October 1952, the new regime carried out one of its major aims, the expropriation of the holdings of the three giant tin companies, Patiño, Aramayo, and Hochschild, which had previously dominated not just the Bolivian economy but its politics as well. The mines had been turned over to a new government agency, Comibol, run by the tin miners union whose leader Juan Lechin was a wildly ambitious opportunist employing socialist rhetoric to incite and hold his followers. Meanwhile, a far more important transformation was taking place in the countryside where about 80 percent of the mostly Indian population lived, still "debt peons" in 1952, and either landless or possessing only tiny plots of a miniscule fraction of an acre. Often the Indians took the initiative themselves in seizing land, which began a genuine agrarian reform program even before the September 1953 official expropriation of large estates for Indian communities. The MNR government also abolished peonage and tried to integrate the Indians into modern society by such measures as granting them full citizenship rights. This was, in short, a full-fledged, sudden, radical, social revolution unprecedented in Bolivian history, much more comprehensive than anything Arbenz had done, and comparable in Latin America only with what had occurred in Mexico after 1910. It was precisely the kind of revolution which leftists claim the United States is inevitably and adamantly against.

Nevertheless, the United States did help Bolivia, so much so that for a while the Bolivian–U.S. working relationship was the closest among nations in this hemisphere.[13] What made the difference in the response of the United States to events in Bolivia as compared to those in Guatemala was the difference in attitudes expressed by the Bolivians. The Bolivians were promoting and protecting their own home-grown revolution, not an imported alien foreign ideology. Pragmatism, not dogmatism, characterized the behavior of the small revolutionary group seeking to usher in a better life for the majority of their illiterate, backward fellow countrymen. The MNR leadership realized that they needed to market their tin and to buy goods as well as to acquire all kinds of aid and assistance for effecting meaningful improvements. There was only one likely source for the massive amount of help Bolivia so desperately needed, and that was the United States. Therefore, Bolivians set out to win a favorable American response to their requests for aid.

If the United States required reassurance about the MNR's intentions and ideology, the Bolivian government was swift to offer it. Ambassador Victor Andrade spent his early days in Washington reassuring the outgoing Truman and the new Eisenhower administration that the Bolivian government was not communist. On the loaded issue of expropriation, President Victor Paz Estenssoro and Andrade took special care to explain and to insist that the MNR government was not against private property per se, but was only against what it felt were the iniquitous Big Three tin companies and the Andean landowners whose land was needed to benefit the majority. Moreover, smaller mining companies and foreign-owned properties were not touched. Nevertheless, it seemed advisable to the MNR leaders to promise not to expropriate any more property. Indeed, these leaders were quick to grasp the significance of an indemnity to Eisenhower: in

June 1953, they decided to negotiate a compensation settlement with the Big Three as quickly as possible.[14]

This last move had the desired effect of convincing the American government that the MNR was sincere in its statements that, while it was reformist, it was not communist. As a result, the United States, despite its already large stockpile of tin, purchased more of the metal from the financially strapped Bolivians and promised more economic assistance on July 6, 1953.

At the same time, Milton Eisenhower returned from his trip to Latin America with fervent advice for his brother: the promotion of "rapid peaceful social change is the only way to avert violent revolution in Bolivia; physical strife would be the surest way of giving the Communists control."[15] Such considerations, as well as the humanitarian evaluation of the country's problems, persuaded Eisenhower to respond quickly (October 1, 1953) and favorably to Paz' appeal for help to stave off starvation and imminent economic collapse.[16] Eisenhower provided Bolivia with an immediate $9 million worth of food and other necessities as well as promised technical and other assistance to develop the agrarian sector and to diversify the economy.[17] Massive aid of a variety of kinds continued during the entire Eisenhower administration, averaging about $20 million a year from 1953 through 1960, mostly in outright grants despite the President's distaste for this kind of assistance.[18]

American appraisal of the policy of gentle persuasion found it generally successful by 1956, though perhaps displaying an amusing lack of perception about who had influenced whom:

Although [the Bolivian government] was crudely Marxian and Socialist in orientation when it assumed power four years ago, it is now considerably more moderate and responsible. We have tried through various devices, . . . to reorient the leaders of the Bolivian Government and labor movement toward a greater appreciation of the possible benefits of our type of society.[19]

Although the Revolution of 1952 was not to solve all of Bolivia's political problems, socially and fiscally it proved to be a tremendous success on its own terms in the 1950s and 1960s. Eisenhower in 1957 was quite complimentary: "Bolivia can continue to provide the peoples of the Americas with an example of the concrete results which initiative, determination and cooperation on the part of Government and people can accomplish in the face of economic adversity."[20] Bolivia also proved something else. As Ambassador Andrade pointed out in 1955,

The relationship between my own country of Bolivia and the United States since 1952 is heartening to all who hope . . . [for] cooperation which helps both the weak and the strong. This relationship today refutes a favorite Communist theory—that a strong capitalistic state always exploits weaker nations if it can.[21]

Consequently, both before and after 1954, Bolivians were in a unique position to fully appreciate the reasons for the difference in American responses between their revolution and the Arbenz regime in Guatemala and comprehend that it was indeed communism, not revolutionary transformation, which the United States opposed.

VENEZUELA

The Eisenhower administration was bracketed by two sets of revolutions, Bolivia and Guatemala early in his presidency, and Venezuela and Cuba toward the end, when an ailing Dulles was replaced by Christian A. Herter.

The revolution in Venezuela in 1958 was undoubtedly the most successful revolution in twentieth-century Latin America because it established a genuine democratic republican form of government in that country which has thus far proved strong enough both to deal with Venezuelan socioeconomic problems and to overcome the communist terrorism attempting to destroy its democratic system. However, in 1958 no one could be sanguine about hopes for such a future. After the unsavory military dictator Marcos Pérez Jiménez had been ousted in January, Washington was perturbed about the extent of communist activity in the new volatile political climate in Venezuela as well as the anti-American militancy of many of the demonstrators. Particularly ominous to the United States was the fact that one of the presidential candidates for the December election in 1958, Rear Admiral Wolfgang Larrázabal, was supported by a coalition in which the Communist party was the most conspicuous member. Larrázabal was so strong a contender for the presidency that Herter as acting Secretary of State, on November 21, urged the Secretary of Commerce to postpone announcing new reductions in oil imports at least until after the elections on December 7. Nationalist Venezuelans interpreted such reductions as attributable not to the economic recession in the United States but to American displeasure with the revolutionary government and, therefore, as "damaging to Venezuela's national interests." The idea of cutting back 20 percent in oil imports

would give the Communists an almost insuperable political advantage if they are announced before the elections. Moreover, it would seriously undermine the campaigns of Admiral Larrázabal's two opponents for the presidency, either of whom would be acceptable to us.[22]

The U.S. government was, therefore, vastly relieved when the Democratic Action leader Rómulo Betancourt won the hotly contested presidential election in December and made every effort to establish cordial relations with the new President.[23]

Betancourt reciprocated the friendly attitude and consistently reiterated his government's commitment to democracy and to friendship with the United States: "In Venezuela we have a regime which constitutionally respects the right to private property, which is moving toward social justice through an evolutionary revolution . . . and a government which is frankly and decidedly part of the

Western World.[24] Betancourt's idea of an "evolutionary revolution" included comprehensive social and economic changes by which to reform and to modernize Venezuela and to improve its people's lives. Those who are unimpressed by Washington's support for Bolivia, where actual American investment was rather small, and who persist in citing Arbenz as proof that the United States will oppose any revolutionary government that proposes to reduce sizable foreign investment invariably are silent about the programs instituted by Betancourt and his successors and American reaction to them. One of Democratic Action's major objectives was the nationalization of the petroleum industry, transferring it from foreign to Venezuelan ownership. Betancourt, a nationalist, wanted the oil revenues in order to finance the extensive reform program. (Venezuelans referred to this as "sowing the oil.") The Venezuelan President was at the same time a careful man who refused to expropriate the industry overnight, fearing such action would disrupt production and reduce revenue at a time when Venezuela was deeply in debt thanks to Pérez Jiménez' incredible mismanagement, profligate spending, and accumulation of an enormous personal fortune. Betancourt preferred the policy of gradual transference by ending the granting of concessions to foreign companies and continually increasing taxes and other payments to boost Venezuela's share from 60 percent in 1959 to complete ownership. The oil companies, like the U.S. government, accepted the inevitability of ultimate nationalization and found that they could work with Betancourt.

As for his other reforms, in 1960 Betancourt initiated the far reaching Venezuelan agrarian reform program whereby the government purchased and distributed land to landless farmers. In addition, the government provided technical assistance and training as well as credit. Rural housing and education improvements were undertaken in hopes of diminishing the flood of migrants into the already overcrowded cities. Efforts were also made to improve living and working conditions in the cities, along with ambitious policies promoting industrialization, health, and public work projects.

Betancourt thus typified the kind of "good" revolutionary preferred by the American government. As Herter declared, " . . . the democratic constitutional government of President Betancourt is in the forefront of the moderate reform movement in Latin America, as opposed to the proponents of violent revolutionary change."[25] Consequently it was Washington's earnest desire that Betancourt "will be able to continue effectively to overcome the efforts of various extremists of both the right and the left to overthrow his Government by violence, emphasizing our support for the principles of constitutional government."[26]

Indeed, the juxtaposition of the Venezuelan Democratic Revolution of 1958 and the Cuban Communist Revolution of 1959 (although the Cuban was not as honest about its intentions) made Betancourt and Fidel Castro the champions of two entirely different solutions to Latin American political, social, and economic problems. The communists did not want Betancourt to succeed; therefore, from the beginning and throughout his administration, they attempted to disrupt and to subvert his government and to force him to adopt repressive measures that would stain his reputation as a democratic leader. By 1960, radical terrorists had formed the Revolutionary Leftist Movement (MIR), while the Venezuelan Community party pledged loyalty to Castro—both groups launched guerrilla warfare against Betancourt with Castro's active aid and encouragement. Actually, Venezuela had even greater problems with Cuba than did the United States, which made Betancourt an ever closer ally of the Americans. Eisenhower and Herter realized that "Venezuela is a key country in our relations with Latin America. . . . [Betancourt, whose] moderate, democratic constitutional Government is under attack by pro-Castro elements in Venezuela needs all of the public support we can give him."[27]

In addition, Washington stood ready to provide whatever help it might be asked for, help which eventually included loans (during the early days when Venezuela was in financial difficulties) and assistance in counterinsurgency later on.

CUBA

The problem with responding to signals being sent by the opposition is that a very shrewd and clever man can sufficiently confuse and befuddle his audience (especially if they underestimate him) by sending enough contradictory messages and outright lies to postpone effective action being taken against him. Thus, Fidel Castro consistently managed to outmaneuver the Cuban dictator Fulgencio Batista, his erstwhile revolutionary allies who were not communists, and the U.S. government. Before his advent to power on January 1, 1959, Castro promised one kind of revolution, similar to what Venezuela was establishing. After January 1, he began instituting quite another revolution with mass executions, postponed elections, and open ties with communists.

In hindsight it appears that Castro's move should have been clear, but he sold an image of himself as a genial, simple agrarian reformer. Eisenhower later insisted that only on the eve of Batista's fall in late 1958 was he given positive evidence that "Communists and other extreme radicals appear to have penetrated the Castro movement. . . . If Castro takes over, they will probably participate in the government."[28] Although the President hoped that a viable alternative to both Batista and Castro would materialize, the American government made no effort to affect the ensuing course of events. In fact, the United States recognized the new regime rather quickly on January 7 after being assured that the rebel government intended "to comply with the international obligations and agreements of Cuba."[29] Within the week, Cuba initiated propaganda attacks against the United States.[30]

This did not prevent the irrepressible Castro from making an unofficial visit to the United States seeking loans. Since the Cuban was busily creating a new dictatorship, Eisenhower refused to see him, but Castro did meet with Richard Nixon on April 19, and their discussion convinced the Vice-President that Castro really was a communist.[31] However, Castro recovered from his fumble with Nixon and was accepted as a noncommunist reformer by several other American analysts, though he did not succeed in obtaining loans. Herter's report to Eisenhower indicated befuddlement as well as deep concern; nevertheless, he recommended continuing the usual wait-and-see policy:

On balance, despite Castro's apparent simplicity, sincerity and eagerness to reassure the United States public, there is little probability that Castro has altered the essentially radical course of his revolution. . . . Castro remains an enigma and we should await his decisions on specific matters before assuming a more optimistic view than heretofore about the possibility of developing a constructive relationship with him.[32]

Eisenhower decided to give the Cuban situation a year to crystallize.[33] However, it would not be a year before Castro made his intentions perfectly obvious. Within a month, on May 17, 1959, perhaps in a deliberate commemoration of the anniversary of communist weapons arriving in Guatemala, Cuba instituted an agrarian reform bill that did *not* provide compensation for the property it was seizing.[34] The situation went steadily from bad to worse from the American viewpoint. Finally, on January 26, 1960, Eisenhower strenuously protested the Cuban propaganda offensive which he said attempted "to create the illusion of aggressive acts and conspiratorial activities aimed at the Cuban government and attributed to United States officials."[35]

It does appear that if the President had not already been considering covert activities against Castro, the Cubans had suggested the need for such a move, perhaps by following the same path that had proved successful against Batista, that of escalating difficulties through constant pressure and attacks until provoking retaliation which they could then claim proved their initial accusations. Thus, Castro eventually achieved his intention of casting Cuba in the rule of a martyred country being abused by the American colossus. In the dilemma of how to handle Castro, the Eisenhower administration resorted to the Guatemalan model, completely forgetting Cuba was not Guatemala, that the Soviet leadership was not the same in 1960 as in 1954, that Castro was not Arbenz, and, furthermore, that Castro had undoubtedly been fully briefed on what had happened in Guatemala by his friend, the Argentine communist Ernesto Guevara, who had witnessed the downfall of Arbenz. Instead of tailoring a plan to Cuban realities, the United States drifted with the Guatemalan plan, despite the dearth of uniformity and cooperation among the various Cuban refugee groups, as well as the lack of a single leader who could rally most of the exiles behind him.

On March 17, 1960, Eisenhower gave the Central Intelligence Agency orders "to begin to organize the training of Cuban exiles, mainly in Guatemala, against a possible future day when they might return to their homeland."[36] This order was undoubtedly induced by Cuba's agreement with the Soviet Union, signed in February, to exchange sugar for Soviet military equipment and monetary loans. It was not until July 6 that Eisenhower reacted publicly to the Cuban-Soviet trade agreement by announcing the reduction of the sugar quota that the United States would guarantee to buy from Cuba. Although outraged Cubans appeared to regard the American market as a natural right of which they were being unjustly deprived, Eisenhower did not believe American money should be used to support a government that has "embarked upon a deliberate policy of hostility toward the United States."[37] The President continued to delay going beyond economic sanction, however, on the grounds "that we would first have to prove to the Organization of American States, beyond any shadow of a doubt, that Cuba had become a Communist base; otherwise, resentment at 'arrogant intervention' could lead to serious difficulties for us in Latin America."[38] However, Castro and the communists did not hesitate to intensify the crisis. On July 9, Castro confiscated all American-owned property in Cuba, even while he declared that the United States was preparing to invade the country. The Soviet Union immediately issued a public declaration promising to come to Cuba's aid if that happened.

Eisenhower quickly denounced the Soviet offer which

underscores the close ties that have developed between the Soviet and the Cuban governments. It also shows the clear intention to establish Cuba in a role serving Soviet purposes in this hemisphere . . . [and] reflects the effort of an outside nation and of international Communism to intervene in the affairs of the Western Hemisphere.[39]

His words echoed by the ministers at the meeting of the Organization of American States in August where the Soviet intervention was condemned. The ministers also declared that the "acceptance of such an offer would constitute a threat to inter-American unity."[40]

Nonetheless, despite ever closer ties between Cuba and the Soviet Union in 1960, no concrete measures were taken to oust Castro and the communists from Cuba. There was, for example, no *cordon sanitaire* or blockade and ostracism of Cuba of the type suggested by Betancourt to deal with dictators. The United States was to learn once again that the weight of its displeasure, or that of the Organization of American States, or that of the disorganized dissidents in exile would not bring down a government. American resolve had to be firm, too. The conclusion is inescapable that the Cuban communist regime survived primarily because the United States would not risk a confrontation with the Soviet Union in 1960.

In the waning days of his presidency, confronted with such impotence, Eisenhower became quite testy because of the humiliations and pressures brought on by Castro. On one occasion in a staff meeting, an irritated Eisenhower expressed his profound wish "to see [Castro and other Latin dictators] sawed off."[41] This was undoubtedly the reason behind Eisenhower's last major policy decision as President. On January 2, 1961, the Cuban government reduced the number of American diplomats it would permit in Cuba to eleven and ordered the other seventy-six, accused of being spies, to leave within forty-eight hours. This time Eisenhower reacted immediately. On January 3, just seventeen days before he left office, an irked and provoked Eisenhower denounced "this calculated action . . . the latest of a long series of harassments, baseless accusations, and vilifications."[42] The President formally severed all American diplomatic relations with

Cuba, effective immediately. Such swift and decisive action, while correct, was not necessarily to be expected from a generally cautious, careful President.

CONCLUSIONS

Eisenhower was always perturbed by the attraction which communism held for so many underdeveloped nations. He observed that ''Communism masquerades as the pattern of progress, as the path to economic equality, as the way to freedom from what it calls 'Western imperialism,' as the wave of the future.''[43] He realized that the free world had to find a way

to convince a billion people in the less developed areas that there is a way of life by which they can have bread *and* the ballot, a better livelihood *and* the right to choose the means of their livelihood, social change *and* social justice—in short, progress and liberty. The dignity of man is at stake.[44]

To many Latin Americans, as to many people everywhere, basic survival took precedence over what appeared to be the esoteric ideal of freedom. The distinction between democracy and communism seemingly had little relation to their daily lives or concerns. Even further removed were the struggles between the United States and the Soviet Union for the survival of their basically inimical, different ways of life. To be sure, some Latin Americans were genuine converts to communist ideology and would use people's needs to attain political power. It was incumbent upon the United States in pursuing its ''own enlightened self-interest'' to do its best to thwart such efforts and intentions, keeping in mind Machiavelli's sage observation that

Moreover, a prince . . . must become the leader and defender of the less powerful neighboring states. . . . He must also be on guard lest by any chance some foreigner equal to him in power should enter them. Such an event always comes about through the help of discontented inhabitants who willingly admit a foreign power either through excessive ambition or through fear. . . . It is in the nature of things that as soon as a powerful foreigner enters a province, all the weaker powers in it will become his allies through envy of those who have been ruling over them.

Indeed, in the late summer of 1960, Eisenhower had boldly declared that the United States would never permit an American state to be taken into the Soviet orbit. On January 12, 1961, in his final State of the Union message, the President linked a bitter admission about communism dominating Cuba with a reference to the earlier, more satisfactory removal of Arbenz. It was, under the circumstances, almost wistful. Perhaps what the American experiences in Guatemala and Cuba prove best is that a government cannot survive if a majority of its own people do not support it and, conversely, that it will easily weather foreign displeasure, not to say overt hostility, if most of the people do.

In the conclusion to his last presidential message, Eisenhower referred to Cuba as one of the issues necessitating "delicate handling and constant review."[45] Such had been Eisenhower's watchwords, which resulted in a policy of reaction, not of initiative, and subject to the limitation implicit in such an approach. Still, this method had permitted governments, especially the revolutionary governments in Latin America, to make their position as friend or foe, as democratic or communistic, as constructive reformers or authoritarian dictators perfectly clear. Hence, Eisenhower believed the method amply justified his administration's subsequent responses to the various governments in Latin America.

NOTES

1. Dwight D. Eisenhower, *The White House Years: Mandate for Change, 1953–1956* (Garden City, N.Y.: Doubleday, 1963), p. 420.
2. Dwight D. Eisenhower, *The White House Years: Waging Peace, 1956–1961* (Garden City, N.Y.: Doubleday, 1965), p. 517.
3. Dwight D. Eisenhower to John Foster Dulles, June 20, 1952. Dwight D. Eisenhower Library Archive, Abilene, Kansas (hereafter referred to as Abilene): A.W.-Dulles-Herter–1.
4. Under Juan José Arévalo, from 1944 to 1950, communists had infiltrated all the major unions, education, student organizations, and the government bureaucracy. They were his most reliable supporters because, although they thought he was too moderate, nevertheless he was useful to them. The results of the 1950 election were obviously vital to the communists. The popular opponent of Arbenz, Francisco Arana, was assassinated by "persons unknown"; Guatemalans were not stupid, and held Arévalo and Arbenz responsible.
5. John E. Peurifoy, U.S. ambassador to Guatemala, in testimony before the Subcommittee on Latin America of the House Select Committee on Communist Aggression stated the Eisenhower administration's position in October 1954. See U.S. House of Representatives Subcommittee on Latin America of the Select Committee on Communist Aggression, Ninth Interim Report, *Communist Aggression in Latin America*, p. 124.
6. Even his original promise of private farms, each of which would contain approximately 40 acres, was scarcely adequate for the needs and wishes of the people for their own land since the plots would have been miniscule and obviously insufficient to provide adequately for the needs of a family. Still, Arbenz hoped to win the allegiance of the landless farmers by this measure. Furthermore, it was a move designed to please nationalists who loathed the power and wealth of the unpopular United Fruit Company, known locally as "the octopus."
7. See, for example, Dwight D. Eisenhower to Alfred Gruenther, November 30, 1954, and Dwight D. Eisenhower to William Robinson, August 4, 1954, Abilene: August and November 1954.
8. Castillo Armas and Miguel Ydigoras Fuentes were the major opposition leaders. Neither Guatemalan particularly liked or trusted the other; in fact, one of the main problems for Arbenz' opponents and one of Arbenz' greatest allies was the indisposition of the opposition to compromise and cooperate with each other. This significant fact accounts for the survival of many a dictator or unpopular leader. The majority may not like

him, but they cannot all agree on whom to support to oust him either. In this case, the CIA decided Castillo Armas was the best choice for leadership of this projected movement, and Ydigoras Fuentes finally decided to go along with him.

9. John Foster Dulles statement in U.S. Department of State (*American Foreign Policy, 1950–1955, Basic Documents*, Vol. 1, p. 1310). Dulles delivered a major speech on the matter on June 30, 1954, in which he categorically declared: "The master plan of international communism is to gain a solid political base in this hemisphere, a base that can be used to extend Communist penetration to the other peoples of the other American Governments. It was not the power of the Arbenz government that concerned us but *the power behind* it." J. F. Dulles address, June 30, 1954, Department of State, *Bulletin* 31 (July 12, 1954): 43–45.

The U.S. government went out of its way to emphasize that most Guatemalans were not communists. The problem was that a few were, and "Communists always operate in terms of small minorities who gain positions of power." This had happened with Arbenz. Moreover, the massive arms shipment indicated a danger beyond the Guatemalan borders because Guatemala already was "the heaviest armed of all the Central American States. Its military establishment is three to four times the size of that of its neighbors. . . . By this arms shipment a government in which Communist influence is very strong has come into a position to dominate militarily the Central American area" (Department of State press release, May 25, 1954; Department of State, *Bulletin* 30 [June 7, 1954]: 873–74). The American military, including President Eisenhower, did not believe that the Guatemalan armed forces had "any legitimate, normal requirements" for so many arms and that they would only be necessary if Arbenz envisioned an aggressive war against his neighbors (*Mandate for Change*, p. 424).

10. It is emphasized, for instance, in the campaign speech Eisenhower delivered at Wilmington on October 29, 1954 (see *Public Papers of the Presidents*, 1954, Washington, D.C., 1960, pp. 1001–1006) and in his final State of the Union message, January 12, 1961. See Robert L. Branyan and Laurence H. Larsen, *The Eisenhower Administration, 1953–1961. A Documentary History*, 2 vols. (New York: Random House, 1971), p. 1348, and throughout *Mandate for Change*.

11. State of the Union message, January 6, 1955, *Public Papers of the President, 1955* (Washington, D.C.: 1959), pp. 7–30.

12. *Mandate for Change*, p. 426.

13. Geography proves as much or as little an explanation as one wishes in this case since, although Bolivia is located far away from the United States, it is situated in the middle of South America and therefore occupies a vital strategic location with long and indefensible borders with five other countries. Ernesto Guevara found this fact especially enticing some years later.

14. It was expedient since American stockholders had invested extensively in Patiño and held perhaps a 10-percent interest in the nationalized properties. While Assistant Secretary for Inter-American Affairs John Moors Cabot believed that pressure had been brought to bear on the Bolivian government to secure compensation, the Bolivians were keenly aware that payment in such cases is always expected and that the U.S. Congress will not authorize foreign aid unless it has been forthcoming.

15. Milton Eisenhower's Report on Latin America, to Dwight D. Eisenhower, November 18, 1953, Abilene: Whitman, Name Series, 13.

16. Victor Paz Estenssoro to Dwight D. Eisenhower, October 1, 1953, Abilene: A. W. International File 4-Bol. (3). Paz concluded his plea with the reminder that "it concerns the

furnishing of aid to a people who, as is the case in Bolivia, are sincerely pledged to improve the democratic institutions inherent in the free world, to which they firmly adhere, and who furthermore support the principles of mutual security which govern the nations of the Western Hemisphere."

17. Dwight D. Eisenhower to Victor Paz Estenssoro, October 14, 1953, Abilene: A. W.-International File 4-Bol. (3). Dulles felt that it was expedient to publicize Eisenhower's role in providing American assistance as much as possible to "have maximum psychological impact" in Bolivia and in "Latin America as a whole," obviously to offset Guatemalan propaganda. Dulles memo to Dwight D. Eisenhower, October 13, 1953, Abilene: A.W.-International File 4-Bol. (3). At the same time, the State Department did not want Eisenhower to make any hasty promises; therefore, when meeting with Ambassador Victor Andrade, he was cautioned to stick to what had already been arranged.

18. Cole Blasier, "The United States and the Revolution," in James M. Malloy and Richard S. Thorn, eds., *Beyond the Revolution: Bolivia Since 1952* (Pittsburgh: University of Pittsburgh Press, 1971), pp. 53–110. See especially p. 83.

19. State Department memo—Fishburn to Hoghland, July 13, 1956, Abilene: Central Files—Official File 853–163, Bolivia.

20. Dwight D. Eisenhower to Hernan Siles Zuazo, April 22, 1958, Abilene: Central File 4-Bol. (3).

21. Andrade speech given in Des Moines, Iowa, November 12, 1955.

22. Christian A. Herter to Lewis L. Strauss, Secretary of Commerce, November 21, 1958, Abilene: A. W.-Dulles-Herter–8, November 1958. Animosity toward the United States was largely the result of Washington's uncritical acceptance of Pérez Jiménez' assurances of friendship for the United States and opposition to communism. Pérez Jiménez' anticommunism appears to be mostly for foreign consumption. Within Venezuela one of the few sources of active support Pérez Jiménez had enjoyed came from one faction of the communists.

23. Herter memo to Dwight D. Eisenhower, December 17, 1958, Abilene: White House Office-Staff Sec.-International File 17-Ven. (1).

24. Robert J. Alexander, *The Venezuelan Democratic Revolution* (New Brunswick, N.J.: Rutgers University Press, 1964). Betancourt's speech is on pp. 137–38.

25. Herter memo to Dwight D. Eisenhower, November 2, 1960, Abilene: A. W.-International File 50-Ven. (1). Of course, the achievements of the democratic regime in Venezuela largely came after Eisenhower's administration had ended. For example, by 1969 about three-fourths of the families who were landless in 1960 had received land under the agrarian reform program.

26. Ibid. The "right" refers to Dominican dictator Rafael Leonidas Trujillo whose hatred for and opposition to Betancourt led him to plot an assassination attempt in 1960, which fortunately failed in its execution.

27. Herter memo to Dwight D. Eisenhower, October 31, 1960, Abilene: A. W.-International File 50-Ven. (1).

28. *Waging Peace*, p. 521.

29. Department of State, *Bulletin* 40 (January 26, 1959): 128.

30. Department of State, *Bulletin* 11 (February 2, 1959): 162–163.

31. Nixon believed that Castro was "a dangerous threat to our peace and security," that "he looked like a revolutionary, talked like an idealistic college professor and reacted like a Communist," and that "Castro is either incredibly naive about communism or is under

communist discipline.'' Nixon believed the latter to be the more likely. Branyan and Larsen, *The Eisenhower Administration*, pp. 1163–65.

32. Herter memo to Dwight D. Eisenhower, April 23, 1959, Abilene: A.W.-Dulles-Herter 9 April 1959 (2).

33. Ibid., with D.D.E. scribbled note in margin.

34. Department of State, *Bulletin* 40 (June 29, 1959): 958–59.

35. Branyan and Larsen, *The Eisenhower Administration*, pp. 1168–70.

36. *Waging Peace*, p. 533.

37. *Public Papers of the President, 1960–1961* (Washington, D.C.: 1961), pp. 526–63. Also see *Waging Peace*, p. 535.

38. *Waging Peace*, p. 535.

39. *Public Papers, 1960–1961*, pp. 567–68.

40. *Waging Peace*, p. 538.

41. Minutes, Abilene: White House Office-Staff Secretary 4–1960 (March-May) (6). Eisenhower expressed the same idea less colloquially but equally fervently on other occasions as to the Venezuelan Ambassador Falcon Briceño. See Memo, November 30, 1960, Abilene: A.W.-International File 50-Ven. (1).

42. *Public Papers, 1960–1961*, p. 891. In *Waging Peace*, he declared this Cuban act was the ''last straw'' (p. 613).

43. *Public Papers of the President, 1959* (Washington, D.C., 1961), p. 257.

44. Ibid., pp. 257–58. The italics are Eisenhower's.

45. *Public Papers, 1960–1961*, pp. 913–30.

20

Dwight D. Eisenhower and the State of Israel: Supporter or Distant Sympathizer?

Isaac Alteras

On September 27, 1948, Dwight D. Eisenhower, at the time president of Columbia University, was awarded an Honorary Degree of Humane Letters by the neighboring Jewish Theological Seminary of America. At the ceremonies he was praised for his role as Supreme Commander of the Allied Expeditionary Forces in Europe when he led the fight that ended the terror of the Nazi onslaught. His military accomplishments were lauded for the high moral standards they embodied, such as "statesmanship, tolerance and humaneness . . . [for being] a soldier of intellectual integrity with a love for peace and his fellow man." It was quite appropriate for the Jewish Theological Seminary of America, the spiritual and intellectual center of American Conservative Judaism, to so honor Eisenhower, for his humanity was clearly demonstrated by his humane treatment of Jewish survivors of the Holocaust.

Eisenhower's aversion to Adolf Hitler and Nazism first became known to his Jewish friends in 1938 in Manila, the capital of the Philippines. There, as a young major, he assisted Douglas MacArthur in training the Phillipine Army. At a social function he was astonished to hear American businessmen and some members of the Spanish community express admiration for Hitler. Impressed by his condemnation of Nazism, his Jewish friends asked him to take the job of relocating Jewish refugees from Nazi Germany in places such as China, Indochina, Indonesia, and elsewhere in Asia. The job carried with it a very handsome salary of $60,000 a year plus expenses, with a promise to place the first five years of salary in escrow to be paid to him in full if for any reason he had to leave the job. Apart from the tempting monetary reward, as Eisenhower later recalled, the job offered a challenge: "it would have been a pretty wonderful thing to resettle these poor people who were driven out of their homelands."[1] Despite its advantages, however, Eisenhower turned it down, and the only explanation he gave was that he wanted to continue his military career. Perhaps, as Stephen Ambrose suggests, given Hitler's ambitions Eisenhower might have already foreseen the coming storm. With the United States in no position to stay out of the war, it would be his duty to lend a hand to the military effort needed to end Nazi tyranny.[2]

On May 8, 1945, the war in Europe was over. As the Allied troops converged from the east and west, they marched through the showplaces of Nazi horror, Maidanek, Buchenwald, Auschwitz, Dachau, and Belsen. Eisenhower visited some of those sites and wrote to his wife Mamie on April 15, 1945, of what he saw, "I never dreamed that such cruelty, bestiality and savagery could really exist in this world! It was horrible."[3] On the same day he dispatched the following telegram to George Marshall, the Chief of Staff of the Army:

The most interesting although horrible sight that I encountered during the trip was a visit to a German internment camp near Gotha. The things I saw beggar description. While I was touring the camp I encountered three men who had been inmates and by one ruse or another had made their escape. I interviewed them through an interpreter. The visual evidence and the verbal testimony of starvation, cruelty and bestiality were so overpowering as to leave me a bit sick. In one room, where they were piled up twenty or thirty naked men killed by starvation. George Patton would not even enter. He said, he would get sick if he did so. I made the visit deliberately in order to be in a position to give first hand evidence of these things, if ever in the future, there develops a tendency to charge these things merely to propaganda.[4]

In this same interest, Eisenhower invited reporters, British Members of Parliament, and American congressmen to visit the concentration camps and see for themselves.

After V-E Day Eisenhower was appointed military governor of Germany as well as the Commander of American troops in Europe. In this role he assisted Jews fleeing from Poland, Rumania, Hungary, and those who survived the concentration camps. All were desperately seeking refuge in displaced persons camps under Allied supervision with the hope of finding new places of residence rather than return to their former homelands. Since the Jewish survivors had received far harsher treatment from the Nazis than non-Jews and were suffering from malnutrition and disease, Eisenhower ordered that they be placed in separate camps to receive special rehabilitation treatment. The treatment included avoiding overcrowding, improved sanitary conditions, sufficient food, and adequate medical services.[5] According to Judah Nadich, Eisenhower's adviser on Jewish Affairs in the European Theater of Operations, the General's personal appearances lifted the morale of the survivors who saw in him a symbol of hope and a better future. When David Ben-Gurion, at the time chairman of the Executive of the Jewish Agency and later the first Prime Minister of Israel, visited those displaced persons camps in October 1945, he thanked Eisenhower on behalf of the Jewish people for his role in defeating Nazism as well as for his humaneness toward the survivors of the Holocaust.[6]

The overwhelming majority of the Jewish displaced persons refused to return to their countries of origin and preferred Palestine instead. At Ben-Gurion's urgings, Eisenhower agreed to provide them with farms for agricultural pioneer training on land requisitioned from the German population. Eisenhower also expanded educational and cultural programs in Hebrew in order to prepare them for a useful life in Palestine. Weekly, he sent military planes to Palestine to bring Hebrew books, agricultural instructors, and teachers. The same planes carried mail between the refugees and their relatives in Palestine, thereby stimulating family reunions.

Eisenhower's human approach toward Jewish survivors of the Holocaust did not translate in subsequent years to support for the creation of a Jewish state in Palestine, the future homeland of many displaced persons. Nor as President did he support Israel's position in the Arab-Israeli conflict. The reasons for the differences in attitude are not difficult to ascertain. In helping Jewish survivors of the Nazi terror, he acted as a humanitarian, in line with his basic character of decency and tolerance. The future of Palestine and the creation of a Jewish state were controversial political questions and were closely tied to what he and the military believed to be American interests in the Middle East.[7]

Thus, as Chief of Staff of the Army Eisenhower advised the Joint Chiefs of Staff against any action that would commit U.S. troops in Palestine or "orient the peoples of the Middle East (i.e., the Arabs) from Western Powers, as the United States has a vital security interest in that area." He also stressed the military importance of the control of Mideast oil, "this being the one large undeveloped resource in a world which may come to the limits of its oil resources within this generation . . . a great part of our military strength as well as our standard of living is based on oil."[8] This preoccupation with oil led President Eisenhower to seek better relations with Arab countries, to the chagrin of Israel and its supporters in the United States. For the same reason, as Chief of Staff, Eisenhower could not be convinced that a Jewish state in Palestine would serve American military and political interests in the Middle East.[9] When the late Secretary of the Treasury Henry Morgenthau, Jr., a supporter of the Zionist cause, requested Eisenhower to meet the political adviser for the Jewish Agency for Palestine to discuss possible military measures to defend Jewish and Arab states in view of pending British withdrawal, Eisenhower shunned any kind of involvement. He answered Morgenthau's request by sending him elsewhere, stating "we now have a Department of National Defense, such conversations should be held with someone above me."[10] Presumably he meant James Forrestal, the Secretary of Defense whose opposition to a Jewish state in Palestine was well known.

As Commander of NATO forces in Europe, Eisenhower expressed in private the desirability of winning the friendship of Arab peoples as military allies of the Western world in the struggle against communism.[11] Only in the final weeks of the presidential campaign did Eisenhower begin to praise Israel as "democracy's outpost in the Middle East . . . every American who loves liberty must join the efforts to make secure forever the future of the newest member of the family of nations." On October 18, 1952, in a letter to Rabbi Hillel Silver, a leading Zionist and lifelong Republican, Eisenhower praised Israel "for the great things it had accomplished . . . the hard work of its pioneers, the vision and quality of the work of resettlement and reclamation which they are so energetically prosecuting." He promised, if elected, to work for the establishment of peace between Israel and the Arab world and the extension of political and economic aid to all countries in the Middle East.

Early in his administration, President Eisenhower told an official delegation representing the American Zionist Council headed by its chairman Louis Lipsky, "our government has only the friendliest feelings for Israel and the Arab states and intends to use its offices to bring about peace in the Middle East." The same sentiments were expressed in an interview which the President gave on July 8, 1953, to Rabbi Silver.

Indeed, as President, Eisenhower had attempted to bring about peace between the Jewish state and its Arab neighbors. On October 16, 1953, in an attempt to prove that the United States was an "objective friend" of all countries in the Middle East, he announced the appointment of Eric Johnston as his personal envoy to the region to seek a comprehensive program to develop the Jordan River and water resources on a regional basis. The President's initiative to bring about economic cooperation between Israel and its neighbors was based on the hope that the successful Marshall Plan experience in Europe could be emulated in the Middle East, and that economic remedies and cooperation would alleviate political problems. In January and March of 1956, he sent a special emissary, Robert Anderson, to the Middle East, on a most sensitive and secret mission to attempt to persuade Egypt and Israel to conclude a peace agreement.[12] Unfortunately, both attempts ended in failure owing mainly to Arab unwillingness to recognize and make peace with Israel.

Although the President's utterances and actions to resolve the Arab-Israeli conflict were commendable, they could not, as the recent declassified documents show, conceal the fact that the President and his administration went out of their way to minimize the importance of the U.S.-Israeli relationship. While Zionist leaders were told about his desire to bring about peace in the region, the President also assured Prince Faisal, the Foreign Minister of Saudi Arabia, that the United States would attempt to correct the mistakes of the previous administration and win Arab friendship.

In pursuing this policy, the President and John Foster Dulles, the Secretary of State, were in full agreement. Eisenhower greatly admired and trusted Dulles' diplomatic skills and judgments, and there existed as close a cooperation as possible between them in the conduct of foreign policy. In the words of William Bragg Ewald, Jr., Eisenhower's former speechwriter and a member of the small White House Staff, they "were two men who thought like one." When they differed, Dulles would at times have his way, and his recommendations on the Middle East would be accepted by the President, as in the Suez Crisis of October-November 1956.[13]

Like Eisenhower during his days as Chief of Staff of the Army, Secretary

Dulles viewed the Arab Middle East as a region of great strategic, political, and economic importance to the free world, since it contained petroleum resources vital to Western security and economic well-being. He believed that if the Soviets gained a Mideast position from which they could restrict this oil supply, the "Western Europeans' will to resist communist collaboration would be greatly weakened."[14]

Accordingly, the Arab-Israeli conflict had given the Soviet Union its greatest opportunities to exploit Arab grievances and win Arab favor. Since the Arabs believed that the State of Israel had been established with Western and especially American support, any cooperation from them against the Soviets could be gained only by downplaying the U.S. relationship with the Jewish state. However, any attempt by the United States to turn the clock back on the existence of Israel would be, in the words of a National Security Memorandum, "unrealistic, politically impracticable and morally dubious."[15] Short of reneging on the American commitment to Israel's right to exist, both in rhetoric and in action, the Eisenhower administration was obsessed with the need to prove how its policy differed from that of Truman.

Eisenhower and Dulles defined their approach to the Middle East as "friendly impartiality" toward both Israel and the Arab states as distinct from Truman's "special relationship" with Israel. Both felt that Truman had gone overboard in favor of Israel because of Zionist pressures and personal preferences. Now, American foreign policy would not be influenced by internal considerations. For the sake of balance, "the Arab interest would be upgraded, Israel would be looked after but downgraded."[16] The task would be made easier, since Eisenhower had won the presidency in 1952 without the support of American Jewish voters, 75 percent of whom had voted for Adlai Stevenson.

On May 9, 1953, Secretary Dulles left Washington for a three-week visit to the Middle East, in his words, "to renew old friendships and make new ones." Dulles was reported to have assured Saeb Salem, the Lebanese Prime Minister, of his objectivity in the Arab-Israeli conflict. A majority of Jews had voted against him when he ran for the Senate in 1949, as they had voted against Eisenhower in 1952. The United States, Dulles continued, wanted to recapture the Arab world's friendship.[17]

Upon his return, Dulles made the following observation in a memorandum to the President about the trip to Israel and the Arab states:

The Israeli factor and the association of the United States in the minds of the people of the area with French and British colonial and imperialistic policies are millstones around our neck. Today the Arab people are afraid that the United States will back the new State of Israel in aggressive expansion. They are more fearful of Zionism than of Communism and they fear lest the United States become the backer of expansionist Zionism.[18]

The policies which the United States pursued with full presidential backing were designed to get rid of the "millstones" in order to save the region for the

United States. Those policies included attempts to disengage from Israeli positions pertaining to the conflict with the Arabs. The United states found it necessary to convince the Arabs that it was capable of acting independently of other
Western states and Israel. On June 1, 1953, Dulles proposed that the United States
help strengthen the interrelated defense of the Middle East countries so that a
security system "could grow from within." Given that the Arab states did not
recognize Israel, it would be excluded from any such defense system. Dulles
called for the return of some Palestinian refugees to the "area presently controlled
by Israel" and indirectly appealed for the internationalization of Jerusalem.[19] The
Israelis interpreted such phrases as questioning their territorial integrity as well as
their right to Jerusalem. All in all, from the Israeli perspective such pronounce-
ments caused shock, bewilderment, and outcries of American appeasement of the
Arabs.

Other administration actions during the second half of 1953 confirmed the
pro-Arab trend in American policy. On July 20, Assistant Secretary of State
Henry Byroade told a congressional committee that the United States intended to
supply larger quantities of arms to Arab states than to Israel. On July 28, Secretary
Dulles protested in strong terms the transfer of the Israeli Foreign Ministry Office
from Tel-Aviv to Jerusalem as negating existing U.N. resolutions. The United
States deplored the Israeli attack on the Jordanian village of Qibya during October
14–15 in which fifty-three Arabs were killed without looking into the reasons why
the raid took place.[20] On October 20, as a result of Israel's refusal to comply with
the request of the Chief of Staff of the U.N. Truce Supervision Organization
(UNTSO) to suspend work on its hydroelectric project on the upper Jordan River,
the United States canceled aid to Israel. The aid was reinstated once Israel had
agreed to suspend work on the project, but the United States had for the first time
used economic power to coerce Israel, thereby making its pursuit of an independent policy all but impossible. On April 14, 1954, the United States announced
that its part-in-aid to Israel for fiscal 1955 would be reduced to $52.2 million
"because Israel was nearer to self-support and no longer required the large sums
that had been made available the previous years."[21] While Israel appreciated the
compliment, the announcement was unwelcome news, for Israel's economic
planning was tied to an increase rather than a reduction in economic aid.

Furthermore, the arms deal between Egypt and Czechoslovakia concluded in
September 1955 meant that Egypt would receive substantial quantities of arms
including jet aircraft, tanks, and naval vessels from the Soviet Union in exchange
for cotton and rice. This agreement would upset the balance of military power in
the area which the United States, Britain, and France had been trying to uphold
since 1950. Israel's reaction to the Egyptian-Czech deal was to apply to the United
States for arms to offset the Egyptian buildup. But the State Department with full
presidential approval refused to accede to Israel's request on the theory that such
a course would lead to an arms race which it assumed Israel could not win. More
importantly, it would be detrimental to U.S. interests, because the Arab world
would perceive it as a change in U.S. policy of neutrality in the Middle East. Only

pressure from American public opinion had finally forced Dulles, on April 11, 1965, to approve France's sale of an additional twelve French Mystere IV jets to Israel.[22]

The State Department, that is, John Foster Dulles, spoke and acted with the full authority of the President. The President was kept informed and consulted about every basic decision made by the Secretary of State and was intimately involved in the decision-making process to the minutest detail. This was so much the case that when American Zionist leaders and others friendly to Israel criticized what they viewed as pro-Arab tilt in American Mideast policy, Eisenhower tried to calm Dulles and urged him to disregard the protests. Thus, on October 28, 1953, Eisenhower wrote to Dulles: "The political pressure from the Zionists in the Arab-Israeli controversy is a minority pressure. My Jewish friends tell me that except for the Bronx and Brooklyn the great majority of the nation's Jewish population is anti Zion."[23]

The President believed the statement of his Jewish friends, thereby showing limited knowledge or understanding of American Jewry's attitudes and concerns for Israel.[24] In all likelihood, that is because Eisenhower had never been exposed to Jewish political pressures before his presidency, as he might well have had he served in Congress as many Presidents did before reaching the Oval Office. He came to the White House from a military career, and when as President he first encountered Jewish clout, he acted defensively as if provoked. In a Cabinet meeting on November 12, 1953, when the subject of the Middle East came up, Eisenhower told those present that he would "never use foreign policy for domestic political advantage as Truman had done."[25] Furthermore, he viewed his predecessor's action in recognizing Israel as having been carried out too hastily. In 1955, Eisenhower offered the opinion that the "difficulties of the past ten years resulted from that decision."[26]

In researching the documents of the Eisenhower presidency, one is hard put to find instances of the late President's sympathy with Israel's plight. The single exception then becomes important. Late in the afternoon of March 13, 1956, Anderson directly reported to the President on the failure of his mission to bring about peace between Israel and Egypt. He told the President that he had made no progress whatsoever in his basic aim, which was to arrange a meeting between Gamal Abdel Nasser and Ben-Gurion. Nasser, said Anderson, "proved to be a complete stumbling block. He is apparently seeking to be acknowledged as the political leader of the Arab world." While the Israeli leaders were eager to talk with Egypt, they were unwilling to make the territorial concessions demanded by Nasser and showed immense distrust of the Egyptian leader. Eisenhower sympathized with Israel's predicament: "Israel a tiny nation, surrounded by enemies, is nevertheless one we have recognized and on top of this it has a very strong position in the heart and emotions of the Western world because of the tragic suffering of Jews throughout two thousand five hundred years of history."[27]

Despite such sentiments, the President would not accede to Israel's demand for arms. On the contrary, he took a very harsh stand toward Israel when, in collusion with Britain and France, it attacked Egypt on October 29, 1956. Eisenhower ignored Nasser's unwillingness to make peace, the constant attacks on Israeli settlements by Egyptian-supported *fedayeen*, and the Egyptian blockade of the Straits of Tiran. The President found a measure of opportunism in the timing of Israel's military action. Referring to the upcoming presidential elections in the United States, Eisenhower wrote to his boyhood friend "Swede" Hazlett:

The Administration had realized that Ben Gurion might try to take advantage of the pre-campaign period to launch a war because of the importance that so many politicians in the past have attached to our Jewish vote. I gave strict orders to the State Department that they should inform Israel that we'd handle our affairs exactly as though we didn't have a Jew in America. The welfare and best interests of our country were to be the sole criteria on which we operated.[28]

Eisenhower was furious that the British, French, and Israelis would have recourse to what he considered eighteenth-century methods of settling disputes. He insisted on an immediate halt to the operation and withdrawal from Egyptian territory. When Israel refused to withdraw without adequate security guarantees, the administration proceeded with plans for the imposition of sanctions against Israel as a means of bringing about its unconditional withdrawal from the Sinai. According to Sherman Adams, Eisenhower's Chief of Staff, the United States could no longer tolerate any further delays in the Israeli response to withdraw. In his words, such action by Israel "would endanger western influence by convincing Middle Easterners that U.S. policy toward the area was in the last analysis controlled by Jewish influence in the United States."[29] In conversations with Adams, the President went so far as to prefer a U.N. resolution that would call on U.N. members to suspend not just governmental aid but also private assistance to Israel.[30]

Only strong public and congressional criticism of administration policy prevented the imposition of sanctions and forced it to provide Israel with a measure of security guarantees prior to the withdrawal of its forces from Egyptian territory. As a result of the intervention by Lyndon Johnson, who at the time was Senate Majority Leader, the President went along with an amendment to the Eisenhower Doctrine on the Middle East. That amendment tried to allay Israeli security fears by stating that the United States strongly supported the independence, sovereignty, and territorial integrity of all countries in the Middle East.

By mid–1957, the strain in American-Israeli relations subsided. It became apparent to the President and his administration that despite its condemnation of the British, French, and Israeli attack on Egypt and its successful effort to save Egypt from a military debâcle, Nasser showed no gratitude for American favors. On the contrary, he rejected the Eisenhower Doctrine and undermined American interests in the region. Washington viewed Nasser as the Soviets' principal vehicle and ally. He and not Israel stood in the way of checking the spread of Russian influence in the area. In view of the frequent crises in the Middle East owing to Nasserite subversion of pro-Western governments, the United States began to appreciate Israel as the only stable pro-Western country in the region. The improvement in the relationship between the two countries was expressed in increases of American aid for development purposes, culminating with an unofficial visit by Ben-Gurion to the White House in August 1960—the final months of the Eisenhower presidency.

Thus, it is quite evident that—as a General—when Eisenhower first encountered the Jewish problem he manifested sympathetic understanding, viewing it as a humanitarian question. Israel as a state was a different matter, however. Even though he admired its democratic system and the pioneering spirit of its people, these qualities could not override what he considered to be America's national interests. Rightly or wrongly, in his judgment preserving those interests required distancing the United States from its support of Israel, while still maintaining a commitment to its right to exist as a state. Anything less would have been morally wrong and in all likelihood politically untenable. Furthermore, contrary to previously held views, recent evidence suggests that the President was in complete control of policies regarding the Arab-Israel conflict, with John Foster Dulles a faithful servant.

In assessing the feelings toward Israel of three Presidents, Truman, Eisenhower, and Kennedy, Israel's first Prime Minister, David Ben-Gurion, said of Eisenhower: "Every man who has had the privilege of meeting President Eisenhower comes immediately under the impact of his high moral purpose and his devotion to peace. He is a very warm and responsive man, always anxious to be understanding and helpful."[31] These kind words are a true portrayal of Eisenhower the man and less a reflection of his policies in regard to Israel.

NOTES

1. Ann Whitman, Diary Series, Box 9 (file 2), January 15, 1958. Deposited at the Eisenhower Presidential Library, Abilene, Kansas. For a more complete account of this episode, see D. D. Eisenhower, *At East: Stories I Tell to Friends* (New York: Eastern Acorn Press, 1981), pp. 229–30.

2. Stephen Ambrose, *Eisenhower: A Life*, Vol. 1, *The Soldier and the Candidate 1890–1952* (New York: Simon and Schuster, 1983), p. 110.

3. John S.D. Eisenhower, *Letters to Mamie* (Garden City, N.Y.: Doubleday and Co., 1978), p. 248.

4. *The Papers of D. D. Eisenhower, The War Years*, Alfred D. Chandler, Jr., ed., Vol. 4 (Baltimore: Johns Hopkins University Press, 1970), document 2418, pp. 2615–16; Ambrose, *Eisenhower*, p. 371; see also Harry Butcher, *My Three Years with Eisenhower* (New York: Simon and Schuster, 1946), pp. 815–16.

5. Judah Nadich, *Eisenhower and the Jews* (New York: Twayne, 1953), p. 41.

6. *Ben Gurion Looks Back*, in talks with Moshe Perlman (New York: Simon and Schuster, 1965), p. 114.

7. From mid–1945 through 1948, the question concerning the future of Palestine led to dissension within the Truman administration. The President and his advisers took a

supportive attitude toward the Jews in Palestine. During 1945 and 1946, Truman urged the British to allow 100,000 Jewish displaced persons to enter Palestine, something they refused to do in large measure because of Arab opposition. On October 4, 1946, the President called for a separate Jewish state that would be situated in an adequate area and would control its own immigration and economic policies. Then in November 1947 the President overruled the advice of the State Department in having the United States urge other countries to vote in favor of the partition of Palestine into a Jewish and Arab state (November 19, 1947). Finally, on May 14, 1948, to the surprise and chagrin of the American U.N. Delegation Truman recognized the State of Israel. Arrayed against the White House policies were the State Department, the Pentagon, and the British who viewed the President's action as alienating the Arab world and damaging Western interests in the Middle East. For a thorough discussion of this controversial subject, see John Snetsinger, *Truman, the Jewish Vote and the Creation of Israel* (Stanford, Calif.: Hoover Institute Press, 1974); Zvi Ganin, *Truman, American Jewry and Israel, 1945–1948* (New York: Holmes and Meier Publisher, 1979); Michael Cohen, *Palestine and the Great Powers, 1945–1948* (Princeton, N.J.: Princeton University Press, 1982); Kenneth Bein, *March to Zion: U.S. Policy and the Founding of Israel* (Texas A & M University Press, 1980).

8. *The Papers of D. D. Eisenhower*, Vol. 7, Memo by Eisenhower to the Joint Chiefs of Staff, June 18, 1946, pp. 1137–38.

9. Ibid., Vol. 8, Letter by Eisenhower to Lauris Norstad, June 24, 1947, pp. 1178–79.

10. Ibid., Vol. 9, Eisenhower to John Hersey Michaelis, December 8, 1947, p. 2122.

11. Nadich, *Eisenhower and the Jews*, p. 11, and interview with the author.

12. This mission was put together by John Foster Dulles and his brother Allen, then head of the CIA, and was very secret. There were guarded phone calls, traveling was done in disguise, and Anderson's dictated cables reporting on his meetings with Nasser and Ben-Gurion reached Dulles through special channels—CIA operatives in Cairo and Jerusalem. The documents relating to this mission have not been declassified yet. For the most recent information on the mission, see William Bragg Ewald, Jr., *Eisenhower the President: Crucial Days, 1951–1960* (Englewood Cliffs, N.J.: Prentice-Hall, 1981), pp. 194–99. See also Donald Neff, *Warriors at Suez, Eisenhower Takes America into the Middle East* (New York: Simon and Schuster, 1981), pp. 133–36; 168–69.

13. Ewald, *Eisenhower the President*, p. 211.

14. White House Office, National Security Council Series, Box 12, NSC 5428, Progress Report, May 17, 1956. U.S. Policy Toward the Middle East. These recently declassified documents are located at the Eisenhower Library in Abilene, Kansas.

15. White House Office, National Security Council Series, Arab-Israeli Problem, NSC 5428, box 12, July 23, 1954, p. 34.

16. Abba Eban, Oral History, Interview, p. 15. Deposited at the Mudd Library, Princeton University, Princeton, N.J.: see also Herbert S. Parmet, *Eisenhower and the American Crusades* (New York: Macmillan Co., 1972), pp. 476–77.

17. *Time*, Vol. 61, May 25, 1953. The story was immediately denied by John Katzenberg, a member of the U.S. delegation. This denial notwithstanding, the fact remained that U.S. policies in subsequent years were in line with the spirit of that report.

18. Report on the Near East, Department of State *Bulletin* 28 (June 15, 1953): 834.

19. Ibid., pp. 831–35.

20. The Security Council of the United States at the initiative of Western powers censured Israel and asked its government "to bring those responsible to account." Abba

Eban, the Israeli representative, told the Council that Israel suffered 421 persons killed and wounded in Jordanian infiltration raids since 1950.

21. Ernes Stock, *Israel on the Road to Sinai 1949–1956* (Ithaca, N.Y.: Cornell University Press, 1967), p. 65.

22. *D.D.E. Diaries, Dulles-Herter Series*, Box 5, Telephone Conversation with Gordon Gray, April 12, 1956.

23. *D.D.E. Diaries, Dulles-Herter Series*, box 1, October 26, 1953.

24. For a discussion about the feeling of American Jews toward Israel during this period, see Marshall Sklare and Mark Vost, *The Riverton Study* (New York: American Jewish Committee, 1957); see also Melvin Urofsky, *We Are One American Jewry and Israel* (Garden City, N.Y.: Doubleday and Co., 1978).

25. Robert J. Donovan, *Eisenhower, The Inside Story* (New York: Harper and Row, 1956), p. 67.

26. As quoted in Blanche Cook Wiessen, *The Declassified Eisenhower, A Divided Legacy* (Garden City, N.Y.: Doubleday and Co., 1981), p. 191.

27. *Eisenhower Papers as President*, Ann Whitman File, Box 9, March 13, 1956.

28. *D.D.E. Diaries*, Box 20, November 2, 1956. See also D. D. Eisenhower, *Waging Peace; The White House Years, 1956–1961* (Garden City, N.Y.: Doubleday and Co., 1965), p. 56; Neff, *Warriors at Suez*, p. 396.

29. Sherman Adams, *Firsthand Report: The Story of the Eisenhower Administration* (New York: Harper and Bros., 1961), p. 665.

30. Ibid.

31. Amram Ducovy, *David Ben Gurion in His Own Words* (New York: Fleet Press Corp., 1968), p. 68.

21

Congress and the Middle East: The Eisenhower Doctrine, 1957

Philip J. Briggs

U.S. rivalry with the Soviet Union in the Middle East provided one of the earliest incidences of Cold War conflict between the two superpowers following World War II. The first complaint the Security Council of the United Nations received was supported by the British and lodged by the Iranian government against the Soviet Union on January 19, 1946. Soon thereafter, the Iranians charged the U.S.S.R. with keeping their troops in Iranian Azerbaijan past the agreed upon date for their withdrawal. The Soviet Union retaliated by claiming that British troops in Greece and Indonesia were a threat to peace. However, the Security Council, by a vote of 8 to 3 overruled a Russian request that the Iranian dispute not be placed on the agenda. All Soviet troops were evacuated from Iran on May 6, 1946, after President Harry S Truman sent Premier Joseph Stalin an ultimatum stating that he "would send troops if he [Stalin] did not get out."[1]

During that same year, the Soviet Union also sought an agreement whereby British influence would be eliminated in Turkey and strategic bases commanding the Dardanelles Straits would be obtained. Strongly backed by the United States, which quickly dispatched a naval task force to the Mediterranean, the Turks rejected these proposals.

The following year the United States adopted the Truman Doctrine which was aimed at stopping communist-supported partisans in Greece through the unilateral intervention of American economic and military aid. Via the implementation of this policy, governments friendly to the United States were maintained in both Greece and Turkey. The Truman Doctrine was also a general statement of American foreign policy which substantially differed from the nation's pre-World War II isolationism. The policy of isolationism itself had given way to collective security as the new foreign policy only four years before (1943), as a result of congressional approval of the Fulbright and Connally Resolutions.[2]

As Britain formally terminated its Palestine mandate, Jewish leaders proclaimed the State of Israel on May 14, 1948. The Truman administration demonstrated its sympathy for a Jewish homeland in the Middle East by immediately recognizing the new state—despite State Department opposition. Arab League armies immediately attacked Israel and were decisively defeated in a short but bloody war. By 1949, Egypt signed an armistice with Israel, and other Arab states quickly followed suit. The armistice was shaky at best: border raids continued, with the Arabs refusing to recognize the existence of Israel and vowing to eventually destroy the new Jewish state in a war of annihilation.

American political commitments in the Middle East rose sharply during May 1950 when through American initiative a Tripartite Declaration with Britain and France was announced guaranteeing the shaky Israeli-Arab armistice. Arab resentment of the new Jewish state continued to manifest itself, however, and on June 17 five Arab states signed a collective security pact followed by a prohibition against Israeli shipping through the Suez Canal imposed by Egypt on July 19.

By 1951, the forces of nationalism were sweeping across the Middle East. On March 15, Iran nationalized the British-held Anglo-Iranian Oil Company. In Egypt, potentially the most powerful Arab state, Parliament abrogated the treaty that had assigned the defense of the Suez Canal to the British. London answered by reinforcing its Suez garrison with Washington backing the British position. In October, Egypt turned down an opportunity to participate in an Anglo-American-French-Turkish Middle East Command which was to defend the whole area against communism. During 1952, the Egyptian King Farouk was ousted in an army coup that vowed a campaign against corruption and colonialist forces in Egypt. By April 1954, Colonel Gamal Abdel Nasser had risen to lead the military clique that ruled Egypt; his policies were anti-Israeli and anticolonial, with an ultimate goal of pan-Arab unity.

The year 1954 also saw the development of an American protectorate over oil-rich Iran on the Soviet Union's borders. Iran had been gripped by an economic paralysis and faced bankruptcy after it seized the Anglo-Iranian oil fields and British technicians left the country. Via a coup organized by the Central Intelligence Agency, Premier Mohammed Mossadegh was overthrown during August 1953 and an oil accord was promulgated during 1954 between Washington, London, and Teheran. Through this agreement, the Anglo-Iranian Oil Company formally lost its monopoly, but the United States gained substantial concessions for its own oil concerns. According to one high American oil corporation official involved, it had been a "most profitable patriotism."[3]

DULLES AND THE MIDDLE EAST

John Foster Dulles dominated the formulation of American foreign policy during his tenure as Secretary of State in the Eisenhower administration with the strong backing of the President. Innovations in policy such as the Formosa

Resolution of 1955 were Dulles' in conception and motivated by a fervent anticommunism.[4]

Dulles also jealously guarded the right to determine who could speak for the administration on American foreign policy. To this end, President Eisenhower admonished Cabinet members during the 1956 Middle East war that "it is the Department of State which is to be the public spokesman for the Executive Branch on foreign affairs, especially during the present delicate international situation." At the same time, Dulles guarded the flow of foreign policy information to other administration members. During March 1957, he met Cabinet members' requests for more information with an agenda memorandum stating that while he would be "happy to makes some remarks" on the general international situation, he would "not go into detail about the Middle East."[5]

It was Dulles' judgment that any possible communist penetration of the area could best be prevented by establishing yet another regional security organization such as the recently completed Southeast Asia Treaty Organization (SEATO) in 1954. In addition, the Secretary was concerned with the effect of rising Arab nationalism on American access to Middle East oil. Consequently, on November 22, 1955, Britain, Turkey, Iran, Iraq, and Pakistan announced the establishment of the Baghdad Pact. Although the United States initiated this arrangement and participated in some of its key committees, it did not sign the Pact for fear that a formal American alliance with Iraq would antagonize Egypt and Israel.[6]

The existence of the Pact inadvertently triggered an outcome which Dulles had wanted to avoid: retaliation by both Egypt and Syria in the form of their cultivation and acceptance of Soviet economic and military aid. Nasser was embittered over the growing role of the United States in the Middle East as it threatened his goal of Arab leadership. Thus, the bond between certain Arab states and the Soviet Union grew stronger.

During September 1955, a Czech arms deal with Egypt was announced, and Israeli Prime Minister Moshe Sharett reacted by instructing his Embassy in Washington to shift its emphasis from gaining a U.S. security guarantee to the supply of arms for Israel. What followed was a "hint from a CIA source which reached Jerusalem through a highly secret channel, intimating that if Israel hit Egypt upon the arrival of the Soviet weapons, America would not protest."[7]

In November 1955, David Ben-Gurion formed a new government serving as both Prime Minister and Defense Minister of Israel. Addressing the Knesset on November 2, 1955, Ben-Gurion reminded his nation's adversaries, especially Egypt which blocked Israeli shipping through the Suez Canal and was in the process of seeking the same effect through the Red Sea Gulf, that: "Our aim is peace—but not suicide."[8]

Dulles now sought to counteract Nasser's increasing alienation by making a joint offer with the British government of $70 million to Egypt during December 1955 for building the High Aswan Dam and, on the other hand, by denying the sale of arms to Israel the following month. Israel sought these arms to counterbalance the military shipments which Egypt was receiving from Soviet sources. Washington also continued to pressure London to complete the withdrawal of its large garrison from Suez as agreed to with Egypt the previous year.

Dulles also dispatched the Texas oil magnate and later Secretary of the Treasury, Robert Anderson, to negotiate between Israel and Egypt for the purpose of reaching a compromise of political and territorial settlement. The Secretary tried to link these negotiations to support for the High Dam—which only made Nasser furious, and the mission failed.[9]

During February, Cairo came tentatively to terms with the International Bank for Reconstruction and Development for an additional loan with which to build the Aswan Dam. However, Middle East tensions continued to rise as young King Hussein of Jordan dismissed General John Bagot Glubb as Commander of the Arab Legion on March 2, 1956, and insisted that all British advisers and troops leave Jordan. During the spring of 1956, Nasser was actively seeking more aid for his High Dam project, and he continued to cultivate his position in the Arab world as champion of Arab nationalism and major proponent of anti-imperialist and anti-Israeli policies.

Bloody raids continued to be mounted from the Sinai Peninsula and the Gaza Strip into Israel. On April 19, the U.N. Secretary General Dag Hammarskjöld was able to announce a cease-fire on the Egyptian-Israeli frontier. However, King Hussein of Jordan signed a military accord with Syria on May 31 and appointed a pro-Nasser premier, completing an increasingly hostile encirclement of Israel.

Nasser continued a buildup of arms from the Soviet Union with the avowed intention of annihilating Israel. He also recognized the People's Republic of China, hinted that the Russians would, under favorable terms, underwrite the costs of the Dam, sent aid to anti-British guerrillas on Cyprus and their counterparts in French Algeria, and celebrated the final British withdrawal from Suez on June 13 as a triumph for Arab nationalism.

The following month the State Department stunned Nasser with an announcement that it would not finance the Aswan Dam. Both London and the International Bank quickly concurred in this decision. The U.S.S.R. announced it never had offered aid to build the dam. Nasser struck back swiftly on July 27 by nationalizing the Suez Canal and announcing that compensation to the stockholders would be made and revenues from the canal would be used to build the dam. Dulles' decision led directly to war. It was made without specific directives from Eisenhower or consultation with other members of the Cabinet, though there was significant opposition in the Congress to funding the Dam.

CONGRESS AND THE HIGH DAM

By 1956, the Republicans had long been castigating the Democrats for overspending, thus making it doubly difficult for them to argue that the Congress, with its Democratic majorities since the 1954 midterm elections, should support such a huge and controversial undertaking as the High Dam. It was also an election year, and the enormous amount of ongoing funding required for the Dam was unpopular with the Congress. Senators and Representatives prefer annual appropriations that are based on yearly justifications, not the kind of long-term commitment of funds that was required for the Dam.[10]

Democratic Senator J. William Fulbright of Arkansas was incorrect when he later claimed that opposition to the project "was confined to the Committee on Appropriations." A most important link existed between the United States' China policy and funding for the High Dam. Nasser's recognition of the People's Republic of China during May 1956 triggered a strong response from the China Lobby (advocates of the Republic of China on Taiwan). Republican Senate Minority Leader William Knowland of California was the outspoken head of the powerful China Lobby who quickly narrowed Dulles' options via some friendly advice. The Minority Leader told the Secretary that the foreign aid bill was soon to be voted on in Congress, and it contained two controversial-country programs—assistance to Nasser who was drawing closer to communism and assistance to Tito of Yugoslavia who had broken away from Moscow. Knowland strongly disliked both men and suggested that the entire foreign aid bill would be jeopardized if the administration insisted on aid for both. Under the circumstances, Dulles chose aid for Yugoslavia.[11]

Knowland was not a Progressive Republican in the Eisenhower mold, and his strong views on China were well known. Only the year before in Senate debate, he had used the extremist tactic of accusing Oregon Senator Wayne Morse of having endangered the security of the United States, because Morse had previously claimed that passage of the Formosa Resolution "would legalize the position of the proponents of a preventive war." Nevertheless, Morse characterized subsequent passage of a Mutual Defense Treaty with the Republic of China as a "treaty with Knowland." However, the outspoken Morse also opposed funds for the Dam. He disliked the financing of a giant dam in Egypt instead of one or several dams in the Northwest United States.[12]

Additional congressional opposition existed on behalf of Israel. Abba Eban, Israeli Ambassador to the United States at that time, has since recorded that American funding of the Dam was "more than Israel could afford. Here was Nasser getting arms from Moscow. He would now get the Dam from America." As a result, according to Eban, Nasser "would become insufferable through the sheer extremity of arrogance." Thus, he added in the same interview, "Israeli influence, I will say quite frankly, was exercised against American support of the Dam." Although Eban described his country's influence as "not a very ponderable thing," the Ambassador added that "it counts and certainly in that context there were many in the Senate and the House who opposed the Aswan Dam proposal in Israel's interest."[13]

There was also important opposition from the Cotton Lobby in the Congress whose influence has probably been underestimated in relation to the Dam proposal. Cotton-growing states are almost exclusively found in the South, including Texas, but the Southwest and southern California also contain areas of high yields. During the 1950s, the United States remained the number one producer of ginned cotton in the world. However, American cotton exports were temporarily hurting in 1955, with exports down about 2 million bales from what they had been in 1950. American cotton producers quite naturally opposed funding the High Dam for fear it would lead to significantly greater cotton exports and increased competition from Egypt. Moreover, their Southern representatives in the Eighty-fourth Congress (1955–1957) were heavily represented in positions of power and thus able to defend their interests. Under the circumstances, the opposition of King Cotton could not be overlooked.[14]

DULLES AND THE DOCTRINE

By the end of August 1956, British, French, and Israeli representatives were meeting in secret to coordinate their plans for an attack on Egypt. The Suez Canal was viewed as vital to British economic interests, with 25 percent of the island nation's total imports traversing the Canal. It was also "an oil pipeline, an economic lifeline," according to a *London Star* editorial on July 27. Finally, Canal revenues were a significant source of funds for the British treasury. French motivations were more political and military—to strike back at a government that was supporting the Algerian rebels in their bitter struggle against France.[15]

A severe miscalculation was in the making, however. The United States was not informed of the secret arrangements for war being made by the three states. Shimon Peres, the Israeli Director General of the Ministry of Defense, returned from France on September 25 where the meetings were taking place. He reported that the French "do not think the United States will interfere; as for the Soviet Union, they just cannot guess what the reaction will be."[16]

The administration did have at least some inkling of the impending attack when an overflight of the eastern Mediterranean by Francis Gary Powers (of later U–2 fame) discovered a large military buildup on the Island of Malta. Moreover, American Ambassador to Israel Edward B. Lawson cabled Washington that "an enormous mobilization in Israel" with "tanks on all the roads" was occurring. On October 27, Ambassador Eban was called to the State Department. With Dulles and his advisers grouped around a great map of the Israeli-Jordan frontier, the Ambassador was confronted with Lawson's observations and the question—was not Israel preparing for war? However, Eban had not yet been notified of his government's final war decision, and the administration remained in the dark.[17]

Events in the Soviet bloc countries of Eastern Europe became closely related to the imminent Middle East War. In an effort to increase his personal power and allow the Soviet economy to expand by removing Stalinist restrictions, Nikita Khrushchev had detailed Stalin's crimes against the Communist party at the Twentieth Party Congress in February 1956. As a result of this de-Stalinization process, liberal forces in Poland and Hungary were seeking greater independence from Moscow. On October 29, 1956, the Israeli Army attacked and almost completely destroyed the Egyptian Army. On October 30, England and France delivered ultimatums to Egypt and Israel to keep their armies away from the canal. When Nasser rejected their ultimatums, the previously planned British-French intervention began. The resulting war gave the Kremlin an ideal time period for counteraction in Eastern Europe. As Anglo-French columns advanced into the Suez Canal area during the first week in November, the Hungarian rebellion was suppressed by Soviet tanks.

Eisenhower's initial reaction to the Middle East War may be summarized in one word—furious. He called Downing Street directly and delivered a tirade to one of the Prime Minister's aides whom he mistook for Anthony Eden. By the time the Prime Minister got on the phone, the President hung up. Ambassador Eban has also recalled that, in the absence of Dulles, who had entered the hospital on November 3, "we had to deal with Eisenhower in his full righteous fury."[18]

The Soviet Union suggested a Moscow-Washington joint effort to settle the crisis on November 5 which the United States rejected. However, under enormous pressure from the United Nations, the Soviet Union, and most significantly the United States, the ailing Eden announced a British-French cease-fire would take place at midnight, November 6. That same day Eisenhower easily defeated his Democratic opponent in the presidential election, Adlai E. Stevenson, with a popular vote lead of over 9 million and more than six times as many electoral votes (457 to 73). Yet despite the President's popularity, both houses of Congress remained firmly in control of the Democratic opposition.

After having played an important role in destroying the Middle Eastern colonial power of England and France, the administration became convinced that a power vacuum was developing in the Middle East which the Soviet Union would attempt to fill. As Vice-President Richard Nixon would later note: "For better or worse, the colonial empires were disintegrating. The great question in the 1950s was who would fill the vacuum." In addition, even though the administration did not wish to identify its role in the area with former colonial traditions, Nasser's pan-Arab ambitions were feared as much as the presumed Russian threat. Therefore, it was not the purpose of U.S. foreign policy "or of the involved oil companies to push too far a unified Arab world, to abdicate the hold over the oil concessions, or to allow any further British-French vacuums to remain unfilled."[19]

The administration was also faced with the problem of whether or not to stand with the majority at the United Nations and vote for withdrawal of all belligerent forces, or abstain from voting in order not to further exacerbate relations with its North Atlantic Treaty allies. At the November 16 Cabinet Meeting, State Department legal adviser Herman Phleger, speaking for Dulles, reported that "Nasser had assured the United States that he had no intent at present of permitting the entry of volunteers and thus flaunt the UN position, but he reserved judgment as to the future should the French and British not withdraw promptly." Under the circumstances, Dulles was convinced that the U.N. position was the legal position, and the United States voted on November 24 for a resolution ordering a "forthwith" withdrawal of all invaders.[20]

The oil interests had warned the State Department that rushing oil to Western Europe to replace its cutoff supplies might endanger American oil holdings in the Middle East whose leaders sided with Nasser. Therefore, "the diplomatic strategy was to promise oil but to go slow in delivery, first ensuring the end of the conflict and the withdrawal from Egypt of the invading armies." Under these American pressures, England and France completely backed down, and by December 22 all of their troops had evacuated Suez. Their withdrawal only heightened Washington's conviction that a dangerous power vacuum was developing in the Middle East.[21]

Dulles now decided on a plan in the tradition of the Formosa Resolution of 1955. Still recuperating in his room at Walter Reed Hospital, he formulated a resolution in which the Congress would be asked to share responsibility in promulgating a new defense doctrine aimed at stopping any overt communist aggression in the Middle East. Prior congressional approval was to be obtained via a joint resolution to assist area nations in defending against aggression "from any country controlled by international communism." The President would be authorized to use force in meeting any attack if assistance was requested under Article 51 of the U.N. Charter. Broad economic and military aid totaling $200 million would also be made available to any such state upon request. Thus, the Eisenhower Doctrine was born.[22]

A BIPARTISAN STRATEGY

Administration efforts were aimed at quickly gaining bipartisan support from the Congress for the joint resolution. Eisenhower presented it first to Republican congressional leaders on the last day of 1956. The following day leaders of both parties in the Senate and the House were brought in for consultation in an effort to gain their approval and insure prompt attention for the resolution when the Congress convened its first session of the new year. The President assured Republican leaders that the resolution implied no intention to enter local conflicts in the Middle East in which the question of communist aggression was not involved. He assured the Democratic leaders that if Congress would grant him the authority to use military force if necessary in the Middle East, he believed he would never have to use it. Eisenhower then stated the power vacuum thesis that motivated his administration: "I just do not believe that we can leave a vacuum in the Middle East and prayerfully hope that Russia will stay out."[23]

The administration was soon confronted with strong criticism of the proposed resolution from within Democratic party ranks. Adlai E. Stevenson was applauded by both Republicans and Democrats as he sat in the diplomatic gallery at the opening session of the Senate on January 3. He issued a statement criticizing the administration's Middle East proposal in which he claimed the President "is evidently trying frantically to fill the vacuum his own policies helped create before Russia does." Stevenson also warned that Eisenhower "was going to ask for another military blank check, this time the right to send our forces to fight in the Middle East."[24]

Two days later, Eisenhower countered with a special message to Congress on the proposal emphasizing his personal responsibility over its military provision. He claimed that "Russia's rulers have long sought to dominate the Middle East," but they would have nothing to fear from the United States in the Middle East or elsewhere as long as they "do not themselves first resort to aggression. That statement I make solemnly and emphatically."[25]

Overseas, the British Foreign Office welcomed the resolution in brief general terms, but a *London Times* editorial on January 7 observed that "it comes very late, that it is fearfully vague in parts, and that it is largely irrelevant to the main causes of the Middle East upheavals, tensions and dangers." Yet, the editorial continued, "when everything has been said against it, it can be welcomed as a step forward."[26]

Another prominent Democrat attacked the proposal on January 10. Former Secretary of State Dean Acheson, while testifying before the House Foreign Affairs Committee, referred to it as being "not only unnecessary but undesirable." He claimed the President already possessed the power to use the military and to dispense aid. What was needed, according to Acheson, was a Vandenberg-type resolution that would simply express the "sense of the Senate" and in that way strengthen the hand of the Executive. The joint resolution, he concluded, was an "undesirable exercise of the legislative power of Congress." Furthermore, it was "vague" and did not direct itself at the greater threat in the area which was subversion.[27]

Alternative resolutions were quickly introduced in both the House and Senate. House Speaker Sam Rayburn circulated a substitute among his colleagues that was aimed at specifying more exactly those Middle Eastern countries the United States would be pledged to defend. Eisenhower balked at this suggestion claiming that, as in the Formosa Resolution, exact boundaries of the American commitment could not be specified lest the enemy feel free to attack elsewhere. In addition, Dulles did not approve of the Rayburn proposal, claiming it would look like an effort to establish an "American protectorate" over the Middle East countries.[28]

In the Senate, Foreign Relations Committee member William Fulbright also offered an alternative. The Fulbright approach was related to Acheson's suggestion to formulate a Vandenberg-type resolution that would simply be an expression of the "sense of the Senate" and would not result in a law as would passage of a joint resolution signed by the President. The Fulbright approach would also have eliminated any specific authorization of aid. His alternative expressed the concern of Senators who were against granting the President the right to use force in advance as he saw fit, plus the allocation of $200 million in aid for unspecified purposes.[29]

Dulles, who returned to his State Department office during December, testified before the combined Senate Foreign Relations and Armed Services Committees on January 14. The Secretary was "strongly and skeptically examined" by this key Senate group—mainly on his contention that some Arab states needed economic assistance. Democratic Senator Richard B. Russell of Georgia, Chairman of the Armed Services Committee, commented that the Middle East had very considerable "liquid assets," referring to the enormous oil resources of the region. Nevertheless, Dulles applied pressure for approval. He urged action claiming that "every day's delay means that the Soviet is getting that much deeper into the area." More ominously, he claimed that if they either gutted or rejected the administration's resolution, "the responsibility for peace or war would lie with them."[30]

Congress was also concerned that two of America's closest allies in NATO (Great Britain and France) deeply resented the administration's Middle East policies, with the result that unity in the Atlantic Alliance had almost been destroyed. Friends of Israel in Congress were watching closely as pressure from the United Nations and Washington mounted on Israel to pull its armies back to their prewar frontiers. These developments, as well as the State Department's efforts to effect a friendlier posture toward certain Arab states during this period, later played a significant role in contributing to senatorial reluctance to pass the resolution. U.N. pressure on Israel mounted further on January 17 when the General Assembly recalled several previous resolutions (November 2, 4, 7, 24, 1956), and once again noted that Israeli forces had not withdrawn from Egypt.

On January 23, Israel announced that it would not withdraw its forces from the Gaza Strip or from the Gulf of Aqaba strongpoint unless the United Nations dispatched forces to these areas to insure they would not be used as a basis for future Arab attacks on Israel. That same day Eisenhower held a news conference during which he attempted to defend the economic portions of the resolution that were now heavily under fire in the Senate. He claimed that if the economic aid section of the proposal was not approved it "would destroy what we are really trying to do." In answer to the recurring criticism that the President already possessed constitutional authority to employ the armed forces, he commented that a strong expression from Congress was needed to make it plain that the nation is "largely one in our readiness to assume burdens, and where necessary, to assume risks to preserve the peace."[31]

The Dulles-authored Middle East Resolution dovetailed well with the second basic rule Eisenhower used as a guide in his decision-making. According to Presidential Assistant Sherman Adams, those two rules were: "Don't make mistakes in a hurry and secondly, if you do, share them." Thus, upon approval of the Eisenhower Doctrine the Congress would share with the President responsibility for American foreign policy in the Middle East—especially in the advent of war.[32]

Despite congressional criticism, the House Democratic leadership moved to bring the resolution, unchanged, to a vote the following week. However, the real battle was to take place in the Senate where deliberations would be slower and more critical and where Secretary Dulles' policies and performance in particular were to be severely criticized.

DULLES UNDER FIRE

Secretary Dulles testified before a Foreign Relations Committee different from that over which Democratic Senator Walter George of Georgia had presided during the Eighty-fourth Congress. George had retired, and the administration could no longer count on his prestigious leadership to dominate the committee and successfully guide key administration proposals such as the Formosa Resolution of 1955 through the Senate. The Chairman of the Foreign Relations Committee was now the elderly Theodore Francis Green, a Rhode Island Democrat whom Carl Marcy (the Committee's Chief of Staff) described as possessing ''quite a different kind of mind from his predecessors. He was quite interested in details and not that interested in policy.''[33]

As a result, younger, more liberal members of the Committee, especially Senator Fulbright, were making themselves heard. Fulbright's strong criticism of Dulles' policies in the Middle East were based on two primary reasons. The first reason is an observation by Carl Marcy that Fulbright believed Dulles ''tended not to appreciate the depth of Arab nationalism and confused Arab nationalism with communism.'' Second, he shared Adlai E. Stevenson's stated view in correspondence that ''the world has lost confidence in Dulles.''[34]

Dulles was also faced with the implication that his Middle East policies may have been tinged with an anti-Israeli bias. Republican Senator Jacob K. Javits of New York noted that these charges began in 1953 when the administration cut off aid to Israel because of a retaliatory raid it conducted against Egypt. By 1956, according to Javits, ''Dulles was at a really very, very low ebb with the Jewish people and with many, many other people in the country at that time.'' In his sharp disagreement with the Secretary over Middle East policy, Javits recalled leading large delegations of congressmen, ''I mean large—50 to 60,'' to confront Dulles. Senator Javits felt he played a key role in the transformation of Dulles' attitude. Javits believed Dulles' policies began to sound less suspect when he offered economic aid to both the Arab states and Israel, held Nasser to his commitments, canceled Nasser's Aswan Dam funds, and developed a growing understanding of the ''vital character'' of Israel. This last point was driven home to Dulles later during the Lebanon crisis (1958), when, according to Javits, ''Israel turned out to be the most reliable country, by far, and not only reliable but effective.'' Thus, by the late 1950s, Javits described Dulles as becoming ''a hero in the relations between Israel and the United States.''[35]

During the early 1957 hearings on the resolution, Senator Fulbright led the attack on Dulles by reading a lengthy indictment of his policies while the Secretary sat on the witness stand before the combined Senate Foreign Relations and Armed Services Committees. Fulbright criticized the Secretary's ''reluctance to be specific'' as to what would be done with the requested funds. He also noted that

Britain and France were "grievously wounded by our policies." Fulbright then characterized the resolution as a "blank check for the administration to do as it pleased with our soldiers and with our money." He described Dulles' performance as being "harmful to our interests" and "calculated to weaken the influence of the free world in the Middle East," as well as disastrous to NATO. The Senator stated that no "vote of confidence in the stewardship of Secretary Dulles" should be given before more information was available. More specifically, he proposed on January 24 that Dulles furnish the joint committee with an official White Paper on American policy in the Middle East before a committee vote on the resolution was taken.[36]

The resolution's implications for Congress' power to declare war was of special concern to a number of Senators including Democratic Senator Estes Kefauver of Tennessee, a member of the Armed Services Committee. He stated that the congressional right and duty to declare when the United States should be at war was being delegated, under the resolution, "to people who are going to decide it on facts which may or may not be convincing enough to the Senate." When Kefauver asked for assurances that the President would ask for a declaration that a state of war existed before American armed forces were committed, Dulles stated flatly: "Not prior to their use; no, sir." This could not be done, according to Dulles, because the purpose of the resolution was to "make clear that the Armed Forces will be available to resist open, armed aggression by a country controlled by international communism." Senator Morse also pressed Dulles on this issue. Morse asked if the Secretary of State thought "the power vested in the Congress to declare war carries with it the power to rescind any act of the President that may lead to war." Dulles answered by stating he knew of "no way in the world" to rescind acts of the President once they had been taken.[37]

Dulles attempted to strike back at his critics during his testimony on January 25. He objected to the Fulbright White Paper proposal claiming that "any investigation of his policies and this country's relationship with Britain and France in the Suez crisis of last autumn" would cause an "infinite delay" of the administration's plan and to "irreparable damage" to the country's association with France and Great Britain. He then resorted to the familiar time-is-running-out argument to demonstrate his concern regarding a Russian attack and thus spur the Senate to action. He cited "desperate appeals from Iran, Iraq, Turkey and Pakistan seeking assurances that the United States would come to their aid in case of Russian attack." However, Dulles also undiplomatically indicated he preferred that British and French troops be deployed in Europe rather than in the Middle East if a real emergency with the Soviet Union arose, claiming he would "rather not have a French and a British soldier beside me." By this blunder, he further exacerbated strains in the Atlantic Alliance which a number of Senators were accusing him of having provoked in the first place.[38]

The attack on Dulles and his policies continued to mount. Democratic Senator Sam J. Ervin, Jr., of North Carolina suggested during the January 25 hearings that if the United States had become a member of the Baghdad Pact it would have insured this country of "at least five" committed allies, Dulles retorted that the United States did not join the Baghdad Pact because it didn't wish to become "embroiled in Arab politics." Ervin then noted that the administration's resolution might very well "embroil" the United States in Arab politics anyway.[39]

On January 28, the *New York Times* reported that criticism against the Secretary of State "was apparently beginning to create a serious question as to Mr. Dulles' future prestige and influence with Congress and in the eyes of other nations." The same article also reported that during a televised interview Senator Fulbright stated he would vote against the resolution "unless Mr. Dulles' conduct of foreign policy were investigated first." It was also reported that Senator Hubert Humphrey (D-Minn.) felt Congress had "no choice" other than to give the administration some military and economic aid for the Middle East, but he contended the resolution "is not directed at the real danger of Communist infiltration of the Middle East." He then added: "We are being prescribed the wrong medicine and I'm afraid we need to change doctors."[40]

Eisenhower came to the defense of his Secretary of State on January 29. To a meeting of legislative leaders at the White House, he noted that Dulles felt very "down" because of his slip of the tongue regarding fighting next to British and French soldiers. He then told how he had begun to press Dulles' critics to be more specific about these "supposed blunders of Foster's." At the same time, a potential deadlock between the Senate and the Secretary over the requested White Paper information was averted when Senator Green, Chairman of the Joint Committee hearings, informed Dulles that: "The committees desire such information, but they will not delay action on Senate Joint Resolution 19 pending receipt of such information."[41]

The following day at a press conference, the popular President strongly reiterated his support for Dulles, claiming that the Secretary had personal approval from him for all of his Middle East negotiations "from top to bottom." That same day Speaker Sam Rayburn, in cooperation with the Republican floor leader Joseph W. Martin, Jr., of Massachusetts, successfully steered the resolution to a vote in the House. It passed decisively, 355 to 61. A bipartisan mixture of 188 Democrats and 167 Republicans had backed the administration's resolution; 35 Democrats and 26 Republicans had opposed its passage. The opposition was primarily a mixture of isolationist Republicans and liberal Democrats.[42]

THE SENATE BALKS

Throughout December and January, the administration applied pressure on England, France, and Israel to withdraw their troops from the occupied territories. The State Department's efforts to meet the now crucial oil needs of Western Europe were deliberately slow in order not to offend anticolonial Arab leaders who might jeopardize American oil industry holdings in the Middle East. Under these pressures, England and France evacuated their forces, but Israel did not. Instead, Israel sought guarantees that it would not be subject to renewed terrorist raids, as well as assurance that free transit in the Gulf of Aqaba would be maintained. Israeli Prime Minister Ben-Gurion made it clear that Israel's armies would not withdraw without such guarantees. However, King Saud of Saudi Arabia had obtained a pledge from the administration that Israel would leave the occupied territories "unconditionally."[43]

In February 1958, the United States proposed a U.N. resolution stipulating that Israel withdraw from both the Gaza Strip and Gulf of Aqaba "without further delay." A second American resolution proposed that following such withdrawal, a U.N. force be stationed on the armistice line. On February 3, the Israeli Cabinet reiterated its position: Israel would not withdraw without guarantees against Arab terrorist raids and a guarantee that the right of free transit in the Gulf of Aqaba would be protected.[44]

The Israeli Embassy and its press officials soon began a strong campaign of presenting their side of the question to the American people. These spokesmen contended that as far as their nation was concerned, only Aqaba and Gaza remained real trouble areas; their arguments were aided by the high esteem in which the American public held the recently victorious Israeli armies. In addition, Democratic party leaders Lyndon B. Johnson, Hubert H. Humphrey, and J. W. Fulbright sympathized with the Israeli position.[45]

It was now becoming increasingly clear to the administration that the Senate did not agree with its determination to have Israel withdraw without guarantees and under a growing implied threat of sanctions. Under these conditions, the Senate might choose to deliberate a very long time on the resolution whose quick passage Dulles continued to insist was vital in his effort to fill the Middle East "power vacuum."

An important defection in Republican party ranks over this issue occurred on February 6 when Senate Minority Leader Knowland voiced his criticism of the administration's "double standard" policy, referring to the recent Soviet intervention in Hungary. Knowland declared that punishing Israel while ignoring the Soviet Union's aggression would be both "immoral and unsupportable."[46]

Behind the scenes Herman Phleger, State Department Deputy Secretary Robert Murphy, and Dulles worked with Israeli Ambassador Eban on a proposal. The result of their collaboration was the Department *aide mémoire* of February 11 which Eban believed was the "turning point in the whole affair because we could get out of Aqaba and Gaza and yet get our main interests." Its stipulations were as follows:

1. The Israeli government should withdraw from both Sharm el-Sheikh guarding the Gulf of Aqaba, and the Gaza Strip in accordance with U.N. recommendations.

2. The Egyptian government should respect the right of passage of all ships through the Gulf of Aqaba.

3. The United States would support the principle of free passage through Aqaba.[47]

In the meantime, the Foreign Relations and Armed Services Committees continued to scrutinize the administration's resolution. They finally agreed on a substitute proposal that would back the administration's use of force if it was in accordance with previous treaties including the U.N. Charter. The original resolution included an authorization to commit troops against any overt aggressor. Thus, many Democrats felt they had eliminated an authorization for "blank-check" military authority via the substitute proposal. The committee vote on the authorization issue was made along party lines, with fifteen Democrats lining up behind it and thirteen Republicans voting against the modification.[48]

On February 14, the administration announced it would accept the substitute resolution. Eisenhower made this decision on the advice of Senate Republicans who warned him that to insist on the administration version might only provoke a losing fight on the floor of the Senate. Majority leader Lyndon B. Johnson let it be known that he "strongly" hoped the President would accept the substitute as the Democrats also wished to avoid a head-on confrontation. Johnson stressed that the substitute resolution could be used abroad with all the force the President could have used for the administration version. In addition, according to the future Commander in Chief, the granting of authority to commit troops by Congress contained in the original resolution would have "created a precedent for a weaker Presidency."[49]

This was a significant breakthrough in the deadlock between the executive and congressional branches over the resolution. Via their substitute proposal, the majority Democrats had divested themselves of some anxiety over the authorization issue raised in the original resolution. Nevertheless, passage of the resolution would still give credence to the prior consent argument for military action which many Senators feared. Although the Senate was moving closer to voting on the resolution, the administration's position on the question of Israeli withdrawal and the possible use of sanctions would block final approval until it was resolved.

On February 15, the Israeli government rejected the *aide mémoire* because it lacked sufficient guarantees, especially that Egypt be forbidden to return to Gaza. On February 17, a White House statement was issued justifying the contents of the *aide mémoire* and the administration's growing pressure on Israel to withdraw. Soon thereafter, Democratic leader Johnson sent a letter to Dulles vigorously protesting the possible use of sanctions against Israel by the United Nations. He especially attacked the double standard being used on the Soviet Union and Israel, claiming that "Israel has in large part complied with the directives of the U.N.; Russia has not even pretended to be polite." On February 19, the Senate Democratic Policy Committee endorsed Johnson's statement and called on the President to "resist any United Nations attempts to impose sanctions on Israel."[50]

In the meantime, Dulles saw Eban on the rejected *aide mémoire*. The Israeli Ambassador has recalled that Dulles said "he thought we would take this thing like a shot, instead of which we were bargaining and haggling, and meantime the situation was getting worse." Dulles also stated: "If you and I can't work this out, then we are no use at all. Can't you get your people to see that this is the turning point?" Eban explained that he "couldn't possibly succeed by cable"; instead, he would return to Israel if the United States could hold up any action at the United Nations for three or four days. Eban had himself been recalled on February 18, and American U.N. Ambassador Henry Cabot Lodge approached the President of the General Assembly, saying that the situation should be kept in abeyance.[51]

Although there was no common agreement on the wording of the resolution, a major schism had developed between the administration and the Democratic-controlled Senate over the question of sanctions. The Democrats and a number of leading Republicans had no intention of endorsing a resolution that would be interpreted as supporting administration policies that might include sanctions against Israel.

Eisenhower and Dulles attempted to meet this critical concern on February 20 by calling together in the Cabinet Room at the White House a bipartisan group of congressional leaders. In a meeting described as "tense and strained," Eisenhower first explained why his administration was in favor of pressuring Israel to comply with the U.N. demand for unconditional withdrawal. He reiterated his belief that Russian influence would increase among the Arabs if Israel did not pull back its forces. "And then the whole thing might end up in a general war," the President added. He concluded by stating that nobody wants to impose sanctions, "but how else can we induce Israel to withdraw to the line agreed on in the 1949 armistice? The Arabs refuse to discuss a permanent settlement until that move is made." Senate Majority Leader Johnson quickly reminded Eisenhower and Dulles that both he and Minority Leader Knowland were not in favor of sanctions against Israel. "After all," Johnson added, "there are times when Congress has to express its own views." Eisenhower responded that he "certainly had no objection to that." Staring at the President with a wry smile, Johnson said, "Thank you."[52]

Eisenhower then turned the meeting over to Dulles. The Secretary added that on crucial questions such as the use of sanctions the world believed Israel could control American policy because of the strong support it had in the United States. He claimed that the Arabs were therefore watching the United States closely and "if we confirmed this belief, they would feel compelled to turn to Russia." However, in spite of all the administration's protestations and admonitions that a vote on sanctions at the United Nations was unavoidable and the United States would have to take a stand, senatorial support for sanctions was not obtained. According to Sherman Adams, "They were anxious to let Eisenhower have all of the credit for this declaration." That night the President took his case to the people via national television; he referred to his earlier meeting with congressional leaders, but not to the disagreement over sanctions. Although he spoke in general terms, he left no doubt as to what his final decision would be if left "no choice but to exert pressure on Israel to comply with the withdrawal resolution."[53]

THE SENATE CONSENTS

On February 21, the deadlock began to break when Israeli Prime Minister Ben-Gurion stated his government would make further efforts to come to an understanding with the United States. Ambassador Eban obtained from Ben-

Gurion new directives for reaching an understanding regarding the doctrine of free maritime passage and the maintenance of a force in Gaza to prevent the Egyptian Army from returning. Eban explained these conditions to Dulles upon his return on February 24, recalling that they ''were really in the spirit of the February 11th memorandum.'' Dulles responded: ''I think we have settled this.'' A memorandum was drawn up by Eban and Dulles in which Israel received American assurances that the Gulf of Aqaba would remain open, as well as promises that the United States would exert all effort to make Gaza a U.N.-administered area. On March 1, the Israeli Foreign Minister Golda Meir announced to the General Assembly that Israel was ''now in a position to announce its plans for a full and complete withdrawal.'' On March 4th, Ben-Gurion ordered Israeli forces to pull back from Gaza and Sharm el-Sheikh.[54]

In the meantime, an additional modification was made in the resolution with reference to the commitment of armed forces by the President. An amendment to the previously approved amendment that had eliminated the word ''authorized,'' substituted ''Constitution of the United States'' for ''Charter of the United Nations.'' The change was proposed by Senator Joseph O'Mahoney, Democrat of Wyoming, and received Senate approval on February 28 by and 82 to 0 vote. The final wording of this section of the Eisenhower Doctrine now read with reference to the employment of armed forces: ''*Provided*: That such employment shall be consonant with the treaty obligations of the United States and with the Constitution of the United States.''[55]

On March 5, 1958, two months from the day Eisenhower had originally asked Congress for passage of the joint resolution, it received Senate approval, 72 to 19. The opposition on the final roll call was made up of a small number of liberal Democrats, a larger group of Southern Democrats, and three conservative Republicans. The opposition's main effort centered on an amendment sponsored by Senator Morse. It stipulated that, if the President intended to use the armed forces, he must first give the Congress a justification for their use, or, in case of an emergency and the Congress was not so notified, he must immediately request approval or disapproval from the Congress after the troops had been committed. The Morse proposal was defeated by a 64 to 28 vote with both future Presidents, Lyndon B. Johnson and John F. Kennedy, voting with the majority.[56]

On March 7, the House brought their version of the resolution into line with that of the Senate by a vote of 350 to 60. Debate among the Representatives was concerned ''almost as much with ill-concealed resentment at the Senate, for having rewritten the House version, as with the basic issue of the policy itself.'' Two days later the President signed the joint resolution into law.[57]

SUMMING UP

John Foster Dulles dominated American foreign policy formulation during the Eisenhower administration with the strong backing of the President. The Secretary's refusal to fund the High Dam was a turning point in Middle East history, and his decision was undoubtedly motivated in part by Nasser's growing relationship with the Soviet Union. However, congressional opposition to funding the dam was substantial and has been underestimated as a contributory factor in Dulles' final decision.

Congressional opposition was strong and broadly based. Its most significant element was probably the China Lobby whose spokesman was the Senate Republican Minority Leader. It may still have been possible for the administration to overcome opposition to funding the Dam, but much goodwill with the Congress would have been expended in any such effort over an issue that had strong opponents in both political parties.

The President's reaction to the Suez War has been underestimated. Ike was in a wrath about the whole matter, with the result that American opposition was a key factor in the eventual British-French withdrawal and Anthony Eden's subsequent resignation. However, the demise of European power in the Middle East left what the administration believed was a power vacuum that must be filled immediately. The resulting Middle East Resolution was a Dulles contrivance in the mold of the Formosa Resolution and in line with Eisenhower's penchant for sharing responsibility for major decisions.

Congressional approval of the resolution proved to be a most difficult task, with significant resistance occurring at several junctures. The first hurdle was Senator Fulbright's demand for a White Paper before any "vote of confidence" could be given on Dulles' policies. Senator Green's letter to Dulles accepting the White Paper information *after* action on the resolution overcame this obstacle. Second, the presidential employment of armed forces which was authorized in the original text was changed by two amendments which provided that any such employment be "consonant with the treaty obligations of the United States and with the Constitution of the United States." Finally, the *aide mémoire* formulated by Ambassador Eban and members of the State Department, including Dulles, broke the final deadlock over Israeli withdrawal and the possible use of sanctions.

The Congress therefore played a substantial role in American Middle East policy during this period. First, it heavily influenced the decision to reject funding the High Dam in 1956—a decision that led directly to war. Second, although the Eisenhower Doctrine was clearly an administration formulation, the Senate modified its wording and would not give it final approval until the administration had given certain guarantees to Israel.

In addition to Dulles, several key actors emerged in the development of the Doctrine. Senator Fulbright is easily identifiable as Dulles' chief critic in the Senate, although he did not see the depths of his colleague's opposition to funding the Dam. Israeli Ambassador Eban, whose joint authorship of the *aide mémoire* and skillful diplomacy broke the final impasse between his government and the administration, played an important role. Senator Knowland, whose opposition to both the Dam and any possible sanctions against Israel, played a pivotal role. Majority Leader Johnson's similar opposition to sanctions brought highly important additional pressure on the administration. Senator Morse's last ditch effort to eliminate any prior consent loopholes in the resolution is notable considering the later and continuing conflicts in executive-congressional relations over the war powers.

The position of Israel was quite different from that of either of its two European allies in the Suez War. Israel had acted under mounting threats and attacks against its vital national interests and not the essentially colonial interests that motivated Britain and France. It was therefore logical that Israel would resist withdrawal without guarantees and that its friends in the Senate would support its position under the circumstances.

Finally, the President's backing of Dulles in this policy area "from top to bottom" gave the forceful Secretary of State greater strength in dealing with the Congress. Yet, congressional influence was surely demonstrated in the development of the Eisenhower Doctrine.

NOTES

1. John C. Campbell, *Defense of the Middle East: Problems of American Policy*, rev. ed. (New York: Harper and Brothers, 1960), p. 33.

2. The Fulbright and Connally Resolutions are examined in Philip J. Briggs, "Congress and Collective Security: The Resolutions of 1943," *World Affairs* 132, No. 4 (1970): 332–44.

3. Robert Engler, *The Politics of Oil: A Study of Private Power and Democratic Directions* (New York: Macmillan Co., 1961), p. 209.

4. Dulles' central role in the formulation of American foreign policy and the Formosa Resolution are examined in Philip J. Briggs, "Congress and the Cold War: U.S.-China Policy, 1955," *China Quarterly*, No. 85 (1981): 80–95.

5. Washington, D.C., The White House, Minutes and Agenda of the Cabinet, November 16, 1956, and March 29, 1957.

6. Congressional Quarterly, Inc., *The Middle East: U.S. Policy, Israel, Oil and the Arabs*, A Contemporary Affairs Report, 4th ed. (Washington, D.C.: Congressional Quarterly, Inc., 1979), p. 37.

7. Moshe Sharett, *Yeoman Ishi* (Personal Diary) (Tel-Aviv: Sifriyat Maariv, 1980), Vol. 4, pp. 1180–88, as cited in Avi Shlaim, "Conflicting Approaches to Israel's Relations with the Arabs: Ben-Gurion and Sharett, 1953–1956," *Middle East Journal* 37, No. 2 (1983): 193.

8. David Ben-Gurion, *Israel: A Personal History* (Tel-Aviv: American Israel Publishing Co., 1971), p. 449.

9. Chester L. Cooper, *The Lion's Last Roar: Suez, 1956* (New York: Harper and Row, 1978), p. 95. Cooper was an assistant to Central Intelligence Agency Director Allen Dulles. Beginning in 1955, he acted as liaison between the American and British analytical intelligence services.

10. Cooper, *The Lion's Last Roar*, p. 94.

11. *Congressional Record* 103 (1957): 14706; Cooper, *The Lion's Last Roar*, p. 96.

12. See Briggs, "Congress and the Cold War," pp. 90–94: Cooper, *The Lion's Last Roar*, p. 95.

13. Ambassador Abba Eban, recorded interview, Rehovot, Israel, May 28, 1964, John Foster Dulles Oral History Project, Princeton University Library, pp. 30–31.

14. Townsend Hoopes, for instance, describes cotton proponents as "most curious" in *The Devil and John Foster Dulles: The Diplomacy of the Eisenhower Era* (Boston: Little, Brown, 1973), p. 331; cotton export figures in the National Advisory Commission on Food and Fiber, *Cotton and Other Fiber Problems and Policies in the United States* (Washington, D.C.: U.S. Government Printing Office, 1967), p. 113. On Southern representation, see Donald R. Matthews, *U.S. Senators and Their World* (New York: W. W. Norton, 1973), p. 165.

15. London *Star* quote and reference to British economic interests in Cooper, *The Lion's Last Roar*, p. 107.

16. Peres' assessment in Major-General Moshe Dayan, *Diary of the Sinai Campaign* (New York: Harper and Row, 1966), p. 25.

17. Robert H. Ferrell, ed., *The Eisenhower Diaries* (New York: W. W. Norton, 1981), pp. 330–31; Eban, recorded interview, pp. 33–34, Lawson's cable as referred to by Eban.

18. Cooper, *The Lion's Last Roar*, p. 167; Eban, recorded interview, p. 36.

19. *The Memoirs of Richard Nixon*, 2 vols. (New York: Warner Books, 1978), 1:166; Engler, *The Politics of Oil*, p. 260.

20. Minutes of the Cabinet, November 16, 1956. On November 10, the Soviet Union warned that it would allow Russian volunteers to join Egyptian forces if a withdrawal did not take place.

21. Engler, *The Politics of Oil*, p. 261.

22. Text of resolution as passed by Congress in U.S. Congress, House, *Collective Defense Treaties*, H. Doc., 90th Cong., 1st Sess., 1967, p. 199. The genesis of Article 51 is explained in Philip J. Briggs, "Senator Vandenberg, Bipartisanship and the Origin of U.N. Article 51," *Mid America: An Historical Review*, 60, No. 3 (1978): 163–69.

23. As quoted in Sherman Adams, *Firsthand Report: The Story of the Eisenhower Administration* (New York: Harper and Brothers, 1961), pp. 271–72.

24. Walter Johnson, ed., *The Papers of Adlai E. Stevenson: Toward a New America, 1955–1957*, 8 vols. (Boston: Little, Brown, 1976), 6:402–403. Democratic-Liberal Senator Herbert H. Lehman of New York had referred to the Formosa Resolution as a "blank check" in a Senate speech two years earlier.

25. Adams, *Firsthand Report*, p. 272.

26. *The Times*, (London), January 7, 1957.

27. *New York Times*, January 11, 1957. The Vandenberg Resolution, 1948, was approved in support of U.S. association with regional and other collective arrangements (NATO, 1949).

28. Dwight D. Eisenhower, *The White House Years: Waging Peace, 1956–1961*, 2 vols. (New York: Doubleday and Co., 1965), 2:180–81.

29. *New York Times*, January 12, 1957.

30. Ibid., January 15, 1957.

31. Ibid., January 24, 1957.

32. Author interview with Sherman Adams in Hanover, New Hampshire, November 14, 1967; also quoted in Briggs, "Congress and the Cold War,"pp. 82–83.

33. Author interview with Carl Marcy, Washington, D.C., December 12, 1967.

34. Ibid.; see Stevenson letter dated January 24, 1957, to Fulbright and reference to the Senator's response in *The Papers of Adlai E. Stevenson*, 6: 434–35.

35. Senator Jacob K. Javits, recorded interview, Washington, D.C., March 2, 1966, John Foster Dulles Oral History Project, Princeton University Library, pp. 12–15.

36. Hearings before the Senate Committees on Foreign Relations and Armed Services

on S. J. Res. 19 & H. J. Res. 117, *The President's Proposal on the Middle East*, 85th Cong., 1st Sess., 1957, pp. 216–19.

37. Ibid., pp. 268–69.

38. *New York Times*, January 26, 1957; Adams, *Firsthand Report*, p. 274.

39. *New York Times*, January 26, 1957.

40. Ibid., January 28, 1957.

41. Adams, *Firsthand Report*, p. 274; full text of Senator Green's letter dated January 19, 1957, reprinted in *Congressional Record* 103 (1957): 14702.

42. Adams, *Firsthand Report*, p. 275; *New York Times*, January 31, 1957.

43. Herman Finer, *Dulles Over Suez: The Theory and Practice of His Diplomacy* (Chicago: Quandrangle Books, 1964), p. 478.

44. *New York Times*, February 2, 1957; Finer, *Dulles Over Suez*, p. 469.

45. Ibid., p. 470.

46. Ibid., p. 475.

47. Eban, recorded interview, p. 41; *New York Times*, February 12, 1957.

48. Ibid., February 14, 1957.

49. Ibid., February 15, 1957.

50. Finer, *Dulles Over Suez*, pp. 476–77.

51. Eban, recorded interview, pp. 43–44.

52. Adams, *Firsthand Report*, pp. 180–82.

53. Ibid., pp. 283–86.

54. Ibid., pp. 286–87: Eban, recorded interview, pp. 44–45; Finer, *Dulles Over Suez*, pp. 486–87.

55. *Congressional Record*, 103 (1957): 2800–2802.

56. Ibid., pp. 3121–29.

57. *New York Times*, March 8, 1957.

22

"No More Koreas": Eisenhower and Vietnam

David L. Anderson

"We want no more Koreas with the United States furnishing 90% of the man-power."[1] This unanimous declaration by eight legislative leaders succinctly summarized the opinion of Congress in April 1954, as President Dwight D. Eisenhower pondered an American response to war in Indochina. In a striking parallel, prominent members of Congress now cry "No more Vietnams" as the Reagan administration assesses U.S. options in conflicts around the world. Both historical and contemporary debates often reduce complicated problems to simplistic aphorisms. Eisenhower was aware of what in today's jargon might be called the "Korea syndrome," but his Indochina decisions in 1954 were much more complex than the congressmen's negativism. The United States avoided war in 1954, and the President let it appear that Congress had a major role in that outcome. In reality, the administration made its own policy determinations. By giving credit to Capitol Hill for policy recommendations, Eisenhower was cleverly attempting to maneuver Congress into supporting an interventionist policy.

By the spring of 1954, events in Indochina had evolved to the point where a simple yes-or-no choice was not possible on the question of employing U.S. military forces in the region. On March 13, the decisive battle of France's war against the communist Vietminh began at Dienbienphu. This bloody fight quickly turned into a French military disaster, and the Eisenhower administration urgently weighed the possibility of armed American involvement in order to forestall a communist success. Whatever course the United States took had sweeping global implications far beyond Vietnam. If the United States rushed to France's rescue in the name of anticommunism, Washington would be aiding what American officials themselves had labeled a colonial war to reestablish French influence over its former Asian empire. Conversely, not to join the French on the basis of

anticolonialism was to risk the likelihood of a major communist success in
Southeast Asia.[2]

On becoming President in 1953, Eisenhower had adopted Harry Truman's
policy of providing material assistance to the French while simultaneously lobby-
ing Paris to guarantee unconditionally the future independence of Vietnam, Laos,
and Cambodia. By Ike's second year in office, however, this approach was
straining under new realities. The French public was tired of the war, and
Washington feared that Paris might give up entirely the anticommunist fight in
Asia. At the same time, the United States was trying to overcome French opposition to the rearmament of West Germany as part of the European Defense
Community (EDC). To encourage French ratification of the EDC and to shore up
the wavering war effort in Indochina, the Eisenhower administration was paying
80 percent of the French war costs by 1954. Despite this increased aid, French
leaders still insisted, over American objections, that Indochina be included in
international negotiations to begin at Geneva on April 26.[3]

Both the French and Vietminh wanted a major victory to strengthen their
bargaining positions at the Geneva Conference. The French commander chose the
place for the battle—the village of Dienbienphu in an isolated mountain valley in
northern Vietnam. His plan was to put a large, fortified garrison in this remote site
as bait to lure the elusive Vietminh guerrillas into a set-piece battle. Supposedly
French firepower could then destroy much of the enemy's main battle force. The
Vietminh took the bait but quickly besieged the garrison with a force outnum-
bering the French by two to one.[4]

At the weekly meeting of the National Security Council (NSC) on March 18,
President Eisenhower did not exhibit any particular sense of urgency over the
fighting at Dienbienphu. Although U.S. intelligence sources rated the French
chances of holding out as about 50–50, the soldier-President expressed doubt that
the military situation was that bad. Since the French had planes, napalm, and
heavily fortified positions, he reasoned that the two to one numerical advantage
of the Vietminh was not very significant. The French were in a tight spot, but at
this meeting and at subsequent sessions Ike gave every indication that militarily
the situation was manageable.[5]

Scarcely forty-eight hours after this NSC meeting, the administration's attitude
toward Indochina became much graver. On March 20 General Paul Ely, Chairman of the French Chiefs of Staff, arrived in Washington and confronted Eisenhower and his advisers with an ominous reality. Ely did not request immediate
U.S. intervention nor divulge any startling military information. Rather, the
General delivered a blunt warning that "a major defeat would have serious
adverse effects" on French public opinion. Ely consciously avoided a defeatist
tone, but his words galvanized the administration into action. Although the
possibility of a complete French withdrawal from Indochina had concerned Washington for months, such a decision now appeared imminent.[6]

Before President Eisenhower could consider pulling the French "chestnuts out
of the fire," as he later put it, he had to determine what specific action the United

States could contemplate taking. After lengthy conversations with Ely, Chairman of the Joint Chiefs of Staff Admiral Arthur Radford urged the President to "be prepared to act promptly and in force possibly to a frantic and belated request by the French for U.S. intervention."[7] On the other hand, Secretary of State John Foster Dulles believed that some caution was in order. Although not ruling out armed intervention, Dulles advised Eisenhower that any American military engagement must be assured of success because "a defeat would have worldwide repercussions."[8]

If the United States decided to take military action, the most likely form would be a massive, conventional air strike on the Vietminh positions at Dienbienphu. Although the use of American ground troops was, in Ike's words, an "ever-present, persistent, gnawing possibility," such deployment was never advocated by anyone within the administration, and, in fact, Army Chief of Staff General Matthew Ridgway actively opposed it. Similarly, the use of nuclear weapons was never seriously contemplated. Admiral Radford, a naval aviator, strongly supported a conventional air strike. He had complete confidence that a saturation-type raid involving perhaps 350 carrier-based aircraft as well as heavier bombers from Okinawa and the Philippines could save Dienbienphu. The plan has usually been identified as Operation Vulture, but Radford himself never heard of that code name until Ely used it in a conversation in late April.[9]

Although in later years Eisenhower scoffed at the usefulness of bombing at Dienbienphu, his initial reaction to Radford's proposal was not so negative. On March 24 he confided to Dulles that he "did not wholly exclude the possibility of a single strike, if it were almost certain this would produce decisive results."[10] In the same conversation, he stressed that "political preconditions" would be necessary for any U.S. involvement in the Indochina fighting. The next day the President provided a general outline of these prerequisites to the National Security Council. He acknowledged that "Congress would have to be in on any move by the United States to intervene in Indochina." He was also especially concerned that other nations, including Asian countries, participate "in a broadened effort to save Indochina."[11] These conditions remained central to Ike's thinking throughout the Dienbienphu episode. He was willing to involve the United States directly in Southeast Asia, but he wanted to avoid Truman's error of going out on a limb alone without Congress or allies.

It might appear that these qualifications were evidence of the President's unspoken desire to avoid any U.S. action, but such was not the case. At the same meeting, Eisenhower asked the NSC staff for further study of the use of "ground forces to save Indochina from the Communists." The old soldier in the White House was obviously not timid about considering all options. One alternative that he would not accept, however, was to do nothing. When Secretary of Defense Charles Wilson asked "whether it would be sensible to forget about Indochina for awhile," the President responded "that the collapse of Indochina would produce a chain reaction which would result in the fall of all of Southeast Asia to the Communists."[12] Now famous as the Domino Theory, Ike's assessment revealed the strategic importance he placed on Indochina in the global battle against communism.

It is apparent that in late March Eisenhower was considering strong action in Indochina, including the possibility of an air strike or even ground combat forces. Yet in May Dienbienphu fell, and in July the Geneva Conference implicitly recognized the existence of a communist government in North Vietnam; both happened without the United States firing a shot. What restrained the President? Numerous theories have been proposed and include (1) congressional opposition; (2) allied, especially British, reluctance; and (3) General Ridgway's warnings about pursuing land wars in Asia. Townsend Hoopes has even concluded that the President simply had ''a feeling in his bones.''[13] Ike's remarks at the March 25 NSC meeting suggest that the need for allies and the need to satisfy Congress were the most critical considerations, but these mutually reinforcing constraints did not mean that Eisenhower let others make this decision.

During the closing days of March, the French position at Dienbienphu deteriorated rapidly and presented the administration with the need to act quickly, if at all. As late as March 26, Washington believed that the approaching rainy season in northern Vietnam would end the fighting before the Vietminh assault could achieve success. Since the French were almost totally dependent on parachute drops for resupply and reinforcement, however, the worsening weather was hurting Dienbienphu's defenders more than the attackers. If his air raid plan was to have any chance of success, Radford concluded that now was the time to act. His convictions were so strong that on March 31 he recommended an immediate U.S. offer of assistance to the French despite the unanimous dissent of the other service chiefs, who had a variety of reservations about the proposed mode of intervention.[14]

Meanwhile, Secretary of State Dulles was also declaring that the time was now for resolute action in Southeast Asia. In a widely publicized address on March 29, he characterized the Vietminh as Soviet and Chinese communist puppets and warned that their success would be ''a grave threat to the whole free community.'' The United States should not passively accept this danger, he argued, but should meet it with ''united action.'' Dulles did not specify the form of this ''united action,'' but his speech conveyed three messages: (1) The United States was determined to oppose communist expansion in Southeast Asia as a vital strategic imperative; (2) the public should be prepared for possible U.S. intervention in Indochina; and (3) preferably, such intervention should be multilateral rather than unilateral.[15]

The President concurred with Dulles' statements; the two men had even consulted on the drafting of the speech. Eisenhower was also well aware, however, that ''united action'' was only a vague formula unsupported by any specific arrangement with other nations. The rapidly changing battlefield situation at Dienbienphu meant that there might not be time to secure even an ad hoc alliance. On the morning of March 29, before Dulles' speech, Ike had advised Republican congressional leaders in a regular weekly briefing that ''at any time within the space of forty-eight hours, it might be necessary to move into the battle of Dien Bien Phu in order to keep it from going against us.'' The reference to forty-eight hours is notable, since that is the amount of time Radford had estimated would be necessary to launch an air strike. If this contingency should arise, the President bluntly told the legislators, ''I will be calling in the Democrats as well as our Republican leaders to inform them of the action we're taking.''[16] Ike's use of the word ''inform,'' rather than ''consult,'' revealed no inclination to defer to Capitol Hill on his matter.

By April 1, Eisenhower was ready to make his decision, and he was not going to delegate it either to Congress or to the National Security Council. At the Council meeting on the morning of April 1, the President was toying with Radford's air strike plan. He specifically brought up the disagreement between Radford and the Joint Chiefs of Staff over the air attack. He termed this question one for ''statesmen,'' and even though he could ''see a thousand variants in the equation and very terrible risks,'' he declared that the intervention decision had to be confronted. When Dulles then tried to turn the discussion to specifics, Eisenhower abruptly dropped the issue and announced that he would pursue it after the meeting with a small group in his office.[17]

Although there are no records of this meeting or even a list of participants in the Eisenhower Library or the Department of State files, it must have been a dramatic session. Dulles was present, and from his telephone conversations later in the day it is clear that (1) ''something fairly serious had come up,'' (2) ''time was a factor,'' and (3) there was need for an urgent meeting of the bipartisan congressional leadership.[18] The tenor of these conversations following on the heels of the NSC meeting implies the imminent possibility of implementing Radford's plan. In fact, shortly after the private session in his office, the President confided to two luncheon guests that the United States ''might have to make decision to send in squadron from 2 aircraft carriers off coast to bomb Reds at Dien Bien Phu.'' He immediately added that ''of course, if we did, we'd have to deny it forever.''[19]

That last comment raises several questions about the President's decision to bring the congressional leadership ''in on'' the Vietnam deliberations at this point. Did Eisenhower want a formal authorization from Congress to use armed force in Vietnam? If so, why would legislatively sanctioned action have to be denied forever? Did he want something from Congress other than a joint resolution? The confusion over the President's motives derives from the ambiguous nature of his relationship with Capitol Hill. He later wrote that ''we have a constitutional government and only when there is a sudden, unforeseen emergency should the President put us into war without congressional action.''[20] Dienbienphu was not a sudden development, and there is no reason to doubt Eisenhower's sincere respect for the constitutional role of Congress in decisions for war. On the other hand, he had little respect for the legislature's wisdom on international affairs. In February, the administration had managed to abort the Bricker Amendment that would have nullified executive authority in foreign policy. Privately, Eisenhower complained of the lack of congressional support, especially among Republicans, for his foreign policies. He had called the Dienbienphu decision one for "statesmen," and he did not include the leaders of Capitol Hill under that label.[21]

The meeting between administration representatives and congressional leaders was set for Saturday, April 3. Eisenhower was not to be present because this confidential session was not intended to make any decisions. In preparation for the meeting, he conferred on Friday with his two principal spokesmen—Secretary Dulles and Admiral Radford. Dulles arrived at the Friday meeting with a draft congressional resolution that authorized the President, at his discretion, "to employ the Naval and Air Forces of the United States to assist the forces which are resisting aggression in Southeast Asia."[22] The President agreed with the content of the draft but did not want it submitted to the congressmen. The Saturday session was only "to develop" congressional thinking. Meanwhile, he wanted the administration's own position clarified before developing that of Congress. Dulles' proposal for united action, which would require time for international consultations, conflicted with Radford's recommendation for an immediate strike. The Admiral resolved this difference by making a significant concession. He declared that it was now too late for an air attack to save Dienbienphu itself. He still maintained that armed intervention might be needed in Indochina, but its use no longer depended on the Dienbienphu timetable. The meeting than adjourned with the suggestion that congressional support would "fill our hand" in negotiations with other nations on joint action.[23]

In terms of decision-making, the role of the five Senators and three Representatives who arrived at the State Department the next morning was only peripheral. The administration was already leaning toward an effort to arrange allied, not unilateral, military intervention against the Vietminh, and the allied approach was also the unanimous recommendation of the legislators. Declaring that they wanted "no more Koreas," they informed Dulles that he must first secure definite commitments of support from America's allies before Congress would authorize the President to employ armed forces in Indochina. Basically, the congressional leaders were only underscoring the preference for united action that Eisenhower and Dulles had expressed from the beginning of the Dienbienphu deliberations.[24]

How significant, then, was this April 3 meeting? A few months later, journalist Chalmers Roberts published an account of this secret session with the tantalizing title, "The Day We Didn't Go to War." Presumably using information leaked by one of the congressmen present, Roberts recreated a scene in which very possibly only the forceful dissent of the legislators prevented U.S. bombers from taking off for Dienbienphu. This scenario now seems greatly overdramatized, since Admiral Radford had already disclaimed the usefulness of bombing Dienbienphu. Robert F. Randle's more scholarly speculation that Eisenhower and Dulles arranged the meeting primarily to divert Radford's bombing alternative is also unsupported by the record. Radford, in fact, reasserted at the April 3 meeting that it was too late for airpower to save Dienbienphu. George Herring in his highly regarded book *America's Longest War*, writes that "The April 3 session doomed VUL-TURE," but it appears that Radford may have doomed the plan himself.[25]

In a telephone conversation on the afternoon of April, 3, Eisenhower and Dulles did not seem especially surprised about the outcome of the meeting. The Secretary reported that it had gone "pretty well," although he noted that there were "some serious problems" with the congressional insistence on allies. Neither Ike nor Dulles "blame[d] the Congressmen for this thought," however, and agreed that it was quite understandable. Perceiving that British cooperation would greatly ease this concern, they decided to being work immediately on a personal message from the President to British Prime Minister Winston Churchill. Congressional hesitancy was more of a diplomatic complication than a policy determinant.[26]

On Sunday evening, April 4, Eisenhower made his basic policy known in a private White House gathering with Dulles, Radford, and a few others. According to his assistant Sherman Adams, the President agreed "to send American forces to Indo-China under certain strict conditions." There were three provisions—none of which included any reference to a congressional resolution. Eisenhower specified that (1) any intervention must be multinational and include Asians, (2) France must agree to stay in the war, and (3) the future independence of Vietnam, Laos, and Cambodia must be guaranteed to avoid any hint of colonialism.[27] At almost exactly the same time as this meeting, Eisenhower's personal message to Churchill was being sent and an urgent request for U.S. air support was arriving from Paris. The next day Dulles, with Ike's approval, wired the French that there would be no unilateral U.S. action in Indochina and no action "without a full political understanding with France and other countries," that is, Eisenhower's three conditions.[28]

In this April 5 message to Paris, Eisenhower and Dulles also declared that "Congressional action would be required" for U.S. military involvement. Eisenhower, however, never pressed Congress for any specific authorization. Later, in his memoirs, he graciously credited Congress with the three preconditions for involvement, and Dulles claimed immediately that they "emerged" from his April 3 meeting with congressional leaders. These criteria had been developed by the administration long before the April 3 session, however. Moreover, neither Dulles' minutes of the meeting nor Roberts' account mentions such criteria. Congress received more retrospective credit for shaping U.S. policy in Indochina than it deserved.[29]

President Eisenhower was trying in late March and early April to obtain congressional approval for armed American intervention in Indochina without running the gauntlet of a formal vote. His weekly White House briefings of Republican leaders, Dulles' united-action speech, and the April 3 meeting were all moves to bring key congressional leaders into the decision-making without giving them a voice. The President had just fought a battle with powerful members of his own party over executive authority in foreign affairs, and he was trying to circumvent another clash. On the morning of April 5, about an hour before Dulles telegraphed the negative response to Paris, Eisenhower told the Secretary that "some kind of arrangement" with Congress would be necessary for the United States to enter the fight. He did not mention a congressional resolution, and the next day he told the NSC that the administration would have to fight "like dogs" to get an intervention vote from Capitol Hill.[30]

Eisenhower's interest in Radford's air strike plan suggests that the President was prepared to commit U.S. airpower to Indochina, provided that his preconditions were met. It could be argued that congressional opposition intimidated the administration, but another more likely scenario is that the administration was trying to finesse Congress. The initial moves did not work before the battlefield conditions at Dienbienphu collapsed. As of early April, however, the French war in Indochina was not over, and there was still time for more gambits. Eisenhower's letter to Churchill was one of these, and there would be others leading to the master stroke—the Southeast Asia Collective Defense Treaty signed in September 1954. With the so-called SEATO treaty, Eisenhower was successful in neutralizing congressional concerns about the essentially unilateral burden of American's last war, but in his jockeying with Congress he created the legal rationale for America's next war. The dictum "no more Koreas" had Congress and the President looking back over their shoulders instead of forward toward where they were headed.

NOTES

1. "Memorandum for the File of the Secretary of State," April 5, 1954, in U.S. Department of State, *Foreign Relations of the United States, 1952–1954*, 13 (Washington, D.C.: U.S. Government Printing Office, 1982), p. 1224. Hereafter cited as FRUS.

2. For the background of the Indochina crisis of 1954, see George C. Herring, *America's Longest War: The United States and Vietnam, 1950–1975* (New York: John Wiley and Sons, 1979), pp. 1–29.

3. Ibid.; Herbert S. Parmet, *Eisenhower and the American Crusades* (New York: Macmillan Co., 1972), pp. 353–64.

4. For the details of the battle, see Bernard B. Fall, *Hell in a Very Small Place* (Philadelphia: J. B. Lippincott, 1967).

5. "Memorandum of Discussion . . . of the National Security Council, . . . March 18, 1954," FRUS, pp. 1132–33; "Memorandum of Discussion . . . of the National Security Council, . . . April 6, 1954," FRUS, p. 1253; Dwight D. Eisenhower, *The White House Years: Mandate for Change, 1953–1956* (New York: Signet, 1963), pp. 449–50.

6. "Memorandum for the Record by Captain G. W. Anderson, USN," March 21, 1954, FRUS, pp. 1137–40; James C. Hagerty Diary, March 20, 1954, James C. Hagerty Papers, Dwight D. Eisenhower Library; Victor Bator, *Vietnam: A Diplomatic Tragedy* (Dobbs Ferry, N.Y.: Oceana, 1965), p. 31.

7. "Memorandum by the Chairman of the Joint Chiefs of Staff (Radford) to the President," March 24, 1954, FRUS, p. 1159.

8. "Memorandum by the Secretary of State to the President," March 23, 1954,

FRUS, p. 1141; "Memorandum of a Conference at the White House, . . . May 5, 1954," FRUS, p. 1469.

9. Eisenhower, *Mandate for Change*, p. 418; Matthew B. Ridgway, *Soldier: The Memoirs of Matthew B. Ridgway* (New York: Harper and Brothers, 1956), pp. 274–78; Arthur W. Radford, *From Pearl Harbor to Vietnam: The Memoirs of Admiral Arthur W. Radford*, edited by Stephen Jurika, Jr. (Stanford, Calif.: Hoover Institution Press, 1980), pp. 393–94; *The Pentagon Papers*, Gravel edition (Boston: Beacon Press, 1971), 1, 97–98; "Memorandum for the File by the Chairman of the Joint Chiefs of Staff (Radford)," April 24, 1954, FRUS, p. 1397; "Memorandum by the Special Assistant to the President for National Security Affairs (Cutler) . . . ," April 30, 1954, FRUS, p. 1447.

10. "Memorandum of Conversation, by the Secretary of State," March 24, 1954, FRUS, p. 1150; Eisenhower, *Mandate for Change*, p. 450; Chester L. Cooper, *The Lost Crusade: America in Vietnam* (New York: Dodd, Mead, 1970), p. 73.

11. "Memorandum of Discussion . . . of the National Security Council, . . . March 25, 1954," FRUS, pp. 1167–68; Radford, *From Pearl Harbor to Vietnam*, p. 396.

12. "Memorandum of Discussion . . . of the National Security Council, . . . March 25, 1954," FRUS, pp. 1167–68, Radford, *From Pearl Harbor to Vietnam*, p. 396.

13. Townsend Hoopes, *The Devil and John Foster Dulles* (Boston: Little, Brown, 1973), p. 211. For a summary of the factors involved in the President's decision, see Herring, *America's Longest War*, pp. 29–36.

14. Hagerty Diary, March 26, 1954; "Memorandum by the Joint Chiefs of Staff to the Secretary of Defense [Wilson]," March 31, 1954, FRUS, pp. 1198–99; "Ambassador at Saigon [Heath] to the Department of State," April 1, 1954, FRUS, pp. 1199–1200; Memoranda by General Ridgway, Admiral Carney, General Twining, and General Shepherd, April 2, 1954, FRUS, 1220–23.

15. John Foster Dulles, "The Threat of a Red Asia," Department of State Bulletin (April 12, 1954): 539–42.

16. Quoted in Richard Nixon, *RN: The Memoirs of Richard Nixon* (New York: Grosset and Dunlap, 1978), p. 151; "Memorandum of Conversation, by the Secretary of State," March 24, 1954, FRUS, p. 1150.

17. "Memorandum of Discussion . . . of the National Security Council, . . . April 1, 1954," FRUS, pp. 1201–1202.

18. Ibid., p. 1202 n.3

19. Hagerty Diary, April 1, 1954. The importance of such private and informal Oval Office meetings in Eisenhower's decision-making process is discussed in Anna Kasten Nelson, "The 'Top of the Policy Hill': President Eisenhower and the National Security Council," *Diplomatic History* 7 (1983): 307–26.

20. Eisenhower, *Mandate for Change*, p. 418.

21. Ibid., pp. 340–48; Hagerty Diary, April 20, 1954; Robert H. Ferrell, ed., *The Eisenhower Diaries* (New York: W. W. Norton, 1981), pp. 269–70.

22. "Draft Prepared in the Department of State," April 2, 1954, FRUS, pp. 1211–12.

23. "Memorandum of Conversation, by the Secretary of State," April 2, 1954, FRUS, pp. 1210–11.

24. "Memorandum for the File of the Secretary of State," April 5, 1954, FRUS, pp. 1224–25.

25. Ibid.; Herring, *America's Longest War*, p. 32; Chalmers M. Roberts, "The Day We

Didn't Go to War," *Reporter*, September 14, 1954, pp. 31–35; Robert F. Randle, *Geneva 1954: The Settlement of the Indochina War* (Princeton, N.J.: Princeton University Press, 1969), pp. 63–64, 118–19.

26. "Memorandum of Telephone Conversation Between the President and the Secretary of State," April 3, 1954, FRUS, p. 1230.

27. Sherman Adams, *Firsthand Report: The Story of the Eisenhower Administration* (New York: Harper and Brothers, 1961), p. 122.

28. "Secretary of State to the Embassy in France," April 5, 1954, FRUS, p. 1242; "Ambassador in France (Dillon) to the Department of State," April 5, 1954 [received April 4, Washington time], FRUS, pp. 1236–38; "Secretary of State to the Embassy in the United Kingdom," April 4, 1954, FRUS, pp. 1238–41.

29. "Secretary of State to the Embassy in France," April 5, 1954, FRUS, p. 1242; "Memorandum of Discussion . . . of the National Security Council, . . . April 6, 1954," FRUS, p. 1254; Eisenhower, *Mandate for Change*, p. 420; Parmet, *Eisenhower and the American Crusades*, pp. 367–68.

30. "Memorandum of Presidential Telephone Conversation, . . . April 5, 1954," FRUS, pp. 1241–42; "Memorandum of Discussion . . . of the National Security Council, . . . April 6, 1954," FRUS, pp. 1253–54.

REVIEWING THE
EISENHOWER YEARS

23

Eisenhower Revisionism and American Politics

Anthony James Joes

"Eisenhower is clearly emerging," writes Mary McAuliffe, "as one of the most important presidents of this century."[1] Probably everyone is aware that such a sentiment is symptomatic of profound changes in the perception of President Eisenhower, not least in the ranks of the academic community. In a poll conducted in 1962 by Arthur Schlesinger, Jr., among American historians on the subject of presidential performance, Dwight Eisenhower placed twentieth, tied with Chester Alan Arthur and behind Benjamin Harrison and Rutherford B. Hayes. A similar poll a few years later found Eisenhower still languishing in a lowly place in the view of historians, especially with regard to "significance of achievement."[2] In stark contrast, a poll by Professor Robert Murray appearing in the December 1983 issue of the *Journal of American History* ranked Eisenhower as number eleven, ahead of Kennedy, Cleveland, and even Polk.

Prescinding from the question of what such polls tell us, if anything, about presidential merit, we learn much from them about opinion within the academic community. The clear shift of such opinion regarding Eisenhower is both result and cause of recent scholarly writings about him. All are aware that this newer scholarship has proceeded in a decidedly pro-Eisenhower direction, but not everyone has grasped how great a distance Eisenhower revisionism has traveled, especially in the past five or six years. This chapter will therefore not present a chronology of developments in the Eisenhower literature, a task ably performed by others.[3] Rather, we will examine certain books that have been deliberately chosen to emphasize the extent of Eisenhower revisionism.[4]

In the following two sections, we will examine vintage and widely read indictments of the Eisenhower presidency. While the authors were not professional academicians, their books were quite representative of "informed opinion'' about Eisenhower, and arguments and even phrases similar to theirs can be found in the more strictly ''academic'' writings of the time.[5]

THE ANTI-EISENHOWER PERSPECTIVE

In 1958, Marquis Childs published *Eisenhower: Captive Hero*, a thoroughgoing and relentless indictment. According to Childs, Eisenhower's ''lack of knowledge and experience'' before he became President meant that ''he brought to the office so little preparation for what is surely the most difficult and demanding position in the world today.'' Rather, ''he had brought to his high office a civics-textbook concept of the coordinate powers of the three branches of the federal government.'' The key to the failure of his administrations, he said, lay in Eisenhower's intellectual and personal deficiencies: ''he was a man little given to reflection'' one ''whose interest in politics [was] at most academic.'' Eisenhower had ''no understanding of the uses of patronage and power'' and ''seemed to regard the presidency almost as a ceremonial office.'' ''The evidence points to his intense dislike for most of the aspects of the job of president''; consequently ''his seeming indifference to the office he held became more and more apparent.''[6]

Eisenhower surrounded himself in his Cabinet, according to Childs, with men equally unprepared and simplistic in their thinking: they all shared

an orthodoxy based on simple precepts which had filtered down out of the eighteenth and nineteenth centuries. This is the familiar stuff of chamber of commerce speeches: the best government is the least government, anything that interferes with the freedom of business to make profits is inherently evil, a balanced budget is the most vital requirement of sound government, deficit financing and high spending will bankrupt the nation.[7]

In the domestic field, ''the administration apparently felt no responsibility for coming to the rescue of innocent victims of McCarthy in government.''Eisenhower also failed, after *Brown* vs. *Board of Education*, to go on a speaking tour of the South appealing for ''order and reason''; he might at least have gone on television ''with an appeal to all the people for patience and understanding.'' Things worsened in the first months of his second term: ''if he was concerned over the state of the nation or the world he showed no sign of it.''During the Little Rock crisis Eisenhower went off to play golf, and by the midpoint of the second term ''one clearly sensed again the old drift of inaction.''[8]

Eisenhower performed no better, Childs maintains, in the field of foreign affairs. Even his seeming triumph of ending the inherited stalemate in Korea was really a serious reverse: ''the cost of that settlement was very great; half of the peninsula ceded to the Communists. But the American people were never made aware of what this loss meant or of the tragic miscalculations that had led up to it.'' Neither were the readers of Childs' book. Eisenhower was, moreover, the mere puppet of his Secretary of State. ''No president in history delegated so much of his constitutional authority over the conduct of foreign policy as Eisenhower was to do''; indeed, ''the record of the administration in this department becomes, therefore, largely an account of the Dulles policy and its successes and failures.'' President Eisenhower, in this supreme area of foreign relations, ''had defaulted on his responsibilities.'' As a consequence, ''Europe was no longer in a trusting or for that matter a forgiving mood.''[9]

Even in the area of national defense, where Eisenhower might have been supposed to know something, there was nothing but failure. Childs indicts an unaccountable lack of alarm in the Eisenhower circle over the Sputnik launching in 1957. All Eisenhower was capable of were ''glib assurances that all was well and that a free society was bound to outdo a slave society.'' ''The President's reputation in the field in which he had spent his life was further shaken'' when the ''generals and admirals sought to bring their case before the country'' for more and more money. Eisenhower's military budgets, while increasing in dollar terms, were getting smaller each year in terms of percentage of gross national product (GNP). America under his false leadership was ''trading tail fins and chromium for national security.''[10]

''Declining in both authority and prestige'' under Eisenhower, ''the office of President . . . resembled much more what it was in the late nineteenth century, when a ceremonial president was content to let the tides of economic destiny have their way.'' The two Eisenhower administrations were, in summary, ''a national tragedy.''[11] (Miraculously, the sadly diminished prestige of the presidency did not deter its passionate pursuit in 1960 by Johnson, Kennedy, Nixon, Rockefeller, Stevenson, Symington, and other connoisseurs of power.)

Emmet J. Hughes mounted an attack on Eisenhower in his *Ordeal of Power* (1963) that was perhaps more destructive than the Childs book because it was sprinkled throughout with professions of the author's personal regard for his subject. A sometime speech writer for Eisenhower, Hughes noted that ''the fondness for simplification, so evident in the candidate of 1952, would be no less a mark of the president, for all his life in office. History . . . however, was not presenting its problems in simple shapes or compact packages.'' Eisenhower's poor leadership record was rooted in his ''slightly disdainful aloofness from aggressive politics,'' an ''aversion to rough political combat,'' and most of all to ''the President's basic assumption that many heads are better than one—especially one's humble own.''[12]

Alas, this tendency to seek advice brought Eisenhower no help. ''His principal campaign advisers in 1952, brother Milton Eisenhower and Herbert Brownell, were inadequate: ''zeal never stirred in these councils. Debate was never profound. Panic was unknown, passion would have seemed strange.'' His Cabinet members held only a few ''elemental principles'' of ''simplicity.'' They believed above all in preserving American ''economic strength,'' especially the ''soundness of the dollar.'' Uncannily, ''they steadfastly believed that the less government did, the more the people would prosper and progress.'' The principal power in this unimpressive Cabinet, Treasury Secretary George Humphrey, ''arrived in

Washington with an intellectual baggage uncluttered with complexities." He and
other Cabinet advisers sorely needed "a collision with a sufficient number of
realities."[13]

"The remarkable political naiveté of the President" increased the administration's "intellectual and moral confusion"; "the presidential will" was often
"slack and unsure." Consequently, "the whole political life of the Eisenhower
administration" showed "the film of irresolution and vacillation" and consisted
of "half-acts and the broken gestures, the halting assertions and the hesitant
rebuttals."[14] The Eisenhower record had no bright spots: all was a composite of
uncertainty, ignorance, and failure, from the domestic field, in which Eisenhower
demonstrated a "basic insensitivity" on "the whole issue of civil rights" to "a
foreign policy" made up of "the negative or the passive."[15] Sinking below mere
incompetence, the Eisenhower administration ultimately became "ridiculous."
"I knew there was much to mourn here, even to ridicule. There were the narrow
and shallow beliefs, about the structure of government . . . the frayed
prejudices . . . the worn clichés . . . the solemn incantations . . . the political
superstitions." "There was sadly much, indeed, that seemed laughable."[16] In its
final years this ridiculous administration lapsed into "a self-absolving helpless-
ness." In summary, "the 1950s were essentially a lost decade."[17]

THE REVISIONIST PERSPECTIVE

Now that we have examined briefly the vintage anti-Eisenhower position, let us
turn to some very recent works by distinguished academic authorities on the
Eisenhower presidency, the first a professor of politics at Princeton, the second a
professor of history at Texas.

When Fred Greenstein formed his first evaluation of President Eisenhower in
the 1950s, a great deal of information now at hand was not available, and most of
the academic analysis of Eisenhower was being done by Stevenson Democrats.
Predictably, Greenstein saw Eisenhower as a "good-natured bumbler, who
lacked the leadership qualities to be an effective president." Today, the author
affirms the dramatic contrast between that view and "the centerpiece of my
present knowledge—that behind Eisenhower's seeming transcendence of politics
was a vast amount of indirect, carefully concealed effort to exercise influence,"
an effort that Greenstein maintains was very often successful.[18] Greenstein is thus
a self-confessed revisionist vis-à-vis his own earlier ideas, an uncommon stance
for an academic to take.

Greenstein notes in the beginning that built into the very structure of the
presidency is a serious ambiguity: the contrast between the President as Head of
State and the President as Chief of Government; that is, between the universal
father and symbol of unity, and the political leader who must take the heat. "The
unique characteristic of Eisenhower's approach to presidential leadership was his
self-conscious use of political strategies that enabled him to carry out both
presidential roles without allowing one to undermine the other." Eisenhower

"was fully aware that his popularity was essential to his ability to exercise influence over others," especially recalcitrant congressional figures. Hence, he saw the need to preserve his popularity by avoiding public political muscle-flexing, and surrounding himself with those who were willing to take the inevitable political flak.[19] Eisenhower worked out a self-conscious strategy that allowed him to use political power while appearing to be above the sweaty political arena. This strategy included "hidden-hand" leadership, "instrumental" use of language (including deliberate ambiguity and fogginess at press conference), basing actions on an analysis of the personalities of the people affected, selective delegation of authority, studious abstention from "engaging in personalities" in public, and efforts to build support for the administration across party and class lines.[20] An example of Eisenhower combining "selective delegation" and "personality analysis" was the choice, often lamented by critics, of Charles Wilson to be Secretary of Defense. Since Eisenhower intended to make his own defense policy, what he wanted was an experienced manager to administer the Defense Department, which was exactly what he got in Wilson.[21]

Along this same line, Greenstein challenges the belief that Eisenhower was the tool of John Foster Dulles in foreign policy. Indeed, it was Eisenhower's strongly felt views on foreign policy and the unacceptable position taken by Senator Taft on many international issues, that pushed him into the contest for the 1952 GOP nomination. President Eisenhower knew, moreover, that Dulles gave the impression to the world of an austere and not very likable Cold Warrior. This image, along with his immense knowledge and experience, made Dulles very valuable to Eisenhower; Dulles was a foil against which Eisenhower could appear as the "warm champion of peace."[22]

Many criticized Eisenhower for his preference for "Cabinet government"; frequent Cabinet meetings, where Eisenhower allegedly played a passive role, were a fateful symptom of his "weak" presidential leadership. But Greenstein shows that there was no formal voting in the Cabinet, and Eisenhower did the summing up. Indeed, the Cabinet often met to discuss an issue on which the President had already made up his mind. Eisenhower used these meetings primarily to build support. He believed that frequent consultation created team spirit and lessened the tendency of Cabinet members to engage in backstabbing and information leaking. His second purpose was to educate: through these Cabinet sessions, in which complex issues were thoroughly aired, Treasury Secretary George Humphrey became converted to foreign aid. (The famous 1957 incident in which Humphrey attacked the Eisenhower budget as likely to produce a "hair-curling" depression was, as Greenstein shows, a nonevent manufactured by the media.) Eisenhower also held regular meetings of the National Security Council (NSC). Wishing security questions to be considered in light of economic realities, the President invited the Secretary of the Treasury and the Director of the Bureau of the Budget to these meetings. Eisenhower always corrected and amended the Record of Action of the NSC, making clear that he was the ultimate decision-maker. Greenstein rejects the image of an Eisenhower cut off by a faintly menacing coterie from the events of the day: "in all, official and unofficial associates combined to provide Eisenhower with at least as diverse a flow of information and advice as any of the other modern presidents."[23]

Most of the criticism of Eisenhower on the domestic front was generated by his dealings with Senator Joseph McCarthy. During the 1952 campaign, candidate Eisenhower deleted an indirect attack on McCarthy in the Senator's home state at the urgent request of Republican Governor Walter J. Kohler, Jr.; this was perhaps the best known episode in the relations between the two men. Greenstein paints the complexity both of the McCarthy problem and Eisenhower's methods in coping with it.

President Harry S Truman's tactic of publicly brawling with McCarthy merely gave McCarthy, in Eisenhower's view, the headlines he craved, and also increased the suspicion in the public mind that something must be amiss if a President could so easily and so often be aroused to public anger. By not "indulging in personalities," Eisenhower could lower the media temperature and maintain the "above the fray" image that was to prove so useful to him politically. Other considerations also indicated that an indirect approach to McCarthy would be the best. The Wisconsin Senator was revered by a large segment of the Republican electorate and by many Democrats as well; as late as January 1954, the Gallup Poll showed that Americans approved of McCarthy 51 percent to 29 percent. Many would presumably be totally alienated by a White House "persecution" of their hero who was perceived as only trying to get at subversives in the federal government. (Recall that in 1945 the Canadian government had revealed the existence of a highly ramified Soviet espionage operation in the United States; Americans were, moreover, waging war against communist aggressors in Korea.) Eisenhower well remembered the Roosevelt "purge" fiasco in the 1938 senatorial primaries. Besides, having preached for so long about the importance of respecting the separation of powers, he felt he was not in a position to lead an open presidential assault against a Senator. Even McCarthy's enemies would not all cooperate in such a venture. In 1954, when McCarthy was down and almost out, a resolution to strip him of his committee chairmanship, introduced by Vermont Republican Ralph Flanders, failed because this attack on the seniority principle scandalized powerful Southern Democrats.[24]

Eisenhower's strategy for dealing with McCarthy consisted in publicly ignoring him, depriving him of his favorite issue by carrying out an effective internal security program, and undermining him by indirect methods.[25] Eisenhower's successful insistence on the confirmation of Charles Bohlen as Ambassador to Russia early in 1953 was a clear defeat for McCarthy, and in June of that year Eisenhower indirectly but unmistakably criticized the Senator when he advised undergraduates at Dartmouth: "Don't join the bookburners."

McCarthy played into Eisenhower's hands, however, when he attacked the Army. Knowing that this issue was one on which McCarthy could impale himself, Eisenhower decided to move quietly but massively against him. The Army-McCarthy hearings, opening on April 12, 1954, were the beginning of the end for the Wisconsin Republican. Eisenhower instructed Press Secretary James Hagerty to work with "certain key people" in the media to mobilize public opinion behind the Army. He directed GOP National Chairman Leonard Hall and Defense Secretary Wilson to attack McCarthy's charges against the Army as false. In May 1954, at the height of the hearings, the President warned a Columbia University audience of "thought control" by "demagogues thirsty for personal power and public notice"; nobody had any doubts about the object of that thrust. At press conferences, Eisenhower would attack McCarthy without using his name, thus avoiding an open breach with the Senator's Republican admirers. But after these conferences Hagerty would make it clear to the press exactly what, and whom, Eisenhower had meant.[26]

In the end, McCarthy destroyed himself, with several telling assists from the White House. Eisenhower's choice of indirect methods in this affair "rejected a course of action that, it can plausibly be argued, would have perpetuated McCarthy's influence." The President's methods did not please liberal opinion-makers but, Greenstein concludes, "it is difficult to see how, at least for the purpose of defusing McCarthy, another technique would have worked faster and more decisively in the context of the times."[27]

Except for periods of grave national crisis during which, presumably, a bipartisan majority would emerge, "Eisenhower's leadership style is not suited to effecting major political change"; yet "we should note that other approaches normally do not succeed either." Whether or not a President is an "activist," all modern occupants of the White House have run into the complexities of modern politics and the checks and balances of the American system. Thus, "the modest sort of change Eisenhower favored has been the rule rather than the exception in presidential politics."[28]

Greenstein dispenses with the commonly held view that Eisenhower could "get away" with his political style because the 1950s were a calm period. Eisenhower was President during years of real danger and upheaval (see below). One reason why the politics of the period seem calm to us today, Greenstein writes, was that Eisenhower tried intentionally to defuse issues; the calmness was of the President, not of the times.[29]

The Eisenhower record, like that of all modern Presidents, is a tally sheet of wins and losses: Eisenhower did not achieve his cherished goal of a permanent reduction of East-West tensions, nor was he able to place his chosen successor in the White House in 1960. But there were victories as well: the long-delayed Saint Lawrence Seaway, the highly ramified interstate highway system, the first civil rights legislation since Reconstruction. Above all, Eisenhower's record consists of what he prevented: there was no rollback of New Deal legislation, no further advance of the welfare state, and most of all, no intervention in another war.[30]

Greenstein observes that it is highly unlikely that any future President will come into office after having been a national hero for nearly a decade. But future Presidents would do well to imitate Eisenhower's technique of group consultation, which helped to clarify policy goals and identify means to attain them. "In retrospect, it can be seen that a number of Kennedy decisions might have profited from more formal analysis.'' Above all, Greenstein concludes, we need to study more about this ''unexpectedly fascinating presidency.''[31]

Most Presidents-elect, observes Robert Divine in *Eisenhower and the Cold War*, have little experience in foreign affairs; as in the cases of Truman and Johnson, this inexperience can lead to ''overreaction and tragedy.'' In contrast, Dwight Eisenhower had little training in domestic politics but possessed a ''broad background in international matters.'' Consequently, ''he achieved little at home—no sweeping reforms or significant legislation. Instead, his accomplishments came abroad. For eight years, he kept the United States at peace, adroitly avoiding military involvement in the crises of the 1950s.''[32]

As Allied Commander in Europe, Eisenhower not only directed the conquest of Adolf Hitler, but also handled with great skill the often conflicting demands and expectations of Roosevelt, Churchill, De Gaulle, and Marshall. Eisenhower ''delighted in winning over potentially hostile individuals,'' and manifested a ''latent talent for diplomacy'' and ''an instinctive ability at public relations.'' World War II ''would serve ever after as Eisenhower's point of reference in world affairs,'' from which he derived his rejection of isolation and appeasement. From these experiences evolved Eisenhower's basic principles for conducting U.S. foreign policy: the United States must make no major move without the support of key allies, and the President must take no major initiative overseas without the explicit support of Congress.[33]

From these principles arose Eisenhower's refusal to intervene in Vietnam. Believing in the Domino Theory in Southeast Asia, Eisenhower nevertheless resisted the temptation to involve this nation unilaterally in the Indochina War as France faltered. ''If we intervened alone in this case we would be expected to intervene alone all over the world.'' He believed that ''no western power can go into Asia militarily except as one of a concert of powers.'' Since most of the United States' major allies were opposed to any serious effort in Vietnam, Eisenhower wrote North Vietnam off, replacing the French in the south through the vehicle of SEATO.[34]

Rejecting the myth of Dulles as the real power behind the foreign policy throne, Robert A. Divine maintains that ''in essence, Eisenhower used Dulles.'' Eisenhower never accepted the pure Dulles doctrine on ''liberation'' and ''massive retaliation.'' During an NSC meeting on the Lebanon intervention, the President interrupted Dulles with a terse ''Foster, I've already made up my mind. We're going in.'' Feeling less at home in Far Eastern affairs, Eisenhower relied heavily on Dulles here, and both men ''were blinded by the prevailing belief that monolithic Communism lay behind the turmoil of the orient.'' This ''misconception doomed American policy.'' Nevertheless, when the Quemoy-Matsu crisis erupted in the fall of 1954, Eisenhower rebuffed calls from such leaders as Republican Senate Majority Leader William Knowland for a blockade of Mainland China.[35]

Eisenhower reacted furiously to the Anglo-French and Israeli invasion at Suez; he thought it would help turn the whole Third World against the West and allow the Russians to pose as the protectors of the Arabs. When the fighting stopped, Israel refused to evacuate the Gaza Strip. Eisenhower feared that this intransigence would increase Russian influence in the area and threaten the flow of oil, thus endangering Britain and France and bringing World War III closer. When the Senate balked at administration efforts to apply sanctions to the Israelis to force them out of the Strip, Eisenhower sternly took to the airways; the Israelis and their friends in the Senate backed down, Gaza was evacuated, the Suez Canal reopened, and the flow of oil resumed.[36]

Eisenhower feared that after Suez U.S. credibility in the Middle East was at stake. Wishing to reassure small American allies in that area, and all over the world, he devised the Eisenhower Doctrine, under which, with congressional authorization, of course, a President could dispatch economic and military aid, including troops, to any country threatened by "overt armed aggression by any nation controlled by international Communism." The murder of the King, Crown Prince, and Prime Minister of Iraq provided a testing ground. Fearing for the flow of oil to Europe and anxious for a show of real force to keep wavering Arab groups in line, Eisenhower sent 14,000 U.S. troops into Lebanon and moved into the Persian Gulf to back up Kuwait. This strong action reaped good rewards. "The President's determination to make Lebanon a display of America's resolve in the Middle East impressed Arab leaders. [Iraq's] General Abdul Karim Kassem was quick to assure the European leaders that there would be no interruption in the flow of oil." If at times Eisenhower "confused the danger from Arab nationalism with that from Soviet Communism, at least he had a clear sense of the strategic value of Persian Gulf oil and acted boldly to protect that vital national interest."[37]

In 1953, Eisenhower told his newly sworn-in head of the Atomic Energy Commission that "the world simply must not go on living in the fear of the terrible consequences of nuclear war." Divine identifies the "overriding aim" of Eisenhower's foreign policy as the reduction of Cold War tensions and the achievement of détente with the Soviets. His "pursuit of peace was the dominant feature of his presidency, and the failure to secure it his greatest disappointment." His "Atoms for Peace" address at the United Nations won worldwide praise, and at the 1955 Geneva Summit Eisenhower emerged as "the world's most eloquent spokesman for peace" and "the nation's single most valuable asset in the continuing struggle with the Soviet Union."[38]

In Divine's appraisal, "far from being the do-nothing president of legend, Ike was skillful and active in directing American foreign policy." Indeed, "what some perceived as excessive caution and even indecision would prove in time to be admirable qualities of patience and prudence." The author concludes: "Tested by a world as dangerous as any American leader has ever faced, Eisenhower used his sound judgment and instinctive common sense to guide the nation safely through the first decade of the thermonuclear age."[39]

EISENHOWER REVISIONISM: BACKGROUND

The contrast between the Childs-Hughes view of Eisenhower, on the one hand, and that of Greenstein and Divine, on the other, is arresting. It amounts not to the revision of the first view by the second so much as to its repudiation. Such a radical reversal on so many fundamental points in so short a time constitutes a small but veritable revolution. These deep divergences were foreshadowed and paralleled by the cleavage between the Childs-Hughes school and the public opinion of the 1950s. However great the disdain of the intelligentsia, Americans liked Ike, and twice chose him President by landslides that buried long-standing sectional, class, and religious divisions. Many believe that if it had not been for the U–2 contretemps—if Eisenhower, in other words, had been able to complete his second term with a love feast with Khrushchev in Paris followed by a triumphal tour of the U.S.S.R. in the summer before the 1960 election—Vice-President Nixon would have been assured of victory in that contest, which he almost won anyway. Hughes himself concedes that had Eisenhower been able to run in 1960 he would have treated Senator Kennedy to "an electoral rout." *Eisenhower revisionism therefore represents the convergence, after more than twenty years, of the professoriate with the electorate, with the professors traversing by far most of the territory.*

No doubt this development is all to the good for a society that seeks a broad consensus on fundamentals; a democracy can scarcely afford to have its professors and its voters permanently regarding each other with annoyed incomprehension. Besides, the direction, if not the magnitude, of the movement of scholarly opinion toward Eisenhower was predictable.

But the inescapable question arises: Why was such a convergence between the intelligentsia and the electorate necessary in the first place? Why were so many of those who sought to inform and shape American consciousness so wrong for so long?

The reluctance of so many wordsmiths to give Eisenhower any recognition is not explained by the "tranquility" of the 1950s. President Eisenhower inherited a stalemated and unpopular war in Korea, along with brewing crises in Guatemala and Iran. The collapse of the French before the Vietminh required some momentous decisions. Soviet tanks in Budapest and Israeli tanks in the Sinai threw up frightening clouds of Russian-American confrontation. Asia boiled and bubbled from Iraq and Lebanon to Quemoy and Matsu, while the United States was soon to be challenged in its own back yard by Castro. All these trials and threats developed within a context of possible thermonuclear exchange. At home, Eisenhower faced deep divisions within his own party, dating from the year of the Bull Moose and still apparent in his day; the staggering implications of *Brown* v. *Board of Education*; the first portentous stirrings of the civil rights revolution; another revolution (that is, probably the correct word) in American agriculture, and, neither last nor least, the boil on the body politic raised by the junior senator from Wisconsin. The 1950s were not placid; they were turbulent and dangerous.

Yet we were given to believe that in the midst of this turmoil, the general peace and economic advances that characterized Eisenhower's two administrations developed by accident.

Nor was the Eisenhower record unimpressive under that very rubric to which one might have expected students of politics to be most alert: electoral success. Before Eisenhower's nomination in the summer of 1952, the GOP had lost five straight presidential elections. After that date, it was to win six of the next nine (through 1984), and very nearly win two others. The year 1952 thus marked the beginning of a real transformation in U.S. politics. But how many, instead of perceiving or even suspecting this, viewed the Eisenhower landslides as mere aberrations, as evanescent as they were annoying?

Eisenhower's difficulties with the intellectual community resulted in part from (1) the nature of his accomplishments and (2) the nature of his observers. "Nearly all of Eisenhower's foreign policy achievements," writes Divine, "were negative in nature. He ended the Korean War, he refused to intervene militarily in Indochina, he refrained from involving the United States in the Suez crisis, he avoided war with China over Quemoy and Matsu, he resisted the temptation to force a showdown over Berlin, he stopped exploding nuclear weapons in the atmosphere."[40]

Because Eisenhower's accomplishments consisted to such a degree in preventing things from happening, or reversing undesirable trends, or in extricating the country from some foreign mire, Eisenhower became, perhaps unavoidably, a victim of that tendency among human beings which Charles de Gaulle, identified some years ago: to remember leaders not by the deeds they perform or the goods they deliver, but by the aspirations they proclaim and the visions they describe. Eisenhower, with his eight years of general peace, relative prosperity, and electoral success, was a bore and a failure; Woodrow Wilson, in contrast, whose foreign policy collapsed twice, whose administration ended by sinking into a swamp of intransigent dogmatism, and whose political heirs were resoundingly repudiated at the polls—Wilson is regarded even today as one of the very greatest Presidents.

The nature of Eisenhower's achievements is related directly to his worldview and his political style, a view and a style that place him squarely in that part of the American political tradition represented in the last century by the Whigs. As Wilfred E. Binkley wrote a generation ago, "more than any other party, the Whigs were compelled to cultivate the fine arts of tolerance of the conflicting interests of the nation." He described the Whigs as both "the party of commerce and finance" and of the "poor white mountaineers of Eastern Tennessee," a fairly accurate description of the GOP of the 1950s.[41] Daniel Webster was animated by an "image of an American working class of 'emerging capitalists,' " a desire for a "sound federal fiscal system," and a "conservative view of the world which gave social and political stability a higher value than the eradication of evil."[42] Henry Clay labored mightily to prevent the political temperature from rising to the danger point. Finally, the Whigs won both of their presidential victories behind popular military heroes. With his respect for the prerogatives of the Congress, his view of the political process as the reconciliation of discordant interests, his preference for diplomacy rather than military solutions in foreign affairs, his penchant for internal improvements like the interstate highway system and the Saint Lawrence Seaway, Eisenhower was a latter-day Whig.

That Eisenhower was indeed an heir of the Whigs—the party of Webster and Clay and young Abraham Lincoln, the party of union and moderation, whose demise heralded civil war—did not endear him to the intellectual community. In the 1960s, the word "Whig" was used as an epithet and an accusation against him.[43] Most of the men and women studying and writing about the presidency in the 1950s and 1960s were Stevenson Democrats. This was not a fatal malady in itself, but the differences between Eisenhower and Stevenson were exaggerated out of all proportion, not only in light of future contests such as 1964, 1972, and 1980, but even of past contests such as 1932 or 1896. The tendency of many journalists and academicians to overdramatize the contrast between Eisenhower and Stevenson is disturbing. One of its consequences was to ascribe Eisenhower's great victories to the preference of the electorate for Eisenhower's smile over Stevenson's brains, a viewpoint with profoundly antidemocratic implications. This elitism, tendency for Manichean thinking, and search for a presidential messiah among the intelligentsia reached a crescendo in the late 1960s and early 1970s, during which time the divorce, the mutual incomprehension, and mutual distaste between the intelligentsia (for the most part) and the citizenry reached a degree reminiscent of Tsarist Russia early in this century.

By the mid–1980s, the activist presidency had lost much of its attraction and glamor. More is involved here, perhaps, than the obvious trauma of Vietnam and Watergate, the growing doubt that the federal government can create or even define the Great Society, the increasing suspicion that Camelot was something of a Potemkin village. Americans have been dismayed by what Greenstein calls "the manifest difficulties Eisenhower's successors had in maintaining effectiveness, even at the minimum levels of winning and serving out second terms."[44] In contrast, Eisenhower sought consensus behind limited aims, often expressed in terms of preventing bad things from happening, and reaped real achievements and popular affection. These Whiggish methods look more and more effective to observers of the American political process. "The essence of Eisenhower's strength," writes Robert Divine, "and the basis for any claim to presidential greatness, lies in his admirable self-restraint."[45] One cannot escape the suspicion that, had they possessed more of this Eisenhower self-restraint, the presidencies of Lyndon Johnson and Richard Nixon would have been quite different, along with the lives of all of us.

Assuming, for the moment, that most of the statements in this chapter are more or less true, what are the practical implications? Two come easily to mind.

First, the disenchantment among wide strata of the electorate with presidential messianism is perhaps one of the largest and most important political facts of the

1980s. So is the scholarly burnishing of the Eisenhower reputation; these two phenomena reinforce and legitimate one another. It is not unreasonable to expect that this dual process can have a most significant effect on the strategies of major White House aspirants through the 1980s, and perhaps beyond.

Second, the utter failure of so great a segment of the intelligentsia to understand Eisenhower and to grasp his appeal to their fellow citizens interfered with the communications process in this democracy. This was not the last or perhaps the most serious such failure. They should not and cannot be swept under the rug. It is very important to identify and analyze the roots of the mistakes of those days. But it is even more important to take satisfaction that such mistakes can be and are being corrected. Above all, everyone in their chosen field of labor should periodically examine themselves to ensure that partisanship, preconception, and prejudice do not so crowd out respect for facts and a sense of the tentativeness of human opinion in their own writings that they become proper objects for the revisionist scholars of the future.

NOTES

1. Mary S. McAuliffe, "Eisenhower, the President," *Journal of American History* 68 (1981): 632.

2. Gary M. Maranell, "The Evaluation of Presidents: An Extension of the Schlesinger Polls," *Journal of American History* 57 (1970).

3. Gary W. Reichard, "Eisenhower as President: The Changing View," *South Atlantic Quarterly* 77 (1978): 265–82; McAuliffe, "Eisenhower, the President," pp. 625–32; Vincent P. De Santis, "Eisenhower Revisionism," *Review of Politics* 38 (1976): 190–208.

4. Marquis Childs, *Eisenhower: Captive Hero* (New York: Harcourt, Brace, 1958); Emmet John Hughes, *The Ordeal of Power: A Political Memoir of the Eisenhower Years* (New York: Atheneum, 1963); Fred I. Greenstein, *The Hidden-Hand Presidency: Eisenhower as Leader* (New York: Basic Books, 1982); Robert A. Divine, *Eisenhower and the Cold War* (New York: Oxford University Press, 1981).

5. See, for example, Thomas A. Bailey, *Presidential Greatness* (New York: Appleton-Century, 1966), pp. 325–28; Greenstein, *The Hidden-Hand Presidency*, p. 139.

6. Childs, *Eisenhower*, pp. 300, 292, 179, 208, 214, 227, 271, 218, 281.

7. Ibid., p. 163.

8. Ibid., pp. 181, 245, 249, 259, 273.

9. Ibid., pp. 203, 188, 286.

10. Ibid., pp. 258–61, 264.

11. Ibid., pp. 291, 286.

12. Hughes, *The Ordeal of Power*, pp. 148, 63, 27, 134.

13. Ibid., pp. 23, 60, 71, 78.

14. Ibid., pp. 267, 269, 139.

15. Ibid., pp. 242, 344.

16. Ibid., pp. 88, 146.

17. Ibid., pp. 310, 335.

18. Greenstein, *The Hidden-Hand Presidency*, pp. 137–39, vii, viii.

19. Ibid., pp. 5, 99.

20. Ibid., pp. 57–58.

21. Ibid., pp. 83.

22. Ibid., pp. 87 ff; 47–49, 90, 92.

23. Ibid., Ch. 4; pp. 121, 132, 150.

24. Ibid., Ch. 5.

25. Ibid., p. 170.

26. Ibid., pp. 220–21.

27. Ibid., pp. 157, 227.

28, Ibid., pp. 230, 229.

29. Ibid., pp. 231–32.

30. Ibid., pp. 248, 230.

31. Ibid., pp. 29, 242, 248.

32. Divine, *Eisenhower and the Cold War*, pp. vii, viii.

33. Ibid., pp. 7, 6, 10, 55.

34. Ibid., pp. 51, 41–44.

35. Ibid., pp. 21, 99, 33, 57–58. The old view of Eisenhower as the tool or junior partner of Dulles is also rejected by, *inter alia*, Richard H. Immerman in his "Eisenhower and Dulles: Who Made the Decisions?," *Political Psychology* 1 (1979): 21–38, and Peter Lyon, *Eisenhower: The Portrait of a Hero* (Boston: Little, Brown, 1974).

36. Divine, *Eisenhower and the Cold War*, pp. 85–88, 93–96.

37. Ibid., pp. 91, 102, 104.

38. Ibid., pp. 105, 111, 122, 123.

39. Ibid., p. 155.

40. Ibid., p. 154.

41. Wilfred E. Binkley, *American Political Parties: Their Natural History*, 4th ed. (New York: Alfred A. Knopf, 1963), pp. 171–73.

42. Irving H. Bartlett, *Daniel Webster* (New York: W. W. Norton, 1978), pp. 172, 244.

43. See, for example, Erwin C. Hargrove, *Presidential Leadership: Personality and Political Style* (New York: Macmillan Co., 1966), and Stuart Gerry Brown, *The American President: Leadership, Partisanship and Popularity* (New York: Macmillan Co., 1966).

44. Greenstein, *The Hidden-Hand Presidency*, p. vii.

45. Divine, *Eisenhower and the Cold War*, p. 154.

24

Eisenhower and Soviet-American Relations: Robert Fedorovich Ivanov's *Dwight Eisenhower*

Alexej Ugrinsky

On any given subject, a view from outside the ordinary circle of consideration is always valuable. When it involves Soviet-American relations and the place of Dwight David Eisenhower in their development during the years of the Cold War, a Soviet point of view is invaluable. We are fortunate in that Robert Fedorovich Ivanov's recently published book, *Dwight Eisenhower*, offers an illuminating glimpse at how a Russian scholar, an "Americanist," and knowledgeable visitor to this country, views Eisenhower the Soldier, the President, and the Statesman. The author has kindly allowed me to translate his remarks on some of the book's major topics.

After two rather sympathetic chapters devoted to Eisenhower's childhood and youth in Abilene (Chapter 1) and to his pre-World War II Army career (Chapter 2), Ivanov turns to his main topic, World War II (Chapter 3). He writes that in 1942 the military leaders of the United States, statesmen, and politicians were full of admiration for the heroic deeds of the Red Army fighting the Germans, a view shared by the Supreme Commander of the U.S. Army.[1] Following the decisive battles at Moscow and Stalingrad, which proved that the Red Army was fully capable of driving the German aggressors off Russian soil and of liberating the European nations, Eisenhower turned to the leaders of the Western Alliance, stressing to them the importance of reaching the European countries ahead of the Russians.[2]

Regarding Eisenhower's personal conduct as Supreme Commander and leader of men, Ivanov claims that "Ike" was always easily accessible, and that those who worked with him throughout the war noted how deeply he cared for his soldiers and officers. His personal inspection of military units is viewed as proof of his deep concern, and Ivanov points out that Eisenhower once rejected an Italian villa which was assigned to him, ordering that it be made a resthome for the men in his command. This became common knowledge in the Army. The men knew that their Supreme Commander worked as hard as they did, slept only four hours a night, and often suffered from high blood pressure.[3]

Of the severe battles in the Ardennes region in December 1944, which at least temporarily stopped the advances of the Western forces, Ivanov says, the Soviet High Command did everything possible to relieve the pressure. American historians admit that the advances of the Soviet armed forces aided the British and American forces significantly in shoving back the Germans in the Ardennes.[4] In March 1945, Eisenhower established direct connection with the Soviet High Command. On his own initiative, he sent a message through the U.S. Military Mission to Stalin, informing him that it was his goal to cut off the Ruhr region from the rest of the Reich and that he hoped to accomplish this by April 1. He stressed, however, that the success of this operation would depend on the closest possible coordination with the efforts of the Soviet armed forces. Stalin replied very quickly, agreeing with the proposed plan of action. Churchill and his British military leaders were highly critical of this move by Eisenhower, and so on April 21, 1945, when he sent another message to the Soviet High Command, Eisenhower yielded to the criticism and this time did not mention the Soviet Supreme Commander by name.[5] Instead, he informed the Soviet High Command of the decision to stop his forces at the River Elbe.[6]

Ivanov's next significant entry concerns the meeting of Eisenhower and General Georgi Koustantinovich Zhukov on May 7, 1945, after the defeat of Germany. Ivanov writes: "We greeted each other like soldiers, Zhukov remembered, like friends. Eisenhower took both my hands, looked at me for a long time and said, 'So, that's how you look.' Zhukov expressed his thanks to Eisenhower and to the Allied brothers-in-arms, and declared his satisfaction with the fruitful cooperation of the armed forces and allied nations during the war. After exchanging reminiscences of the war, the two turned to discussing questions of the activity of the Control Council."[7] This led to the first collision with U.S. General of the Army Carl Spaatz, who vehemently objected to the assigned air corridors for the U.S. Air Force. Eisenhower, however, intervened, stopping Spaatz with the stern reminder, "I did not authorize you to raise the question of U.S. Air Force flights."[8]

Eisenhower had high regard for General Zhukov's military talent. He later wrote that during the long years of the war Zhukov was always placed in the decisive sectors of the front which made it clear to Eisenhower that he was considered an extremely capable military leader. On Zhukov's side, his impressions of the visit to Eisenhower's headquarters in July 1945 are summarized by his remembering: "We left Frankfurt with the hope of continued friendly and coordinated action in the four-power control of Germany."[9]

In his official statements, Eisenhower paid high tribute to the role which the Soviet people and the Soviet armed forces had played in the destruction of German fascism. On the occasion of the twentieth anniversary of the Red Army, he sent a message to the Soviet soldiers and officers stating his belief that "by stopping the German war machine, the Red Army has demonstrated to the world a supremely heroic deed, unique in history. I salute the officers and soldiers of the Red Army."[10] Similarly warm feelings were extended toward the Soviet representatives and to the Soviet people as well. Eisenhower was one of the very few U.S. leaders to have direct contact during the war years with Soviet representatives. In the summer of 1945, he remarked to Harry Butcher, his naval aide, that

the Russians, having had few encounters with the Americans and the British even during the war, do not understand us, and we do not understand them. However, the more contacts we have with the Russians in the future, the more they will understand us and the better our cooperation will be. The Russians are strong yet simple in their policies and to yield only causes them to be suspicious. We will be able to work together with Russia if we continue our friendly cooperation established first between our High Commands.[11]

Later, at the end of 1945, Eisenhower declared publicly,

If the American people would have the opportunity to get to know the Russian people, and they us, I am sure we could cooperate and hold each other in high esteem. I have closely cooperated with Zhukov and others. I hold them in high esteem. I always got along with them. I have no doubts regarding friendly relations between our country and the Soviet Union. Naturally there will be some friction in our relations, but in the long run agreements can be reached.[12]

General Eisenhower remembered his deep impressions of the U.S.S.R. during his visit to Leningrad in August of 1945. During one of the receptions held in Leningrad, Zhukov invited Eisenhower's son to offer a toast. The young lieutenant responded with a toast to the most important Russian in World War II, the simple Russian soldier of the great Red Army. In offering this tribute, John Eisenhower expressed his own and his father's opinion. Dwight Eisenhower later stressed that this toast was received with greater enthusiasm and applause than any he heard during his days in Russia.[13] It should also be remembered that during Eisenhower's meeting with Zhukov on June 10, 1945, Zhukov awarded the Allied Commander the highest Russian medal, the Order of Victory, and that earlier, in February 1944, Eisenhower was awarded the Order of Suvorov.[14]

Ivanov points out that the anti-Hitler coalition was the first such cooperation in world history between nations of differing socioeconomic systems. This fact cannot be overemphasized, he says, especially in our time when, notably in the West, such cooperation is declared impossible.[15]

In remembering the Eisenhower visit to the USSR in August 1945, General Zhukov recalled that it was Stalin who, during the Postdam Conference, spoke of the possibility of inviting Eisenhower to Russia. "He was to be my guest," Zhukov explained, "because we shared the position of having been outstanding military leaders in World War II." On August 11, 1945, the two arrived in Moscow to view the athletes' festival. The head of the Soviet General Staff, Alekseil Antonov, formally invited Eisenhower and two members of the U.S.

delegation to join Stalin on the official podium atop the Lenin Mausoleum. During the five-hour parade, Eisenhower and Stalin stood side by side, and a lively conversation developed with the help of an interpreter.[16]

One final moment of shared emotions to which Ivanov points is the reception which Averell Harriman arranged to honor Eisenhower's visit at which news of the defeat of Japan was received. Here was yet another mutual victory, hailed by the Soviet guests and their American hosts.[17]

In Chapter 4, Ivanov deals with the Eisenhower presidency, and, in considering Eisenhower's role as Commander of NATO, raises some interesting questions. Ivanov asks:

Did Eisenhower really believe in the possibility of the U.S.S.R. attacking the U.S.A.? The author of this book has read hundreds of confidential letters of the General, stored in the library that bears his name. In these letters he has firmly expressed that he does not believe in the danger of military aggression by the U.S.S.R. The President's brother, Milton Eisenhower, also replied to this question with great emphasis: "I have never heard my brother say or express the fear that the U.S.S.R. might attack the USA. I consider that such fears never entered his mind." If, however, Eisenhower did not believe there was such a danger, then the following question assumes even greater importance: Why did he so emphatically support the NATO position? There could only be one answer, that by taking an active part in the formation of this aggressive military block, Eisenhower had demonstrated convincingly his solidarity with the reactionary circles within the West. The importance of the European region for American foreign policy was then, and is still, enormous. This was now a part of the world where, after the formation of NATO, the interests of the two diametrically opposed economic systems were clashing. At stake were, after all, American investments.[18]

Eisenhower had correctly predicted the opposition of other European powers to the entry of the Federal Republic of Germany into NATO, however, and it was against the strict opposition of France (with the United States and Great Britain overruling) that the Federal Republic of Germany was indeed rearmed.[19]

On the topic of Eisenhower the candidate, Ivanov writes: "He approached the campaign in the military manner. He once said, 'It is the task of a general to correct the bedlam created by diplomats, and for the diplomats to spoil it all again.' "[20] "During the campaign Eisenhower uttered many sober judgments on international politics. To a trusted few, he expressed his personal conviction that there was no chance that he could see of winning a third World War. It is impossible to occupy Russia, Siberia, and China; therefore, America could never fill the vacuum created by a retreat of the communists. As a professional soldier he knew what catastrophes a new war could lead to, and claimed the only chance to win such a war is to prevent it."[21]

Of the Korean conflict Ivanov writes, "Eisenhower was sober enough as a military and political leader to understand that the widening of the conflict could be extremely dangerous, as the Soviet Union and Korea were bound by treaty.[22] On November 3, Eisenhower declared the matter of peace to be "most precious in the eyes of free people, and the foremost task of the new administration will be the ending of this tragic conflict which touches every American home and carries the danger of a third World War.''[23] Here, too, Eisenhower acknowledged the importance of the role of the U.S.S.R. On June 19, 1952, Eisenhower said, ''I came to the conclusion that the Korean problem cannot be solved completely until we reach the necessary understanding with Russia on basic issues.''[24]

Regarding the future prospects of relations between the United States and China, Eisenhower again had some sober views. According to Ivanov, while speaking at a press conference on August 4, 1954, the President remarked, ''Could anyone present in the winter of 1944/45 have imagined, when we were fighting in the Ardennes, that a time would come when we would look at the Germans, and then at the Japanese, as people with whom we could cooperate closely?'' This was a hint at the possibility of a change in United States-China relations, a thinly veiled hint.[25] As to the question of China's possible entry into the United Nations, Ivanov quotes Special Aide Robert Gray as follows: ''For the Red Chinese it would be an incredible political victory, if they would get the right to represent 640 million Chinese at the United Nations.'' John Foster Dulles played an especially active role in this matter, and Ivanov claims that a whole row of documents in the Dulles archives is proof of his influence.[26]

U.S. interest in Soviet-Chinese relations increased drastically after the death of Stalin, according to Ivanov. On March 10, 1953, Henry Wallace closed his letter to the President with the following questions: ''Would it not be the best solution to declare after the funeral of Stalin, 'Stalin is dead, long live free and peace-loving China, which participates in trade with all countries'?''[27] On June 1, 1953, President Eisenhower, echoing his comment of a year before, declared to a group of senators, ''Communist China is not yet a member of the U.N. But it would be foolish to completely tie our hands on this matter for the future. Remember 1945 when Germany was our deadly enemy. Who would have thought that a few years later Germany would be our friend?''[28]

On the matter of Central America, Ivanov writes that during the Eisenhower presidency the United States had actively supported all dictatorships in Latin America, especially the bloody dictator Anastasio Somoza of Nicaragua. However, on the reasons for the Latin American problem, Ivanov writes, ''Eisenhower had stated, not without reason, that the fundamental problem in Latin America is illiteracy and poverty.''[29] Toward the end of his life, according to Ivanov, Eisenhower had to admit to himself the failure of his policies in that region. He declared in 1965 that he had no doubts whatever that revolution in Latin America was inevitable.[30]

Regarding the Geneva Conference of 1955, Ivanov writes: ''During the opening of the Conference, Eisenhower again spoke warmly about his brother-in-arms and member of the Soviet delegation, Georgi Konstantinovisch Zhukov.'' (Journalists noted that Eisenhower spoke about Zhukov for seventeen minutes.) Eisenhower's main proposal at Geneva was the ''Open Sky Policy,'' which was not adopted. The Soviets' main position was that the partnership of the

Federal Republic of Germany in NATO "presented serious problems in solving the German problem." Dulles reacted as follows, according to Ivanov, "The point of view of the U.S. is, that the neutrality policy is not applicable to a country of the type that Germany is."[31] Yet Geneva was no failure; Ivanov writes:

After the meetings in Geneva the international atmosphere warmed up decidedly. There disappeared from the pages of American newspapers and journals the rather crude anti-Soviet slogans, so familiar to readers in the long years of the Cold War. The American press even reported that the Eisenhower Administration had issued clear directives to stop the sharp polemics directed toward the U.S.S.R.[32]

On the launching of Sputnik by the U.S.S.R. in 1957, Ivanov writes: "Eisenhower had openly declared that the light emitted by the Soviet Sputnik was positively blinding and required the introduction of essential correctives into U.S. policy toward the Soviets." Even before Sputnik, however, according to Ivanov, Eisenhower was thinking of closer scientific cooperation with the U.S.S.R. Milton Eisenhower remembers that after the election of 1956, the President said, "It would be nice to send 15,000 U.S. students to the U.S.S.R. to study, and to invite in return an equal number of Soviet students." He even called Dulles on this matter. Dulles, however, rejected the idea and stressed the primary necessity of extensive political negotiations first.[33]

In July 1959, Vice-President Richard Nixon visited the Soviet Union to open the U.S. trade exhibit in Moscow. In his speeches on Soviet radio and television and to U.S. media after his return, Nixon stressed the need for peaceful coexistence between the two nations. He even made a number of practical suggestions directed toward the development of better relations between the United States and the U.S.S.R. in a number of areas. Specifically, he declared, "Let us join forces in the exploration of space; let us fly together to the moon," quoting a Soviet worker from Novosibirsk. But Nixon's position, according to Ivanov, must also be seen in the light of the election campaign of 1960 which was then looming.[34] Earlier in this same chapter, Ivanov says of Nixon that when he became Eisenhower's running mate he was a young Republican senator of the state of California who did not have any special credentials—except for being an ardent anticommunist.[35]

In the course of conversations this author had with Milton Eisenhower, the latter brought up the question of the post-White House relations between the President and the Vice-President. For eight years Nixon enjoyed his fullest trust, which was only natural, according to the President's brother and, since Nixon's daughter married his grandson, the Watergate scandal, unprecedented in the history of the U.S., touched the Eisenhower family deeply.[36]

Of this relationship, Milton Eisenhower, said,

I said before, that my brother and I agreed on everything. That was not quite true. My views were different on Nixon. Nixon had lied to the American people for a whole year about the Watergate matter. A moraly firm person would not have conducted himself in this way. I am glad President Eisenhower died before this scandal developed. It would have shaken my brother deeply.[37]

Milton Eisenhower is quoted by Ivanov on the subject of another disagreement between himself and his brother. It has to do with the downing of the U–2 plane in May of 1960. He quotes Milton Eisenhower as saying, "Already several months before the incident Eisenhower had ordered the stopping of the flights. But interested U.S. Government institutions had insisted on their continuation. The President did not force the issue. He later accepted full responsibility. I disagreed with him. The President said: 'Should I have found a scapegoat?' " Milton Eisenhower concluded the remembrance, "This was a fine lesson for us."[38] Five years later the President wrote in his memoirs: "Our biggest mistake was naturally our too hasty and wrong [untrue] declaration. I personally regret that, but all other decisions were basically correct." These words by the President, Ivanov comments, unfortunately show that he merely regretted the fact that the United States had to bear the full moral and political responsibility for this incident, which, Ivanov claims, can justly be compared with the more recent Korean Airliner incident of September 1, 1983.[39]

In his concluding pages Ivanov writes:

The year 1960 was coming to a close. And with it his active political life. Nine more years he was to live, to work on his papers and his memoirs. Eisenhower's name is forever connected with the greatest event in the history of mankind, the crushing of German Fascism. Tens of millions of dead and maimed, the destruction of colossal material structures . . . that was a heavy price to pay for victory. But it was not in vain. The victory of the Allies was the salvation of mankind from the brown plague of fascism. Eisenhower entered the White House in a very difficult period of world crisis caused by the U.S. aggression in Korea. It should further be noted that the American public connects with the name of President Eisenhower the ending of that war.[40]

Soviet readers, too, are primarily interested in the foreign policy aspects of his activities. And this interest, in our opinion, is not merely historical. The great hopes and crushed hopes of the period of the Eisenhower presidency have a direct connection to the proper understanding of the complexities of contemporary Soviet-American relations, watched with the greatest interest by the Soviet and foreign public.

"In our opinion," Ivanov continues, "that is a question of the utmost importance. The general public will play a great role in the further development of Soviet-American relations and in many ways the future of all of mankind depends on it. In his speech at the July 1983 forum of the Central Committee of the Communist party of the U.S.S.R. Iu. Andropow said, 'Our goal is not simply the prevention of war. We strive towards basically healthier international relations and the strengthening of all good beginnings in these relations.' The main area in which this problem of global and historical importance must be solved is in the area of Soviet-American relations."[41]

The following presents excerpts from three review articles of Ivanov's book:

The author, directing himself toward the many foes of a Soviet/American cooperation, claims that Eisenhower—in confidential documents—firmly expressed his disbelief in the myth of a "Soviet threat." This new book by the well-known Soviet scholar will be of great interest to many readers.[42]

Today reactionary forces in the U.S. attempt to bring about a second "Cold War." However, such a "hard-course" lacks, just as the one before did, all historical perspective. Proof of this was the foreign policy of the U.S. during the Eisenhower presidency. In the 1950s it became evident that nobody won the "Cold War" and that all were losers. This remains the most convincing argument against the new political "adventurism" presently conducted by the U.S. Robert Ivanov's book is about U.S. policies of the recent past. But it leads also to a deeper understanding of the present aggressive policies of the U.S.[43]

Robert Ivanov quotes President Eisenhower in one of his official speeches as saying "We cannot avoid each other. We must understand other nations. We must consider it our foremost duty to comprehend what they are thinking and what this means to us." The reasons for a more constructive policy toward the Soviet Union—which became even more noticeable during the presidency of John F. Kennedy—were (1) the growing economic and military strength of the Soviet Union, which left fewer hopes for "hard-course" advocates in the U.S. and (2) the evident failure of "confrontation-oriented" policies of the U.S. to weaken the Soviet Union. Eisenhower, and even to a certain degree his fanatically anti-Soviet Secretary of State John Foster Dulles, began to look at the issues more soberly. Will such a sobering-up also occur in the United States of today?[44]

NOTES

1. Robert Fedorovich Ivanov, *Dwight Eisenhower* (Moscow: Mysl,' 1983), p. 65.
2. Ibid., p. 73.
3. Ibid., p. 83.
4. Ibid., p. 105.
5. Ibid., p. 106.
6. Ibid., p. 109.
7. Ibid., p. 110.
8. Ibid., p. 111.
9. Ibid.
10. Ibid.
11. Ibid., p. 112.
12. Ibid.
13. Ibid., p. 113.
14. Ibid., p. 117
15. Ibid., p. 118.

16. Ibid., p. 121.
17. Ibid., p. 122.
18. Ibid., pp. 130–31.
19. Ibid., p. 133.
20. Ibid., p. 141.
21. Ibid., p. 144.
22. Ibid., p. 149.
23. Ibid., p. 150.
24. Ibid., p. 154.
25. Ibid., p. 171.
26. Ibid., p. 174.
27. Ibid., p. 175.
28. Ibid., p. 176.
29. Ibid., p. 177.
30. Ibid., p. 178.
31. Ibid., p. 191.
32. Ibid., p. 192.
33. Ibid., p. 211.
34. Ibid., p. 215.
35. Ibid., p. 141.
36. Ibid., p. 162.
37. Ibid., p. 163.
38. Ibid., p. 218.
39. Ibid.
40. Ibid., p. 273.
41. Ibid., p. 274.
42. N. Mostovets, "R.F. Ivanov, *Dwight Eisenhower*," *Sovetskaia Rossiia*, May 17, 1984.
43. A. A. Obukhov, "R. F. Ivanov, *Dwight Eisenhower*," *Novaia i Noveishaia Istoriia*, no. 6, 1984.
44. Iu. Oleshchuk, "Is a Sobering-up Coming? R. F. Ivanov, *Dwight Eisenhower*," *Mirovaia Ekonomika i Mezhdunarodnye Otnosheniia*, no. 9, 1984.

DWIGHT D.
EISENHOWER

SOLDIER • PRESIDENT • STATESMAN

THIRD ANNUAL PRESIDENTIAL CONFERENCE
MARCH 29–31, 1984

Election night

With Churchill and Bernard Baruch, January 5, 1953.

HOFSTRA
UNIVERSITY

HEMPSTEAD, NEW YORK 11550

HOFSTRA UNIVERSITY
CULTURAL CENTER

Director
JOSEPH G. ASTMAN
Associate Director & University Curator
PETER D'ALBERT
Assistant Directors & Conference Coordinators
NATALIE DATLOF
ALEXEJ UGRINSKY

Secretaries
MARILYN SEIDMAN
ATHELENE A. COLLINS

Assistants
JO-ANN GRAZIANO
MICHAEL E. HURLEY
MICHAEL R. JAKOB
DORIS KEANE
NEL PANZECA
SINAIDA U. WEBER

GALLERIES

DAVID FILDERMAN GALLERY
MARGUERITE M. REGAN
Assistant to the Dean of Library Services

NANCY E. HERB
ANNE RUBINO

TENTH FLOOR COMMITTEE
ROBERT MYRON
Professor of Art History
Chairman, Department of Art History

LINDA ANDERSON
Curator

DONALD H. SWINNEY
Professor of Drama
Director, John Cranford Adams Playhouse

PETER D'ALBERT
Hofstra University Cultural Center

HAROLD A. KLEIN
University Relations

EMILY LOWE GALLERY
GAIL GELBURD
Director

MARY WAKEFORD
Directorial Assistant

SUSANN ROSS
Hofstra University Organizer for the Winston S. Churchill Exhibition

MUSICAL ORGANIZATIONS

AMERICAN CHAMBER ENSEMBLE
BLANCHE ABRAM
NAOMI DRUCKER
Directors

HOFSTRA STRING QUARTET
SEYMOUR BENSTOCK
Artistic Coordinator

Cover Design: Jesse Hirschberger, Department of Fine Arts Student

THIRD ANNUAL PRESIDENTIAL CONFERENCE
DWIGHT D. EISENHOWER
SOLDIER • PRESIDENT • STATESMAN

March 29–31, 1984

Conference Director	ERIC J. SCHMERTZ *Dean, Hofstra University School of Law*
Deputy Director	HAROLD A. KLEIN
Hofstra University *Cultural Center Director*	JOSEPH G. ASTMAN
Assistant Directors & *Conference Coordinators*	NATALIE DATLOF ALEXEJ UGRINSKY

Hofstra University Eisenhower Conference Committee: Faculty Members

BRUCE ADKINSON
Political Science

RICHARD T. BENNETT
Government Relations

BERNARD J. FIRESTONE
Political Science

JOHN DeWITT GREGORY
Law

PAUL F. HARPER
Political Science

LOUIS KERN
History

WILLIAM F. LEVANTROSSER
Political Science

HARVEY J. LEVIN
Economics

JOHN L. RAWLINSON
History

HERBERT D. ROSENBAUM
Political Science

RONALD H. SILVERMAN
Law

LYNN TURGEON
Economics

JOHN E. ULLMANN
Management and Marketing

ROBERT C. VOGT
Political Science

HAROLD L. WATTEL
Economics

JACOB WEISSMAN
Economics

Hofstra University Eisenhower Conference Committee: Student Members

ROBERT A. WILSCHEK,
Student Coordinator
GINA MARIE CASTELLI
JIM DAGUANNO
WALKER GLANARY
DONNA GIORDONO
TONY IADEVAIA
JON KAIMAN
LIZABETH LYNNER

GINA RICCIO
DEBORAH ROBBINS
LOUIS SEPULUEDA
HELAINE SONNENSCHEIN
MARK TROMPETER
MARK WERLE
JANE WILLIAMS
EILEEN SPRINGS

German Club
MICHAEL R. JAKOB, *President*
RONALD JUNDA, *Vice President*
STEFANI DANA, *Secretary*
PATRICIA BECK, *Secretary*

Gold Key
THERESA PLUNKETT, *President*
FRANCINE GETMAN, *Vice President*
KURTIS FERTMAN, *Treasurer*
ROBIN ROY, *Secretary*
BESSE ROMANO, *Historian*

DWIGHT D. EISENHOWER PRESIDENTIAL CONFERENCE
INTERNATIONAL HONORARY COMMITTEE

Co-Chairmen:
Honorable Milton S. Eisenhower
Ambassador John S.D. Eisenhower

Hon. Sherman Adams
Hon. H. Meade Alcorn, Jr.
Dr. Stephen E. Ambrose
H.E. Hans G. Andersen
Hon. John B. Anderson
Marian Anderson
Hon. Robert B. Anderson
V. Adm. Evan Peter Aurand, USN (Ret.)
Dr. Robert F. Bacher
Amb. George W. Ball
Hon. Ezra Taft Benson
Hon. Ezra Taft Benson
Michael R. Beschloss
Dr. Hans A. Bethe
Owen F. Bieber
Col. Earl H. Blaik, USA (Ret.)
Justice William J. Brennan, Jr.
Hon. Herbert Brownell
William F. Buckley, Jr.
Amb. Ellsworth Bunker
Chief Justice Warren E. Burger
Adm. Arleigh Burke, USN (Ret.)
Amb. Arthur F. Burns
Dr. James MacGregor Burns
Hon. Hugh L. Carey
Hon. William Carney
Hon. Jimmy Carter
Hon. William J. Casey
Hon. Jacques Chaban-Delmas
Hon. Winston S. Churchill, M.P.
Hon. George L. Clark, Jr.
Gen. Mark W. Clark, USA (Ret).
Hon. Clark M. Clifford
Joseph D. Coffee, Jr.
Hon. Peter F. Cohalan
Hon. Barber B. Conable, Jr.
Hon. Maurice Couve de Murville
Hon. Mario M. Cuomo
Hon. Alfonse M. D'Amato
E. Clifton Daniel, Jr.
Margaret Truman Daniel
Hon. Harry Darby
Amb. Arthur H. Dean
Hon. Michel Debré
Sir Roy Denman
Hon. C. Douglas Dillon
Hon. Robert J. Dole
Hon. Pete V. Domenici
Hedley Donovan
Hon. Thomas J. Downey
Hon. Eleanor Lansing Dulles
John R. Earnst
Anne Eisenhower
Barbara T. Eisenhower
Dwight David Eisenhower II
Julie Nixon Eisenhower
Mary Jean Eisenhower
Susan Eisenhower
H.E. Sükrü Elekdağ
Hon. Frank J. Fahrenkopf, Jr.
Hon. Edgar Faure
Hon. Gerald R. Ford
Amb. Evan G. Galbraith

Amb. John Kenneth Galbraith
Hon. Robert Garcia
Lt. Gen. James M. Gavin, USA (Ret.)
Amb. Arthur J. Goldberg
Hon. Barry Goldwater
Gen. Andrew J. Goodpaster, USA (Ret.)
H.E. Allan Gotlieb
Hon. Robert K. Gray
Hon. William S. Green
Hon. Thomas S. Gulotta
Gen. Alexander M. Haig, Jr., USA (Ret.)
Hon. Bryce N. Harlow
Dr. Karl G. Harr, Jr.
Amb. Arthur Adair Hartman
Hon. Orrin G. Hatch
Hon. Mark O. Hatfield
Rt. Hon. Edward Heath, M.P.
H.E. Knut Hedemann
Hon. John Heinz
H.E. Peter Hermes
Hon. Oveta Culp Hobby
Dr. R. Gordon Hoxie
Hon. Daniel K. Inouye
William E. Jackson, Esq.
Hon. Jacob K. Javits
Hon. Max M. Kampelman
H.E. Nicolas A. Karandreas
Hon. Jack Kemp
Dr. James R. Killian, Jr.
Dr. Grayson L. Kirk
Hon. Henry A. Kissinger
H.E. Thomas Klestil
Hon. Melvin R. Laird
Dr. Arthur Larson
David Laventhol
Hon. Paul Laxalt
Hon. Louis J. Lefkowitz
Lewis E. Lehrman
Gen. Lyman L. Lemnitzer, USA (Ret.)
Hon. Norman F. Lent
Hon. John V. Lindsay
Amb. Henry Cabot Lodge
Amb. John Davis Lodge
Amb. John J. Louis, Jr.
H.E. Dr. Jan Hendrik Lubbers
Amb. Clare Boothe Luce
H.E. Dr. Joseph M.A.H. Luns
Rt. Hon. Harold Macmillan, M.P.
Amb. William B. Macomber
Alain Malraux
Madeleine Malraux
Amb. Mike Mansfield
H.E. Gabriel Mañueco
Hon. William McChesney Martin
Hon. Charles McC. Mathias, Jr.
H.E. Leonardo Mathias
Hon. John J. McCloy
Tex McCrary
Adm. Wesley L. McDonald, USN
Hon. George McGovern
Hon. Raymond J. McGrath
Hon. Robert S. McNamara
Hon. Edwin Meese III
Hon. Robert E. Merriam
Drew Middleton
Mary Jane McCaffree Monroe

Hon. E. Frederick Morrow
Hon. Bill D. Moyers
Hon. Daniel Patrick Moynihan
Hon. Robert J. Mrazek
Hon. Edmund S. Muskie
Aksel Nielsen
Hon. Richard M. Nixon
William S. Paley
Hon. Basil A. Paterson
Hon. Charles H. Percy
Hon. Samuel R. Pierce, Jr.
Dr. Emanuel R. Piore
Hon. Francis T. Purcell
Lt. Gen. Elwood R. Quesada, USAF (Ret.)
Amb. Maxwell M. Rabb
Dr. Isidor I. Rabi
R. Adm. William E. Ramsey, USN
Hon. Charles B. Rangel
Hon. Elliot L. Richardson
Gen. Matthew B. Ridgway, USA (Ret.)
Victor Riesel
H.E. Eric da Rin
Gen. Bernard W. Rogers, USA
Hon. William P. Rogers
Hon. William J. Ronan
H.E. Meir Rosenne
Hon. Eugene T. Rossides
Hon. W. W. Rostow
Hon. James Rowe, Jr.
Celia Sandys
Edwina Sandys
Hon. Raymond J. Saulnier
David F. Schoenbrun
Hon. Maurice Schumann
Gen. C.V.R. Schuyler, USA (Ret.)
Lt. Gen. Willard W. Scott, Jr., USA
Amb. William W. Scranton
Eric Sevareid
Hon. Bernard M. Shanley
Hon. Rocco C. Siciliano
Michael I. Sovern
Adm. Sir William Staveley
Hon. Thomas E. Stephens
Hon. Adlai E. Stevenson
Justice Potter Stewart, (Ret.)
Hon. William H. Sullivan
C.L. Sulzberger
Gen. Maxwell D. Taylor, USA (Ret.)
Walter N. Thayer
Gen. James A. Van Fleet, USA (Ret.)
Hon. Cyrus R. Vance
Gen. John W. Vessey, Jr., USA
Amb. James J. Wadsworth
Hon. Robert F. Wagner
Hon. Allen Wallis
Amb. Vernon A. Walters
Gen. Albert C. Wedemeyer, USA (Ret.)
Hon. Caspar W. Weinberger
Hon. Theodore S. Weiss
Ann C. Whitman
Gen. John A. Wickham, Jr., USA
Dr. John E. Wickman
Rt. Hon. Lord Wilson
Hon. Pete Wilson
H.E. Sir Oliver Wright
Dr. Herbert F. York
Lord Zuckerman

Director's Message to our Guests

The year 1985 will mark Hofstra University's 50th anniversary.

With this Conference on Dwight D. Eisenhower, following conferences on Franklin D. Roosevelt and Harry S. Truman over the last two years, Hofstra University is established as a leading historical, scholarly and commemorative center for the study of the lives, careers and administrations of the Presidents of the United States who held office during the years of our University.

For at least a year, those of us responsible for the Dwight D. Eisenhower Conference have been immersed in the events, the personalities and the global impact of the Eisenhower legacy. Things we knew before have been affirmed. Some things we thought we knew have been re-examined and reformed and are now better understood. And we learned much that we did not know.

Our search for knowledge was aided by many—Eisenhower biographers, military colleagues, former Eisenhower officials and friends, leaders of other governments, and of course, the Eisenhower family. We are enormously grateful to all of them for their invaluable and good-spirited assistance.

We concluded that Dwight Eisenhower's career was threefold: his military achievements, his Presidency, and integral to both, his statesmanship. Hence, the *Soldier, President, Statesman* title of this Conference.

We have tried to develop panels, forums, roundtables and addresses dealing with those three aspects of his life. We have done so in multiple ways—through the presentation of papers by Eisenhower scholars, with the participation of important public figures who were center stage during the Eisenhower years, and with the inclusion of more contemporary national and international dignitaries and distinguished representatives of the media, who can responsibly assess the Eisenhower record and, we hope, intriguingly speculate on how Dwight Eisenhower would have dealt with current national and international issues.

One of the facts that emerged from our studies was that as a military hero, as President, and as a human being, people of all walks of life whether supporters or opponents, regardless of nationality, ideology, economic, social or educational status, remember Dwight D. Eisenhower with a uniform respect, admiration, acclaim and warmth probably unsurpassed by any other American or world figure in modern history.

We hope our Conference meets the test of doing justice to the Eisenhower memory.

We welcome our guests and we hope our three days together will be enjoyable, intellectually rewarding and historically significant.

ERIC J. SCHMERTZ
Dean, Hofstra University School of Law
Director, Dwight D. Eisenhower Conference

THIRD ANNUAL PRESIDENTIAL CONFERENCE
DWIGHT D. EISENHOWER
SOLDIER • PRESIDENT • STATESMAN

PROGRAM

Pre-Conference Event
Wednesday, March 28, 1984
7:30 PM

DAVID FILDERMAN GALLERY
HOFSTRA UNIVERSITY
SOUTH CAMPUS

A FOUNDERS' DAY CELEBRATION

Master of Ceremonies	*Matthew Kupec,* Director, Alumni Relations
Greetings and Remarks	*James M. Shuart,* Class of '53 President, Hofstra University
Alumnus of the Year Award	*Emil V. Cianciulli,* Class of '52 Chairman, Hofstra University Board of Trustees
Address	*Eric J. Schmertz* Dean, Hofstra University School of Law Director, Dwight D. Eisenhower Conference "The Making of a Presidential Conference"
Exhibits	Advance Showing of the Dwight D. Eisenhower Art, Book, and Manuscript Exhibits.

RECEPTION

Thursday, March 29, 1984
STUDENT CENTER THEATER
NORTH CAMPUS

In this Conference program the biographical identifications of the speakers, where appropriate, are limited to the Eisenhower years. See *About the Speakers* for more expanded descriptions of their careers.

9:00 a.m.	*Registration*
10:00 a.m.	
Opening Ceremonies	Student Center Theater
Presiding	*Eric J. Schmertz,* Dean Hofstra University School of Law Director, Dwight D. Eisenhower Conference
Welcome	Recognition of the Honorable Milton S. Eisenhower *James M. Shuart,* President, Hofstra University
Greetings	*Dean Eric Schmertz*
	Joseph G. Astman, Director Hofstra University Cultural Center
	D. David Eisenhower II
Keynote Address	*Andrew J. Goodpaster* General, United States Army (Ret.) Defense Liaison Officer and Staff Secretary to President Eisenhower, 1954-1961 Chairman, Dwight D. Eisenhower World Affairs Institute, Washington, D.C.
	"Reflections on the Eisenhower Years"
Invitational Address	*Stephen E. Ambrose* Alumni Distinguished Professor of History University of New Orleans
	"The Eisenhower Presidency: An Assessment"
11:30 a.m.	*Lunch:* Student Center, North Campus

Refer to page 30 for Conference Exhibits Schedule

12:30-2:30 p.m.
Panel I

FOREIGN POLICY

Moderator/Commentator:
William F. Levantrosser
Professor of Political Science
Hofstra University

David L. Anderson
Professor of History & Political Science
Indiana Central University

"'No More Koreas': Eisenhower and Vietnam"

STUDENT CENTER, DINING ROOMS ABC

J. Gerrit Gantvoort
Professor of History
State University of New York at Oneonta

"Lifting the American Iron Curtain:
Cultural Exchange with the Soviet Union
and National Security, 1955-56"

J.P. Rosenberg
Professor of Political Science
Kansas State University

"Dwight D. Eisenhower and the Foreign Policy-
Making Process"

Kenneth W. Thompson
Director, White Burkett Miller Center of Public Affairs
University of Virginia

"The Eisenhower Foreign Policy: An Appraisal"

2:30-4:00 p.m.
Panel II a

THE MIDDLE EAST

Moderator/Commentator:
Jacob Weissman
Professor of Economics
Hofstra University

Isaac Alteras
Professor of History
Queens College/CUNY

"Dwight D. Eisenhower and the State of Israel:
Supporter or Distant Sympathizer?"

Philip J. Briggs
Professor of Political Science
East Stroudsburg University

"Congress and the Middle East:
The Eisenhower Doctrine, 1957"

Alexander M. Polsky
Princeton University
and
American Enterprise Institute,
Research Assistant

"Dulles Over Suez? President Eisenhower and the
Crisis of 1956"

Coffee Break

Thursday, March 29, 1984
STUDENT CENTER, DINING ROOMS ABC

2:30-4:00 p.m.
Panel II b:

THE THIRD WORLD AND
NON-ALIGNED NATIONS

Moderator/Commentator:
Robert C. Vogt
Associate Professor of Political Science
Special Advisor to the Provost for Academic Affairs
Hofstra University

Henry W. Brands, Jr.
Instructor of History
Austin Community College

"The Specter of Neutralism: Eisenhower, India
and the Problem of Non-Alignment"

James M. Keagle, Captain, USAF
Professor of Political Science
United States Air Force Academy

"The Eisenhower Administration, Castro, and
Cuba, 1959-61"

Loretta Sharon Wyatt
Professor of History
Montclair State College

"Reform, Yes; Communism, No! Eisenhower's
Policy on Latin American Revolutions"

Coffee Break

4:15-6:00 p.m.
Panel III a

CIVIL RIGHTS

Moderator/Commentator:
Herbert D. Rosenbaum
Professor of Political Science
Hofstra University

Robert F. Burk
Professor of History
University of Cincinnati

"Dwight D. Eisenhower
and Civil Rights Conservatism"

James C. Duram
Professor of History
Wichita State University

"Whose Brief? Dwight D. Eisenhower,
His Southern Friends, and
the School Segregation Cases"

Michael S. Mayer
Professor of History
University of Alabama

"'Regardless of Station, Race or Calling':
Eisenhower and Race"

4:15-6:00 p.m.
Panel III b: *ECONOMIC AND SOCIAL POLICIES*

Moderator/Commentator:
John E. Ullmann
Professor of Management & Marketing
Hofstra University

Sheri I. David
Adjunct Assistant Professor of History
Hofstra University

"Eisenhower and the American Medical
Association. A Coalition Against the Elderly"

Theodore P. Kovaleff
Assistant Dean
Columbia University School of Law

"The Politics of Antitrust during the 1950's"

Jared C. Lobdell
Professor of Economics
Muskingum College

"Eisenhower, Hoover, Corporatism,
and the Military-Industrial Complex"

Raymond J. Saulnier
Professor Emeritus of Economics
Barnard College, Columbia University
Chairman, President Eisenhower's Council
of Economic Advisers, 1956-1961

"Distinguishing Features
of Eisenhower's Economic Strategies"

6:00 p.m.   *Dinner:* Student Center, North Campus

Thursday, March 29, 1984
STUDENT CENTER, DINING ROOMS ABC
7:30 P.M.

Roundtable

STAFF RECOLLECTIONS
EISENHOWER THE POLITICIAN

Moderator/Commentator:
William B. Ewald, Jr.
Special Assistant to Secretary of the Interior, 1959-1960
Special Assistant on the White House Staff, 1954

H. Meade Alcorn, Jr.
Chairman, Republican National Committee,
1957-1959
General Counsel, Republican National
Committee, 1959-1961

Robert K. Gray
Appointments Secretary
to President Eisenhower, 1958
Secretary of the Cabinet, 1959-1960

Robert E. Merriam
Deputy Assistant
to President Eisenhower, 1958-1961
Deputy Director of the Budget, 1955-1958

L. Arthur Minnich
Assistant Staff Secretary
under President Eisenhower, 1953-1960

E. Frederic Morrow
Executive Assistant
to President Eisenhower, 1953-1961

Vernon A. Walters
Lieutenant General, United States Army (Ret.)
Ambassador-at-Large
Aide to President Eisenhower at SHAPE 1951-1956
Staff Assistant to President Eisenhower at the
White House.

Refreshments

Friday, March 30, 1984
STUDENT CENTER, DINING ROOMS ABC

9:00-10:30 a.m.
Panel IV a

THE COMMANDER-IN-CHIEF

Moderator/Commentator:
Bruce Adkinson
Associate Professor of Political Science
Hofstra University

Morris Honick, Historian
Supreme Headquarters Allied Powers Europe
SHAPE, Belgium

"The Role of General Eisenhower as Supreme
Allied Commander Europe"

William B. Pickett
Professor of Humanities
Rose-Hulman Institute of Technology

"Eisenhower as Student of Clausewitz"

James D. Weaver
Professor of Politics
Marymount College

"Eisenhower as Commander-in-Chief"

Coffee Break

9:00-10:30 a.m.
Panel IV b

REASSESSMENTS

Moderator/Commentator:
Herman A. Berliner
Dean, School of Business
Hofstra University

R. Gordon Hoxie
President, Center for the Study of the Presidency

"Eisenhower and the Rating Game"

Anthony James Joes
Professor of International Relations
Saint Joseph's University

"Eisenhower Revisionism and American Politics"

Duane Windsor
Professor of Administrative Science
Rice University

"Eisenhower's 'New Look' Reexamined:
The View from Three Decades"

Coffee Break

Friday, March 30, 1984
STUDENT CENTER, DINING ROOMS ABC

10:30-12:00 noon
Panel V a

THE CANDIDATE

Moderator/Commentator:
Lynn Turgeon
Professor of Economics
Hofstra University

Steve M. Barkin
Professor of Journalism
University of Maryland

"Eisenhower and Robinson: The Candidate
and the Publisher in the 1952 Campaign"

Joseph M. Dailey
Professor of Communications
Carroll College

"The Reluctant Candidate:
Dwight D. Eisenhower in 1951"

L. Richard Guylay
Director of Public Relations
for Eisenhower Presidential Campaign,
Republican National Committee, 1955-1956

"The Eisenhower Campaigns: 1952 and 1956"

10:30-12:00 noon
Panel V b

THE WHITE HOUSE AND
THE FEDERAL SYSTEM

Moderator/Commentator:
Ronald H. Silverman
Professor of Law
Hofstra University School of Law

Gerard E. Giannattasio
Assistant Law Librarian
Hofstra University School of Law

Linda R. Giannattasio
Associate
Milbank, Tweed, Hadley & McCloy

"Eisenhower, Constitutional Practice
and the Twenty-fifth Amendment"

Phillip G. Henderson
Professor of Political Science
University of Maryland Baltimore County

"Organizing the White House
for Effective Leadership: Lessons from
the Eisenhower Years"

Carl Lieberman
Professor of Political Science
University of Akron

"The Eisenhower Administration
and Intergovernmental Relations"

12:00-1:00 p.m.   *Lunch:* Student Center, North Campus

Refer to page 30 for Conference Exhibits Schedule

STUDENT CENTER THEATER

1:00-3:00 p.m.
Forum   *THE SCIENCE ADVISORY COMMITTEE,*
                                       REVISITED

Moderator/Commentator:
William T. Golden
Treasurer and Director
American Association for the Advancement
of Science
Consultant, U.S. Atomic Energy Commission
1950-1958

Robert F. Bacher
Professor Emeritus of Physics
California Institute of Technology
Member, President's Science Advisory
Committee, 1953-1955

Hans A. Bethe
Professor Emeritus of Physics
Cornell University
Member, President's Science Advisory
Committee, 1956-1960

Emanuel R. Piore
Vice-President and Chief Scientist, (Ret.)
International Business Machines Corporation
Member, President's Science Advisory
Committee, 1959-1962

Isidor I. Rabi
Professor Emeritus of Physics
Columbia University
Member, President's Science Advisory
Committee, 1957-1968 (Chairman, 1957)

Friday, March 30, 1984
STUDENT CENTER THEATRE

3:15-3:45 p.m.
Introduction   President Shuart

International Address   The Honorable Edgar Faure
                                  Premier of France 1952; 1955-1956

                                  "Dwight D. Eisenhower and France"*

                                  *M. Faure will address the Conference in French.
                                  Written English translations will be provided
                                  at the time.*

3:45-5:45 p.m.
Forum   INTERNATIONAL TURMOIL:
                                  THROUGH THE EISENHOWER PRISM

                                  Moderator/Commentator:
                                  C.L. Sulzberger
                                  Author and Former Columnist,
                                  The New York Times

                                  Barton J. Bernstein
                                  Professor of History
                                  Stanford University

                                  "The Far East: Korea and Indo-China"

                                  Blanche W. Cook
                                  Professor of History
                                  John Jay College of Criminal Justice/CUNY

                                  "Central America"

                                  Robert F. Ivanov
                                  Professor of History
                                  Institute of World History
                                  Academy of Sciences of the USSR
                                  Moscow, USSR

                                  "The Soviet Union"

                                  William H. Sullivan
                                  Foreign Service Officer: Japan, Italy,
                                  The Netherlands, Burma, 1950-1959
                                  UN Advisor,
                                  Bureau of Far Eastern Affairs, 1960-1963

                                  "The Middle East"

                                  John J. McCloy
                                  United States Military Governor
                                  and High Commissioner for Germany, 1948-1952

                                  "Eisenhower's Guildhall & D-Day Speeches"

Evening Program
RECEPTION, EXHIBITS, BANQUET

7:00 p.m.	*David Filderman Gallery,* *Hofstra University Library,* South Campus
Exhibits	Reception and Opening of Dwight D. Eisenhower Art, Book and Manuscript Exhibits
Introductions	*Harold A. Klein* Deputy Director of Dwight D. Eisenhower Conference Director, University Relations
Greetings	*John E. Wickman* Director, Dwight D. Eisenhower Library Abilene, Kansas
Remarks	*John L. Pendergrass,* M.D. "Eisenhower Political Buttons: A Collection"
8:00 p.m.	*DWIGHT D. EISENHOWER PRESIDENTIAL* *CONFERENCE BANQUET*
Banquet	Student Center Main Dining Room, North Campus
Presiding	*James M. Shuart* President Hofstra University
Introductions	*Eric J. Schmertz* Dean, Hofstra University School of Law Director, Dwight D. Eisenhower Conference
Introduction of Banquet *Speaker*	*The Honorable William J. Casey* Director, Central Intelligence Agency
Banquet Address	*The Honorable Clare Boothe Luce* Ambassador to Italy, 1953-1957 "The Eisenhower I Knew"
Concert	The Cadet Chapel Choir of the U.S. Military Academy at West Point Director: John A. Davis, Jr.

Evening Program Continued

Musical Selections

Alma Mater—U.S. Military Academy .... *Reinecke-Kuecken-Mayer*
God Bless America .... *Irving Berlin*
Yearnings.. *John Carter*
Oh, What a Beautiful Morning........................ *Rodgers & Hammerstein*
Let's Begin Again .... *John Rutter*
Battle Hymn of the Republic .... *Steffe-Wilhousky*

THE CADET CHAPEL CHOIR
U.S. MILITARY ACADEMY
WEST POINT, N.Y.

DR. JOHN A. DAVIS, JR., *Director*
CPT. ROBERT DUNN, *Officer-in-Charge*
CADET JERRY GREEN '84, *President*
CADET MILLICENT WRIGHT '84, *Vice President*
CADET CHARLES GARDNER '85, *Secretary*

The Cadet Chapel Choir is probably the oldest cadet musical group at West Point, having been organized prior to 1850 by Dr. Martin Philip Parks, an 1826 USMA graduate, who also served as Chaplain and Professor of Geography, History and Ethics from 1840-1846. The Choir sings regularly at West Point Chapel services and represents the Academy at the annual service for the Army in the Washington Cathedral. For special academic occasions and interfaith programs the Cadet Chapel Choir joins the Catholic and Jewish Cadet Choirs. Some members of the Choirs also sing the with Cadet Glee Club, which is performing in Maryland this weekend. The Cadet Choir has had two directors since 1911— Frederick Mayer, who retired in 1954, and John A. Davis, Jr., who succeeded him.

Saturday, March 31, 1984
STUDENT CENTER, DINING ROOMS ABC

8:00-9:00 a.m.	*Continental Breakfast*
9:00 a.m. *Introduction*	Dean Schmertz
Invitational Address	*Susan Eisenhower*
	"Eisenhower: Public Perception and the Man"
9:30-11:00 a.m. *Panel VI*	*THE SEARCH FOR PEACE*
	Moderator/Commentator: Burton C. Agata
	Max Schmertz Distinguished *Professor of Law* Hofstra University School of Law
	John Kentleton Professor of History University of Liverpool
	"Eisenhower, Churchill and the 'Balance of Terror'"
	David F. Schoenbrun Senior Lecturer New School for Social Research News Analyst of Independent Network News
	"Eisenhower: 'Man of Peace'" (From *America Inside Out,* McGraw-Hill, September 1984)
	D. Cameron Watt Stevenson Professor of International History London School of Economics
	"Eisenhower and Churchill: The Race to the Summit, 1952-54"
11:00 a.m. **Introduction**	*President Shuart*
International Address	*The Right Honorable Lord Wilson of Rievaulx* Member, House of Lords Prime Minister of Great Britain, 1964-1970; 1974-1977
	"The World that Dwight D. Eisenhower Inherited"
11:30 a.m.	Brunch Student Center

Refer to page 30 for Conference Exhibits Schedule

Saturday, March 31, 1984
STUDENT CENTER, DINING ROOMS ABC

12:30-2:30 p.m.
Forum

PRESIDENTIAL BIOGRAPHERS

Moderator/Commentator:
Michael D'Innocenzo
Professor of History
Hofstra University

Robert H. Ferrell
Professor of History
Indiana University

"The Eisenhower We Did Not Know"

Fred I. Greenstein
Professor of Politics
Princeton University

"Eisenhower and the Hidden-Hand Presidency"

Herbert S. Parmet
Distinguished Professor of History
Queensborough Community College/CUNY
The Graduate Center/CUNY

"Adjusting to the Fifties:
A Stevensonian Faces Eisenhower"

2:30-4:30 p.m.
Roundtable:

EISENHOWER:
SOLDIER AND STATESMAN

Moderator/Commentator:
Louis W. Koenig
Professor of Government
New York University

Arthur H. Dean
Special Ambassador to Korea (for Post-
Armistice Negotiations at Panmunjom),
1953-1954

Justus B. (Jock) Lawrence
Colonel, Army of the United States (Ret.)

Lyman L. Lemnitzer
General, United States Army (Ret.)

Roundtable Continued

> *William B. Macomber*
> Special Assistant to Secretary of State
> John Foster Dulles, 1955-1957
> Assistant Secretary of State for
> Congressional Relations 1957-1962
>
> *Harold E. Stassen*
> Partner, Stassen Kostos & Mason
> Former Governor State of Minnesota, 1938-1945
> Special Assistant to President Eisenhower with
> cabinet rank to direct studies of United States
> and world disarmament, 1955-1958
> Assistant Chief of Staff to Admiral William F.
> Halsey, 1943-1945.

4:45 p.m.
Forum:

> *DWIGHT D. EISENHOWER*
> *AND THE PRESS*
>
> Moderator/Commentator:
> *Tex McCrary*
> Producer, "The President's Week," NBC, 1953
> Co Chairman,
> The "Eisenhower Bandwagon," 1952
>
> *Victor Riesel*
> Newspaper Columnist
> Field Newspaper Syndicate
>
> *Sarah McClendon*
> White House Correspondent since the
> Roosevelt Administration

6:30 p.m.
Program Closing

> *Dean Schmertz*

6:45 p.m.

> *Reception*
> Emily Lowe Gallery, South Campus
>
> "Painting as a Pastime"
>
> The Paintings of Winston S. Churchill
> An Exhibition organized
> by The Royal Oak Foundation
>
> Curated by *Edwina Sandys* and *Celia Sandys*
>
> Hofstra University organizer for the Exhibition:
> Susann Ross

About the Speakers
MEMBERS OF THE EISENHOWER FAMILY

D. David Eisenhower II
Author, forthcoming three volume biography, *The Eisenhower Years*
(publication of Volume I, Spring 1985)
Lecturer, University of Pennsylvania

Susan Eisenhower
Communications and Public Relations Consultant for profit and non-profit
organizations.

PUBLIC FIGURES AND THE PRESS
H. Meade Alcorn, Jr.
Partner, Tyler, Cooper & Alcorn
General Counsel, Republican National Committee, 1959-1961
Chairman, Republican National Committee, 1957-1959

Robert F. Bacher
Professor Emeritus of Physics
California Institute of Technology
Member, President's Science Advisory Committee, 1953-1955
Member, Atomic Energy Commission, 1946-1949
Head of Experimental Physics Division, Los Alamos Laboratory Atomic
Bomb Project, 1943-1945

Hans A. Bethe
Professor Emeritus of Physics
Cornell University
Member, President's Science Advisory Committee, 1956-1960
Member, Presidential Study on Disarmament, 1958
Director of Theoretical Physics Division, Los Alamos Laboratory Atomic
Bomb Project, 1943-1946
Recipient of numerous science awards including Nobel Prize in Physics, 1967

William J. Casey
Director, Central Intelligence Agency
Under Secretary of State for Economic Affairs, 1973-1974
Chairman, Securities and Exchange Commission, 1971-1973
Former Partner, Hall, Casey, Dickler & Howley

Arthur H. Dean
Partner and Counsel, Sullivan & Cromwell, 1929-1979
Chairman, U.S. Delegation to 18-Nation Disarmament Conference, Geneva,
1962
Chairman, U.S. Delegation to the Conference on Discontinuance of Nuclear
Weapons Tests, Geneva, 1961-1962
Special Ambassador to Korea (for Post-Armistice Negotiations at
Panmunjom), 1953-1954

William B. Ewald, Jr.
Program Director Communications Studies
IBM Corporation
Assistant to Dwight D. Eisenhower in the preparation of his memoirs,
   Mandate for Change and *Waging Peace,* 1961-1965
Special Assistant to Secretary of the Interior, 1959-1960
Special Assistant on the White House Staff, 1954

Selected Publications: *Eisenhower the President: Crucial Days, 1951-1960*
                                    (1981)
                             Forthcoming: *Who Killed Joe McCarthy?* (April 1984)

Edgar Faure
Attorney. Author. Member of l'Academie francaise
Mayor of Port-Lesney-Grange-de-Vaivre, 1983—
President of the National Assembly, 1973-1978
Premier of France, 1952; 1955-1956
Deputy of the National Assembly, 1946-1958

Selected Publications: *La Politique francaise du petrole* (1939)
                             La Disgrace de Turgot (1961)
                             Philosophie d'une reforme (1969)
                             *L'Ame du combat; pour un nouveau contrat
                                social* (1969)
                             Ce que je crois (1971)

William T. Golden
Treasurer and Director of the American Association for the Advancement
   of Science
Vice-President and Trustee, American Museum of Natural History
Consultant, U.S. Atomic Energy Commission, 1950-1958
Member of Taskforce, Commission on Organization of Executive Branch of
   the Government (Hoover Commission), 1954-1955
Special Consultant to President Truman to review organization of
   government science activities, 1950-1951 (led to creation of President's
   Science Advisory Committee)
Adviser to Director of Bureau of Budget on organization of National Science
   Foundation, 1950-1951
Assistant to Commissioner, U.S. Atomic Energy Commission, 1946-1950

Andrew J. Goodpaster
General, United States Army (Ret.)
Chairman, Dwight D. Eisenhower World Affairs Institute, 1983—
President, Institute for Defense Analyses, 1983—
Superintendent, United States Military Academy at West Point, 1977-1981
Commander-in-Chief United States Forces, Supreme Allied Commander,
   Europe, 1969-1974
Member, United States Delegation to the Paris Negotiations with North
   Vietnam, 1968
Defense Liaison Officer and Staff Secretary to President Eisenhower,
   1954-1961
Commander, 48th Engineer Combat Battalion, 5th Army, 1943-1944

Robert K. Gray
Chairman, Gray & Company
Secretary of the Cabinet, 1959-1960
Appointments Secretary to President Eisenhower, 1958

L. Richard Guylay
Director of Public Relations for Presidential Campaigns,
   Republican National Committee, 1956, 1964, 1968

Justus B. (Jock) Lawrence
Colonel, Army of the United States (Ret.)
Author
Presidential Appointee, U.S.O. Corporation, 1960
Delegate, 10th General Conference, UNESCO, Paris, 1958
Chief Public Relations Planner, SHAPE (NATO), 1951-1952
Chief Publications Officer, European Theatre of Operations,
    U.S. Army, 1943-1945
U.S. Aide to Admiral Mountbatten, 1942-1943

Lyman L. Lemnitzer
General, United States Army (Ret.)
Supreme Allied Commander, Europe, 1963-1969
Commander-in-Chief, United States European Command, 1962-1969
Chairman, Joint Chiefs of Staff, 1960-1962
Chief of Staff, U.S. Army, 1959-1960
Commander-in-Chief, Far East and U.N. Commands, 1955-1957
Commanding General Far East and 8th U.S. Army, 1955
Commanding General 11th Airborne Division, 7th Infantry Division
    (in Korea), 1951-1952
Head of U.S. Delegation to Military Committee of the Five (Brussels Pact)
    Powers, 1950
Assistant to Secretary to Defense, 1949-1950
Deputy Commandant, National War College, 1947-1949
Commanding General, Allied Force Headquarters England, 1942

Clare Boothe Luce
Member, President's Foreign Intelligence Advisory Board, 1973-1977; 1982—
Ambassador to Italy, 1953-1957
Member of Congress, 1943-1947
Author and Playwright

Selected Publications: *The Women* (1937)
                         Kiss the Boys Goodbye (1938)
                         Margin for Error (1939)
                         Slam the Door Softly (1970)

Sarah McClendon
White House Correspondent since the Roosevelt Administration
Founder and Director of McClendon News Service
Publisher of *Sarah McClendon's Report*
Columnist, "Sarah McClendon's Washington"

John J. McCloy
Partner, Milbank, Tweed, Hadley & McCloy
Chairman, American Council on Germany
Chairman, President's General Advisory Committee on Arms Control,
    1961-1967
United States Military Governor and High Commissioner for Germany,
    1949-1952
President, World Bank, 1947-1949
Assistant Secretary of War, 1941-1945

Tex McCrary
Chairman, Texcomm
Chairman, Estee Corporation
Producer, Congressional Medal of Honor Dedication by President Ronald
    Reagan, 1984
Producer, "The President's Week," NBC, 1953
Co-Chairman, The "Eisenhower Bandwagon," (which launched the
    Eisenhower Campaign), 1952

William B. Macomber
President, Metropolitan Museum of Art
Ambassador to Turkey, 1973-1978
Deputy Under Secretary of State, 1969-1973
Ambassador to Jordan, 1961-1964
Assistant Secretary of State for Congressional Relations, 1957-1962
Special Assistant to Secretary of State John Foster Dulles, 1955-1957

Robert E. Merriam
Partner, Alexander Proudfoot Company
Deputy Assistant to President Eisenhower, 1958-1961
Deputy Director of the Budget, 1955-1958

L. Arthur Minnich
Foreign Service Reserve, (Ret.)
Assistant Staff Secretary under President Eisenhower, 1953-1960
Office of the Chief of Staff of the War Department, 1944-1946

E. Frederic Morrow
Consultant. Retired Banker
Executive Assistant to President Eisenhower, 1953-1961

Emanual R. Piore
Vice-President and Chief Scientist, Ret.
International Business Machines Corporation
Member, President's Science Advisory Committee, 1959-1962
Member, National Science Board, 1961
Head, Electronics Branch, Office of Naval Research, 1946-1947
Head, Special Weapons Group, Bureau of Ships, U.S. Navy, 1942-1944
Member, National Academy of Sciences
Member, National Academy of Engineering
Recipient of numerous science awards

Isidor I. Rabi
Professor Emeritus of Physics
Columbia University
Vice-President, International Conference on Peaceful Uses of Atomic Energy,
	Geneva, 1955, 1958, 1964, 1971
Member, President's Science Advisory Committee, 1957-1968
	(Chairman, 1957)
Consultant, Science Advisory Committee, Ballistic Research Laboratory,
	Aberdeen, 1939-1965
Member, NATO Science Committee, 1958—
Chairman, Science Advisory Committee, ODM, 1953-1957
Consultant, Los Alamos Science Laboratory, 1943-1945; 1956—
Recipient of numerous science awards including Nobel Prize in Physics, 1944

Victor Riesel
Daily National Syndicated Columnist,
Field Newspaper Syndicate
Television and Radio Broadcaster and Commentator
Lecturer at Universities throughout the world
Former President, Overseas Press Club
Interviewer of all Presidents since Harry S. Truman including
	President Eisenhower
Recipient of twenty-three newspaper awards

Raymond J. Saulnier
Professor Emeritus of Economics
Barnard College, Columbia University
Public Governor, American Commodities Exchange, 1978-1980

Saulnier continued   Member, The Consumer Advisory Council
                                of the Federal Reserve Board, 1976-1979
                             Public Governor, American Stock Exchange, 1965-1977
                             Member Presidential Commission on Financial Structure and Regulation
                                (Hunt Commission), 1970-1973
                             Chairman, President Eisenhower's Council of Economic Advisers,
                                December 1956-January 1961
                             Chairman, Cabinet Committee on Government Activities Affecting Costs
                                and Prices, 1959-1960
                             Chairman, Cabinet Committee on Small Business, 1956-1960
                             U.S. Representative to the Economic Policy Committee
                                of OECD, 1956-1960
                             Director, Financial Research Program, National Bureau of Economic
                                Research, 1946-1953

                             Selected Publications: *Contemporary Monetary Theory* (1938)
                                                    Federal Lending and Loan Insurance, co-author, (1953)
                                                    The Strategy of Economic Policy (1963)
                                                    Numerous articles for economic journals
                                                    Currently at work:
                                                    *Toward Stability and Balance: The U.S. Economy
                                                       under Eisenhower, 1953-1960* (tentative title)

David F. Schoenbrun
Senior Lecturer, New School for Social Research
News Analyst of Independent Network News
Author, *America Inside Out* (to be published, September 1984)
Chief Washington Correspondent, CBS News, 1960-1964
Chief Paris Correspondent, CBS News, 1945-1960

Harold E. Stassen
Partner, Stassen Kostos & Mason
Former Governor State of Minnesota, 1938-1945
Director, Mutual Security Administration, 1953
Director, Foreign Operations Administration, 1953-1955
Deputy, U.S. Representative on UN Disarmament Commission, 1955
Special Assistant to President Eisenhower with cabinet rank to direct studies
    of United States and world disarmament, 1955-1958
Assistant Chief of Staff to Admiral William F. Halsey, 1943-1945
United States Delegate to San Francisco Conference of UN, 1945
A signer of the UN Charter
Chairman, National Governors' Conference, 1940-1942

William H. Sullivan
President, The American Assembly, Columbia University, 1979—
Ambassador to Iran, 1977-1979
Ambassador to the Philippines, 1973-1977
Ambassador to Laos, 1964-1969
UN Adviser, Bureau of Far Eastern Affairs, 1960-1963
Foreign Service Officer: Japan, Italy, The Netherlands, Burma, 1950-1959

C.L. Sulzberger
Author
Former Columnist, *The New York Times*
Overseas Press Club, Award for Best Book on Foreign Affairs, 1973
Recipient Pulitzer Prize citation, 1951
Overseas Press Club, Award for Best Consistent Reporting, 1951

Selected Publications: *What's Wrong with U.S. Foreign Policy* (1958)
                       A Long Row of Candles (1969)
                       An Age of Mediocrity (1973)
                       Seven Continents and Forty Years (1977)

Vernon A. Walters
Lieutenant General, United States Army (Ret.)
Ambassador-at-Large
Senior Advisor to the Secretary of State, 1981
Aide to President Eisenhower at SHAPE Headquarters in Paris, 1951-1956
Special Project Officer at the NATO Standing Group in Washington, D.C.,
   1956
Staff Assistant to President Eisenhower at the White House
Participated in many Summit Meetings of the Post-War Period

Lord Wilson of Rievaulx
Member, House of Lords
Member, House of Commons, 1945-1983
Prime Minister of Great Britain, 1964-1970; 1974-1977
Leader of the Opposition, 1963-1964; 1970-1974
Leader, Labour Party, 1963-1976

Selected Publications: *New Deal for Coal* (1945)
                        In Place of Dollars (1952)
                        The War on World Poverty (1953)
                        The Relevance of British Socialism (1964)
                        The Labour Government, 1964-70 (1971)
                        A Prime Minister on Prime Ministers (1977)
                        The Chariot of Israel (1981)

INVITED SCHOLARS

Isaac Alteras
Professor of History
Queens College/CUNY

Stephen E. Ambrose
Alumni Distinguished Professor of History
University of New Orleans
Dwight D. Eisenhower Professor of War and Peace,
Kansas State University, 1970-1971

Selected Publications: *Halleck: Lincoln's Chief of Staff* (1962)
                        Duty, Honor, Country: A History of West Point (1966)
                        The Papers of Dwight D. Eisenhower: The War Years,
                           5 volumes, Assoc. ed., (1970)
                        The Supreme Commander: The War Years of
                           General Dwight D. Eisenhower (1970)
                        Crazy Horse and Custer: The Parallel Lives of
                           Two American Warriors (1975)
                        Ike's Spies: Eisenhower and the Espionage
                           Establishment (1981)
                        Eisenhower: Soldier, General of the Army,
                           President-Elect, 1890-1952, Vol. I (1983)
                        Numerous articles and reviews

David L. Anderson
Professor of History & Political Science
Indiana Central University

Steve M. Barkin
Professor of Journalism
University of Maryland

Barton J. Bernstein
Professor of History
Stanford University
Selected Publications: *Towards a New Past* (1968)
                      Politics and Policies of the Truman
                        Administration (1970)
                      Twentieth-Century America (1973)
                      The Atomic Bomb (1976)
                      Numerous articles on the Eisenhower Presidency

Henry W. Brands, Jr.
Instructor of History
Austin Community College

Philip J. Briggs
Professor of Political Science
East Stroudsburg University

Robert F. Burk
Professor of History
University of Cincinnati

Blanche W. Cook
Professor of History
John Jay College of Criminal Justice/CUNY
Selected Publications: *Crystal Eastman on Women and Revolution,* ed.,
                        (1978)
                      The Declassified Eisenhower: A Divided Legacy of
                        Peace and Political Warfare (1981)
                      Forthcoming: A biography of Eleanor Roosevelt

Joseph M. Dailey
Professor of Communications
Carroll College

Sheri I. David
Adjunct Assistant Professor of History
Hofstra University

James C. Duram
Professor of History
Wichita State University

Robert H. Ferrell
Professor of History
Indiana University
Selected Publications: *Peace in Their Time* (1952)
                      American Diplomacy in the Great Depression (1957)
                      George C. Marshall (1966)
                      Off the Record: The Private Papers of
                        Harry S. Truman, ed., (1980)
                      The Eisenhower Diaries, co-author, (1981)
                      Dear Bess, ed., (1981)
                      The Diary of James C. Hagerty, ed., (1983)
                      Forthcoming: *Truman: A Centenary*
                        Rememberance, (1984)

J. Gerrit Gantvoort
Professor of History
State University of New York at Oneonta

Gerard E. Giannattasio
Assistant Law Librarian
Hofstra University School of Law

Linda R. Giannattasio
Associate
Milbank, Tweed, Hadley & McCloy

Fred I. Greenstein
Professor of Politics
Princeton University
Henry Luce Professor of Politics, Law and Society, 1973-1981
Princeton University

Selected Publications: *Personality and Politics: Problems of Evidence,*
Inference, and Conceptualization (1969, rpt. 1975)
The Dynamics of American Politics, co-author, (1976)
The Evolution of the Modern Presidency:
An Annotated Bibliography, co-author, (1977)
The Hidden-Hand Presidency:
Eisenhower as Leader (1982)
The Reagan Presidency: An Early Appraisal,
ed., (1983)
Numerous articles and reviews

Philip G. Henderson
Professor of Political Science
University of Maryland Baltimore County

Morris Honick
Historian of Supreme Headquarters Allied Powers Europe (SHAPE)
Allied Staff of the Headquarters, 1955—
Member, International Institute for Strategic Studies of London

R. Gordon Hoxie
Founder and President, Center for the Study of the Presidency
Assistant to the Provost, Columbia University during the
Eisenhower Presidency
Former President of C.W. Post College and Chancellor of
Long Island University
Served as a Consultant to the Department of Defense and the Department
of State
Editor, *Presidential Studies Quarterly*
Author, Contributor, Editor of more than one dozen volumes on the
American Presidency

Robert F. Ivanov
Professor of History
Institute of World History
Academy of Sciences of the USSR
Moscow, USSR

Selected Publications: *The Struggle of Negroes for Land and Freedom in the*
South of the USA, 1865-1877 (1958)
The Civil War in the USA, 1861-1865 (1960)
Abraham Lincoln and the Civil War in the USA (1964)
V.I. Lenin on the United States of America (1965)
The Republican Party of the USA, 1854-1972 (n.d.)
Dwight Eisenhower (1984)

Anthony James Joes
Professor of International Relations
Saint Joseph's University

James M. Keagle, Captain, USAF
Professor of Political Science
United States Air Force Academy

John Kentleton
Professor of History
University of Liverpool

Louis W. Koenig
Professor of Government
New York University
Office of Intelligence Research, Department of State, 1950
Foreign Affairs Taskforce of the First Hoover Commission, 1948-1949

Selected Publications: *The Chief Executive* (1981)

Theodore P. Kovaleff
Assistant Dean
Columbia University School of Law

Selected Publications: *Business and Government During the Eisenhower
                        Administration* (1980)

Carl Lieberman
Professor of Political Science
University of Akron

Jared C. Lobdell
Professor of Economics
Muskingum College

Michael S. Mayer
Professor of History
University of Alabama

Herbert S. Parmet
Distinguished Professor of History
Queensborough Community College/CUNY
The Graduate Center/CUNY

Selected Publications: *Aaron Burr: Portrait of an Ambitious Man,*
                        co-author, (1967)
                       *Never Again: A President Runs for a Third Term
                        (1968)*
                       Eisenhower and the American Crusades (1972)
                       The Democrats: The Years After FDR (1976)
                       Jack, The Struggles of John F. Kennedy (1980)
                       JFK, The Presidency of John F. Kennedy (1983)

John L. Pendergrass
Physician, Green-Herring-Pendergrass Eye Clinic
Collector of Eisenhower memorabilia

William B. Pickett
Professor of Humanities
Rose-Hulman Institute of Technology

Alexander M. Polsky
Princeton University, Student
American Enterprise Institute, Research Assistant

J.P. Rosenberg
Professor of Political Science
Kansas State University

Kenneth W. Thompson
Director and Professor, White Burkett Miller Center of Public Affairs
University of Virginia

Selected Publications: *Principals and Problems of International Politics,*
                        Co-author with Hans J. Morgenthau
                        (1950, rpt. 1982)
                        Political Realism and the Crisis of World Politics:
                        An American Approach to Foreign Policy
                        (1960, rpt. 1982)
                        American Diplomacy and Emergent Patterns
                        (1962, rpt. 1983)
                        Morality and Foreign Policy (1980)
                        Masters of International Thought (1980)
                        The President and the Public Philosophy (1981)
                        Winston Churchill's World View:
                        Statesmanship and Power (1983)

D. Cameron Watt
Stevenson Professor of International History
London School of Economics

Selected Publications: *Personalities and Policies: Studies in the Formulation*
                        of British Foreign Policy in the Twentieth Century
                        (1965)
                        Hitler's Mein Kampf, ed., (1969)
                        Too Serious a Business: European Armed Forces and
                        the Onset of the Second World War (1975)
                        Succeeding John Bull: America
                        in Britain's Place, 1900-1975, (1984)
                        Numerous articles and contributions on the history of
                        international relations.

James D. Weaver
Professor of Politics
Marymount College

John E. Wickman
Director, Dwight D. Eisenhower Library
Original documents on display at this Conference courtesy of the
  Dwight D. Eisenhower Library

Duane Windsor
Professor of Administrative Science
Rice University

Loretta Sharon Wyatt
Professor of History
Montclair State College

MODERATORS AND COMMENTATORS:
HOFSTRA UNIVERSITY FACULTY

Bruce Adkinson
Associate Professor of Political Science

Burton C. Agata
Max Schmertz Distinguished Professor of Law

Herman A. Berliner
Dean, School of Business

Michael D'Innocenzo
Professor of History

William F. Levantrosser
Professor of Political Science

Herbert D. Rosenbaum
Professor of Political Science

Ronald H. Silverman
Professor of Law

Lynn Turgeon
Professor of Economics

John E. Ullmann
Professor of Management & Marketing

Robert C. Vogt
Associate Professor of Political Science
Special Advisor to the Provost for Academic Affairs

Jacob Weissman
Professor of Economics

Conference Exhibitions Schedule

David Filderman Gallery, Hofstra University Library
DWIGHT D. EISENHOWER BOOK, MANUSCRIPT & MEMORABILIA EXHIBIT
March 28–May 15, 1984

Thursday, March 29—10:00 a.m.–5:00 p.m.
Friday, March 30—10:00 a.m.–8 p.m.
Saturday, March 31—1:00 p.m.–5:00 p.m.
Sunday, April 1—1:00 p.m.–5:00 p.m.
Monday, April 2—10:00 a.m.–5:00 p.m.
Tuesday, April 3—10:00 a.m.–9 p.m.
Wednesday, April 4—10:00 a.m.–5:00 p.m.

For remainder of exhibit the following hours are in effect:
Monday–Friday—10:00 a.m.–5:00 p.m., (516) 560-5974

Hofstra University Library–10th floor
DWIGHT D. EISENHOWER ART EXHIBIT, *March 28–April 12, 1984*
Same schedule as David Filderman Gallery, (516) 560-5974

Emily Lowe Gallery
THE PAINTINGS OF WINSTON S. CHURCHILL, *March 25–April 4, 1984*
"Painting as a Pastime"
An Exhibition organized by The Royal Oak Foundation

Short Documentary Film Show
"A Place in the Country"—15 min.
"Churchill the Man"—20 min.

Films shown every day for the duration of the Exhibit at 12:00 noon and upon request.

Same schedule as David Filderman Gallery

*Exhibition Catalogue available for sale at the Emily Lowe Gallery. Proceeds
will go towards The Royal Oak Foundation and Hofstra University.*
(516) 560-5672

Selected Greetings from Dignitaries
who are unable to attend the Conference:

BALTIMORE, MARYLAND

Dear President Shuart:

I have just reviewed in detail Hofstra University's program on President Eisenhower as military and political leader. It is massive and impressive.

I am glad that many of the scholars who will speak did not in 1961 have a high opinion of President Eisenhower's stewardship in the White House, for he was not a conventional, assertive-type leader. But research has brought about a turn of a hundred and eighty degrees in scholarly opinion, so now intellectuals and the general public join in their admiration of the contributions he made in maintaining peace, avoiding inflation, aiding a growing economy, wisely maintaining relations with the USSR which avoided an arms race, refusing to enter the Vietnam war, improving relations with many nations, and firmly establishing an efficient system of Federal administration.

Recently one of the older and best known columnists in the United States called me to say that in his long career he had only one regret. He had been unfair to President Eisenhower in the 1950's, for he did not really know the creative methods the President used in maintaining leadership in domestic and international affairs. "Now," he said, "I am one who applauds all he did."

I am so sorry that my health prevents my being with you....And my congratulations to you and your colleagues at Hofstra University for the superb program you have arranged.

> Sincerely,
> MILTON S. EISENHOWER
> President Emeritus
> The Johns Hopkins University

KIMBERTON, PENNSYLVANIA

"I do...applaud what you are doing. It may very well be that my father's philosophy of government and his methods of implementing that philosophy constitute a more lasting legacy than many of his more concrete contributions to our society, with the big exception of keeping us out of war with the Soviet Union during a period before the balance of terror made general war completely unthinkable...."

I wish you the very best for a highly successful occasion."

> Sincerely,
> JOHN S.D. EISENHOWER

KANSAS CITY, KANSAS

"...anything that carries the Eisenhower label is very important to me. I will be pleased to be a part of this program honoring our friend and most distinguished American."

> Sincerely,
> HARRY DARBY

WASHINGTON, D.C.

"I wish you well in your planned conference."

> Very Cordially Yours,
> ELEANOR LANSING DULLES

SHAPE, BELGIUM

To the Conference Participants:

"Today Allied Command Europe continues the efforts of one of America's greatest military leaders, General of the Army Dwight D. Eisenhower. When he served as Supreme Commander of the Allied Expeditionary Force in the Second World War, General Eisenhower established the standard for leadership in an alliance. In December 1950 when he was called to be the first Supreme Allied Commander Europe in the newly formed NATO, he again demonstrated his consummate skill in directing an allied effort. That his command, Allied Command Europe, continues today to assist NATO in maintaining peace with freedom through collective resolve is a testament to the inspiration of its first commander.

General Eisenhower possessed that essential quality of military leadership: character. Unlike some in history who have found rapid elevation to high command in wartime overwhelming, General Eisenhower never lost his sense of balance. In peace and in war he remained sensitive to the particular demands of the personalities and nations with whom he served. He harnessed the abundant and diverse talents of those he commanded and directed their efforts toward the common goal. General Eisenhower valued consensus more than national pride, cooperation more than personal exercise of power. Our freedom today owes much to this sensible man. Our greatest tribute to him will be to strive to continue in this tradition of leadership."

> BERNARD W. ROGERS
> General, United States Army
> Supreme Allied Commander Europe

CARLE PLACE, NY

"The Eisenhower Conference is timely; his presidency is now viewed in a much broader and favorable perspective, and his contributions as the Nation's Chief Executive are now only beginning to be fully appreciated. Hofstra University should be commended for selecting Dwight D. Eisenhower as the focus of its Third Annual Presidential Conference."

> Sincerely,
>
> WILLIAM J. RONAN
> Vice Chairman
> CCX, Inc.

Congress of the United States
House of Representatives
WASHINGTON, D.C.

"As Hofstra University approaches its 50th year, it should feel a great sense of accomplishment in the contribution it is making to both our nation and the international community through its Annual Presidential Conferences."

> Sincerely yours,
>
> JACK KEMP
> Member of Congress

Belgian Embassy
WASHINGTON, D.C.

"May I. . .take this occasion to wish you every possible success with this event."

> Sincerely yours,
>
> J. RAOUL SCHOUMAKER
> Ambassador of Belgium

Congress of the United States
House of Representatives
WASHINGTON, D.C.

"I did admire President Eisenhower tremendously as a noble gentleman and a great leader of our country.

Please accept my best wishes. . . ."

Very Sincerely,
CLAUDE PEPPER
Member of Congress

Congress of the United States
House of Representatives
WASHINGTON, D.C.

"The conference should prove interesting and enlightening, and attract the attention of international scholars. President Eisenhower's years in office and as a general during World War II will provide a wealth of information for the Conference.

With best wishes."

Sincerely,
ROBERT GARCIA
Member of Congress

PARIS, FRANCE

"Je suis très honoré par cette proposition et vous en remercie sincèrement. Je l'accepte bien volontiers dans le souvenir du Grand Président des Etats-Unis qu'a été le Président Eisenhower."

MAURICE COUVE DE MURVILLE

United States Army
WASHINGTON, D.C.

"Your organization's decision to memorialize such a great man is indeed commendable.

. . . I join in the belief that the character of President Eisenhower should be emulated by us all.

Best wishes for a rewarding and productive conference."

Most sincerely,
JOHN A. WICKHAM, JR.
General, United States Army
Chief of Staff

VIENNA, AUSTRIA

"May I assure you that I have the highest regard and admiration for the late President Dwight D. Eisenhower. He was a great soldier and an outstanding President of your country. He certainly played a special role not only in the history of your nation but also of the world. I congratulate you on your initiative and I am sure that the 3rd Annual Conference will be a great success.

With warm regards and best wishes."

Yours sincerely,
DR. KURT WALDHEIM

WASHINGTON, D.C.

"I wish you well in your undertaking."

Sincerely,
W. AVERELL HARRIMAN

The Institute for Advanced Study
PRINCETON, NEW JERSEY

"I admired President Eisenhower in many ways and am pleased that he is to be honored...."

Very sincerely,
GEORGE KENNAN

United States Senate
WASHINGTON, D.C.

I am proud to be part of a conference honoring a truly great citizen, President Eisenhower. His career of service as a Soldier, President, and Statesman gives him a unique place in the history of the world.
You have my very best wishes."

Sincerely,
PETE V. DOMENICI
United States Senator

United States Navy
WASHINGTON, D.C.

"I was privileged to be the first Commanding Officer of the USS DWIGHT D. EISENHOWER and in that capacity, to form a close relationship with the Eisenhower family. I am pleased at the opportunity to build upon that relationship and to support the Conference honoring one of our truly great individuals, Dwight D. Eisenhower."

Sincerely,
WILLIAM E. RAMSEY
Rear Admiral, U.S. Navy

CBS, Inc.
NEW YORK, NY

"Nothing could give me greater pleasure than to be associated with an event honoring the memory and achievements of President Eisenhower."

Sincerely yours,
WILLIAM S. PALEY

Embassy of the United States of America
BERN, SWITZERLAND

"I send you my best wishes for the success of your conference on President Eisenhower."

Sincerely,
JOHN DAVIS LODGE
Ambassador

Royal Netherlands Embassy
WASHINGTON, D.C.

"We in the Netherlands continue indeed to consider Dwight D. Eisenhower, who played such a special role in the liberation of our country in 1945, as one of the great statesmen and leaders of our time."

Sincerely yours,
J.H. LUBBERS
Ambassador of the Netherlands

Hudson Institute
WASHINGTON, D.C.

"Best wishes to you in your continued success with the Annual Presidential Conferences. Your efforts enhance the dignity of the Office of the Presidency and contribute to the esteem in which our Presidents have been held by the international community."

Sincerely,
ALEXANDER M. HAIG, JR.

Turkish Embassy
WASHINGTON, D.C.

"The Turkish people have always appreciated the efforts of President Eisenhower to establish the United States as the leader of Western democracies. His intentions for creating a strong alliance, of which Turkey is a member, have been the cornerstones of all NATO member policies."

Sincerely,
SUKRU ELEKDAG
Ambassador of the Turkish Republic

Supreme Court of the United States
Chambers of the Chief Justice
WASHINGTON, D.C.

"Please extend my best wishes to all the participants of this conference."

Cordially,
WARREN E. BURGER
Chief Justice

NEW YORK, NY

"I am sure that it will be a very interesting forum and I hope it is a tremendous success. It is a great pleasure to see how much President Eisenhower's record is being recognized and approved by historians and scholars."
With best wishes."

Sincerely,
WILLIAM P. ROGERS
Rogers & Wells

PUTNEY, VERMONT

"I was a great admirer of President Eisenhower and had the privilege of serving under him as Ambassador to India from 1957-61. President Eisenhower visited India in December 1959 and received the most tremendous welcome that any individual before or after him ever received."

Sincerely,
ELLSWORTH BUNKER

WASHINGTON, D.C.

"I have great admiration for the late President Eisenhower...."

Sincerely yours,
ARTHUR J. GOLDBERG

United States Senate
WASHINGTON, D.C.

"I would consider it an honor to be associated with such a fine effort as this...."

Sincerely,
CHARLES McC. MATHIAS, JR.
United States Senator

Embassy of the United States of America
PARIS, FRANCE

"I congratulate...Hofstra University on this excellent initiative, to which I am honored to lend my name and encouragement.
Although 1985 is still 18 months away, I will also take this occasion to congratulate Hofstra on its fiftieth birthday."

Sincerely,
EVAN G. GALBRAITH
Ambassador

30 Rockefeller Plaza
NEW YORK, NY

"Mr. Laurance S. Rockefeller...asked me to convey...his good wishes for what I am sure will be a memorable event."

Sincerely,
GEORGE R. LAMB

The Church of Jesus Christ of Latter-Day Saints
SALT LAKE CITY, UTAH

"It pleases me greatly that you are recognizing the man with whom I served for eight years and whom I loved and admired.
With every good wish for a most successful conference."

Faithfully yours,
EZRA TAFT BENSON
President, Council of the Twelve

Embassy of the United States of America
ROME, ITALY

"Some of my most memorable years were spent serving him in the White House under his remarkable leadership, and I welcome any opportunity to honor him."

Sincerely,
MAXWELL M. RABB
Ambassador

Embassy of the Federal Republic of Germany
WASHINGTON, D.C.

"The post-war period of my country is closely linked to the personality of Dwight D. Eisenhower. As President of the United States he supported the Federal Republic of Germany in finding her place among free western democracies. I can only support your intention to have his place in history honored by the Conference.

Sincerely yours,
PETER HERMES
Ambassador of the Federal Republic of Germany

10 Downing Street
LONDON, ENGLAND

"The Prime Minister...has asked me to pass on her best wishes for the success of your Conference on President Eisenhower...."

Yours sincerely,
TIM FLESHER
Private Secretary to the Prime Minister

Der Bayerische Ministerpräsident
MUNICH, FEDERAL REPUBLIC OF GERMANY

"With all good wishes for the conference and best regards...."

Sincerely,
FRANZ JOSEF STRAUS

Embajada de España
WASHINGTON, D.C.

"Such conferences are essential to the further understanding of global modern history. I would be delighted to be part of this undertaking."

Sincerely,
GABRIEL MAÑUECO
El Embajador de Espana

CBS News
NEW YORK, NY

"...I wish you every success with the Conference.

Sincerely,
WALTER CRONKITE

Le Maire de Bordeaux
FRANCE

"J'ai moi-même bien connu Dwight D. Eisenhower à la fois lorsqu'il était mon Chef suprême, dans la dernière partie de la Deuxième Guerre Mondiale et ensuite lorsqu'il avait établi son Quartier Général à Louveciennes.

De toute manière soyez certain que je forme voeux fervents pour le plus grand succès de cette Troisième Conférence Présidentielle."

JACQUES CHABAN-DELMAS

North Atlantic Treaty Organization
BRUSSELS, BELGIUM

"...all my best wishes for a fruitful meeting...."

Yours sincerely,
DR. JOSEPH M.A.H. LUNS
Secretary General

Chairman of the Joint Chiefs of Staff
WASHINGTON, D.C.

"Best wishes in your efforts to honor one of our Nation's greatest soldier-statesmen."

Sincerely,
GENERAL JOHN W. VESSEY, JR.
Chairman
Joint Chiefs of Staff

Executive Office of the Secretary-General
United Nations
NEW YORK, NY'

"On behalf of the Secretary-General [Javier Pérez de Cuéllar], I should like...to convey to you his best wishes for a most successful and memorable presidential conference."

Yours sincerely,
ALVARO DE SOTO
Special Assistant to the Secretary-General

COLORADO SPRINGS, COLORADO

"It is an honor to support the Hofstra University 3rd Annual Conference in honor of Dwight D. Eisenhower."

Sincerely,
COLONEL EARL H. BLAIK, USA (Ret.)

Program of Conference

The generous patrons of this conference

AVON PRODUCTS, INC.
GARDEN CITY HOTEL
HAROLD & JULIET KALIKOW FOUNDATION
HEMPSTEAD PLAZA HOTEL
L.F. O'CONNELL ASSOCIATES, INC.
MACK COMPANY
SGS NORTH AMERICA INC.
SHEET METAL WORKERS' INTERNATIONAL ASSOCIATION
SUOZZI, ENGLISH & CIANCIULLI

Hofstra University student sponsoring groups

POLITICAL AFFAIRS CLUB
NEW COLLEGE COMMUNITY GOVERNMENT
STUDENT UCAM
HOFSTRA COLLEGE YOUNG DEMOCRATS
STUDENT GOVERNMENT ASSOCIATION

For creating a special Eisenhower poster we thank

MME FRANÇOISE GILOT

We gratefully acknowledge the cooperation of the following organizations:

Aspen Institute for Humanistic Studies
Washington, D.C.

British Consulate General
New York, NY

British Embassy
Washington, D.C.

Cultural Services of the French Embassy
New York, NY

Dwight D. Eisenhower Library
Abilene, KS

Dwight D. Eisenhower World Affairs Institute
Washington, D.C.

Eisenhower National Historic Site
Gettysburg, PA

Embassy of the United States of America
Paris, France

French Embassy to the United States
Washington, D.C.

Gray & Company
Washington, D.C.

Harry S. Truman Library
Independence, MO

Institute for the Study of the Presidency
New York, NY

International Research and Exchanges Board (IREX)
New York, NY

Nassau Library System
Uniondale, NY

The National Archives
Washington, D.C.

NATO Information Service
Brussels, Belgium

NBC-TV
New York, NY

New York Public Library
New York, NY

The New York Times
New York, NY

The Royal Oak Foundation
New York, NY

Suffolk Cooperative Library System
Bellport, NY

United States Department of State
Office of Protocol
Washington, D.C.

United States Military Academy
West Point, NY

United States Mission to the United Nations
New York, NY

USSR Academy of Sciences
Moscow, USSR

The Wilson Quarterly
Smithsonian Institution
Washington, D.C.

*Credit for the success of the Conference goes to more people than can
be named herein, but those below deserve special commendation:*

HOFSTRA UNIVERSITY OFFICERS:
James M. Shuart, *President*
Sanford S. Hammer, *Provost & Dean of
  Faculties*
Robert C. Vogt, *Special Advisor to the Provost
  for Academic Affairs*
Robert A. Davison, *Acting Dean, Hofstra
  College of Liberal Arts & Sciences*
ARA SLATER:
Tony Interniocola, *Director, Dining Services*
Dawn Smith, *Assistant Director/Catering
  Manager*
DAVID FILDERMAN GALLERY
Marguerite M. Regan, *Assistant to the Dean of
  Library Services*
Nancy E. Herb
Anne Rubino
DEPARTMENT OF ART HISTORY
Robert Myron, *Chairman*
Linda Anderson, *Curator*
DEPARTMENT OF COMMUNICATION
  ARTS
William R. Renn, *Chairman*
Kit Hunt, *Faculty Program Coordinator WRHU*
DEPARTMENT OF DRAMA
James Van Wart, *Chairman*
Donald H. Swinney, *Director of John Cranford
  Adams Playhouse*
DEPARTMENT OF FINE ARTS
David T. Jacobs, *Chairman*
Warren Infield, *Professor of Fine Arts*
DEPARTMENT OF MUSIC
Edgar Dittemore, *Chairman*
DEPARTMENT OF POLITICAL SCIENCE
Paul F. Harper, *Chairman*
Marilyn Shepherd, *Senior Executive Secretary*
DEVELOPMENT OFFICE
Rochelle Lowenfeld, *Assistant to the President
  for Development*
Corey Geske, *Assistant Director of Development*
Alice Castle, *Administrative Assistant to the
  Director of Development*
Joan Tiedge, *Senior Executive Secretary*
Eileen Meserole, *Senior Clerk*
EMILY LOWE GALLERY
Gail Gelburd, *Director*
Mary Wakeford, *Directorial Assistant*
Susann Ross, *Hofstra University Organizer of
  Churchill Exhibit*

HOFSTRA UNIVERSITY LIBRARY
Charles R. Andrews, *Dean*
Wayne Bell, *Associate Dean*

OFFICE OF THE SECRETARY
Robert D. Noble, *Secretary*
Margaret Mirabella
Stella Sinicki, *Supervisor, Special Secretarial
  Services*
Jack Ruegamer, *Director, Art & Printing
  Production*
Vicki Anderson
Veronica Fitzwilliam
Doris Brown, *Supervisor, Printing Department
  & Staff*
Dolores Pallingayan, *Administrator of Mail
  Services & Staff*
George McCue, *Supervisor of Mail Room*

OPERATIONAL SERVICES
James Fellman, *Vice President of Operational
  Services & Staff*

PLANT ENGINEERING & MAINTENANCE
Richard J. Drury, *Director of Physical Plant &
  Staff*

PUBLIC SAFETY &
  TELECOMMUNICATIONS
Robert L. Crowley, *Director*
Ed Bracht, *Deputy Director*
Margaret A. Shields, *Operations Manager*

SCHEDULING OFFICE:
Charles L. Churchill, *Assistant Facilities
  Manager*
Dorothy Fetherston, *Director*

SCHOOL OF LAW:
Stuart Rabinowitz, *Vice Dean*
Robert L. Douglas, *Assistant Dean*
Betty Presti, *Executive Assistant to the Dean*
Secretarial Staff of the Dean's Office
Staff of the Xeroxing Office

TECHNICAL & MEDIA SERVICES
Elizabeth Weston, *Media Services Librarian*
William Gray

UNIVERSITY RELATIONS
Harold A. Klein, *Director*
James Merritt, *Assistant Director*
M.F. Klerk, *Editor/Writer*
Frances B. Jacobsen, *Administrative Assistant*

HOFSTRA TODAY

HOFSTRA UNIVERSITY has been nationally recognized as a center for cultural activity and intellectual enrichment. In December of 1983 the National Endowment for the Humanities (NEH) awarded a Challenge Grant of $450,000 to the University in support of the Hofstra Cultural Center. Since 1976 the Cultural Center has conducted 21 international conferences and is the source of ongoing literary and historical conferences, seminars, and exhibits encompassing all forms of the arts.

Hofstra has the only Phi Beta Kappa chapter at a private university on Long Island, an honor shared by only 10 per cent of *all* colleges and universities. Furthermore, the quality of higher education at Hofstra has been recognized by one of the major publishers of colleges guides—Barrons. During the last decade Hofstra has raised its admissions standards and is rated as "very competitive" in the recent edition of *Barron's Profiles of American Colleges.*" Hofstra is also listed in two new and significantly selective guides published by Barrons: *The Most Prestigious Colleges* (227 top-rated colleges) and *The Best, Most Popular, and Most Exciting Colleges* (350 of America's most notable schools).

The following facts illustrate part of the reason Hofstra is included in such selective listings. Hofstra has one of the largest and finest library collections in the country. Over 1,000,000 volumes are available on campus. Only about 5% of all university collections are as large, and 85% have collections only half of this size. The University continues to grow in response to student and faculty needs. Its Television Institute, which will be in operation in the spring of 1985, will be one of the largest and best equipped non-commercial television facilities in the East. Computer facilities at the University were recently expanded through the investment of $1 million so that students now have immediate access to more than 150 remote terminals that are reserved for academic use.

Another highlight of the Hofstra campus is the University Swim Center which features the largest indoor facility for 200 miles around. It is a full size olympic pool (50 meters 8 lanes) and is open almost every day of the year from early morning until late at night. All buildings and activities at the University are fully accessible to physically disabled students.

Almost 60 per cent of the entering freshmen come from the top 20 per cent of their high school graduating classes and represent 25 states and 60 foreign countries. They are served by over 400 full time faculty, of whom 80 per cent hold the highest degree in their field.

As Hofstra prepares to celebrate its 50th anniversary in 1985, it is experiencing a momentum that is propelling it into the front ranks of American higher education.

NOTES:

HOFSTRA UNIVERSITY
CULTURAL CENTER CONFERENCES

George Sand Centennial—November 1976
Heinrich von Kleist Bicentennial—November 1977
The Chinese Woman—December 1977
George Sand: Her Life, Her Works, Her Influence—April 1978
William Cullen Bryant and His America—October 1978
The Trotsky-Stalin Conflict in the 1920's—March 1979
Albert Einstein Centennial—November 1979
Renaissance Venice Symposium—March 1980
Sean O'Casey—March 1980
Walt Whitman—April 1980
Nineteenth-Century Women Writers—November 1980
Fedor Dostoevski—April 1981
Gotthold Ephraim Lessing—November 1981
Franklin Delano Roosevelt: The Man, The Myth, The Era—March 1982
Johann Wolfgang von Goethe—April 1982
James Joyce—October 1982
Twentieth-Century Women Writers—November 1982
Harry S. Truman: The Man from Independence—April 14-16, 1983
John Maynard Keynes—September 22-24, 1983
Romanticism in the Old and the New World-Washington Irving, Stendhal, and Zhukovskii—
   October 13-15, 1983
Espectador Universal: Jose Ortega y Gasset—November 10-12, 1983
Dwight D. Eisenhower: Soldier, President, Statesman—March 29-31, 1984
Victorian Studies—April 13-15, 1984
Symposium on Eighteenth-Century Venice—April 27, 1984
George Orwell—October 11-13, 1984
Friedrich von Schiller—November 8-10, 1984
John F. Kennedy: The New Frontier—March 28-30, 1985
The Future of Higher Education—April 1985
Harlem Renaissance—May 2-4, 1985
Evolution of Business Education—September 19-21, 1985
Eighteenth-Century Women Writers—October 10-12, 1985
Avant Garde Art and Literature—November 14-16, 1985
Lyndon B. Johnson—March 1986
George Sand: Her Life, Her Works, Her Influence—October 1986
Carl Gustav Jung—November 1986
Richard M. Nixon—Spring 1987
Bicentennial of the United States Constitution—Fall 1987
Gerald R. Ford—Spring 1988
Jimmy Carter—Spring 1989
Bicentennial of the French Revolution—Fall 1989
Ronald Reagan—Spring 1990

"Call for Papers" available

HOFSTRA UNIVERSITY has been named the recipient of a $450,000 Challenge Grant from the National Endowment for the Humanities (NEH). Under the terms of the challenge, the funds raised through the Conference will generate an additional contribution by the federal government of one-third of the total raised. A portion of your admission fee will be used toward matching the challenge grant.

Index

About the Editor

JOANN P. KRIEG is Assistant Professor in the American Studies Program of the Department of English at Hofstra University, Hempstead, New York. She is the editor of *Walt Whitman: Here and Now* (Greenwood Press, 1985) and has contributed articles to *Walt Whitman Quarterly Review, British Journal of American Studies, American Transcendentalist Quarterly*, and *New York State Folklore Journal*.

About the Contributors

ISAAC ALTERAS is Associate Professor of History at Queens College of the City University of New York. His current research involves U.S.-Israeli relations, and his most recent publication on the subject, "Eisenhower, American Jewry and Israel," appeared in the *American Jewish Archives*. He is presently completing a book on U.S.-Israeli relations during the Eisenhower presidency.

DAVID L. ANDERSON is Associate Professor of History at the University of Indianapolis. His principal research field is U.S. relations with East and Southeast Asia. He is the author of *Imperialism and Idealism: American Diplomats in China, 1861–1898*.

STEVE M. BARKIN is Associate Professor of Journalism at the University of Maryland and an associate of the University of Maryland Center for Research in Public Communication. His research has concentrated on political communication, broadcast history, and content studies of print and broadcast news. His articles have appeared in *Journalism Quarterly*, *Journal of American Culture*, *Journal of Broadcasting*, and other journals. He is a contributing editor of the *Mass Communication Review Yearbook*.

HENRY WILLIAM BRANDS, JR., is Assistant Professor of History at Vanderbilt University. He graduated from Stanford University and the University of Texas at Austin, and he is the author of *Cold Warriors: Eisenhower's Generation* and various articles.

PHILIP J. BRIGGS is Professor and Chairperson of the Department of Political

Science at East Stroudsburg University in Pennsylvania. His principal research interests are the legislative-executive relationship and the U.S. foreign policy formulation. His articles have appeared in European and American journals, and he has lectured widely as a Commonwealth Speaker for the Humanities Council.

ROBERT F. BURK is Assistant Professor of American History at Muskingum College, in New Concord, Ohio. He was formerly Visiting Assistant Professor of History at the University of Cincinnati. He is the author of numerous articles on civil rights policy and the Eisenhower administration, as well as *The Eisenhower Administration and Black Civil Rights* and *Dwight D. Eisenhower: Hero and Politician*.

JOSEPH M. DAILEY is Associate Professor of Communication at Carroll College where he has taught and directed journalism studies for more than fourteen years. His principal research interest is political communication.

SHERI I. DAVID is Assistant Professor of History at Hofstra University. She is the author of *With Dignity: The Search for Medicare and Medicaid* which documents the history of the Medicare and Medicaid program. Her principal research efforts focus on social policy in recent American history, particularly policy affecting the elderly.

JAMES C. DURAM is Professor of History at Wichita State University where he has taught for the past nineteen years. His research specialization is U.S. constitutional and legal history. Duram has published books on Norman Thomas and Justice William O. Douglas; his most recent book is *A Moderate Among Extremists: Dwight D. Eisenhower and the School Segregation Crisis*.

J. GERRIT GANTVOORT is Assistant Professor of History at the State University of New York, Oneonta, where he teaches courses in Russian history and Soviet-American relations. His research efforts have been directed toward declassification and analysis of material concerning Soviet-American cultural relations during the Eisenhower administration.

GERARD E. GIANNATTASIO is Assistant Director of the Law Library at the Hofstra University School of Law. He is a graduate of Yeshiva University's Benjamin N. Cardozo School of Law and also holds degrees in history and library science. A former Air Force officer, he is a member of the New York and various federal bars, including the Court of Military Appeals.

LINDA R. GIANNATTASIO is a fifth-year associate with the firm of Milbank, Tweed, Hadley & McCloy in New York City. She is a graduate of the Hofstra University School of Law where she was a research editor of the *Hofstra Law Review*. She has pursued graduate studies at Rutgers University where she taught undergraduate courses in English and American literature.

L. RICHARD GUYLAY was Public Relations Director for the Republican National Committee in three Presidential Campaigns, serving Presidents Eisenhower and Nixon. He also was consultant to Senators Robert Taft, Barry Goldwater, Governors Nelson Rockefeller, Malcolm Wilson, and several U.S. senators. He was formerly president of Public Opinion Polls, Inc., and the National Association of P.R. Counsels, and special assistant for Policy Planning for the governor of New York.

ANTHONY JAMES JOES is Professor of Politics and Director of International Relations at St. Joseph's University. He is the author of *Fascism in the Contemporary World*, *Mussolini*, *From the Barrel of a Gun*, and a co-author of *Political Parties of Europe*.

JAMES M. KEAGLE is Professor of Public Policy at the National War College, the National Defense University, and was formerly Associate Professor of Political Science at the U.S. Air Force Academy as well as serving on the faculty of the Graduate School of Public Affairs, University of Colorado, Colorado Springs. His principal teaching and research interests are in the fields of American foreign policy and the presidency. He is co-editor of *Intelligence: Policy and Process* as well as numerous other articles and book reviews.

JOHN KENTLETON is Lecturer in History at the University of Liverpool, England, where he has been Chairman of the Faculty of Arts and Chairman of the American Studies Panel. He has held appointments in the United States, including Visiting Professor in American History at the University of Nevada. He is at present writing a biography of Franklin D. Roosevelt and a history of recent America.

THEODORE PHILIP KOVALEFF is Assistant Dean at the School of Law, Columbia University, and previously held appointments at Barnard College, New York University, and St. John's University. He is the author of *Business and Government During the Eisenhower Administration*, and a number of articles on antitrust in scholarly journals.

CARL LIEBERMAN is Associate Professor of Political Science at the University of Akron, where he teaches courses in American government and politics. He has contributed articles and reviews to various journals and is the editor of two books of readings: *Institutions and Processes of American National Government* and *Government and Politics in Ohio*.

MICHAEL S. MAYER is a Lecturer in History at the University of Auckland in New Zealand and has held positions at the University of Alabama, St. Vincent College, and Princeton University. He has written a biography of Eisenhower's solicitor general and is the author of several articles on Eisenhower and civil rights, including "With Much Deliberation and Some Speed: Eisenhower and the *Brown* Decision" and "Washington Bids Farewell to Jim Crow."

J. PHILIPP ROSENBERG is Assistant Professor of Political Science at Kansas State University. He has conducted extensive research on the role of presidential belief systems in foreign policy crisis situations. He is currently working on a book on the role of presidential belief systems in American foreign policy during the Cold War.

RAYMOND J. SAULNIER is Professor of Economics (Emeritus) at Barnard College, Columbia University. From 1956 to 1960, he was Chairman of President Eisenhower's Council of Economic Advisers. His most recent publication is *The Strategy of Economic Policy*, and he is now completing a book, *The U.S. Economy Under Eisenhower*.

ALEXEJ UGRINSKY is Assistant Professor of German at Hofstra University and Acting Co-Director of the Hofstra University Cultural Center. His earlier works have appeared in the *Journal of Long Island Bookcollectors* and the *Acta of the Congress of the International Association of German Studies*. He is editor of *Lessing and the Enlightenment* (Greenwood Press, 1986).

JAMES D. WEAVER is Professor of Politics at Marymount College in Tarrytown, New York. His principal teaching and research interests involve national security affairs and presidential war powers. He has served as an American Council on Education Government Fellow at the Department of Defense.

DUANE WINDSOR is Associate Professor of Administrative Science in the Jesse H. Jones Graduate School of Administration at Rice University, where he specializes in business and public management. He was previously a member of the faculty at the University of Iowa. His several books include *The Foreign Corrupt Practices Act: Anatomy of a Statute*.

LORETTA SHARON WYATT, Associate Professor of History at Montclair State College in New Jersey, earned her Bachelor's and Master's degrees at the University of New Mexico and her Ph.D. at the University of Florida, and is a member of Phi Beta Kappa. She is a recognized specialist on Latin American history and culture, particularly on the subject of twentieth-century revolutions, as well as on inter-American relations. She has published several articles in historical journals in the area of Latin American culture and political developments.

Hofstra University's
Cultural and Intercultural Studies
Coordinating Editor, Alexej Ugrinsky

George Sand Papers: Conference Proceedings, 1976
*(Editorial Board: Natalie Datlof, Edwin L. Dunbaugh, Frank S. Lambasa,
Gabrielle Savet, William S. Shiver, Alex Szogyi)*

George Sand Papers: Conference Proceedings, 1978
*(Editorial Board: Natalie Datlof, Edwin L. Dunbaugh, Frank S. Lambasa,
Gabrielle Savet, William S. Shiver, Alex Szogyi)*

Heinrich von Kleist Studies
*(Editorial Board: Alexej Ugrinsky, Frederick J. Churchill, Frank S. Lambasa,
Robert F. von Berg)*

William Cullen Bryant Studies
(Editors: Stanley Brodwin, Michael D'Innocenzo)

*Walt Whitman: Here and Now
(Editor: Joann P. Krieg)

*Harry S. Truman: The Man from Independence
(Editor: William F. Levantrosser)

*Nineteenth-Century Women Writers of the English-Speaking World
(Editor: Rhoda B. Nathan)

*Lessing and the Enlightenment
(Editor: Alexej Ugrinsky)

*Dostoevski and the Human Condition After a Century
(Editors: Alexej Ugrinsky, Frank S. Lambasa, and Valija K. Ozolins)

*The Old and New World Romanticism of Washington Irving
(Editor: Stanley Brodwin)

*Woman as Mediatrix
(Editor: Avriel Goldberger)

*Einstein and the Humanities
(Editor: Dennis P. Ryan)

*Available from Greenwood Press